Theological Fragments

Theological Fragments

*Confessing What We Know and
Cannot Know about an Infinite God*

Rubén Rosario Rodríguez

© 2023 Rubén Rosario Rodríguez

First edition
Published by Westminster John Knox Press
Louisville, Kentucky

23 24 25 26 27 28 29 30 31 32—10 9 8 7 6 5 4 3 2 1

All rights reserved. No part of this book may be reproduced or transmitted in any form or by any means, electronic or mechanical, including photocopying, recording, or by any information storage or retrieval system, without permission in writing from the publisher. For information, address Westminster John Knox Press, 100 Witherspoon Street, Louisville, Kentucky 40202-1396. Or contact us online at www.wjkbooks.com.

Unless otherwise indicated, Scripture quotations are from the New Revised Standard Version of the Bible, copyright © 1989 by the Division of Christian Education of the National Council of the Churches of Christ in the U.S.A., and are used by permission.

Book design by Sharon Adams
Cover design by Allison Taylor

Library of Congress Cataloging-in-Publication Data is on file at the Library of Congress, Washington DC.

ISBN-13: 978-0-664-26747-6

Most Westminster John Knox Press books are available at special quantity discounts when purchased in bulk by corporations, organizations, and special-interest groups. For more information, please e-mail SpecialSales@wjkbooks.com.

*And questions are, I suspect,
all we will take with us on our final journeys
through Time and into Night.*

—Neil Gaiman, *The Sandman: Overture*

Contents

Acknowledegments	ix
Introduction	1
1. A Broken and Contrite Theology	17
Heraclitian Flux or Platonic Totality?	18
Toward a Theology of the Barns and Kennels	23
Persistent Postmodern Myths	33
2. The Myth of Theological Totalitarianism	39
Apologetics after Babel	39
Dueling Modernities	41
Toward a Postmodern Apologetics	54
A Fragment of Theology: The Human in Eastern Orthodoxy	63
3. The Myth of the Free Market	67
Three Perspectives on Religion and Economics	71
The New Spirit of Capitalism	86
A Fragment of Theology: Francis of Assisi and the Spirit of Liberation	92
4. The Myth of Human Uniqueness	101
Darwinism and the Doctrine of Creation	105
Theistic Responses to Darwinism	115
A Fragment of Theology: The Hope of Ecofeminist Theology	127
5. The Myth of Political Sovereignty	137
Theopoetics as Political Activism	145
Neoliberalism's False Narrative	153
A Fragment of Theology: Walter Wink's Third Way	158

6. The Myth of Christian Uniqueness	167
Pachyderm Perambulations	177
The Trinity and Religious Pluralism	180
A Fragment of Theology: The Negative Way of Pseudo-Dionysius	190
7. The Myth of Materialism	195
Word and Flesh in the Gospel of John	199
Flesh and Spirit Are One	206
A Fragment of Theology: Disability and the Body of Christ	212
Concluding Unscientific Postscript	215
Bibliography	221
Index of Scripture	243
Index of Names and Subjects	245

Acknowledgements

Contrary to popular opinion, the writing of scholarly books is not a lonely affair but arises from multiple conversations across many years before pen is ever put to paper in the privacy of the author's study—and even then, the work of writing is always interrupted by the welcome intrusions of everyday life.

In a very real sense this book began when I was an undergraduate student in the philosophy department at the College of William and Mary, where I pushed gently against the ideas and opinions of such wonderful role models as Earl McLane, who sparked my love for the writings of Søren Kierkegaard, and the late Lawrence Becker (1939–2018), who encouraged me to study at Union Theological Seminary in New York. The book continued to develop under the mentoring of the late James M. Washington (1948–1997) at Union Theological Seminary, who nurtured my love of Kierkegaard and also shared my love of Neil Gaiman's *The Sandman* comic books, then attained some degree of theological maturity at Princeton Theological Seminary under the tutelage of Daniel L. Migliore, Mark L. Taylor, and Luis N. Rivera-Pagán, who not only served as my dissertation committee, but each in their own way modeled the socially engaged and intellectually rigorous pastoral theology I seek to embody in this work. Along the way I also benefitted from public lectures by such luminaries as John D. Caputo, Richard Rorty, David Tracy, Jacques Derrida, Cornel West, Elaine Pagels, Peter Brown, Jon Sobrino, Martha Nussbaum, Jürgen Moltmann, John Polkinghorne, Catherine Keller, Gustavo Gutiérrez, Serene Jones, David Bentley Hart, Elizabeth Johnson, Willie James Jennings, Rowan Williams, and Kathryn Tanner, to name a few. As I always remind my students, one of the great benefits of higher education is the opportunity to meet and engage the greatest minds alive; so, I always encourage them to avail themselves of as many such opportunities as come their way.

As a theologian who is also an ordained minister of Word and Sacrament in the Presbyterian Church (U.S.A.), I have remained active in the life of the church, having been a member-at-large of the Presbytery of Giddings-Lovejoy in St. Louis since 2004. During that time, I have been a pulpit supply preacher and regularly led adult education classes throughout the greater St. Louis and southwestern Illinois region. I have also served on the Presbytery's Camp and Conference Center Committee, the Presbytery's Dismantling Racism Committee, and the Committee on Nominations, and I currently serve as moderator for the Commission on Preparation for Ministry.

Every book I have ever written has at some point in its gestation been tried and tested in a parish setting. This book is no exception. I want to thank the adult education classes at Trinity Presbyterian Church, Webster Groves Presbyterian Church, First Presbyterian Church of Kirkwood, and Ladue Chapel Presbyterian Church, for continuing to invite me back, and for struggling with me through some difficult subject matter that we might together hear what the Word of God has to say to us today. Academic theology and the church are fellow pilgrims on the journey, and I am a firm believer that each setting is improved by maintaining dialogue and cooperation, despite what some other academic theologians contend.

This project was completed while juggling a full-time teaching load, serving as Coordinator of the Masters Programs, and agreeing to chair a search committee in the Department of Theological Studies at Saint Louis University—all complicated by the strange new world created by the global COVID pandemic. The book reaches completion in part due to the generosity of my department chair, Dr. Daniel Smith, and my dean, Dr. Donna LaVoie, who in 2022 appointed me to the Clarence Louis and Helen Steber Professorship in Theological Studies. I would also like to thank the doctoral students in my Political Theology seminar, taught in Spring 2019 and again in Spring 2022, for accompanying me through many of the texts and issues that eventually made their way into this monograph. I particularly want to thank my research assistant, Michael Thiele, for his help in compiling the bibliography, copyediting proofs, and indexing the book, and my doctoral student, Josh Sturgeon, whose own dissertation project, a post-Evangelical process theology, has been a welcome conversant on many intersecting concerns.

I lack the words to properly thank my editor at Westminster John Knox Press, Robert Ratcliff, without whom this project—and its predecessor, *Dogmatics after Babel* (2018)—would have never seen the light of day. Bob's gifts as a theologian prompted the reflections that eventually produced a viable project, but it is his otherworldly talent as an editor that, like a grain of sand irritating an oyster's soft tissue, nudges authors to produce works of far greater beauty and import than they could have yielded on their own. His track record speaks for itself, my own humble contributions notwithstanding. Suffice it to say, the good this book contributes to the greater discourse exists because of Bob's ability to refine and polish what is raw and unformed. Furthermore,

Bob is a very compassionate and forgiving editor who was willing to extend multiple deadlines when life reared its ugly head and impeded the timely completion of this project. I might be fooling myself, but I like to believe that we long ago transcended the professional author-editor relationship and have entered the far more rewarding—if exponentially more complicated—realm of friendship. Thank you, my friend.

Finally, some mention of the "welcome intrusions of everyday life" alluded to in the first paragraph is due. My wife and I have been blessed with two wonderful children, Isa and Rafe, who during the writing of this book have transitioned from adolescence to adulthood and from childhood to adolescence respectively. Not a day goes by that I do not marvel at the wonderful persons they have become and give thanks for the miracle they embody. Of course, none of this could have been possible without my wife, Betsy, often at great sacrifice to her own research and scholarship. I pray that in the end, when we tally all the good and all the bad, you can say that your life was better for having me in it, because I know for a fact this is the case for me. Thank you. For everything.

Introduction

This is a book for anyone wrestling with the Christian faith—the believer in the pews, the pastor in the pulpit, the theologian in the academy—who *still* identifies with the Christian tradition *despite* its much-publicized demise in the cultural mainstream. I have been and remain all three: believer, pastor, and theologian. While I make no claim to any special insight, I am at a point in my career as a professional theologian—and more importantly, on my journey as a Christian believer—where I can look back and assess with some degree of clarity why so many are leaving the church and no longer identify as Christian. I hope that, by articulating why I continue to follow Christ regardless of the many failings of the institutional church, I can help others sort out their own relationship with Jesus of Nazareth.

I have always considered myself a "church" theologian, mindful of the lessons learned from my first professor of theology, James H. Cone at Union Theological Seminary in New York. On the first day of class Professor Cone reminded his students that as theologians and pastors we are neither set apart nor elevated above the community of faith, but merely fellow pilgrims on the journey of faith. Thus, in our vocation as theologians, we ought always to remain *accountable* to the community of faith: "Doing Christian theology is a task that arises when one's commitment to Jesus Christ grows in the context of a community of faith that is in search of an understanding of God's meaning for their lives in the world today."[1] Many an "academic" theologian has forgotten this. To clarify, Cone does not stress the accountability of the

---

1. James H. Cone, "The Vocation of a Theologian," *Union News* (Winter 1991), 3–4.

theologian to the community in order to undermine academic freedom, or to bind the theologian to church dogma, but in recognition that the prophetic dimension of the theologian's task seeks *to build up the body of Christ* (Eph. 4:12). Granted, pastors and theologians are often called to speak a prophetic word: "There is no way to speak and to do the truth in an oppressive society without offending the people who are responsible for that oppression."[2] Yet Cone cautions that this urgency to preach "prophetically" ought *not* arise from some "desire for notoriety or for status," but from a deep sense of calling to help the community of believers make sense of Christ's good news for their day and age.[3] Nevertheless, *as* a church theologian and a minister of the Word and Sacrament active in the mission of the Presbyterian Church (U.S.A.), I have come to the conclusion that the church's own actions contribute to its demographic demise, which is why so many—including many Christians—no longer consider the church an institution worth defending.

Elizabeth Drescher's analysis of recent survey data concludes that nearly three-quarters of those who now identify as religiously unaffiliated "were raised in families with some religious affiliation, generally in a Christian denomination."[4] She also jokes, "Nones are the overachievers of the US religious landscape"[5]—her point being that if the nation's "religious Nones" were gathered together as a single demographic bloc, they would constitute one of the largest segments of the population, "larger than any Protestant denomination and *all* Mainline Protestant denominations combined."[6] Still, amidst the church's panic over the rise of the religious Nones[7] and the continuing secularization of Western culture,[8] Drescher cautions academics and church leaders not to lose sight of the fact that the Nones are *not* a homogenous group. Consequently, the search for some "quick fix" that will reverse demographic trends is likely to fail, given there is no cohesive entity called the Nones. Rather, scholars of religion have lumped together an uncategorizable plurality under a single rubric for the sake of convenience. Therefore, instead of focusing on what the church can do to bring Millennials and Gen Z back

---

2. Cone, "Vocation," 3.
3. Cone, "Vocation," 3.
4. Elizabeth Drescher, *Choosing Our Religion: The Spiritual Lives of America's Nones* (Oxford: Oxford University Press, 2016), 6.
5. Drescher, *Choosing*, 16.
6. Drescher, *Choosing*, 6.
7. Pew Research Center, "'Nones' on the Rise," October 9, 2012, https://www.pewforum.org/2012/10/09/nones-on-the-rise/.
8. See Callum G. Brown, *Becoming Atheist: Humanism and the Secular West* (London: Bloomsbury Academic, 2017), and Phil Zuckerman, Luke W. Galen, and Frank L. Pasquale, *The Nonreligious: Understanding Secular People and Societies* (Oxford: Oxford University Press, 2016).

into the fold, the church ought to listen to what these Nones are saying, in order to take spiritual inventory and get its own house in order.

Digging deeper into the makeup of this diverse and expanding group, it becomes evident that much of the disaffection among the key 18–29 demographic has to do with their rejection of a traditional church culture that reinforces certain cultural stereotypes, especially in matters of race, gender, and sexuality: "Surveys report that they [Nones] often turn up on the moderate or liberal side of social and political issues. And—being contemporary people with progressive values—surely they would insist on moving away from the stereotype of a male God, and one who is demanding, authoritarian, or punitive. . . . Many interviewees did not like the idea or term 'God' because they connected it with negative masculine stereotypes, such as the demanding, difficult-to-satisfy father, or the capricious king who could just as well smite you as help you."[9] For one Millennial who came out as lesbian in her mid-thirties, the struggle to leave the Catholic Church was complicated by what she saw as internal efforts within Catholicism to challenge the patriarchy:

> There are Catholic feminists. There are lots of women who are trying to change the church "from within." You know, they'll say, "we can't let them"—the male hierarchy—"push us out of our own church." I was like that for a long time. I didn't want to go. I wanted to help make a change.[10]

Ultimately, she left the Catholic Church but continued participating in Catholic spiritual practices. As they did for many members of the Millennial and Gen Z generations, the sex abuse scandals[11] and the role of the church

---

9. Linda A. Mercadante, *Belief without Borders: Inside the Minds of the Spiritual but Not Religious* (Oxford: Oxford University Press, 2014), 95.

10. Drescher, *Choosing*, 74.

11. While the sheer size of the Roman Catholic Church as a global religion has landed the spotlight upon Catholicism, it is important to note that similar sex scandals have plagued every Christian denomination, as well as nondenominational megachurches. For an analysis of the scandal within the Catholic Church, see Michael D'Antonio, *Mortal Sins: Sex, Crime, and the Era of Catholic Scandal* (New York: Macmillan, 2013); The Investigative Staff of the Boston Globe, *Betrayal: The Crisis in the Catholic Church* (Boston: Little, Brown, 2008). For an analysis of sex-abuse scandals across all denominations, see Patrick Parkinson, *Child Sexual Abuse and the Churches: Understanding the Issues* (Oxfordshire, UK: Routledge, 2003). For an exploration of these issues within Evangelicalism, see Emily Joy Allison, *#ChurchToo: How Purity Culture Upholds Abuse and How to Find Healing* (Minneapolis: Broadleaf, 2021). Also see this 2019 Pew Research Center study of US attitudes about the sex abuse scandal, which acknowledges numerous reports of sexual abuse in other religious organizations, including decades of abuse within the Southern Baptist Convention. Claire Gecewicz, "Key Takeaways about How Americans View the Sexual Abuse Scandal in the Catholic Church," Pew Research Center, June 11, 2019, https://www.pewresearch.org/fact-tank/2019/06/11/key-takeaways-about-how-americans-view-the-sexual-abuse-scandal-in-the-catholic-church/.

hierarchy in covering up abuse by priests[12] proved the straw that broke the camel's back: "You know, I stood by the church even through all the sex abuse scandals. At the time, I tried to focus on all the good that was done for the poor by people in Catholic churches—by women religious especially. I didn't excuse the abuse, but I didn't want to throw away all the good, too."[13]

This same pattern is repeated across Christian denominations as the culture, in the wake of the #MeToo movement, no longer tolerates sexual abuse and rape, as demonstrated by the third-party investigation of sexual abuse within the Southern Baptist Convention that documented a systemic cover-up of predatory sexual abuse by clergy and denominational leaders, including the intimidation and slander of accusers and evidence that "staff members were reportedly told not to even engage those asking about how to stop their child from being sexually violated by a minister."[14]

David Clohessy, former executive director of SNAP (Survivors Network of those Abused by Priests), contends that the sex abuse scandals, especially the cover-up by the church hierarchy—while not the only reason—contributes to the exodus of believers from the church: "Generations of Catholics have been raised to respect and revere priests and bishops and trust them implicitly. Even without the scandal, younger people are more skeptical and rightfully so. Most survivors are no longer churchgoers. Very few of their children are."[15] In the words of one young adult interviewed by the same journalist, the church's (lack of) response to the sex abuse scandals "'made me vote with my feet' and leave the church for good."[16]

In a 2020 study, the Public Religion Research Institute (PRRI) noted a leveling off in membership among mainline Protestant and Catholic churches

---

12. As the scandal continues to be investigated, now with greater cooperation from the Catholic hierarchy, the breadth of the conspiracy to cover up abuse by priests is staggering, with new evidence implicating Pope Benedict XIV in the cover-up during his time as archbishop of Munich and Freising. Bill Chappell, "Pope Benedict XVI Failed to Stop Sex Abuse When He Was an Archbishop, Law Firm Says," *National Public Radio* (January 20, 2022). https://www.npr.org/2022/01/20/1074355457/pope-benedict-xvi-sex-abuse-report.

13. Drescher, *Choosing*, 74–75.

14. Russell Moore, "This is the Southern Baptist Apocalypse," *Christianity Today* (May 22, 2022). https://www.christianitytoday.com/ct/2022/may-web-only/southern-baptist-abuse-apocalypse-russell-moore.html. The full report is available here: Guidepost Solutions LLC, "Report of the Independent Investigation: The Southern Baptist Convention Executive Committee's Response to Sexual Abuse Allegations and an Audit of the Procedures and Actions of the Credentials Committee," May 15, 2022. https://www.sataskforce.net/updates/guidepost-solutions-report-of-the-independent-investigation.

15. Kaya Oakes, "How to Make Nones and Lose Money: Study Shows Cost of Catholic Sex Abuse Scandals," *Religion Dispatches* (September 21, 2015). https://religiondispatches.org/how-to-make-nones-and-lose-money-study-shows-cost-of-catholic-sex-abuse-scandals/.

16. Oakes, "How to Make Nones and Lose Money."

after decades of decline while documenting the more recent drop among Evangelical churches, especially white Evangelical churches.[17] Despite tangible panic within Christian denominations, from mainline Protestant to Catholic to Evangelical, the survey data shows an overwhelming majority of Americans still believe in God or some higher power, despite the rise of the religiously unaffiliated.[18] PRRI data also confirms Linda Mercadante's analysis that Nones fit the pattern of those who in previous generations have described themselves as "spiritual but not religious" (SBNR); that is, those who have not fully abandoned religious belief but just left organized religion. In other words, rather than marking the rapid secularization of US society and culture, the growth of religious Nones among the younger generations polled is marked by "an amazing proliferation of spiritual alternatives which both promote and cultivate the significant proportion of the 'nones' who are looking to develop their own spirituality apart from traditional structures."[19]

According to the Pew Research Center, "one-third of Americans say they do not believe in the God of the Bible, but that they do believe there is some other higher power or spiritual force in the universe. A slim majority of Americans (56%) say they believe in God 'as described in the Bible.' And one-in-ten do not believe in any higher power or spiritual force."[20] Yet a closer look at the data from the 4,700 adults polled by Pew in 2018 reveals that for all the vexation with "traditional" biblical language, popular beliefs about God in the US continue to reflect a fairly orthodox consensus: "Overall, about half of Americans (48%) say that God or another higher power directly determines what happens in their lives all or most of the time," and "Nearly eight-in-ten U.S. adults think God or a higher power has protected them."[21] Most telling, a predominance (72 percent) of the religiously unaffiliated—a group that brings together those who identify as atheist, agnostic, or "nothing at all"—still "believe in a higher power of some kind, even if not in God as described in the Bible."[22]

---

17. See Robert P. Jones, Natalie Jackson, Diana Orcés, and Ian Huff, "The 2020 Census of American Religion," Public Religion Research Institute (July 8, 2021). https://www.prri.org/research/2020-census-of-american-religion/.

18. Pew Research Center, "When Americans Say They Believe in God, What Do They Mean?," April 25, 2018, https://www.pewforum.org/2018/04/25/when-americans-say-they-believe-in-god-what-do-they-mean/.

19. Mercadante, *Belief without Borders*, 4.

20. Pew Research Center, "When Americans Say They Believe in God, What Do They Mean?"

21. Pew Research Center, "When Americans Say They Believe in God, What Do They Mean?"

22. Pew Research Center, "When Americans Say They Believe in God, What Do They Mean?"

Consequently, the 2020 Census of American Religion conducted by PRRI substantiates the claim that the demographic "collapse" of institutional religion is stabilizing, for even the most rapid decline—among white Evangelical Christians—has slowed down, while the number of religiously unaffiliated has declined slightly since 2018 (with the numbers among Christians of color and non-Christian religious groups remaining stable).[23] In light of the argument that Western culture is becoming increasingly fragmented, and that a return to an earlier model of cultural Christendom is extremely unlikely (and, I would argue, undesirable), one of the most important points to be gleaned from the PRRI study is that Americans ages 18–29 are not only the most likely to answer "nothing at all" when asked what religion they profess; they also constitute *the most religiously diverse age group* in the United States. As one male Millennial describes his journey,

> I guess I still have a lot of religion in me, you could say. It just comes out differently now. I feel comfortable in a church for the most part, or in a Buddhist temple, or whatever even if I don't exactly believe what they believe. I think it is good when people pray together and sing. All religions have something good in them, even the most small-minded of them. I like that. I like to be open to all of it.[24]

Accordingly, while secularism and atheism account for a small but constant percentage of the global population (especially in Europe and North America), the growth of the religiously unaffiliated in the United States is also attributable to an expanding diversity of religious perspectives and a more religiously pluralistic future, rather than increased secularization alone.[25] In fact, the religiously unaffiliated are projected to decline as a share of the global population (from 16.4 percent in 2010 to 13.2 percent in 2050), while Islam and Christianity will see continued growth. Islam is currently the world's fastest growing religion, while global Christianity continues to grow at a slower pace, so that by 2050 Christianity and Islam combined will account for 64 percent of the world's population.[26] Perhaps most surprising is that by 2050 the atheist state of China could become the world's largest Muslim and Christian nation, given that today the government of China estimates there are over 78 million

---

23. Jones, Jackson, Orcés, and Huff, "The 2020 Census of American Religion," 7–10.
24. Drescher, *Choosing*, 25.
25. See John Micklethwait and Adrian Wooldridge, *God Is Back: How the Global Rise of Faith Is Changing the World* (New York: Penguin, 2009).
26. Pew Research Center, "The Future of World Religions: Population Growth Projections, 2010–2050," April 2, 2015, http://www.pewforum.org/2015/04/02/religious-projections-2010-2050/.

Christians and about 20 million Muslims in China, which according to the Pew Center on Religion and Public Life are very conservative estimates.[27]

Regardless, given that a majority of the religiously unaffiliated in the US were raised within a Christian confessional setting, even if expressing deep dissatisfaction with how the institutional church articulates and embodies its beliefs, conceptions of God among the Nones remain intelligible within the framework of the Western Christian intellectual tradition. Therefore, the church ought to view the rise of the Nones as an opportunity to understand and learn from the challenges and insights embodied in the 18–29 demographic. Christianity is still the largest religion in the US (by far), but the demographic decline signals the breakup of Christian hegemony in the West (Europe and North America),[28] aided by the decentering of power and authority within world Christianity as the churches of the Global South continue to grow and assert their influence on the vestiges of a Eurocentric Christendom.[29] The challenge for the church is not combating the rise and spread of atheism; the challenge for white, Eurocentric Christianity entails accepting and adapting to its greatly reduced place within Global Christianity, as well as the increased competition from non-Christian religions and nontraditional spiritualities.

One challenge I have encountered teaching theology to this youngest generation of students at a private religious university is the fact that more and more students come to my Theological Foundations course—required of all undergraduate students—with little to no knowledge of Christianity, the Bible, or even religion in general. Recognizing that anecdotal evidence has limited value, due to the fact that it is rarely gathered in a manner that is both empirical and verifiable according to the scientific method, twenty years of classroom teaching experience nonetheless provide a unique vantage point from which to observe the rise of the religious Nones. In 2004, when I first started teaching at Saint Louis University (SLU), a Jesuit Catholic university in the midwestern United States, most students in my Theological Foundations

---

27. Pew Research Center, "The Future of World Religions: Population Growth Projections, 2010–2050"; also see Pew Research Center, "The Global Religious Landscape," December 18, 2012, https://www.pewforum.org/2012/12/18/global-religious-landscape-exec/.

28. See Francis Rothery, *Missional: Impossible! The Death of Institutional Christianity and the Rebirth of G-d* (Eugene, OR: Wipf & Stock, 2014); Hugh McLeod and Werner Ustorf, *The Decline of Christendom in Western Europe, 1750–2000* (Cambridge: Cambridge University Press, 2003); Nancy Christie, Stephen J. Heathorn, and Michael Gauvreau, eds., *The Sixties and Beyond: Dechristianization in North America and Western Europe, 1945–2000* (Toronto: University of Toronto Press, 2013).

29. See Philip Jenkins, *The New Faces of Christianity: Believing the Bible in the Global South* (New York: Oxford University Press, 2016); Dyron B. Daughrity, *Rising: The Amazing Story of Christianity's Resurrection in the Global South* (Minneapolis: Fortress, 2018); Elijah Jong Fil Kim, *The Rise of the Global South: The Decline of Western Christendom and the Rise of Majority World Christianity* (Eugene, OR: Wipf & Stock, 2012).

course were Roman Catholic, with previous religious education, whether catechetical instruction in their home parish or theology classes at a Catholic high school. In the years since, I have observed some gradual changes. First, the number of Roman Catholic students with a Catholic high school education began to decrease over time; gradually Protestant students—primarily some form of Evangelical Christian—closed the gap with Catholic students (though 50 percent of SLU undergraduate students still identify as Catholic).

Then, in the last three to five years, non-Christian students at Saint Louis University have become a more visible presence. Some of this can be attributed to shifting demographics, resulting from increased international student recruitment from regions like the Middle East, South Asia, and East Asia, but given that the majority of undergraduate students at Saint Louis University come from US midwestern states, the shift in religious affiliation from Christian to None at SLU follows national patterns for Gen Z students.[30] In other words, given that an overwhelming number of SLU undergraduates, even those who claim "no religious affiliation," at one time identified as Christian, understanding the dissatisfaction with and exodus from Christianity by young people age 18–29 remains a pressing concern for Christian institutions.

Undoubtedly, one of the factors contributing to the rise of religious Nones is simply that while their parents might have been raised Christian, many in *this* generation of students have had little exposure to Christianity, as evidenced from this comment by a first-year student in Theological Foundations: "This year was the first time I have read a bible verse. Growing up, my family never taught me to believe one thing or another, and let me think for myself as I progressed through my public education." For other students, especially those majoring in the natural sciences, there is real resentment about the narrow worldview imposed by their religious upbringing:

> I felt like a chump. There I was thinking I was so smart. You know, all the parents always brag about how much better homeschooled kids do on standardized tests. I did so well on the SATs. I actually had a full academic scholarship. I was that smart. And I also thought the universe was six thousand years old. I actually believed that. . . . Who the fuck sends their kids out into the world thinking that? What was wrong with my parents that they believed these domineering, self-deluded church leaders who told them to teach us this stuff?[31]

---

30. According to the Office of Institutional Research (OIR), only 5 percent of SLU undergraduates in the 2021 incoming class come from outside the United States. See "Saint Louis University: 2021 Profile." https://www.slu.edu/about/key-facts/slu-profile.pdf.

31. Drescher, *Choosing*, 70.

Introduction 9

For many Gen Z students, changes in attitudes concerning institutional religion are grounded in some ideological disagreement or personal disappointment with the church. There is some consensus that "the majority of Nones who retain a belief in a supernatural being or power that acts within human life" conceptualize their faith within an unaffiliated spirituality that "sets any supernatural engagement primarily in the concrete reality of the here-and-now" rather than some "promised eternal hereafter."[32] Because the majority of Nones come from some type of religious background, they inevitably employ religious language when speaking about their views—especially moral beliefs. Yet, what distinguishes this generation is that they retain some degree of faith or spirituality without prioritizing any one confessional tradition, while also tolerating moral and religious pluralism. Meaningful engagement with these students can lead to a rediscovery of faith, even if said faith is located *extra muros ecclesiae* ("outside the walls of the church"), as evidenced by another student's comments:

> I went into this course thinking it was going to be just another Bible study similar to what I have been doing my whole life. I was very pleased to learn that our goal was to actually try and find some answers, analyze, and critique our faith. . . . I not only connected with my past self and began to be intrigued by my religion again, but I learned a lot of useful information about our society as a whole.

Perhaps the widespread panic ignited by the rise of the Nones has been overstated, and the church's response ought to be tempered with caution, since the data shows both a stabilizing decline and a more focused identification of the causes behind the decline.

I have always pursued my vocation as a theologian guided by David Tracy's axiom that the theologian addresses three publics simultaneously: the church, the academy, and the public square.[33] Admittedly, I am at a point in my life where I am having doubts as to the effectiveness of the *ecclesia* in the public discourse. Don't get me wrong—I am fully committed to a vision of Christian "life together" amidst the public square, working with non-Christians to build the common good. But time and experience have taught me to readjust my expectations concerning the efficacy of Christian witness in the contemporary world. Despite identifying as a "political" theologian, I don't believe in five-year plans. Suspicious of authoritarian projects, be they theological or political, I long ago gave up any desire at controlling the powers and

---

32. Drescher, *Choosing*, 248.
33. See David Tracy, *The Analogical Imagination: Christian Theology and the Culture of Pluralism* (New York: Crossroad, 1981), 1–28, 99–135.

principalities (Eph. 6:12) and have redirected my efforts at goading—even shaming—the powers that be into more compassionate behavior. In other words, I am not trying to remake the public square in my image, but simply entering and engaging the public square as a Christian, while focused on the common good. Unfortunately, many Christians in the US seek to blur the lines between church and state and are actively working for the return of Christendom by means of a politically imposed Christian hegemony.[34] Still, the rapid and continuing demographic decline of Christianity over the last decade suggests a near future in which self-identified, practicing Christians no longer constitute a demographic majority of the United States.[35] Which is not to say that secularism has triumphed, but only that Christianity—especially white Christianity—will no longer be the presumed dominant culture.

Contemporary Christianity in the US is undergoing a process of deconstruction. Rooted in the atheist and secular attacks on revealed religion by the great masters of suspicion—figures like Friedrich Nietzsche, Karl Marx, and Sigmund Freud—the concept of deconstruction was popularized via the semiotic analysis of Jacques Derrida, who rejected the static and unchanging essentialism of Platonism.[36] Deconstruction argues that language, especially when applied to abstract concepts like truth, justice, and beauty, is irreducibly complex, ever changing, and in constant flux. Therefore, a deconstructionist approach is intentionally postmetaphysical by limiting meaning to the interrelationships within language, without positing an underlying and corresponding nonlinguistic reality.

---

34. See Frances Fitzgerald, *The Evangelicals: The Struggle to Shape America* (New York: Simon & Schuster, 2017). Fitzgerald traces the evolution of the Christian Right from a populist countercultural movement to a major political player in conservative politics. Also see Benjamin T. Lynerd, *Republican Theology: The Civil Religion of American Evangelicals* (Oxford: Oxford University Press, 2014). Lynerd argues that the Christian Right is promoting an Evangelical civil religion that is increasingly Republican, straight, white, and male, marking the publication of Martin Luther King Jr.'s *Letter from a Birmingham Jail* (1963) as a major break within Evangelical politics, highlighted by "the relative silence of Republican theology in the face of structural injustice" (9). Finally, Andrew L. Whitehead and Samuel L. Perry, *Taking America Back for God: Christian Nationalism in the United States* (Oxford: Oxford University Press, 2020). The authors contend that the overwhelming support Donald Trump has among white Evangelical Christians—despite his all-too-public moral failings—is evidence of yet another transformation within American white Evangelicalism into a form of "Christian nationalism" that works to promote an authoritarian social order, an order in which everyone—Christians and non-Christians, native-born and immigrants, whites and minorities, men and women—is given their "proper" place in society.

35. Gregory A. Smith, "About Three-in-Ten U.S. Adults Are Now Religiously Unaffiliated," Pew Research Center, December 14, 2021, https://www.pewforum.org/2021/12/14/about-three-in-ten-u-s-adults-are-now-religiously-unaffiliated/.

36. See Jacques Derrida, *Of Grammatology*, trans. Gayatri Chakravorty Spivak, corrected ed. (Baltimore: Johns Hopkins University Press, 1997). In this influential volume Derrida introduces the majority of ideas that came to constitute the concept of deconstruction in textual analysis.

Philosopher John D. Caputo, influenced by Derrida, applies a deconstructive hermeneutic to the concepts of God and religion, an approach he calls weak theology. The goal of "weak" theology is not to dismiss or reject God or religious belief, but to recognize the limits of philosophical and theological claims by positing instead an almost mystical understanding of God as an unconditional presence that does not employ coercion when relating to humankind within human history. Caputo gives voice to the struggle many intelligent and educated people of faith have with traditional theism:

> By "God," on the other hand, I do not mean a being who is there, an entity trapped in being, even as a super-being *up there*, up above the world, who physically powers and causes it, who made it and occasionally intervenes upon its day-to-day activities to tweak things for the better in response to a steady stream of solicitations from down below (a hurricane averted here, an illness averted there, etc.). That I consider an essentially magical view of the world. . . . I mean a call that solicits and disturbs what is there, an event that adds a level of signification and meaning, of provocation and solicitation to what is there, that makes it impossible for the world, for what is *there*, to settle solidly in place, to consolidate, to close in upon itself. By the name of "God" I mean the event of this solicitation, an event of deconsolidation, an electrifying event-ing disturbance, the solvent of the weak force of this spectral spirit who haunts the world as its bad conscience, or who breathes lightly and prompts its most inspired moments, all the while readily conceding that there are other names than the name of God. I am trying to save the name of God, not absolutize it.[37]

Dismissive of traditional theism, Caputo's deconstruction of theology nevertheless remains open and receptive to the idea of divine revelation and thus is compatible with theological notions of divine agency as *manifestation*, an experience described by many Christians "as uncanny gift and command, a power not one's own."[38] Caputo's weak theology also resonates with Paul Tillich's notion of the "God above God," a sympathetic critique of traditional theism that "takes seriously the radical doubt experienced by many people. It gives one the courage of self-affirmation even in the extreme state of radical doubt."[39] Tillich's "God above God" transcends confessional Christianity. In Caputo's language, this helps preserve the name of God by not absolutizing it.

---

37. John D. Caputo, *The Weakness of God: A Theology of the Event* (Bloomington: Indiana University Press, 2006), 39–40.
38. Tracy, *The Analogical Imagination*, 371.
39. Paul Tillich, *Systematic Theology*, vol. 2 (Chicago: University of Chicago Press, 1957), 12.

In *Dogmatics after Babel* (2018), I argued that Enlightenment rationalism is modernity's very own Tower of Babel—an imaginary construct designed to stave off uncertainty and chaos through the imposition of a singular, monolithic rationality—whose foundations are just as uncertain as those of the Age of Belief that preceded it.[40] That book developed a critique of modernism's emphasis on truth as a narrowly epistemological concern by promoting narrative knowledge, since rationality is more than merely "getting the facts right"; human rationality originates in the creation of stories that help us cope with the world. The goal of such narratives is not certainty but edification, the moral and/or intellectual improvement of a person through a process of social and cultural formation.

Like Caputo's deconstructed theology, my approach does not seek to impose one narrative above all others but welcomes *many* discourses to the ongoing public conversation on "how best to live"—with the proviso that no single narrative imposes itself as normative for all. *This* book explores what happens when Christians abandon their reliance on metanarratives and embrace the fragmented and incomplete nature of human cognition, aware that the stories we weave are *at best* snapshots of reality—or more accurately, snapshots of some localized reality—while also recognizing that God's manifestation in the world is itself incomplete, fragmentary, and open-ended.

Within US Catholicism, mainline Protestantism, and Evangelicalism the decline in church membership has been accompanied by popularized versions of this deconstruction hermeneutic promulgated by public figures like Richard Rohr,[41] John Pavlovitz,[42] and Rachel Held Evans.[43] Pavlovitz describes his

---

40. Rubén Rosario Rodríguez, *Dogmatics after Babel: Beyond the Theologies of Word and Culture* (Louisville, KY: Westminster John Knox, 2018), xi–xix, 1–33.

41. Richard Rohr, OFM, is a Franciscan priest and writer of popular books on spirituality who founded the Center for Action and Contemplation (CAC) in Albuquerque, New Mexico, in 1986. The CAC is an educational nonprofit organization introducing spiritual seekers to the contemplative Christian path of transformation, founded on certain "prophetic" principles expounded in Rohr's books critical of the institutional church's failure to transform its members and therefore becoming increasingly irrelevant. See Richard Rohr, *Yes, and . . . : Daily Meditations* (Cincinnati: Franciscan Media, 2013) and *The Divine Dance: The Trinity and Your Transformation* (London: SPCK, 2016).

42. John Pavlovitz is a Unitarian pastor and author known for his progressive social and political writings. He worked for nearly a decade as youth pastor at the Good Shepherd United Methodist Church, a megachurch in Charlotte, North Carolina, before being fired for a series of controversial blog postings espousing support for LGBTQ church members and voicing criticism of Christians who voted for Donald Trump in 2016. See John Pavlovitz, *If God Is Love, Don't Be a Jerk: Finding a Faith That Makes Us Better Humans* (Louisville, KY: Westminster John Knox, 2021) and *A Bigger Table: Building Messy, Authentic, and Hopeful Spiritual Community* (Louisville, KY: Westminster John Knox, 2017).

43. The late Rachel Held Evans (1981–2019) was a popular columnist, blogger, and author who chronicled her departure from Evangelicalism due to the movement's close association with the Christian right in the United States. See Rachel Held Evans, *Searching for Sunday:*

journey as a slow and evolving process of self-realization: "It was a gradual deconstruction of my faith. You look at one isolated area of the Bible, for example, then realize, Well, if that doesn't mean what I was taught it meant, what other areas of my spiritual journey was I taking for granted? So you start digging into it, and you find yourself exploring all areas of your belief system."[44]

For Rohr, a septuagenarian Franciscan priest known for running the Center for Action and Contemplation, part meditation retreat part religious school, overcoming the exclusion of Christian incarnational dogma is a major part of his deconstructionist agenda:

> We daringly believe that God's presence was poured into a single human being, so that humanity and divinity can be seen to be operating as one in him—and therefore in us! But instead of saying God came *into* the world through Jesus, maybe it would be better to say that Jesus came *out of* an already Christ-soaked world. The second Incarnation flowed out of the first, out of God's loving union with physical creation. If that still sounds strange to you, just trust me for a bit. I promise you it will only deepen and broaden your faith in both Jesus and the Christ.[45]

According to Rohr, Christianity has become a tribal religion by emphasizing the *uniqueness* of Jesus' incarnation, thereby *excluding* any other vessel of divine manifestation, severing Christ from his mission to unite humanity and divinity, thereby losing "the core of what Christianity might have become."[46]

Rachel Held Evans struggled with leaving the church of her youth, while still strongly identifying as Christian:

> I can find my way around a Bible backward and forward because evangelicals gave me that foundation—I was raised to love and cherish and be hungry for the Bible. But I don't use "evangelical" to describe myself anymore. It's taken on political connotations that I adamantly oppose. Trump has become this figurehead of Christianity, which I think is really harmful. But evangelical is such

---

Loving, Leaving, and Finding the Church (Nashville: Nelson, 2015), and Rachel Held Evans and Jeff Chu, *Wholehearted Faith* (San Francisco: HarperOne, 2021).

44. Amanda Abrams, "How Raleigh's John Pavlovitz Went from Fired Megachurch Pastor to Rising Star of the Religious Left," *INDYweek* (November 22, 2017). https://indyweek.com/news/raleigh-s-john-pavlovitz-went-fired-megachurch-pastor-rising-star-religious-left/.

45. Richard Rohr, *The Universal Christ: How a Forgotten Reality Can Change Everything We See, Hope For, and Believe* (New York: Crown Publishing Group, 2019), 15.

46. Rohr, *The Universal Christ*, 19.

a loosey-goosey term. You ask five evangelicals what it means and you get five different answers."[47]

In all her writings, Evans fought to "change the way Christianity is taught and perceived in the United States," and a major part of her legacy remains "her unwillingness to cede ownership of Christianity to its traditional conservative-male stewards."[48] As David P. Gushee, arguably the highest-profile defector from American Evangelicalism, reflects,[49] the cause of much of the discontent among ex-Evangelicals stems from the "sense that card-carrying American evangelicalism now requires acquiescence to attitudes and practices that *fundamentally* (aha!) negate core teachings of Jesus."[50] For Gushee, Evans, Pavlovitz, and many others who have attracted the public spotlight for criticizing "traditional" Christianity, the goal is "to try to articulate a more faithful version of faith."[51]

Forgotten among all this talk of deconstructing religious beliefs is the painful yet necessary task of *reconstruction*. Unless one simply walks away from the faith—sadly, an increasingly popular alternative—wrestling with belief involves not only critically evaluating church teachings, but also the more painful task of introspection and personal self-improvement. Christian spirituality, however else it is defined, entails a journey of self-discovery mediated by an encounter with a reality beyond the solipsistic confines of the modern self. Whether one envisages their encounter with Jesus of Nazareth as a mystical union with God incarnate, a disciple learning from the wise sage, or a social justice warrior in solidarity with the revolutionary hero, Jesus' impact on Western culture cannot be denied. As this culture fragments, it also reconfigures itself. Christianity must do the same.

---

47. Donna Freitas, "Ex-Evangelical Rachel Held Evans Still Cherishes Her Bible," *Publishers Weekly* (May 9, 2018). https://www.publishersweekly.com/pw/by-topic/industry-news/religion/article/76494-ex-evangelical-rachel-held-evans-on-feminism-and-the-bible.html.

48. Emma Green, "Rachel Held Evans, Hero to Christian Misfits," *Atlantic* (May 6, 2019). https://www.theatlantic.com/politics/archive/2019/05/rachel-held-evans-death-progressive-christianity/588784/.

49. David P. Gushee is a renowned Christian ethicist and public intellectual who rose to national prominence for his outspoken criticism of US policy on the use of torture techniques during the interrogation of detainees, serving as president of Evangelicals for Human Rights, an organization advocating for an end to torture. However, his break with US Evangelicalism came after the publication of his book *Changing Our Mind*, 2nd ed. (Canton, MI: Read the Spirit Books, 2015), in which he makes an argument—as an Evangelical believer—supporting LGBT inclusion. Gushee chronicles his departure from American Evangelicalism in *Still Christian: Following Jesus Out of American Evangelicalism* (Louisville, KY: Westminster John Knox, 2017).

50. David P. Gushee, *After Evangelicalism: The Path to a New Christianity* (Louisville, KY: Westminster John Knox, 2020), 27.

51. Gushee, *After Evangelicalism*, 27.

Unfortunately, many Christians feel threatened by deconstruction, even when it leads to finding a less toxic form of Christianity to call home, since for many spiritual seekers their struggles are not with following Jesus but with the religious institutions bearing his name. The church feels threatened, but for many Millennials and Gen Z believers it is *only* by deconstructing their religion that they can hold on to their faith. This book is offered as one Christian's journey of reconstruction, with some concern for the wreckage of the institutional church but motivated primarily by pastoral concern for those like me whose encounter with Jesus of Nazareth yields enough meaningful fragments to allow for careful reassembly.

1

A Broken and Contrite Theology

> Most young adults I know aren't looking for a religion that answers all of their questions, but rather a community of faith in which they feel safe to ask them.[1]

Human beings are storytelling animals. From our days as nomadic hunter-gatherers sitting around a campfire staving off the darkness and all its terrors—real or imagined—stories allow us to make sense of a complex and frightening world. Stories help us to cope with and transcend our relative insignificance in an infinite cosmos. Stories also create a sense of community and interdependence.

Since the Enlightenment, modernity has been associated with one overarching grand narrative—science—to the diminution of all others, but most pointedly to the exclusion of religion. Despite growing "incredulity toward metanarratives," scientific knowledge "has always been in conflict with narratives. Judged by the yardstick of science, the majority of them prove to be fables."[2] According to *this* story, scientific knowledge is contrasted with (and considered preferable to) narrative knowledge, because it lends itself to independent verification through repeated experimentation under controlled conditions. In other words, the claims of modern science are demonstrably

---

1. Rachel Held Evans, *Evolving in Monkey Town: How a Girl Who Knew All the Answers Learned to Ask the Questions* (Grand Rapids: Zondervan, 2010), 222.
2. Jean-François Lyotard, *The Postmodern Condition: A Report on Knowledge*, trans. Geoff Bennington and Brian Massumi (Minneapolis: University of Minnesota Press, 1984), xxiv, xxiii.

true or false and accessible to all, whereas the claims of religion are founded on unobservable and unrepeatable events that depend on often-unreliable secondhand accounts. Nevertheless, the reductive methodology of the natural sciences, its practical applications notwithstanding, cannot adequately describe the fullness of human existence. Consequently, any account of human knowledge and cognition—even science—must make room for narrative truth, especially when describing that distinctive kind of practical wisdom that gives life meaning and purpose, while also communicating how best to live.

While explicitly theological narratives were excised from the Enlightenment story, the marginalization of confessional perspectives need not continue, given growing suspicion of and dissatisfaction with the scientific worldview. This discontent is signaled by the loss of belief in historical progress, pessimism that the next generation will be worse off than the previous, and the sustained erosion of "authority" now confronting most established institutions, from churches to universities to governments.

Contemporary counternarratives have arisen in reaction to the naive presumption that all human problems can be resolved by technological advancements, with many postmodern narratives attributing much of their pessimism to the scientific virtues of "progress," "materialism," and "technology." In other words, knowledge (as wisdom) has more to do with the improvement of the self and the preservation of the common good than with epistemological certainty about a collection of facts. Unfortunately, some Christian thinkers have reacted to this discontentment with the Enlightenment's grand narrative by reasserting a distinctly Christian metaphysic: "we live in an era in which pre-modern metaphysical approaches to truth are returning to view, and to a renewed viability."[3] This type of reactionary riposte exposes the stubborn human tendency to construct stories that assert dominance over rival narratives rather than embrace dissensus, but does little to overcome secular suspicions about metaphysical thinking.

HERACLITIAN FLUX OR PLATONIC TOTALITY?

The ancient Hellenized world can be divided into two contrasting and largely incompatible narrative worldviews: the pre-Socratic perspective embodied by the philosophy of Heraclitus (ca. 540–480 BCE), and the Socratic point of view, most fully actualized in the works of Plato (ca. 428–348 BCE). Heraclitus

---

3. Catherine Pickstock, *Aspects of Truth: A New Religious Metaphysics* (Cambridge: Cambridge University Press, 2020), x.

viewed the cosmos as ever changing, chaotic, and in a constant state of flux: "You cannot step twice into the same river, for fresh waters are ever flowing upon you."[4] Legend has it one overenthusiastic disciple of Heraclitus took things a step further, proclaiming, "One cannot do it even once."[5] In other words, the universe presents us with plurality and constant change, challenging the belief that the universe is a rationally ordered place. Despite his disciple's assertion, Heraclitus believed reason attempts to systematize experience into a coherent unity, so the very fact that the human mind can organize the maelstrom of sensory experience reflects a human desire for order, even when such unity includes randomness and change as a necessary and constant aspect of the material universe.

The Platonic Ideal, however, posits that our sensory experiences of a universe in flux are but shadows cast by the real, eternal, and unchanging Forms. According to Plato in *The Republic*, sense perception cannot yield true knowledge, since that which is true is both infallible and real: "as the opinable is to the knowable so the image is to the model it is made like."[6] In other words, that which we represent in thought must have some basis in reality. Since sensory perception is unreliable and fallible, truth does not reside in sense experience but in pure thought—the realm of ideas—a transcendent and unchanging reality from which all our experiences and perceptions originate. Thus, in Plato's *Meno*, Socrates postulates the recollection theory of knowledge, which begins with the presumption that the soul is immortal, that reality is but a lesser shadow of eternal life, and that knowledge is only the recollection of Ideas encountered in the soul's past lives: "As the soul is immortal, has been born often and has seen all things here in the underworld, there is nothing which it has not learned; so it is in no way surprising that it can recollect the things it knew before."[7] In other words, Platonic knowledge is conceived as static, eternal, and all encompassing.

While the stories told within this Platonic framework provide some comfort, subsuming the chaotic messiness of experience under the foundational myth of the eternal and unchanging Forms, the Platonic Ideal is woefully inadequate for describing the expansive diversity of real life. Worse, its drive

---

4. John Burnet, *Early Greek Philosophy* (Whitefish, MT: Kessinger, 2003), 136 (Frags. 41 and 42).

5. Søren Kierkegaard, *Fear and Trembling*, trans. Walter Lowrie (Princeton, NJ: Princeton University Press, 1941), 221.

6. Plato, *Plato's Republic*, trans. G. M. A. Grube (Indianapolis: Hackett, 1974), 165 (510a7–8).

7. Plato, *Meno*, trans. G. M. A. Grube (Indianapolis: Hackett, 1976), 14 (81c5–81d).

to universal sameness can manifest in dangerous totalitarianisms.[8] There is a reductionist tendency in scientific description, traceable to the Platonic Ideal, that seeks to universalize the particular in order to arrive at an orderly set of "laws," which loses sight of the myriad wonders of creation, in its drive to catalog and categorize. In other words, instead of rejoicing in the fact that there are over 3,000 different species of catfish and celebrating what makes each one unique, biological classification systems identify that which unites them as catfish, or more generally, as fish. The science of taxonomy looks at the 60,000–100,000 different species of trees worldwide, then categorizes their leaves into two broad morphological categories, literally missing the forest for the trees. That is to say, the natural world in all its complexity cannot be fully described employing idealized Platonic forms for fish or tree. Rather, the natural world demands an accounting true to its vast biodiversity and astonishing complexity. Without undermining the practical benefits of reductionist taxonomies, there is also room in our conception of scientific knowledge for more expansive aesthetic description.

The same diversity also exists within human cultures and religions. There are over 6,000 different languages spoken in the world today, but no universal language (despite utopian efforts to create one like Esperanto), only local and distinctive languages. Furthermore, no living language is ever fixed and complete, since languages evolve as humans constantly strive to say something new or describe what has never been experienced before. Anthropologists also estimate there are over 4,000 religions in the world. Given that the forces of globalization have "shrunk" the world—whether through the ease of migration or increased interaction via modern technology—religionists need to come to terms with the fact that even if their faith makes absolute demands on *them*, there is no single religion for *all* of humanity. Just as we cannot study language in abstraction but must engage particular languages in order to understand one another, we cannot interact with other cultures and religions as if all cultures and religions are the same.

The drive to "essentialize" humanity into a single universal form not only denies the heterogeneity that constitutes humanity; it also fuels imperialist, totalitarian, and genocidal projects that cannot tolerate diversity and difference, as the horrors of the Holocaust have demonstrated. The seed for this hegemonic tendency can be found in Plato's idealized vision of the state described in *The Republic*, where the *polis* ("city state") exists for the noble

---

8. See chapter 3, "The Dignity of Difference: Exorcizing Plato's Ghost," in Jonathan Sacks, *The Dignity of Difference: How to Avoid the Clash of Civilizations*, repr. ed. (New York: Bloomsbury USA, 2003), 39–56.

purpose of establishing the happiness of its citizens by helping them attain the good life in accordance with the principles of justice. Without knowledge of the good and the just, the individual cannot be moral, and yet not everyone seeks this knowledge. Therefore, one of the principal functions of the state is *paideia* ("education"), to form its citizens into a community of like-minded philosophers: "in the intelligible world the Form of the Good is the last to be seen, and with difficulty; when seen it must be reckoned to be for all the cause of all that is right and beautiful . . . and he who is to act intelligently in public or in private must see it."[9] According to Plato, the Form of the Good is eternal, unchanging, and singular: the objective foundation for building the good life and establishing the just state. Unfortunately, totalitarianism arises from this well-meaning impulse to create social unity ("justice") by imposing one universal perspective ("truth")—to the detriment of human diversity *and* particularity.

For better or worse, the dominant paradigm for Christian systematic theology has been the Platonic Ideal. Consequently, the discipline of systematic theology has, until recently, been characterized as the orderly, rational, and coherent account of Christian beliefs grounded primarily in divine self-revelation mediated through the sacred Scriptures, but also encompassing natural revelation, or that which can be known about God by human reason through observation of the physical universe (in the medieval Christian tradition the Book of Nature was always read alongside sacred Scripture). The *Summa Theologiae* of Thomas Aquinas (ca. 1225–1274) stands as the prime example of an orderly and comprehensive systematic theology that addresses Christian faith under a unifying and ordering principle, beginning with philosophical proofs for the existence of God and from there moving to the attributes of God, which in turn leads to all the major loci of Christian doctrine. The result is as complex and interconnected an architectural whole as the vast medieval cathedrals of his age.

To reiterate, Christian systematic theology was born from the encounter of ancient Greek and Roman philosophies with the Hebraic biblical worldview. Consequently, doctrines seldom mentioned in Scripture, like the notion of a benevolent Providence watching over all creation (which "hardly features at all in the Bible"),[10] became integral to Christian belief. Yet, for the modern believer, asserting that the universe began by random chance, while also affirming the Christian dogmatic claim that everything exists by the authority

---

9. *Plato's Republic*, 170 (517c4–6).

10. David Fergusson, *The Providence of God: A Polyphonic Approach* (Cambridge: Cambridge University Press, 2018), 2.

and design of a benevolent and omnipotent intelligence, leads to contradictions. This tension becomes highly problematic when considering the problem of evil and innocent suffering. Is it the case that God wills evil, and is therefore morally responsible for innocent suffering? Or is it the case that God does not will evil, but is unable to prevent it? Either God is not benevolent, or God is not omnipotent. Neither option is particularly comforting.

Herein lies the conflict with the natural sciences, specifically the Darwinian notion of common descent, which says all life on earth has evolved from a common, single-celled ancestor through a natural, undirected process involving random chance and mutation. How can modern believers continue to assert belief in a divine providence "everywhere active in nature,"[11] when the foundations of modern science imply a process of natural selection divorced from any notion of a guiding—let alone benevolent—rationality? As Charles Darwin argued in a letter to the Harvard botanist Asa Gray, one of Darwin's most ardent supporters in the United States and a devout Presbyterian, "I cannot persuade myself that a beneficent and omnipotent God would have designedly created the *Ichneumonidae* [parasitic wasps] with the express intention of their feeding within the living bodies of caterpillars."[12] Once again, the believer is left with one of two options, either God is not omnipotent and cannot direct and control the process of natural selection, or God is not as benevolent a figure as we have been led to believe.

In the modern era, the coherence and sweeping scope of theological systems have been called into question by the exactness of the natural sciences, bolstered by unparalleled technological progress, so that Christian dogmatic claims no longer occupy a central place in Western intellectual thought. This dislocation of systematic theology in the post-Enlightenment era calls to mind one of the parables of Kierkegaard:

> A thinker erects an immense building, a system, a system which embraces the whole of existence and world-history etc.—and if we contemplate his personal life, we discover to our astonishment this terrible and ludicrous fact, that he himself personally does not live in the immense high-vaulted palace, but in a barn alongside of it, or in a dog kennel, or at the most in the porter's lodge.[13]

---

11. Fergusson, *The Providence of God*, 8.

12. Charles Darwin, letter to Asa Gray, dated 22 May 1860, published by the University of Cambridge as part of the Darwin Correspondence Project. https://www.darwinproject.ac.uk/letter/DCP-LETT-2814.xml.

13. Søren Kierkegaard, *The Sickness unto Death*, trans. Walter Lowrie (Princeton, NJ: Princeton University Press, 1941), 176–77.

Today the ambitious projects of systematic theology stand mostly empty. Has there ever been a *New York Times* bestselling systematic theology? Perhaps it is time for the discipline of theology to abandon the Platonic paradigm, which views knowledge as eternal and unchanging, and embrace the Heraclitian, by acknowledging the open-endedness and provisional nature of dogmatic claims.

This book presents a constructive approach that welcomes the fragmented and incomplete nature of theological knowledge by focusing on personal and spiritual formation of the self in society instead of the institutional survival of the church. Through the critical retrieval of *relevant theological fragments* from across the Christian tradition, theology is better equipped to reach the unchurched and religious Nones in the secularized spaces where they reside—a theology of the barns and dog kennels.

TOWARD A THEOLOGY OF THE BARNS AND KENNELS

To be fair, several exciting and promising systematic theologies have been written recently that manage to resist the totalizing impulse of the Platonic paradigm.[14] While some theologians, especially those identified with Radical Orthodoxy, pursue the postmodern reassertion of a distinctly Christian metaphysics, others affirm the unity of God as simultaneously transcendent to and immanent within creation, such that the transcendence of God need not alienate God from human cultures, even non-Christian cultures.[15]

Rather than rebuild ancient, long-abandoned ruins, theology as I envision it seeks a more modest agenda—a project that limits human theological claims in light of the ineffable mystery of God. In communicating the Christian tradition to a secularized and politically polarized culture, theology must engage the pressing issues of the day, from economic globalization to ecological degradation, from racial and ethnic strife to the breakdown of civil society. This is theology with eyes wide open, aware that its cultural impact is waning, speaking to the religious Nones who are leaving the church in greater and greater numbers, while trying to convince them that Christianity is more than an outmoded metaphysical system that rejects modern science and perpetuates

---

14. See Katherine Sonderegger, *Systematic Theology*, vol. 1, *The Doctrine of God* (Minneapolis: Fortress, 2015) and *Systematic Theology*, vol. 2, *The Doctrine of the Holy Trinity: Processions and Persons* (Minneapolis: Fortress, 2020); Douglas F. Ottati, *A Theology for the Twenty-First Century* (Grand Rapids: Eerdmans, 2020); and Sarah Coakley, *God, Sexuality, and the Self: An Essay "On the Trinity"* (Cambridge: Cambridge University Press, 2013).

15. See Orlando O. Espín, *Idol & Grace: Traditioning and Subversive Hope* (Maryknoll, NY: Orbis Books, 2014).

oppressive structures. So conceived, theology becomes a form of *practical wisdom*, enriched by its encounter with humanist learning and modern political liberalism as it directs itself to the academy, the church, and "those who hover agonizingly at the edges of institutionalized religion."[16]

Which brings us back to the stories we tell. We are witnessing the collapse of the Enlightenment's grand narrative, described by Latin American philosopher Enrique Dussel as an "ideological Totality" that facilitated the conquest and colonization of America, Africa, and Asia by disguising "oppression" behind the promise of "progress,"[17] a reality mourned by some and celebrated by others. While the demise of the modernist metanarrative is all but certain, a question still undecided is whether some other metanarrative will rise to take its place. For the moment, however, David Tracy has opined, "fragments are our spiritual situation."[18] The fragmentation of knowledge need not signal a collapse of social order, though conflicting narratives can generate political upheaval and social unrest—even violence—as evidenced by the US Capitol uprising on January 6, 2021.[19] The modernist metanarrative collapsed because it imposed a unifying totality (white, Eurocentric, colonialist, Christian) upon an unwieldy plurality—the defining myths of many diverse colonized cultures.

While this critical mass of indigenous narratives never coalesced into a single unified resistance, each one contributed to modernity's eventual death from a million paper cuts. The broken fragments of these mythic stories still breathe, their narrative power unabated, despite never occupying a position of privilege as the "apex" narrative, revealing a vast mosaic of story fragments distinguished by ambiguity and uncertainty demanding dialogue and interpretation. Most postmodern religionists recognize theology will never again ascend to its former place as "queen of the sciences," yet still view the collapse of religious certainty into innumerable revelatory fragments with some hope.

My assessment of the contemporary situation reveals that certain narrative fragments have more potency than others; some continue to assert themselves as an "ideological Totality" that must be resisted, while others risk fading into cultural irrelevance but *require* resurrecting. Without embracing every aspect of modern Western thought, we can identify those pieces of the Enlightenment

---

16. Coakley, *God, Sexuality, and the Self*, xv.
17. Enrique Dussel, *A History of the Church in Latin America*, trans. Alan Neely (Grand Rapids: Eerdmans, 1981), 6.
18. David Tracy, *Fragments: The Existential Situation of Our Time: Selected Essays*, vol. 1 (Chicago: University of Chicago Press, 2020), 22.
19. See Drew Harwell, Isaac Stanley-Becker, Razzan Nakhlawi, and Craig Timberg, "QAnon Reshaped Trump's Party and Radicalized Believers. The Capitol Siege May Just Be the Start," *Washington Post* (January 13, 2021). https://www.washingtonpost.com/technology/2021/01/13/qanon-capitol-siege-trump/.

tradition that remain vital and necessary for our age—like democratic pluralism. More germane to the task of Christian theology, these dislocated narrative fragments become an occasion for encountering the divine other, not by accident but by design. In this setting, the stories of Jesus provide an anchor to focus and direct our own narratives. In *Dogmatics after Babel*, I employed the hiddenness of God (*Deus absconditus*) as a guiding hermeneutical principle.[20] A similar concept is found in both Judaism and Islam. Therefore, though the divine hiddenness might sometimes contribute to the believer's loss of faith, God allows human beings to live with incomprehension and confusion, because the full mystery of God can never be contained by human thought: "affirming that there is one God, that this God is known primarily through God's own action, and that even in God's self-disclosure God is not fully known but remains mystery, *demands* a conception of theology as an imperfect and incomplete human endeavor."[21] Consequently, given the fragmented nature of human knowing, itself a consequence of the fact that God never grants full comprehension of the divine, it becomes necessary to proceed with a methodological humility that encourages tolerance, compassion, and patience.

Christoph Schwöbel notes, what "can be known about Jesus by means of the possibilities of human historical reconstruction is not revelation," which is why Karl Barth argues revelation "can only be known where God makes himself [*sic*] known *through creating faith*."[22] To the frustration of generations of New Testament scholars, Karl Barth concludes that any attempt to unearth the historical Jesus behind the canon is misguided, since it ignores the pedagogical intent of the New Testament, which is to enable the believer's confession that Jesus is Lord:

> Whoever says "Jesus Christ" may not say, "It might be possible," but rather, must say, "It *is*." Yet which one of us is in the position to say "Jesus Christ"? *We* must satisfy ourselves with the fact that "Jesus Christ" *has been said* by his first witnesses. Our task is to believe in their witness, to believe in the promise, and to be witnesses of their witness—to be theologians of *Scripture*.[23]

---

20. Rosario Rodríguez, *Dogmatics after Babel*, 131–39.
21. Rosario Rodríguez, *Dogmatics after Babel*, 136.
22. Christoph Schwöbel, "Theology," in *The Cambridge Companion to Karl Barth*, ed. John Webster (Cambridge: Cambridge University Press, 2000), 24 (emphasis added). Though every effort is made to use gender-inclusive language throughout this work, sources cited retain the original wording of the author and/or translator.
23. Karl Barth, "The Word of God as the Task of Theology," in *The Word of God and Theology*, ed. and trans. Amy Marga (London: T. & T. Clark, 2011), 198.

This unyielding dogmatic stance alienated even his friend and former student Dietrich Bonhoeffer, who critiqued this aspect of Karl Barth's thought even while praising his contributions:

> Barth was the first theologian—to his great and lasting credit—to begin the critique of religion, but he then put in its place a positivist doctrine of revelation that says, in effect, "like it or lump it." Whether it's the virgin birth, the Trinity, or anything else, all are equally significant and necessary parts of the whole, which must be swallowed whole or not at all.[24]

As the philosopher Søren Kierkegaard noted, whether one is an eyewitness to the miracles attributed to Jesus or is two thousand years removed from those events, historical facts do not bring one to belief: "Eighteen hundred years makes absolutely no difference; they neither change Christ nor reveal who he was, for who he is is revealed only to faith."[25] The doctrine of revelation informing the exegetical method of Karl Barth, himself deeply influenced by Kierkegaard, looks at the past, present, and future life of Jesus as an internally coherent narrative of God's self-revelation in human history.

According to Barth, this essential unity of the New Testament canon as witness to the life of God incarnate means the biblical authors and the first generation of eyewitnesses can be trusted to provide a reliable account of divine self-revelation, so that all contemporary efforts to interpret these texts as Word of God ought to be read through the matrix of this earliest layer of the Christian tradition. The Greek word *apokalypsis*, translated as "revelation," literally means to uncover or disclose. In Christian theology the term has come to mean knowledge of God disclosed by an act of God, who even in this act of self-revelation remains incomprehensible mystery. On a fundamental level, this means there are limits to what humankind can know about God. Even in God's hiddenness, however, God is *revealed as God wants to be known*: "Knowing the true God in His revelation, we apprehend Him in his Hiddenness."[26] In other words,

> However partial and incomplete our reception of revelation may be, revelation is not partial on the side of God's act. God reveals himself by appearing *in person*, as the Subject of a human life in

---

24. Dietrich Bonhoeffer, *Letters and Papers from Prison*, vol. 8 of *Dietrich Bonhoeffer Works*, ed. John W. de Gruchy, trans. Isabel Best, Lisa E. Dahill, Reinhard Krauss, and Nancy Lukens (Minneapolis: Fortress, 2010), 373.

25. Søren Kierkegaard, *Practice in Christianity*, ed. and trans. Howard V. Hong and Edna H. Hong (Princeton, NJ: Princeton University Press, 1991), 63–64.

26. Karl Barth, *Church Dogmatics*, II/1, ed. G. W. Bromiley and T. F. Torrance, trans. T. H. L. Parker, W. B. Johnston, Harold Knight, and J. L. M. Haire (Edinburgh: T. & T. Clark, 1957), 194.

history. Nothing of God is left behind in this personal act. The
hiddenness of God in revelation is thus not to be conceived of as
though it entailed a division in God—part of God revealed, part
of God hidden.[27]

Which is why for Karl Barth history is the ultimate *locus theologicus* for knowing the living God, since Jesus did not exist as a man distinct and separate from God incarnate, but only as the unity of human and divine in the person Jesus of Nazareth, called the Messiah:

"The content of revelation is *wholly* God." The point here is simply
that God is not just half revealed or partly revealed, so that another
part of his being or attributes or acts will have to remain hidden or
will have to be imparted in some other way than by revelation.[28]

While Barth does not—and cannot—speak about the "historical" Jesus, whom he considers a construct of historicism that fails to capture the fullness of Jesus Christ, Barth emphasizes the importance of encountering Jesus *in* history, which is why my postmodern reconstruction of Christian belief prioritizes the stories of Jesus preserved by the earliest community of believers.

The reconceptualization of the task and method of systematic theology in a more "unsystematic" way is at once truer to the biblical witness, and more sensitive to the pastoral concerns of lived faith in the postmodern era. No more uninhabited palaces. Instead, what is proposed is an approach to the discipline of systematic theology that embraces humility and presents dogmatic claims in a provisional manner, recognizing that God remains mystery, even in God's self-revelation. Furthermore, as a practical discipline, this places the focus on the existential experience of divine guidance, order, redemption, and promise, as mediated by the dynamic presence of the Holy Spirit. Brazilian Presbyterian theologian Rubem Alves—whose 1968 doctoral dissertation for Princeton Theological Seminary, "Towards a Theology of Liberation: An Exploration of the Encounter between the Languages of Humanistic Messianism and Messianic Humanism,"[29] was the first published text to employ the term "theology of liberation"—focused theological reflection around one

---

27. Bruce L. McCormack, "'The Limits of the Knowledge of God': Theses on the Theological Epistemology of Karl Barth," in *Orthodox and Modern: Studies in the Theology of Karl Barth* (Grand Rapids: Baker Academic, 2008), 171–72.

28. Karl Barth, *The Göttingen Dogmatics: Instruction in the Christian Religion*, vol. 1, ed. Hannelotte Reiffen, trans. Geoffrey W. Bromiley (Grand Rapids: Eerdmans, 1991), 91.

29. Published, with a foreword by Harvey Cox, as *A Theology of Human Hope*. The press changed the title in an effort to link Alves's book to the hugely popular and influential book by Jürgen Moltmann, *Theology of Hope: On the Ground and the Implications of a Christian Eschatology* (New York: Harper & Row, 1967).

foundational question: "What does it take to make and keep life human in the world?"[30]

In *Dogmatics after Babel* I asserted, "Dogmatic claims made in the absence of this historical and sacramental praxis of love are devoid of meaning."[31] One reviewer deservedly took me to task for intimating "a third way" of doing theology (beyond the theologies of the Word and the theologies of culture) without adequately articulating this stated goal: "Phrased differently, what is the methodological implication of the indispensability of praxis for establishing dogmatic claims? In what ways does the primacy of praxis push the systematic theologian to redraw thematic lines or to revise categories in dogmatic theology?"[32] What I envisioned in *that* book I am putting into practice in *this* book. Without reducing the Christian faith to the praxis of liberation, I argue that the Christian faith cannot exist *without* acts of justice and compassion. More to the point, I contend the Christian faith is no longer "Christian" if it remains silent in the face of injustice and oppression. In other words, while this guiding axiom does not resolve *all* the conflicts and problems within Christian dogmatics, it stands as a necessary prelude to any future Christian dogmatics. Simply put, a Christian theology unconcerned with making "human life human" *for all persons*, that tolerates attacks on the inherent dignity of even a single human life, is not worthy of the name.

I challenge and reject the epistemological arrogance of traditional systematic theology that we can know God with such absolute certainty we can then make demands of others as if speaking for God. In other words, while I do not question the reality of divine revelation or the fact that our reception of this revelation is guided and facilitated by the work of the Holy Spirit, I am suspicious of the human tendency to take the subjective and local and make it objective and universal. I take the reality of human sinfulness too seriously to allow for the absolutizing of any one theological perspective, because in the end theological discourse is a human activity—an interpretation of divine revelation—not divine speech itself. I do not question the task of theology as the human attempt to speak as truthfully and accurately as possible about God. I challenge the human arrogance that believes any human effort to speak the truth about God is conclusive and final.

Accordingly, I define theology as the open-ended and ongoing effort to speak truthfully and accurately about God as encountered in Scripture, experienced in history, and preserved in the traditions of the church, while acknowledging that God is always known and revealed *as mystery*. Ultimately,

---

30. Alves, *A Theology of Human Hope*, 53.
31. Rosario Rodríguez, *Dogmatics after Babel*, 186.
32. José Francisco Morales Torres, "Review of *Dogmatics after Babel: Beyond Theologies of Word and Culture*," *The Journal of Religion* 101, no. 3 (July 2021): 424–26.

the hiddenness of God demands a theological method rooted in humility yet armed with a hermeneutics of suspicion for critiquing false idols. As such, theology cannot speak with the certainty of the scientific method, and most often is better at pointing out where God *is not* than confidently asserting where God *is*. Nevertheless, theology is charged with pointing believers and seekers toward those locations where God *is most likely* to be encountered.

The Christian life is like a story. We do not write the story but bear witness to it. Yet we are more than mere observers or bystanders, since we are also agents in the story, even though we cannot alter its ultimate end, which is salvation. What becomes evident in reading the Christian story (as told in the Old and New Testaments and the theology of the church fathers) is that when we understand God's plans for us, we see the world in a new way. Sin and fallenness—the realization that things are not what they ought to be—precede our awareness and participation in the Christian story. Accordingly, we live in the hope that God will restore communion, having already overcome sin and death in Christ on the cross. We find our place within the greater story, and in doing so see the world as God's gratuitous gift, so that in and through our engagement with the world we experience genuine communion with God and with one another. We do not come to God alone but in the context of human community. So the Christian story holds communion and plurality in tension; we are isolated individuals who experience life as fragmented, yet we are created for communion.

As agents in this story, we embody the grace and forgiveness God has shown us by extending that grace and forgiveness to others. In *De doctrina Christiana* (397 CE), Augustine called this the "principle of charity," in which the love of God and love of neighbor serve as our guiding principles when reading and interpreting Scripture, such that any reading of Scripture that does not increase our love of God and love of neighbor is mistaken. The Christian life is thus shaped by the love of God, the love of self, and the love of neighbor. Systematic theology developed along Platonic lines; the desire to present our knowledge of God in its totality inevitably led academic theology to neglect that aspect of theological studies traditionally called *spiritual theology*—whose sole purpose is to guide believers along life's journey in their attempt to obey the two great commandments that according to Jesus summarize the entirety of the Law: "'You shall love the Lord your God with all your heart, and with all your soul, and with all your mind.' This is the greatest and first commandment. And a second is like it: 'You shall love your neighbor as yourself.' On these two commandments hang all the law and the prophets" (Matt. 22:37–40).

Without imposing a new authoritarian totality upon the Christian tradition, this book critically examines the surviving fragments of the Christian tradition, exposing those fragments that are false idols—human conceits, beliefs, and practices claiming the authority of revelation but advancing human interests (like white supremacy or patriarchy)—while elevating those fragments that manifest the genuine love and compassion of the living Christ. As I argued in *Dogmatics after Babel*, one sure way of identifying God in the world comes "by tracing the work of the Spirit in God's preferential option for the poor, oppressed, and powerless over against those who exploit, repress, and dehumanize the inherent dignity of their fellow human beings."[33] From this arises a spiritual theology focused on the dual love of God and love of neighbor that "embodies the divine imperative to extend compassion, justice, and hospitality to all, but especially those in greatest need."[34]

Theological discourse, without imposing itself as total and absolute, nevertheless dares speak the truth in all settings and across all disciplines, because it not only recognizes the tendency to make false idols out of our own local theologies; it also recognizes we do this with *all* our intellectual and cultural discourses—including the modern scientific method. As a critique of idolatry, theology undertakes the task of saying where God is not and where God might reside, firm in the belief that "the world is God's, that our world (perceivable, knowable) never matches God's world, and it is God's world, which is to say the world itself, that matters."[35]

But the theological approach taken in this book is not satisfied with the apophatic critique of idolatry alone. Apophatic theology complements the postmodern moment due to the widespread distrust of reason and the radical plurality of perspectives in our day and age, which means theologians can speak with more certainty about what God is *not* than about what God *is*. At the same time, by not offering a positive argument for theistic belief, apophatic theologies fail to provide guidance on how their creative visions become actualized in the theological, political, and moral spheres. This book engages and welcomes the other *as other* from the core Christian commitment to love our neighbor—and our enemy—as ourselves. All great theologians, from Augustine to Aquinas to Calvin, speak about God with both apophatic and cataphatic approaches, while striving for a methodological humility that seeks to listen to God rather than dictate what God is. This means that behind the apophatic critique of false idols must lie a fundamental hermeneutics of trust that affirms God speaks and humankind has the capacity to understand.

Liberation theology is often reduced by its critics to its social and moral praxis. This ignores a rich font for Christian spirituality that can help us more

---

33. Rosario Rodríguez, *Dogmatics after Babel*, 194.
34. Rosario Rodríguez, *Dogmatics after Babel*, 194.
35. Vincent W. Lloyd, *Religion of the Field Negro: On Black Secularism and Black Theology* (New York: Fordham University Press, 2018), 10.

fully tell the Christian story by means of our most basic Christian insight: love of God is inseparable from love of neighbor. Liberationists find God's preferential option for the poor and oppressed within the biblical narrative; the work of liberation is thus not an addendum to the Christian story but part and parcel of the Christian story. A liberationist approach insists there is *no* salvation *without* liberation, then commits itself to embodying the kingdom of God by joining in the struggle to "keep human life human,"[36] confident that in Christlike compassion the true God is known without reducing the gospel to a political act of liberation from oppression.

Christian doctrines do not always fit together like the pieces of a jigsaw puzzle. For example, belief in the overarching providence of God, the belief that divine action is generally directed toward the well-being of the creation, does not align perfectly with the belief that God is favorably disposed to some yet not others. As Jesus states in the Sermon on the Mount, God causes the "sun [to] rise on the evil and on the good, and sends rain on the righteous and on the unrighteous" (Matt. 5:45). Yet, as John Calvin has argued, "not one drop of rain falls without God's sure command."[37] How are these two claims held in tension, each one revelatory of a divine truth, yet together creating irreconcilable contradictions in the mind of the believer? In other words, can we speak of everything that happens—good *and* evil—as willed by God?

A Heraclitian theological method, one that recognizes our knowledge of God is open ended and provisional—or in the language of the seventeenth-century Protestant scholastics, *semper reformanda* ("always being reformed")—does not attempt to build a complete and comprehensive system where all dogmatic claims coexist within a unified whole (the Platonic Ideal) but learns to live with contradiction and inconsistency in recognition of our human epistemological limitations. Believing that the world is created and sustained by God suggests that everything that exists is permitted by God, which runs against the grain of the equally plausible belief that certain things that happen (like the Holocaust) cannot be said to be the will of God. Affirmation of divine providence does not require that the believer reconcile these apparent contradictions, but simply demands trust in the benevolence of God to order things for the well-being of the creation, as implied in this passage from the prophet Jeremiah: "I know the plans I have for you, says the LORD, plans for your welfare and not for harm, to give you a future with hope. Then when you call upon me and come and pray to me, I will hear you. When you search for me, you will find me; if you seek me with all your heart, I will let you find

---

36. Alves, *A Theology of Human Hope*, 53.
37. John Calvin, *Institutes of the Christian Religion*, vol. 1, ed. John T. McNeill, trans. Ford Lewis Battles (Louisville, KY: Westminster John Knox, 2006), 204 (1.16.5).

me" (Jer. 29:11–13). Or, as Martin Luther King Jr. often stated, we live in hope, knowing that "the arc of the moral universe is long, but it bends towards justice."[38]

Accordingly, our theological speculations and dogmatic assertions ought to be made in humble trepidation, fully cognizant that all theological statements are human acts through and through, even while guided and sustained by the work of the Spirit. Furthermore, theological claims entail a promissory, tentative, and as yet unfulfilled dimension, as the apostle Paul reminds us, "For now we see in a mirror, dimly, but then we will see face to face. Now I know only in part; then I will know fully, even as I have been fully known" (1 Cor. 13:12).

Many religious Nones associate organized religion with intolerance and injustice, yet still thirst for spirituality, and while they place greater trust in the natural sciences than they do religious authority, they remain skeptical of all authoritarian uses of reason, including the scientific method. Many leaving organized religion also share postmodern suspicions about evangelism as a discourse "reducible to a strategy of power, and every rhetorical transaction to an instance of an original violence."[39]

This book argues such suspicions are fueled by Christian apologetic efforts to defend propositional truth claims using argumentative logic wielded as a metaphorical club to quell all objections. Instead, I pursue an alternative approach that seeks to persuade rather than coerce. By accentuating the Christian faith's emphasis on the presence of God in struggles for human justice, the preservation of the natural world under the caring providence of the Creator, and the pursuit of spiritual fulfillment through interpersonal relationships not confined to traditional conceptions of family and community, the church can articulate a theology that takes the concerns of religious Nones seriously. By identifying and engaging the most persistent narrative fragments vying for cultural dominance, theology can articulate a series of distinctly theological responses to help non-Christians engage Christian beliefs in a more existentially meaningful and personal way *without* reasserting a totalizing system of belief.

---

38. The phrase "moral arc of the universe" in various forms is a constant theme in King's speeches and sermons. King borrowed the phrase from an 1835 sermon by Theodore Parker entitled "Justice and the Conscience." See Martin Luther King Jr., *A Testament of Hope: The Essential Writings and Speeches of Martin Luther King, Jr.*, ed. James M. Washington (San Francisco: HarperSanFrancisco, 1991), 141, 207, 230, 277, 438. See Theodore Parker, "Justice and the Conscience," *Ten Sermons of Religion* (New York: Charles Francis, 1853), 66–101.

39. David Bentley Hart, *The Beauty of the Infinite: The Aesthetics of Christian Truth* (Grand Rapids: Eerdmans, 2004), 2.

PERSISTENT POSTMODERN MYTHS

Postmodernity is characterized by its plurality. While Europe and North America currently trend toward secularization, the Global South—Latin America, Africa, and Asia—continues to see the growth and expansion of religion, especially Christianity and Islam. Given population trends and immigration patterns, demographic projections anticipate that by the year 2050, the religiously unaffiliated will constitute a declining percentage of the total world population (from 16.4 to 13.2 percent).[40] Instead of forcing these tensions to fit the old and worn-out narrative—premodern religion versus Enlightenment rationalism—a different story needs to be told, one that embraces religious plurality while transcending sectarianism. Theology is afloat and rudderless on a Sargasso Sea of competing, sometimes conflicting narratives; it needs to navigate a distinctly theological yet nonauthoritarian course that meets the challenges of our fractured existence. Instead of building comprehensive systems, theological work ought to be fragmentary, occasional, and open ended; scholarly yet public-facing while engaging the pressing issues of the day.

To that end, I have identified six loci, problematic "myths" shaping the intellectual, political, and religious landscape that the discipline of theology must engage in order to contribute meaningfully to the postmodern discourse: (1) the myth of theological totalitarianism, (2) the myth of the free market, (3) the myth of human uniqueness, (4) the myth of political sovereignty, (5) the myth of Christian uniqueness, and (6) the myth of materialism. By no means exhaustive, this list identifies six major existential crises confronting humanity at this moment in history that accentuate the need for explicitly theological narrative voices in the public discourse.

1. The myth of theological totalitarianism. A theological approach that presumes there is only one "right" dogmatic position ought not to be the *only* theological response to religious pluralism and theological diversity. How can an educated person of faith affirm the dogmatic claims of religion without perpetuating anti-intellectualism, intolerance, or exclusionary sectarianism? This book is suspicious of traditional systematic theologies that seek to impose a singular, rigid, and unbending dogmatic vision for all Christians in all times and in all places. For this reason, the theological subdiscipline of apologetics—the rational defense of Christian beliefs, often by demonstrating the absolute truth of Christianity—comes under special scrutiny. Is a postmodern apologetics possible? Can the Christian faith be articulated in ways that

---

40. Pew Research Center, "The Future of World Religions: Population Growth Projections, 2010–2050," April 2, 2015, https://www.pewresearch.org/2015/04/02/religious-projections-2010-2050/.

are comprehensible—even attractive—to those who do not share the same worldview *without* resorting to coercion?

2. *The myth of the free market.* In *Christianity and the New Spirit of Capitalism* (2020), Kathryn Tanner defends Max Weber's thesis that capitalism has replaced Christianity as the West's foundational narrative, while also positing the story that finance-dominated capitalism is cannibalizing capitalism to create an unsustainable and dystopian zero-sum game that potentially threatens planetary survival. Tanner describes two competing if interrelated metaphysical systems: one in which the market stands absolute and becomes both object of devotion and unquestioned determinant of human behavior,[41] and one that is considered the biblical worldview, whose God "is a jealous God" (Exod. 34:14), which does not tolerate divided loyalties and demands utter devotion. In the end, Tanner's tale is not new, but neither is it an attempt to resurrect the dead letter of Christendom. Rather, it is a cautious critical retrieval of Christian resources for articulating an alternative to the dominant narrative of capitalism, in which the god of the markets is contrasted to the biblical God, who presents a radically different lifestyle and accompanying set of practices. Is the old, old story of redemption powerful enough to overcome modern doubts about a benevolent divine agent guiding human history? Can the biblical God entice the followers of Mammon, who willingly bend the knee to the absolute forces of the market?

3. *The myth of human uniqueness.* The assumption that humanity occupies a special place in the natural order as creatures in the image of God was challenged with the publication of Charles Darwin's *On the Origin of Species* (1859). Darwin's narrative contradicts the theological account of human uniqueness, in which humankind is the "image of God," a "little lower than God," with dominion over "the beasts of the field, the birds of the air, and the fish of the sea" (Gen. 1:26–28; Ps. 8:5–8). The complex evolutionary processes that led to sentient life forms capable of self-awareness, of understanding and predicting complex events, and of reflective decision-making and goal-directed action, themselves mark humankind as *distinct* from other organic life on the planet. Consequently, despite our close genetic proximity to other animal life, we are—for the moment—the only species that continues to refine its natural ability to shape habitats for maximal survival to such a degree that we are affecting evolutionary processes themselves, as evidenced by humanity's impact on global climate change.

A theological defense of human uniqueness acknowledges and embraces the human capacity to transform nature on a broad scale in order to find

---

41. See Kathryn Tanner, *Christianity and the New Spirit of Capitalism* (New Haven: CT: Yale University Press, 2020), 82.

positive solutions for adverse and destructive climate change by encouraging more meaningful dialogue and cooperation between religious beliefs and the natural sciences. Can Christianity continue to affirm human uniqueness in light of the claims of evolutionary theory that all animal life—including human beings—is descended from a common ancestor? Can a Darwinian account of human descent coexist alongside the deeply held belief that humankind has a sacred origin?

4. *The myth of political sovereignty.* The Enlightenment marked the ultimate collapse of biblical and ecclesial authority in the West, giving rise to widespread secularization. Modern political liberalism owes much to John Rawls's grounding of democratic theory within a rational decision-making process.[42] The Rawlsian project is ultimately pragmatic and secular, if not outright atheistic in its methodology. Still, according to Rawls there is no privileged set of beliefs in modern political discourse; all beliefs remain open ended and always subject to revision in search of the ever-elusive greater overall coherence. Unfortunately, the arc of modern politics continues to tilt toward authoritarian encroachment on democratic freedoms, forever haunted by the specter of Carl Schmitt's fetishizing of totalitarian power, contributing to what many view as the breakdown of the modern liberal and democratic order.[43] As Gary Dorrien has opined, "Political theology needs a better genealogy than the Carl Schmitt story it usually tells."[44] An engagement of Nichole M. Flores's *The Aesthetics of Solidarity: Our Lady of Guadalupe and American Democracy* (2021) yields a theological critique of modern democratic liberalism and its institutions as empowering antidemocratic capitalistic oligarchies while also perpetuating white supremacy. What does a Christian theology of the political look like? Can the Christian faith take its proper place in the public square without imposing theocratic authoritarian rule?

5. *The myth of Christian uniqueness.* Not only is Christian theology characterized by a growing doctrinal diversity, but Christianity also exists in a religiously pluralistic cultural context where engagement and interaction with other faiths is unavoidable. In *Formations of the Secular: Christianity, Islam, Modernity* (2003), Talal Asad challenges the normativity of secularizing narratives by arguing that "secular" is a concept grounded in the metaphysical, epistemological, and normative claims of a Christian Euro-American culture. *Dogmatics after Babel* explored the question, "What happens when we stop viewing theological pluralism as a problem to be solved and embrace it as a gift of the Spirit?"

---

42. See John Rawls, *A Theory of Justice* (Oxford: Oxford University Press, 1971).
43. See Carl Schmitt, *Political Theology: Four Chapters on the Concept of Sovereignty*, trans. George Schwab, repr. (Chicago: University of Chicago Press, 2005).
44. Gary Dorrien, *Imagining Democratic Socialism: Political Theology, Marxism, and Social Democracy* (New Haven, CT: Yale University Press, 2019), 2.

John Thatamanil challenges Christian theology to think of religious diversity not as problem but as promise.[45]

One way of preventing the church's limited and all-too-human perspective from becoming a false idol is by undertaking the task of critical self-reflection of Christian beliefs and practices in mutually enriching dialogue with other religions. Comparative theology affirms a wide range of theological voices on the assumption that we can know God better by studying traditions in their particularity, while asserting that no single theological interpretation of divine revelation can claim absolute authority. Can Christian voices accommodate religious pluralism? Or is the Christian narrative—at least in the US context—so entwined with nationalism it is no longer distinguishable from the myth of American exceptionalism?

6. The myth of materialism. While potentially lifesaving organ donation and the harvesting of tendons or bones from cadavers to repair joints in the injured or ailing are practices strictly regulated by the US government, donating one's body to "science" after death is mostly unregulated and has become a multimillion-dollar industry that regularly sells human body parts for profit. Aside from dispelling "romantic notions that the world is going to be a better place by donating their body [to science]," the booming market for donated body parts "has reduced the number of bodies donated to [medical] schools to train students," thereby creating a public health crisis.[46] At the same time, Christianity in the US has become increasingly identified with some form of the prosperity gospel, a movement that measures spiritual growth in terms of material well-being.[47] While it is easy to dismiss the trade in donated bodies as yet another symptom of late-stage capitalism, the underlying narrative about human bodies as little more than a collection of parts for harvesting, sale, and distribution raises questions about the need for a theological anthropology that transcends materiality yet values fleshly embodiment.

In *Poetics of the Flesh* (2015), Mayra Rivera embraces a view of the human as embodied and material over against the Christian tendency to dissociate spirit from flesh, while also fighting the secular tendency to reduce carnality to its material components.[48] Focusing on the Eucharist as a means of sacralizing human bodies—especially enslaved, exploited, traumatized, and marginalized

---

45. See John J. Thatamanil, *Circling the Elephant: A Comparative Theology of Religious Diversity* (New York: Fordham University Press, 2020), 1.

46. John Shiffman and Brian Grow, "U.S. Company Makes a Fortune Selling Bodies Donated to Science," *Reuters* (October 26, 2017). https://www.reuters.com/article/us-usa-bodies-science-specialreport/special-report-u-s-company-makes-a-fortune-selling-bodies-donated-to-science-idUSKBN1CV1J7.

47. See Kate Bowler, *Blessed: A History of the American Prosperity Gospel* (Oxford: Oxford University Press, 2018).

48. Mayra Rivera, *Poetics of the Flesh* (Durham, NC: Duke University Press, 2015), 76.

bodies—Rivera responds to corporeal vulnerability with ethical urgency by valuing this very vulnerability as part of our inherent interconnectedness and interdependency as human beings, without weaving an essentialist narrative or indulging in a pious repristination of past orthodoxies. Can a theology of embodiment overcome the repressive materiality of a contemporary Christianity mired in multiple forms of the prosperity gospel? Can a theological narrative correct the reductionist materialism of the Enlightenment's scientific worldview?

The central argument of this book is that a viable theology—one that appeals to and connects with religious Nones—can be culled from the theological fragments left after the collapse of Enlightenment rationalism. Rather than viewing the Christian religion as a monolithic, ahistorical, and doctrinally pure entity to be defended at all costs, it is better to view religious traditions as local theologies always in flux and constantly negotiating what unites and differentiates them. Rather than imposing artificial unity through coercion, Christian theology needs "a way of reconciliation" that "leads beyond, and ultimately overcomes, all violence."[49] The all-too-common tendency to enforce a theological totalitarianism is not faithful to the biblical witness, because it inadequately considers the hiddenness and ultimate incomprehensibility of God. This book presents a theological framework for engaging the unchurched by challenging the church to abandon traditional notions of evangelism and apologetics and instead to embrace spiritual fragmentation as a means of giving voice to a broken and contrite theology better suited to Christian mission in a fractured world.

---

49. Hart, *The Beauty of the Infinite*, 2.

2

The Myth of Theological Totalitarianism

> When Corinth was threatened with a siege by Philip and all the inhabitants were busily active—one polishing his weapons, another collecting stones, a third repairing the wall—and Diogenes saw all this, he hurriedly belted up his cloak and eagerly trundled his tub up and down the streets. When asked why he was doing that, he answered: I, too, am at work and roll my tub so that I will not be the one and only loafer among so many busy people.[1]

APOLOGETICS AFTER BABEL

To some, the church is a rotting carcass unaware it has died. For Christianity to survive, it needs to do so outside the human institutions we have so badly abused (and used to abuse others). The number of religious Nones in the US—adults who describe their religious identity as atheist, agnostic or "nothing in particular" (Pew Research Center, 2018)—has tripled.[2] The church's response to this perceived crisis is that of Diogenes: a flurry of activity designed to give the impression of working hard, but in the end, "inconceivable for anyone to dream of regarding Diogenes as the savior and benefactor of the city."[3]

---

1. Søren Kierkegaard, *Philosophical Fragments*, ed. and trans. Howard V. Hong and Edna H. Hong, 2nd printing (Princeton, NJ: Princeton University Press, 1987), 6.
2. Pew Research Center, "When Americans Say They Believe in God, What Do They Mean?," April 25, 2018, https://www.pewresearch.org/religion/2018/04/25/when-americans-say-they-believe-in-god-what-do-they-mean/.
3. Kierkegaard, *Philosophical Fragments*, 6.

Substitute church for city and you get a fairly accurate picture of Christianity's paralysis in the face of secularization. Closer analysis reveals that many Nones associate organized religion with intolerance and injustice, while still seeking some form of spirituality. According to the Pew survey, a major reason given by Nones for leaving Christianity is dissatisfaction with the church's position on social and political issues. Regardless of the justification given, however, it has become evident that religious Nones do not respond well to traditional apologetics that provides rational grounds for believing in God and for joining the church. A new approach is needed for the third millennium: an evangelism and apologetics grounded in Christlike praxis.

Recently, a graduate student defended her decision to pursue a doctorate in history rather than theology with this complaint, "You theologians present the faith as it ought to be. I am interested in studying Christianity as it is lived." Her comment exposes the commonly held yet mistaken assumption that Christianity can be reduced to an objectively certain set of propositional truth claims. It is increasingly difficult, however, to maintain Christian beliefs as objectively certain and experientially verifiable when even scientific laws and theories remain tentative and open ended.[4] Still, when pressed, most religious believers defend their faith with the simple answer, "I believe because it is true." A theological approach that presumes there is only one "right" dogmatic position ought not to be the *only* theological response to religious pluralism and theological diversity.

As a Christian theologian, I choose to inhabit the crucible between how the world *ought to be* (the theological) and *how it is* (the historical). Christian theology in the postmodern world needs to recognize that all religious traditions are malleable, evolve over time, and possess a permeable set of constantly negotiated core beliefs that nevertheless unites them as οἰκουμένη.[5] Having rejected traditional systematic theologies that seek to impose a single rigid and unbending dogmatic vision for all Christians in all times and in all places, this chapter explores the possibility of a postmodern approach that embraces plurality and dissensus. Apologetics—the rational defense of Christian beliefs, often by demonstrating the absolute truth of Christianity—thus comes under special scrutiny.

Some contemporary voices, John Milbank and Stanley Hauerwas chief among them, reject or devalue the task of apologetics. However, what they object to most is the *form* traditional apologetics has taken, not its *ultimate goal*. Take this statement by Milbank: "The task of such a theology is not apologetic,

---

4. See Thomas S. Kuhn, *The Structure of Scientific Revolutions: 50th Anniversary Edition*, 4th ed. (Chicago: University of Chicago Press, 2012).

5. The Greek word οἰκουμένη, transliterated as *oikoumenē*, originally meant "[the whole of the] inhabited world," but in Christian usage refers to the church as a unified whole.

nor even argument. Rather it is to tell again the Christian *mythos*, pronounce again the Christian *logos*, and call again for Christian *praxis* in a manner that restores their freshness and originality. It must articulate Christian difference in such a fashion as to make it strange."[6] Hauerwas expresses a similar sentiment by rejecting all human efforts to defend God: "Never think that you need to protect God. Because anytime you think you need to protect God, you can be sure that you are worshipping an idol."[7] Neither thinker desires to overcome the arguments of secular reason by means of rational argumentation, and Milbank even counters that modernity[8] "is only a *mythos* and therefore cannot be refuted, but only out-narrated, if we can persuade people—for reasons of 'literary taste'—that Christianity offers a much better story."[9] To do this—to appeal to the growing number of religious Nones on an aesthetic level—Christian theology needs a way past the grammar of partisan violence, "a way of reconciliation" that leads to inclusion and community.[10] An apologetics for the third millennium, one that appeals to and connects with religious Nones, needs to persuade (beauty) rather than coerce (reason).

DUELING MODERNITIES

Historically, a fundamental assumption of Christian apologetics is the belief that objective truth is both real and knowable. Accordingly, objective and verifiable knowledge of God is not only attainable—whether through natural

---

6. John Milbank, *Theology and Social Theory: Beyond Secular Reason* (Oxford: Blackwell, 1993), 381.

7. See William Cavanaugh, "Faith Fires Back: A Conversation with Stanley Hauerwas," *Duke University Magazine* (January–February 2002), 10–13.

8. Throughout this work I use the terms "modern" and "modernity" to refer to the general shift away from biblical and ecclesial authority toward an increased reliance on human reason in all aspects of human life, from spirituality to politics, originating with the rise of humanism, greatly impacted by the Reformation and ensuing wars of religion, and reaching maturity and cultural dominance with the Enlightenment of the seventeenth and eighteenth centuries. Within systematic theology, modern thought is often traced to the Cartesian "turn to the subject," which Philip Clayton has characterized as *ontotheology*: "the attempt to derive as much knowledge of God as possible from human reason alone" (2). See Philip Clayton, *God and Contemporary Science*, Edinburgh Studies in Constructive Theology (Grand Rapids: Eerdmans, 1997). As Charles Taylor has argued, despite a growing trend toward secularization, "Even in the latter part of the eighteenth century, in the era of the high Enlightenment, genuine atheism was very rare" (309). See Charles Taylor, *Sources of the Self: The Making of the Modern Identity* (Cambridge, MA: Harvard University Press, 1989). Therefore, what has changed in the modern period is not belief in God, so much as our pathways to God, what is considered evidentiary knowledge, and the degree of certainty such knowledge provides.

9. Milbank, *Theology and Social Theory*, 330.

10. David Bentley Hart, *The Beauty of the Infinite: The Aesthetics of Christian Truth* (Grand Rapids: Eerdmans, 2004), 2.

reason or divine revelation—but then becomes the basis for articulating the Christian faith in a universally understandable and objectively defensible way. In an increasingly pluralist and diverse world, reason becomes the main tool in the evangelist's arsenal for both defending Christian beliefs from the onslaught of secularization and convincing the skeptical unbeliever about the "absolute truth" of Christian revelation.

In the modern era, one widely accepted and influential definition of apologetics is that offered by Adam Lord Gifford (1820–1887), who established the Gifford Lectures as part of a bequest to the universities of Edinburgh, Glasgow, St. Andrews, and Aberdeen to "promote and diffuse the study of Natural Theology in the widest sense of the term—in other words, the knowledge of God."[11] According to the terms of Lord Gifford's will, preeminent scholars from a variety of disciplines are, in dealing with their particular area of specialization, to discuss natural theology as a science, "without reference to or reliance upon any supposed special exceptional or so-called miraculous revelation."[12] Since 1888 the Gifford Lectures have featured speakers as diverse as William James, Alfred North Whitehead, Werner Karl Heisenberg, Hannah Arendt, Karl Barth, Carl Sagan, Martha Nussbaum, Eleonore Stump, and Kathryn Tanner, each one reflecting on the subject of natural theology broadly defined.

Some, like Karl Barth, categorically reject natural theology as a viable pathway to genuine knowledge of God, since "God's real revelation simply cannot be chosen by us and, as our own possibility, put beside another, and integrated with it into a system."[13] Other Gifford lecturers, like Alister McGrath, opt for a narrower definition that understands natural theology as arising from within a Christian worldview: "Our inhabitation of the Christian tradition engenders a discipleship of the mind, which leads to an enhanced and deepening grasp of the Christian faith, and consequently results in changes in the way we see and behave toward nature."[14] While others still, like Carl Sagan, seem to embrace Lord Gifford's definition by arguing that natural theology is "theological knowledge that can be established by reason and experience and experiment alone," yet espouse a view of God mostly unrecognizable by the world's religions: "a set of exquisitely powerful physical

---

11. See the official website of the Gifford Lectures: https://www.giffordlectures.org.

12. A brief history of the Gifford Lectures, detailing the terms of Lord Gifford's bequest, is available here: https://www.giffordlectures.org/overview/history.

13. Karl Barth, *Church Dogmatics*, II/1, ed. G. W. Bromiley and T. F. Torrance, trans. T. H. L. Parker, W. B. Johnston, Harold Knight, and J. L. M. Haire (Edinburgh: T. & T. Clark, 1957), 139.

14. Alister E. McGrath, *A Fine-Tuned Universe: The Quest for God in Science and Theology*, the 2009 Gifford Lectures (Louisville, KY: Westminster John Knox, 2009), 31.

principles that seemed to explain a great deal that was otherwise inexplicable about the universe."[15]

The Gifford Lectures stand as an irrefutably *modernist* endeavor employing human reason unaided by divine revelation. While Christian apologetics is ultimately interested in demonstrating the truths of revealed religion, post-Enlightenment it does so employing the tools of scientific reason. According to philosopher and Calvinist theologian John M. Frame, a staunch defender of *presuppositional apologetics*[16] in the tradition of Cornelius Van Til,[17] there are three distinct aspects of apologetics: (1) apologetics as proof, (2) apologetics as defense, and (3) apologetics as offense. Drawing inspiration from the apostle Peter's exhortation, "Always be ready to make your defense to anyone who demands from you an accounting for the hope that is in you; yet do it with gentleness and reverence" (1 Pet. 3:15–16), Frame views apologetics as "a rational basis for faith or 'proving Christianity to be true' . . . in dialogue with unbelievers."[18] Unlike classical models of apologetics (e.g., Augustine, Aquinas, and Anselm), modern presuppositional apologetics does not view reason or logic as a neutral and unbiased arbiter of truth, but assumes that secular reason and revealed religion begin with differing presuppositions about the existence of God and the nature of revealed knowledge. Therefore, rather than argue from a so-called neutral perspective, these Christian apologists evaluate and critique the presuppositions of nonbelievers from an explicitly Christian point of view:

> To tell the unbeliever that we reason with him [*sic*] on a neutral basis, however that claim might help to attract his attention, is a lie. Indeed, it is a lie of the most serious kind, for it falsifies the very heart of the gospel—that Jesus Christ is *Lord*. There is no neutrality. Our witness is either God's wisdom or the world's

---

15. Carl Sagan, *The Varieties of Scientific Experience: A Personal View of the Search for God*, the 1985 Gifford Lectures, ed. Ann Druyan (New York: Penguin, 2006), 147, 149.

16. See C. Stephen Evans, *The Pocket Dictionary of Apologetics & Philosophy of Religion* (Downers Grove, IL: IVP Academic, 2002). Presuppositional apologetics emphasizes "the way all human belief systems depend on unprovable basic assumptions, arguing that biblical faith or its lack crucially shapes our presuppositions. According to such a view, common ground between the believer and unbeliever is limited or nonexistent and apologetic arguments must take the form of explorations of the unbeliever's system of thought so as to reveal contradictions within it due to its faulty presuppositions" (96). This approach is distinguished from Reformed epistemology, as articulated in the work of Alvin Plantinga, Nicholas Wolterstorff, and William Alston, which "characteristically holds that belief in God may be 'properly basic' and does not have to be based on evidence" (100).

17. See John M. Frame, *Cornelius Van Til: An Analysis of His Thought* (Phillipsburg, NJ: P & R Publishing, 1995); Cornelius Van Til, *The Defense of the Faith*, 3rd ed. (Phillipsburg, NJ: P & R Publishing, 1972) and *Christian Apologetics*, 2nd ed. (Phillipsburg, NJ: P & R Publishing, 2003).

18. John M. Frame, *Apologetics: A Justification of Christian Belief*, ed. Joseph E. Torres (Phillipsburg, NJ: P & R Publishing, 2015), 1–2.

foolishness. There is nothing in between. Even if neutrality were possible, that route would be forbidden to us.[19]

Yet, despite this explicit grounding in the revealed Word of God as encountered in the sacred Scriptures, presuppositional apologetics still employs the philosophical reasoning of natural theology as defined by Lord Gifford's differentiation between special and natural revelation.

Presuppositional apologetics shares with natural theology an unyielding faith in the underlying rationality of the cosmos, which the Christian apologist terms *natural*[20] revelation as distinguished from *special*[21] revelation: "Scripture tells us that God has revealed himself [sic] clearly to the unbeliever, even to such an extent that the unbeliever knows God (Rom. 1:21). Although he represses that knowledge (vv. 21ff.), there is at some level of his consciousness a memory of that revelation."[22] A key difference between natural and special revelation is the fact that the former "does not reveal God's plan of salvation, which comes specifically through the preaching of Christ."[23] Despite its absolute foundation in divine revelation and the biblical witness, this approach to Christian apologetics—particularly popular among Evangelical Christians—shares with Enlightenment rationalism and the scientific method an absolute trust in the human ability to uncover and know the rational foundations of the universe:

> As we look at nature with God's help, we see that the heavens really do "declare the glory of God" (Ps. 19:1). We see some of the very interesting ways in which human beings image God. We see how it is that God furnishes the rational structure of the world and of the human mind, so that the two structures are adapted to each other. We see through science the astonishing wisdom of God's plan (see Ps. 104). We see through history and the arts what evils result when people abandon God and what blessings (and persecutions, Mark 10:30!) follow those who are faithful to [God].[24]

---

19. Frame, *Apologetics*, 8.
20. See Evans, *The Pocket Dictionary of Apologetics & Philosophy of Religion*, 49. Natural or general revelation is "knowledge about God that [God] makes possible through the natural world, including general religious experiences of awe and dependence. Defenders of general revelation have usually claimed that it is sufficient only to give us knowledge of the existence of a powerful Creator, though some have argued that the goodness of God can also be seen in the natural order."
21. See Evans, *The Pocket Dictionary*, 110. Special revelation is *salvific* knowledge above and beyond what can be known about God though natural reason, "given by God through particular persons, experiences, writings or historical events."
22. Frame, *Apologetics*, 12.
23. Frame, *Apologetics*, 20.
24. Frame, *Apologetics*, 23.

In other words, secular reasoning and modern Christian apologetics both employ a foundationalist epistemology and as such can be viewed as dueling modernities trapped within the same conceptual framework. Ignoring the apostle Peter's caution to engage in apologetics "with gentleness and reverence" (1 Pet. 3:16), modern Evangelical apologetics has embraced an adversarial stance over against secular reasoning and devoted much of its energy to Frame's third function of apologetics: apologetics as offense. To that end, apologists employ all the tools of logical argumentation to attack "the foolishness of unbelieving thought (Ps. 14:1; 1 Cor. 1:18–2:16)," not only to "answer the objections of unbelievers, but also to go on the attack against falsehood."[25] In practice, this apologetics of attack has all too often meant rejecting doctrinal perspectives that differ from the apologist's own, not granting legitimacy to the point of view of nonbelievers, and closing itself off from the wisdom found in non-Christian religions.

Yet, as the hegemony of Enlightenment rationalism gives way to postmodern critiques, in which the very notion of "absolute truth" gets lost among a multitude of competing and often-contradictory worldviews, even Evangelical Christian apologists begin to question the effectiveness of a "rational defense of Christianity."[26] Elsewhere I have argued that Enlightenment rationalism is modernity's very own Tower of Babel.[27] However, rather than view the plurality of doctrinal perspectives as a divine confusion of tongues—punishment for the human arrogance we call the Enlightenment project—I challenge theologians to view this postmodern Babylon as blessing: "What happens when we stop viewing theological pluralism as a problem to be solved (Babel) and embrace it as a gift of the Spirit (Pentecost)?"[28] That is to say, the postmodern tolerance of difference offers an opportunity to overturn the theological totalitarianism that has characterized much of what passes for Christian evangelization.[29]

In the West, the Enlightenment witnessed the ultimate collapse of biblical and ecclesial authority as the effort to ground all truth—even knowledge of God—upon a rational and empirically verifiable foundation that inevitably

---

25. Frame, *Apologetics*, 1.

26. See John G. Stackhouse Jr., *Humble Apologetics: Defending the Faith Today* (Oxford: Oxford University Press, 2002), 3–37; Timothy R. Phillips and Dennis L. Okholm, eds., *Christian Apologetics in the Postmodern World* (Downers Grove, IL: InterVarsity Press, 1995).

27. See Rubén Rosario Rodríguez, *Dogmatics after Babel: Beyond the Theologies of Word and Culture* (Louisville, KY: Westminster John Knox, 2018), xi–xix, 1–33.

28. Rosario Rodríguez, *Dogmatics after Babel*, xv.

29. By "theological totalitarianism" I mean the tendency in white, Eurocentric forms of Christianity to impose the dominant culture's version of Christianity as normative for all believers, over against dissenting or minority voices. For a case study of this kind of authoritarian imposition of "one right reading," see Rubem Alves, *Protestantism and Repression: A Brazilian Case Study*, trans. John Drury, repr. ed. (Eugene, OR: Wipf & Stock, 2007).

gave rise to increased *secularization*.³⁰ While the political realities driving secularization are varied and complex, the seventeenth-century "wars of religion" following the Protestant Reformation flung Europe into a state of seemingly unending war, contributing to a widespread malaise toward and general mistrust of religion. In its most extreme form, this secularizing trend led to the antireligious fervor of the French Revolution's Reign of Terror (1793–1794), while in its more widespread variant, secularization becomes a political category for relegating religion to the private sphere while elevating secular reason as a "neutral" discourse for arbitrating ideological differences via supposedly democratic processes.

In *A Secular Age* (2007), based in part on the Gifford Lectures presented at the University of Edinburgh in 1998–99 entitled "Living in a Secular Age," Charles Taylor presents a thorough study of secularization. According to Taylor's version of the "secularization thesis," Western society is undergoing a process of secularization marked by religion's retreat away from the public arena into the private sphere, which creates a more pluralistic culture in which religion becomes one option among many. Not only does Taylor describe the withdrawal of religion from the public sphere, he also recognizes an accompanying decline in religious belief and practice *within* the private religious sphere.³¹ Perhaps the most challenging dimension of Taylor's analysis is the contention that religion itself has been changed by secularization to the point that, while the "human aspiration to religion" will not abate, the forms of spiritual practice that allow a deeper engagement with religion have been radically altered.³² Consequently, after carefully tracing the shift from the "élite unbelief of the eighteenth century" to the more egalitarian and prevalent unbelief of the twenty-first century (characterized as "disaffection and distance from religion"), Taylor rejects the master narrative of secularization that says there is an incompatibility between religion and modernism: "I hold that religious longing, the longing for and response to a more-than-immanent

---

30. See Charles Taylor, *A Secular Age* (Cambridge, MA: Harvard University Press, 2007); Jürgen Habermas et al., *An Awareness of What Is Missing: Faith and Reason in a Post-secular Age*, trans. Ciaran Cronin (Malden, MA: Polity Press, 2010); and Talal Asad, *Formations of the Secular: Christianity, Islam, Modernity* (Stanford, CA: Stanford University Press, 2003).

31. See Harvey Cox, *The Secular City: Secularization and Urbanization in Theological Perspective*, rev. ed. (Princeton, NJ: Princeton University Press, 2014). In 1965, Harvey Cox offered an exploration of the relationship between the rise of urbanization and the decline of hierarchical, institutional religion, which locates the Christian faith not in its institutions and governing hierarchies, but in the lived experience of its people. Accordingly, despite official religion's withdrawal from the public realm in the secular age, God remains equally present in both the religious and secular dimensions of life.

32. Taylor, *A Secular Age*, 515.

transformation perspective . . . remains a strong independent source of motivation in modernity."[33]

By contrast, Jürgen Habermas's version of the secularization thesis contends that Western society has already entered a "post-secular" age, in which secular reason, defined as the fallible results of the natural sciences coupled with widespread democratization and egalitarianism in law and morality, while superseding the authority of religion, is now viewed with suspicion. Consequently, he cautions secularism against setting itself up as judge over the truths of religion. By employing the term "post-secular," Habermas argues that on its own, secularity fails to provide a comprehensive and widely convincing "motivational source for normative principles."[34] Two hundred years of secularization have failed to yield an overarching social narrative possessing the same gravitas as long-established religious traditions that appeal to the collective yearning of large groups of people. Accordingly, Habermas employs "post-secular" to describe the new discursive space created when secular reason recognizes that the Enlightenment's exclusion of religion from the public square was misguided.

This "awareness of what is missing" in our secularized age leads Habermas to negotiate a middle ground that incorporates the rich cultural resources of religion without undermining the contributions of secular philosophies to the discourse on human rights, freedoms, and emancipatory political projects. Still, despite a toleration of religious perspectives within the life of the modern democratic secularized state, Habermas's thesis does not adequately account for the worldwide resurgence of religion in recent decades—especially the rise of religious fundamentalism.

Perhaps this is because Habermas expects secular persons to recognize that religion possesses a cognitive content that cannot be dismissed as irrational, while also demanding that religious persons accept the legitimacy of scientific reason and the egalitarian principles of modern law and morality (i.e., embrace the modernist notion of a religiously "neutral" state). The latter is not likely to happen when religious fundamentalisms unilaterally refuse to dialogue with secular forms of reason and actively oppose the secular state.[35] Nevertheless, there is promise in Habermas's call for a constructive dialogue between

---

33. Taylor, *A Secular Age*, 530.
34. Habermas et al., *An Awareness of What Is Missing*, 39.
35. See David Westerlund, ed., *Questioning the Secular State: The Worldwide Resurgence of Religion in Politics* (London: C. Hurst, 1996); Mark Juergensmeyer, *Global Rebellion: Religious Challenges to the Secular State, from Christian Militias to Al Qaeda* (Berkeley: University of California Press, 2008); Christian Joppke, *The Secular State under Siege: Religion and Politics in Europe and America* (Hoboken, NJ: John Wiley & Sons, 2015); Scott W. Hibbard, *Religious Politics and Secular States: Egypt, India, and the United States* (Baltimore: Johns Hopkins University Press, 2010).

theology and postmetaphysical thinking to translate the semantic content of religion in forms more accessible to nonbelievers.

One viable pathway worth exploring is emancipatory praxis, given that religion has done a better job than secularism "to keep awake, in the minds of secular subjects, an awareness of the violations of solidarity throughout the world, an awareness of what is missing, of what cries out to heaven."[36] Ironically, Habermas (to date) has not engaged liberation theology, arguably the most influential theological movement of the past fifty years, which favors both emancipatory praxis[37] and postmetaphysical thinking.[38] This shortsightedness reveals a narrowly Eurocentric perspective, which might help explain the inadequacy of Habermas's "post-secular" typology when dealing with the expansive growth of religion as a public force in Latin America, Africa, and Asia, even while continuing to decline in Europe and North America.

Talal Asad challenges the normativity of secularizing narratives and provides an alternative to both Taylor and Habermas by arguing that "secular" is a concept grounded in the assumptions and claims of Euro-American culture concerning the world and what it means to be human. Asad is particularly critical of Taylor:

> The eminent philosopher Charles Taylor is among those who insist that although secularism emerged in response to the political problems of Western Christian society in early modernity—beginning with its devastating wars of religion—it is applicable to non-Christian societies everywhere that have become modern. This elegant and attractive argument by a highly influential social philosopher demands the attention of everyone interested in this question.[39]

---

36. Habermas et al., *An Awareness of What Is Missing*, 19.

37. See Margaret M. Campbell, *Critical Theory and Liberation Theology: A Comparison of the Initial Work of Jürgen Habermas and Gustavo Gutiérrez* (New York: Peter Lang, 1999). This study commends the seminal work of Latin American liberation theologian Gustavo Gutiérrez as a vehicle for articulating a distinctly Christian bridge between faith and modernity that enables a liberating voice in public affairs consonant with the postsecular reasoning of Jürgen Habermas.

38. By "postmetaphysical thinking" Habermas means a realist and pragmatic approach to human cultural creation, which includes the natural and empirical sciences, that rejects foundationalism and denies the assertion that knowledge can proceed outside of historical and social contexts by standing on some ultimate fixed Archimedean point. In the sense that they also value the local, historicized, and contextual construction of knowledge, thinkers as diverse as John Caputo and Gustavo Gutiérrez can be categorized as postmetaphysical thinking. See Jürgen Habermas, *Postmetaphysical Thinking: Philosophical Essays* (Cambridge, MA: MIT Press, 1992), 28–54.

39. Asad, *Formations of the Secular*, 2.

In other words, given that the very notion of secularization arose in a distinctly Christian context, once this concept is employed for analyzing and critiquing *all* religions—including non-Western, non-Christian religions—great care must be taken, lest the secular critique of religion become another tool of Euro-American colonization and domination of the subaltern other.

According to Taylor's assessment of secularism, the public square has become a marketplace of ideas, where citizens belonging to different religious traditions (or none at all) attempt "to persuade one another to accept their view, or to negotiate their values with one another."[40] Jeffrey Stout, in *Democracy and Tradition* (2004), articulates a very similar argument, advocating for religion's right to participate in the public discourse via democratic processes, even while recognizing the alienating and counterintuitive dimension of introducing confessional perspectives into secularized political discourse, since "in a religiously plural society, it will often be rhetorically ineffective to argue from religious premises to political conclusions."[41]

Yet Talal Asad contends that both Taylor and Stout relinquish a lot of ground to secularization and fail to engage religion qua religion:

> The secularist concedes that religious beliefs and sentiments might be acceptable at a personal and private level, but insists that organized religion, being founded on authority and constraint, has always posed a danger to the freedom of the self as well as to the freedom of others. That may be why some enlightened intellectuals are prepared to allow deprivatized religion entry into the public sphere for the purpose of addressing "the moral conscience" of its audience—but on condition that it leave its coercive powers outside the door and rely only on its powers of persuasion.[42]

In response to this continued marginalization of religion within the public sphere that narrowly limits how religious perspectives participate in public discourse, Asad finds a curious ally in the godfather of Radical Orthodoxy, John Milbank, whose *Theology and Social Theory* (1990) stands as one of the most thorough and consistent refutations of Enlightenment modernism. Over against the hegemonic imposition of Eurocentric Enlightenment rationality, Asad asserts that "'the secular' should not be thought of as the space in which *real* human life gradually emancipates itself from the controlling power of 'religion' and thus achieves the latter's relocation."[43]

---

40. Asad, *Formations of the Secular*, 186.
41. Jeffrey Stout, *Democracy and Tradition* (Princeton, NJ: Princeton University Press, 2004), 65.
42. Asad, *Formations of the Secular*, 186.
43. Asad, *Formations of the Secular*, 191.

John Milbank starkly distinguishes Radical Orthodoxy as an alternative to modern secularism by boldly proclaiming: "It is theology itself that will have to provide its own account of the final causes at work in human history, on the basis of its own particular, and historically specific faith."[44] Contra Taylor, Milbank does not view theology as one among several competing options within the contemporary political discourse but argues instead for an understanding of theology as its own distinct ontology, providing an alternative metanarrative to the modernist secular politics of statecraft. Rather than articulating yet another "political" theology, Milbank is concerned with articulating a "theology of the political." Admittedly, Charles Taylor is not advocating the secularization he describes in great detail, but he does suggest theological claims ought to be filtered through the language of secularism in order to be understood in the secular political arena.

Radical Orthodoxy responds that modernism has developed a secular—and reductionist—explanatory narrative under which all human experiences are subsumed after having been distilled to their universally "common" essence. Whether employing Taylor's "secularization" thesis or Habermas's "post-secular" framework, faith traditions are not analyzed in their particularity, but only in comparison to what they share with other "religions" under the guise of a value-neutral scientific method:

> What is occluded is the real practical and linguistic context for salvation, namely the *particular society* that is the Church. . . . Therefore, they realize that to uphold ecclesial (rather than political or private) practice as the site of salvation involves subscribing to a particular theological interpretation of history and society (an enterprise which they take to be rendered impossible by the Enlightenment and its aftermath). . . . If one takes one's salvation from the Church, if one identifies oneself primarily as a member of the body of Christ, then inevitably one offers the most "ultimate" explanations of socio-historical processes in terms of embracing or refusal of the specifically Christian virtues. . . . Thus if the Enlightenment makes this sort of thing impossible, it also rules out salvation through the Church as traditionally understood.[45]

As a non-Christian thinker, Asad cuts to the heart of the matter by articulating his suspicions about the inadequacy of the secularization thesis in accounting for the rise of Islamism (radical or fundamentalist Islam): "Even though Islamism is situated in a secular world—a world that is presupposed by, among other things, the universal space of *the social* that sustains the

---

44. Milbank, *Theology and Social Theory*, 380.
45. Milbank, *Theology and Social Theory*, 245–46.

nation-state—Islamism cannot be reduced to nationalism."[46] He argues that the secularization thesis "seems increasingly implausible" because "what many would anachronistically call 'religion' was *always* involved in the world of power," since "the categories of 'politics' and 'religion' turn out to implicate each other more profoundly than we thought, a discovery that has accompanied our growing understanding of the powers of the modern nation-state. The concept of the secular cannot do without the idea of religion."[47] Here, while deeply indebted to Milbank's critique of modernity, Asad ultimately parts company with John Milbank, given the latter's exclusivist assertion that "pluralism is better guaranteed by Christianity than by the Enlightenment."[48]

So, for example, in the supposedly secular United States—with its clear-cut constitutional separation of church and state—one encounters a troubling theological narrative (inspired by the Hebrew prophets) interwoven with yet undermining the secular narrative of *universal* human rights that grounds US political institutions. This prophetic language "overlaps in varying measures with rights language (not to be directly equated with human rights language). . . . Unlike human rights discourse, American prophetic language not only draws its vocabulary and imagery from a particular scripture (the Old Testament), but it is also deeply rooted in narratives of the founding of a particular nation (the American)."[49]

Biblical prophetic imagery undergirded the Puritan mythos of a nation founded on religious freedom after fleeing Anglican persecution,[50] energized the nation building of the original thirteen colonies while resisting English despotism,[51] and fueled the westward expansion that gave rise to the ideology of Manifest Destiny.[52] In the collective unconscious of US populism, this biblical language became conflated with the American exceptionalism of Ronald Reagan, who successfully borrowed Puritan preacher John Winthrop's

46. Asad, *Formations of the Secular*, 200.
47. Asad, *Formations of the Secular*, 200.
48. John Milbank, "On Theological Transgression," in *The Future of Love: Essays in Political Theology* (Eugene, OR: Cascade, 2009), 170.
49. Asad, *Formations of the Secular*, 144.
50. See John M. Barry, *Roger Williams and the Creation of the American Soul: Church, State, and the Birth of Liberty* (New York: Penguin, 2012); Robert Louis Wilken, *Liberty in the Things of God: The Christian Origins of Religious Freedom* (New Haven, CT: Yale University Press, 2019); Michael P. Winship and Mark C. Carnes, *The Trial of Anne Hutchinson: Liberty, Law, and Intolerance in Puritan New England* (New York: W. W. Norton, 2013).
51. See James P. Byrd, *Sacred Scripture, Sacred War: The Bible and the American Revolution* (New York: Oxford University Press, 2013); James Darsey, *The Prophetic Tradition and Radical Rhetoric in America* (New York: New York University Press, 1999); Nicholas Guyatt, *Providence and the Invention of the United States, 1607–1876* (Cambridge: Cambridge University Press, 2007).
52. See Anders Stephanson, *Manifest Destiny: American Expansion and the Empire of Right* (New York: Hill & Wang, 1995); Reginald Horsman, *Race and Manifest Destiny: The Origins of American Racial Anglo-Saxonism* (Cambridge, MA: Harvard University Press, 2009).

"city on a hill" speech for his 1980 election eve address: "I have quoted John Winthrop's words more than once on the campaign trail this year—for I believe that Americans in 1980 are every bit as committed to that vision of a shining 'city on a hill,' as were those long ago settlers."[53] Finally, recent scholarship has exposed the white racist ideology at the heart of what Alexis de Tocqueville called the American experiment, rejecting much of what passes for Christianity in the US as an ideology of white supremacy.[54]

Despite a constitutionally mandated separation of church and state that prohibits the establishment of a state religion, the myth that the United States of America is a *Christian* nation persists. The dominant white Eurocentric political discourse—however secularized—is shrouded in theological language. Since 2016, the rise and toleration of white supremacist nationalist movements in US politics, coinciding with the spread of racialized and nativist political conspiracies within US Christianity—especially white Evangelicalism—reveals something deep seated and unnerving about the dominant forms of Christianity and the role of religion in US politics. According to the Rev. Dr. William J. Barber II, leader of a new Poor People's Campaign,[55] American Evangelicalism is becoming culturally irrelevant as a result of its own idolatrous practices:

> I mean, Jesus is very clear. That's the problem for people like [Franklin] Graham and [Jerry] Falwell. They can't debate us publicly because there's no way they can say, "We're against guaranteed health care for all because Jesus was against guaranteed health care for all." Jesus never charged a leper a co-pay! How can you stand up and say God is for the oppression of the poor when Isaiah—in Isaiah 10—says, "Woe unto those who legislate evil and

---

53. Ronald Reagan, "Election Eve Address 'A Vision for America,'" November 3, 1980, The American Presidency Project, UC Santa Barbara. https://www.presidency.ucsb.edu/documents/election-eve-address-vision-for-america..

54. See J. Kameron Carter, *Race: A Theological Account* (Oxford: Oxford University Press, 2008); Jeannine Hill Fletcher, *The Sin of White Supremacy: Christianity, Racism, & Religious Diversity in America* (Maryknoll, NY: Orbis Books, 2017); Eric Weed, *The Religion of White Supremacy in the United States* (Lanham, MD: Lexington Books, 2017); Khyati Y. Joshi, *White Christian Privilege: The Illusion of Religious Equality in America* (New York: New York University Press, 2020); Robert P. Jones, *The End of White Christian America* (New York: Simon & Schuster, 2017) and *White Too Long: The Legacy of White Supremacy in American Christianity* (New York: Simon & Schuster, 2020).

55. Inspired by the 1968 antipoverty campaign organized by the Rev. Martin Luther King Jr. and the Southern Christian Leadership Conference (SCLC), the Poor People's Campaign: A National Call for Moral Revival was founded by Rev. Barber to advocate for "federal and state living-wage laws, equity in education, an end to mass incarceration, a single-payer healthcare system, and the protection of the right to vote." See Jelani Cobb, "William Barber Takes on Poverty and Race in the Age of Trump," *New Yorker* (May 14, 2018). https://www.newyorker.com/magazine/2018/05/14/william-barber-takes-on-poverty-and-race-in-the-age-of-trump.

rob the poor of their right and make women and children their prey?"[56]

Barber is not alone in this assessment of US Christianity. As Christianity transitions from a predominately white European and North American religion to a religion of the Black and brown peoples of the Global South, and as increased globalization brings American Christianity into contact with all the diversity that constitutes world Christianity, US Christians will have to confront much about their religion that is in fact "serving the purposes of another lord."[57] In the words of Miguel De La Torre, "The gospel is slowly dying in the hands of so-called Christians, with evangelicals supplying the morphine drip."[58] Lest we think this idolatrous perversion of the gospel of Jesus Christ is an isolated Evangelical or Protestant phenomenon, Fr. Bryan Massingale diagnoses a similar phenomenon in US Catholicism:

> The only reason that racism continues to persist is because white people benefit from it. If we're always going to have conversations that are predicated upon preserving white comfort, then we will never get beyond the terrible impasse that we're in, and we will always doom ourselves to superficial words and to ineffective half-measures. That difficult truth is something that the Catholic Church in America has never summoned the courage or the will to directly address.[59]

According to Massingale, the pervasive normative whiteness of Roman Catholicism is "a form of idolatry. It's the worship of a false god."[60]

Taken together, these examples confirm the deep impact and ongoing role of explicitly theological beliefs on the formation and perpetuation of US political institutions, and bolster Talal Asad's critique of Taylor's secularization thesis, demonstrating how in the modern era political language has not been exclusively secular but has freely and repeatedly embraced theological

---

56. David Marchese, "Rev. William Barber on Greed, Poverty and Evangelical Politics," in *New York Times Magazine* (December 29, 2020). https://www.nytimes.com/interactive/2020/12/28/magazine/william-barber-interview.html.

57. David P. Gushee and Glenn H. Stassen, *Kingdom Ethics: Following Jesus in Contemporary Context*, 2nd ed. (Grand Rapids: Eerdmans, 2016), xvi.

58. Miguel A. De La Torre, *Burying White Privilege: Resurrecting a Badass Christianity* (Grand Rapids: Eerdmans, 2019), 4.

59. Regina Munch, "'Worship of a False God': An Interview with Bryan Massingale," *Commonweal* (December 27, 2020). https://www.commonwealmagazine.org/worship-false-god.

60. Regina Munch, "'Worship of a False God.'" Also see Bryan Massingale, *Racial Justice and the Catholic Church* (Maryknoll, NY: Orbis Books, 2010).

narratives. The paradigmatic example is the civil rights movement in the US as embodied in the social critique of white Christianity by Martin Luther King:

> "Justice" for King is not primarily a secular legal concept, as it is for Malcolm X, but a religious one—the idea of redemption. To be redeemed and to redeem others was to restore an inheritance—the Judeo-Christian heritage in general and the American expression of it in particular. In this way the prophetic language of the Old Testament was fused with the Salvationist language of the New. To the extent that the civil rights movement presented itself as an instrument of redemption, its project became the moral restoration of the white majority.[61]

Asad is not equating King's emancipatory theology with white Christian nationalism, but simply highlighting how even King's narrative of Black emancipation has been co-opted by the dominant white culture as a project for the "salvation" of white Christians, rather than as a project of Black liberation. Asad is also exposing the hypocrisy of singling out Islamism for imposing theological reasoning onto the secular political sphere when the dominant Euro-American political discourses—however secularized—advance thinly veiled theological agendas. Asad's critique focuses on the "anxiety expressed by the majority of West Europeans about the presence of Muslim communities and Islamic traditions within the borders of Europe" as indicative of an underlying Islamophobia that believes the religion of Islam "commits Muslims to values that are an affront to the modern secular state."[62]

TOWARD A POSTMODERN APOLOGETICS

Philosopher Christina M. Gschwandtner questions the very possibility of a postmodern apologetics:

> *Postmodern apologetics?* Both of these words tend to be loaded and, at times, hotly contested. Both have negative connotations, at least in some circles. And, in fact, they seem diametrically opposed to each other. Is not apologetics a militant defense of traditional Christianity, associated with forced baptisms, mass conversions, and screaming demagogues? And is not postmodernism an equally militant rejection of any such belief, in favor of other beliefs or no particular beliefs at all, either complete and utter relativism that rejects all values and virtues, or a meaningless term thought up by some

---

61. Asad, *Formations of the Secular*, 146.
62. Asad, *Formations of the Secular*, 159, 160.

doomsayers who thought the modern age was over when, really, we are still in the middle of it? If "apologetics" stands for blind and dogmatic faith and "postmodern" for the complete rejection and even suppression of faith, how could the two possibly meet?[63]

She then quickly acknowledges that such widespread and popular views of apologetics and postmodernism are caricatures of a far more complex—and potentially edifying—reality. For the philosopher, "apologetics" refers to "the coherence and value of religious experience and belief in God," including "the question of whether it is possible to have an experience of the divine and what such an experience might look like."[64] Methodologically philosophers in the modern era have sought a high degree of objectivity by minimizing their own foundational presuppositions, yet Gschwandtner grants that such projects can be properly philosophical and still, "at least in some minimalist sense, apologetic projects: projects in defense of God or Christian faith."[65] Admittedly, those apologetic approaches—like Evangelical Christian presuppositional apologetics—that "make statements about Christianity having the *best* or even *only* account of an experience of the divine" are, from her point of view, problematic.[66] Nevertheless, the postmodern moment offers an opportunity for explicitly confessional perspectives to engage in meaningful dialogue with secular philosophies and secularizing radical theologies.

Christian philosopher Diogenes Allen (1932–2013) viewed postmodernism in a positive light, suggesting that the breakdown of the Enlightenment worldview opens the door to reconsidering Christianity as intellectually meaningful for our day and age. Consequently, he directed his arguments at "those still troubled in various degrees by the assumptions of the Enlightenment and to those who are disillusioned with them, but who feel defenseless before the plurality of worldviews and religions and thus do not know how to avoid relativism."[67] Allen is more comfortable than is Gschwandtner reasoning from a position of faith; like her, he rejects the Enlightenment's opposition of faith to reason by affirming the possibility of a philosophical argument in defense of the Christian faith: "Faith, then, is an essential but not the only ingredient in making Christian claims. Reason is used, not only to examine the grounds for Christian claims but also to understand them better."[68] Recognizing that

---

63. Christina M. Gschwandtner, *Postmodern Apologetics? Arguments for God in Contemporary Philosophy* (New York: Fordham University Press, 2013), xvii.
64. Gschwandtner, *Postmodern Apologetics?*, xvii.
65. Gschwandtner, *Postmodern Apologetics?*, xvii–xviii.
66. Gschwandtner, *Postmodern Apologetics?*, xviii.
67. Diogenes Allen, *Christian Belief in a Postmodern World: The Full Wealth of Conviction* (Louisville, KY: Westminster John Knox, 1989), 10.
68. Allen, *Christian Belief*, 16.

faith is a human act and thus fallible, Allen develops an approach that tests the claims of the Christian religion in conversation with secular reasoning. According to Allen, the biggest obstacle toward arguing for the plausibility of the Christian faith in the postmodern world remains the popular misconception that science and religion are mutually exclusive, hostile worldviews.

Unfortunately, most Christian apologists—especially among Evangelical Christians and more traditional Catholics—remain uneasy with modernism and are unlikely to embrace postmodernism, so they clutch to some form of Christian exclusivism, "using a traditional evidentialist and rationalist apologetic strategy that purports to refute postmodernism."[69] The fear among Christian Evangelical apologists is that a move toward a postmodern hermeneutical approach that abandons modern foundationalist epistemologies will inevitably lead to cultural and moral relativism:

> The postmodernist is advocating much more than mere intellectual humility here. The postmodernist is not merely saying that we cannot know with certainty which religious worldview is true and we therefore must be open-minded; rather he [sic] maintains that *none* of the religious worldviews is objectively true, and therefore none can be excluded in deference to the allegedly one true religion.[70]

Even John Stackhouse, an Evangelical apologist receptive and embracing of postmodern critiques of foundationalism, whose work is especially critical of logocentric approaches to apologetics, expresses concerns about the "more sophisticated, and rarer, forms of pluralism-as-relativism" that cannot even "affirm that 'one option is as good as another' because there is no standard of *good* that is not itself the product of one or another opinion."[71] Yet, as the underlying rationality and universality of Enlightenment modes of thinking are eclipsed and left behind, what happens to apologetics when non-Christian interlocutors no longer share the same epistemological and metaphysical assumptions as Christian apologists?

As argued above, secular reasoning and dominant forms of Christian apologetics in the modern era—despite their many differences and oppositional relationship—share the same naive trust in human reason's ability to know and verify objective truth claims. However, when the audience the apologist is attempting to communicate with no longer accepts as true the very possibility

---

69. Timothy R. Phillips and Dennis Okholm, "Introduction," in *Christian Apologetics in the Postmodern World*, 18.
70. William Lane Craig, "Politically Incorrect Salvation," in *Christian Apologetics in the Postmodern World*, 77.
71. Stackhouse, *Humble Apologetics*, 7.

of a universal, transcultural rational discourse, on what basis can the Christian apologist persuade the non-Christian that their position is true or false? As Evangelical Christian apologists engage and critique postmodernism, they are becoming increasingly aware of the ineffectiveness of Christian apologetics: "Isn't this actually a declaration of apologetic failure? Or isn't this simply acknowledging that one lacks the categories to continue a dialogue with the non-Christian?"[72]

For years, Evangelical Christians have used the demographic decline of mainline Protestantism since the Second World War (while Evangelicalism defied predictions and continued to grow)[73] as fodder for the "culture wars" in defense of doctrinal traditionalism.[74] A more recent study, however, indicates that Evangelicalism, especially white Evangelicalism, is currently experiencing a rapid decline, while mainline Protestantism and Catholicism have stabilized their numbers.[75] Not only has the Evangelical population trended older over time, the white Evangelical population has become disproportionately older when compared to white mainline Protestants and white Catholics, most radically among the 18–29 age group. When asked to explain the reasons Evangelical churches—especially white Evangelical churches—have been losing young people at such a dramatic rate (37 percent since 2006), demographer Robert P. Jones argues:

---

72. Phillips and Okholm, "Introduction," in *Christian Apologetics in the Postmodern World*, 18.

73. According to the Pew Research Center's 2014 Religious Landscape Study, Evangelical Christians constituted the single largest Christian tradition in the US (25.4 percent), and while showing a small decline since 2007 (from 26.4 percent), the decline among mainline Protestant (from 18.1 percent to 14.7 percent) and Catholic Christians (from 26.3 percent to 25.4 percent) continues to outpace the loss of membership among Evangelical churches. Nevertheless, all Christian denominations face the demographic challenge that among the younger generations (Millennials and Generation Z) the fastest demographic growth came among those expressing no religious preference (from 16.1 percent to 22.8 percent). See David Masci and Gregory A. Smith, "5 Facts about U.S. Evangelical Protestants," Pew Research Center, March 1, 2018, https://www.pewresearch.org/fact-tank/2018/03/01/5-facts-about-u-s-evangelical-protestants/.

74. Historian Kristin Kobes Du Mez (Calvin College) attributes the emergence of the "culture wars" to the end of the cold war in 1991, arguing that Evangelical Christians embraced a particular brand of hypermasculine, militaristic Christianity they viewed as responsible for defeating Communism; with that threat eliminated, Evangelical leaders transferred their attention to domestic changes in gender roles and sexuality. See Kristin Kobes Du Mez, *Jesus and John Wayne: How White Evangelicals Corrupted a Faith and Fractured a Nation* (New York: Liveright, 2020). Bill O'Reilly, a conservative political commentator, described the culture war as taking place between "Secular-Progressives" and "Traditionalists," and as such an extension of the cold war insofar as secular-progressives seek to remake the US in the image of European social democracies. See Bill O'Reilly, *Culture Warrior* (New York: Broadway Books, 2006).

75. See Robert P. Jones, Natalie Jackson, Diana Orcés, and Ian Huff, "The 2020 Census of American Religion," Public Religion Research Institute (July 8, 2021). https://www.prri.org/research/2020-census-of-american-religion/.

> The positions that White evangelical churches have become known for as they have become more politicized—opposition to same-sex marriage, opposition to abortion, a denial of climate change, anti-immigrant sentiment, anti-Muslim sentiment—are all strongly out of step with the values of younger Americans. . . . And White evangelicals' unequivocal embrace of [former president Donald] Trump also has them at odds with younger Americans. While White evangelical Protestants voted 84 percent for Trump in 2020, only 35 percent of Americans under the age of 30 did the same, according to Pew's validated voter study.[76]

Accordingly, some Evangelical apologists have embraced aspects of postmodern thought in order to think more creatively about ways of communicating their Christian faith, while still accommodating the diversity of existing social worlds and non-Christian religious perspectives. In light of the postmodern critique of totalizing metanarratives, more Christian apologists affirm the need to sever the good news of Jesus Christ from the authoritarian forms of Christian evangelism (what I call theological totalitarianism) that have become indistinguishable from and historically aligned with the violent and oppressive discourses of European colonialism, US imperialism, and white supremacy.[77]

In *Renewing the Center: Evangelical Theology in a Post-Theological Era* (2000), Stanley J. Grenz challenged Evangelical theology to embrace a more inclusive vision of church without abandoning its missional focus through the "critical appropriation of postmodern insights in the evangelical theological task."[78] In this work, Grenz acknowledged the demise of the Enlightenment grand narrative, while contending that narratives still play a crucial role in the postmodern world. So postmodern Christian apologetics must begin with the

---

76. Jennifer Rubin, "Opinion: Why Are White Evangelicals Embracing an Anti-democratic Movement? Because They're Panicking." *Washington Post* (July 12, 2021). https://www.washingtonpost.com/opinions/2021/07/12/white-evangelicals-decline-spurs-an-anti-democratic-movement/.

77. There is a growing movement of self-identified ex-Evangelicals who have captured the popular imagination and are advocating for a radically reconceptualized yet biblically informed Christianity that seeks to liberate Evangelicalism from its own history of toxic masculinity, white supremacy, and militaristic nationalism. See David P. Gushee, *Still Christian: Following Jesus Out of American Evangelicalism* (Louisville, KY: Westminster John Knox, 2017) and *After Evangelicalism: The Path to a New Christianity* (Louisville, KY: Westminster John Knox, 2020); Rachel Held Evans, *Searching for Sunday: Loving, Leaving, and Finding the Church* (Nashville: Nelson Books, 2015) and (with Jeff Chu), *Wholehearted Faith* (San Francisco: HarperOne, 2021); Valerie Tarico, *Trusting Doubt: A Former Evangelical Looks at Old Beliefs in a New Light*, 2nd ed. (Independence, VA: Oracle Institute Press, 2017); Linda Kay Klein, *Pure: Inside the Evangelical Movement That Shamed a Generation of Young Women and How I Broke Free* (New York: Simon & Schuster, 2019).

78. Stanley J. Grenz, *Renewing the Center: Evangelical Theology in a Post-Theological Era*, 2nd ed. (Grand Rapids: Baker Academic, 2006), 29.

realization that the Christian faith is not a single, monolithic story but is best viewed as a broad "mosaic of local theologies."[79] Admittedly, the postmodern turn means the end of rationalistic apologetics, even within Evangelicalism, since no "longer can any one group, tradition, or subnarrative claim without reservation and qualification that their particular doctrinal perspective determines the whole of evangelicalism."[80] While Grenz views postmodernism as marking the end of academic theology—a cultural shift that has moved the church into a post-theological era where theologizing must be done in the midst of the living community of faith—he also believes the surviving theology is, by its very nature, apologetic. The ensuing postmodern apologetics is "post-theological" only insofar as it entails abandoning the logocentric and evidentialist approaches that have characterized Evangelical apologetics in the modern era, in favor of a postfoundationalist local narrative grounded in the lived faith of the church, which "seeks to engage the contemporary context for the sake of the mission of the church which theology must always serve."[81] Grenz reconceives Evangelical apologetics as participation in an ongoing, open-ended conversation with other Christians *and* non-Christians by means of a deep and meaningful engagement of the contemporary culture, firm in the truth of one's own little corner of the larger Christian mosaic. Still, in order to participate in this broad and inclusive conversation, Evangelical apologetics ought no longer to focus on disproving the truth claims of other traditions, but instead focus on making the truth claims of its own theology comprehensible—even attractive—to its non-Evangelical interlocutors.

In 1994, the annual Theology Conference at Wheaton College, entitled "Christian Apologetics in the Postmodern World: Strategies for the Local Church," yielded a volume of essays by leading Evangelical theologians, *Christian Apologetics in the Postmodern World* (1995). Some, like William Lane Craig, defended the traditional model of evidentialist apologetics for refuting the relativism of postmodernism, while others, like Nicola Creegan and James Sire, while intrigued by the postmodern critique of Christianity, in the end rejected key aspects of postmodern thought. Still, some Evangelical thinkers like Brian Walsh, J. Richard Middleton, and Philip D. Kenneson embraced postmodern critiques and appropriated aspects in their defense of Christianity.

John G. Stackhouse Jr.'s essay for this volume, "From Architecture to Argument: Historic Resources for Christian Apologetics," outlines a strategy for a postmodern apologetics more fully realized in his later book *Humble Apologetics: Defending the Faith Today* (2002). The essay recognizes the futility of

---

79. Grenz, *Renewing the Center*, 187.
80. Grenz, *Renewing the Center*, 189.
81. Grenz, *Renewing the Center*, 191.

pursuing logocentric approaches that reduce Christian apologetics to rational argumentation—and more specifically, as models for evangelization—in order to convince the church to abandon argumentative apologetics in favor of an apologetics of *divine encounter*: "the Christian message is fundamentally an invitation extended to human beings—not just human brains—to encounter the person of Jesus Christ rather than to adopt a doctrinal system or ideology, it is only obvious then that establishing the plausibility and credibility of that message will depend on more than intellectual argument."[82] According to Stackhouse, the dominant form of Evangelical apologetics is public debate, which quickly disintegrates into an intellectual (and spiritual) combat in which "there must be a victor and vanquished," and each "side is sorely tempted to glorify itself as entirely right and true and to demonize the other as evil and false."[83] In this context, Stackhouse asks the rhetorical question, "How can this medium of power convey the gospel of grace?"[84] He then argues that the conceptualization of evangelization as combat is antithetical to the preaching of Jesus Christ; he offers in its place acts of justice and charity as a more sure foundation for sharing the Christian message: "It will depend instead upon the Holy Spirit of God shining out through all the lamps of good works we can raise to the glory of our Father in heaven."[85]

This tendency to demonize the other through intellectual domination is neither true to the gospel, nor representative of the richness that is the Christian tradition: "It might even appear impertinent to suggest that such narrowness thus compromises the witness of the church."[86] Consequently, Stackhouse engages in the critical retrieval of those aspects of the Christian tradition better suited to make the Christian faith seem plausible in the postmodern world, other than the narrow "question of the truthfulness of religious claims."[87] Without question, there is a time and place for evaluating theological truth claims, but Stackhouse contends the Christian tradition contains a vast storehouse of resources *beyond* logical argumentation that are better suited for evangelizing the postmodern world, such as architecture, literature, wisdom, justice, charity, and the practices of Christian communal living.

It is telling that Evangelical Christians—specifically Evangelical apologists, who have been most resistant to modernism *and* postmodernism, and who have held out longest in defense of a universally accepted, objectively

---

82. John G. Stackhouse Jr., "From Architecture to Argument: Historic Resources for Christian Apologetics," in *Christian Apologetics in the Postmodern World*, 55.
83. Stackhouse, "From Architecture to Argument," 54.
84. Stackhouse, "From Architecture to Argument," 54.
85. Stackhouse, "From Architecture to Argument," 55.
86. Stackhouse, *Humble Apologetics*, 206.
87. Stackhouse, *Humble Apologetics*, 206.

verifiable, comprehensive system that demonstrates the truth and superiority of Christian belief—have begun to engage and embrace postmodern critiques. For Stackhouse, this cultural shift offers "an opportunity for Christians to shed the baggage of cultural dominance that has often impeded or distorted the spread of the gospel. It may be, indeed, that the decline of Christian hegemony can offer the Church the occasion to adopt a new and more effective stance of humble service toward societies it no longer controls."[88]

While these ideas are only now gaining favor within American Evangelicalism, many twentieth-century Christian thinkers viewed Christianity's marriage of convenience with the dominant secular culture with suspicion. Examples include Karl Barth's break with nineteenth-century liberal Protestantism,[89] Dietrich Bonhoeffer's call for a "religionless Christianity" in a "world come of age,"[90] and the work of liberation theologians, themselves influenced by Bonhoeffer's challenge to rewrite the story of Christianity from "the underside of history."[91] In fact, Bonhoeffer, in his *Letters and Papers from Prison* (1943–45, first published in English in 1953), was keenly aware of the futility of traditional apologetics in light of the rapid secularization of the dominant culture: "Thus the world's coming of age is no longer an occasion for polemics and apologetics, but is now really better understood than it understands itself, namely on the basis of the gospel and in the light of Christ."[92] Decades before John G. Stackhouse Jr., Bonhoeffer, who has become increasingly influential within US evangelical theology,[93] called for the very same break with the dominant culture—and its subsequent distortion of the gospel: "We are moving towards a completely religionless time; people as they are now simply cannot be

---

88. Stackhouse, *Humble Apologetics*, 36.
89. See Karl Barth, *The Epistle to the Romans*, 6th ed., trans. Edwyn C. Hoskins (Oxford: Oxford University Press, 1968); *The Word of God and Theology*, trans. Amy Marga (London: T. & T. Clark, 2011).
90. See Dietrich Bonhoeffer, *Letters and Papers from Prison*, enlarged ed., ed. Eberhard Bethge (New York: Touchstone, 1997), 280–82, 324–29; also see Peter Selby, "Christianity in a World Come of Age," in *The Cambridge Companion to Dietrich Bonhoeffer*, ed. John W. de Gruchy (Cambridge: Cambridge University Press, 1999), 226–45.
91. See Gustavo Gutiérrez, *A Theology of Liberation: History, Politics and Salvation*, rev. ed., ed. and trans. Sister Caridad Inda and John Eagleson (Maryknoll, NY: Orbis Books, 1988), 23–24, 36–42; and Rubem Alves, "Dietrich Bonhoeffer: Teólogo da Vida," in *CEI Suplemento* 22 (1970), 1–4, cited in Raimundo C. Barreto Jr., "Bonhoeffer in Latin American Liberationist Christianity and Theology," in *T. & T. Clark Handbook of Political Theology*, ed. Rubén Rosario Rodríguez (London: Bloomsbury/T. & T. Clark, 2019), 193–210.
92. Bonhoeffer, *Letters and Papers from Prison*, 329.
93. See the published proceedings from the 2012 Wheaton Theology Conference, "Bonhoeffer, Christ and Culture," published as *Bonhoeffer, Christ and Culture*, ed. Keith L. Johnson and Timothy Larsen (Downers Grove, IL: IVP Academic, 2013), esp. the article by Timothy Larsen, "The Evangelical Reception of Dietrich Bonhoeffer," 39–57. See also Eric Metaxas, *Bonhoeffer: Pastor, Martyr, Prophet, Spy* (Nashville: Thomas Nelson, 2011).

religious any more. Even those who honestly describe themselves as 'religious' do not in the least act up to it, and so they presumably mean something quite different by 'religious.'"[94]

In his letters to Eberhard Bethge, Bonhoeffer outlined plans for a book in which, among other topics, he hoped to revise Christian apologetics for a world come of age: "How this religionless Christianity looks, what form it takes, is something that I'm thinking about a great deal, and I shall be writing to you again about it soon."[95] Unfortunately, Bonhoeffer was working on this book when he was moved from Tegel prison to Buchenwald concentration camp, and eventually to Flossenbürg concentration camp, where he was executed on April 9, 1945. All that survives is the exchange of letters between Bonhoeffer and Bethge on the subject of "religionless Christianity" and the three-page outline for the book containing brief descriptions of each chapter.[96] While that book will never be written, Bonhoeffer's insightful analysis of a Christianity struggling for cultural relevance seems prescient and still informs the contemporary theological agenda, in great part because of Bonhoeffer's ability to connect with the reader on a human level in the midst of life's everyday struggles.

This book draws inspiration from Dietrich Bonhoeffer's *Letters and Papers from Prison* in order to reconceptualize Christian apologetics for a "world come of age," in the hope of connecting with religious Nones in the sociocultural places they inhabit. While Bonhoeffer did say that humanity will have to move forward "without recourse to the 'working hypothesis' called 'God,'"[97] his proposed reimagining of apologetics cannot be reached along the path of the "death of God" theology that gave rise to the "Christian atheism" movement associated with Slavoj Žižek, Thomas Altizer, and William Hamilton.[98] Christian atheism—a form of cultural Christianity as moral system that draws its beliefs and praxis from Jesus' life and teachings as recorded in the New Testament, while rejecting the supernatural claims of Christianity—perpetuates the Enlightenment rejection of religious belief as irrational, and as such is still trapped within the paradigm of secular reasoning.[99] Instead, Bonhoeffer wants

---

94. Bonhoeffer, *Letters and Papers from Prison*, 280.
95. Bonhoeffer, *Letters and Papers from Prison*, 282.
96. See Bonhoeffer, *Letters and Papers from Prison*, 278–394. The outline of the proposed book is contained in pages 380–83.
97. Bonhoeffer, *Letters and Papers from Prison*, 325.
98. See Slavoj Žižek, *The Monstrosity of Christ: Paradox or Dialectic?* (Cambridge, MA: MIT Press, 2009); Thomas J. J. Altizer, *The New Gospel of Christian Atheism* (Aurora, CO: Davies Group, 2002); William Hamilton, *A Quest for the Post-Historical Jesus* (New York: Continuum, 1994).
99. Admittedly, Christian atheism encompasses a wide and varied group of thinkers, but I use the term as employed by Brian Mountford in *Christian Atheist: Belonging without Believing* (Winchester, UK: John Hunt, 2011): "a good description of all the people I know who

the church to embrace the marginalization of Christ by the dominant culture; he wants the church to recognize that a *theologia crucis* demands we radically reconsider and reconceptualize Christianity's relationship to the dominant culture; he wants the church to live *in the world* without accommodation *to the world*: "How do we speak (or perhaps we cannot now even 'speak' as we used to) in a 'secular' way about 'God'?"[100] In other words, what Bonhoeffer seeks is a post-Constantinian Christianity, liberated from the yoke of the temporal realm yet immersed in the material world where "Christ is to be at the centre precisely as and not in spite of God's having been edged out of the world on to the cross."[101] This approach embraces the interaction between the political and the theological in order to affirm that *all* aspects of the human condition fall under God's compassionate care and concern, in contradistinction to the secularization thesis (in all its forms) that views religion as receding from the public sphere into the private realm.

A FRAGMENT OF THEOLOGY: THE HUMAN IN EASTERN ORTHODOXY

Christian apologetics cannot deliver on its promise of a universally accepted, objectively verifiable, comprehensive system that demonstrates the truth and superiority of Christian belief. Especially since Millennials and Generation Z, the largest subset of religious Nones, attribute their exodus from institutional religion to the church's hypocrisy, lack of intellectual rigor, and politics of intolerance. A new *apologia* ("speaking in defense") inspired by Dietrich Bonhoeffer's religionless Christianity is needed. Taking cues from radical theology's concept of a "weak" God, theological aesthetics' bold claim that talk of truth and beauty cannot be separated from ethics and social justice, and liberative pneumatology's insistence that God is encountered wherever the work of human liberation takes place, this work reconceptualizes the task and method of evangelization for the new millennium. The approach proposed demands a

---

value the cultural heritage of Christianity—its language, art, music, moral compass, sense of transcendence—without actually believing in God; or, at least without believing in a way that would satisfy Christian orthodoxy, particularly in the metaphysics department" (1). After the author interviewed numerous self-professed Christian atheists, including professional philosophers, "what emerged was a widespread difficulty with the supernatural claims about God, especially the miraculous and the problem of how an omnipotent God could allow evil and suffering in the world. This was counterbalanced by a strong affirmation of the communal beliefs of the life of the Church, a commitment to Christianity's moral compass, and a valuing of the aesthetics of religion—the sense of transcendence that can be felt in response to art, music and the resonant language of the Bible and Christian liturgy" (7).

100. Bonhoeffer, *Letters and Papers from Prison*, 280.
101. Selby, "Christianity in a World Come of Age," 229.

high degree of humility, recognizing that what Christian faith offers the postmodern world is a series of theological fragments, as opposed to a totalizing system of truth that must be accepted in whole, whose efficacy rests not with the church or its institutions but on the work of the Spirit.

The novelist Madeleine L'Engle noted, "We do not draw people to Christ by loudly discrediting what they believe, by telling them how wrong they are and how right we are, but by showing them a light that is so lovely that they want with all their hearts to know the source of it."[102] This same sentiment is echoed in a quote often attributed to Mahatma Gandhi, "I like your Christ. I do not like your Christians. Your Christians are so unlike your Christ," but more likely originating in a comment by Indian philosopher Bara Dada: "Jesus is ideal and wonderful, but you Christians—you are not like him."[103] Ultimately, the sentiment expressed is that logical argumentation does not attract believers—could in fact repel them—and that the most effective method of Christian evangelism and mission is embodying the example of Jesus through Christlike praxis.

The Christian story, especially as it has been preserved in Eastern Orthodox teaching and practice, offers a theological framework for embodying the kind of welcoming and inclusive christopraxis here envisioned. Recognizing that Christ is mediated in a variety of ways by different Christian communities and traditions, the focus on christopraxis ensures that any theology grounded in the fundamental Christ-event finds its ultimate meaning in "Jesus of Nazareth or with early Christian movements that bore witness to the ministry of Jesus."[104] Accordingly, the Orthodox tradition has focused on Christ's act of *kenosis*, or self-emptying (Phil. 2:7), as the lens through which we must relate to the other.[105] In *Communion and Otherness* (2006), Orthodox theologian John D. Zizioulas addresses the fundamental question of how the Christian ought to engage the non-Christian through two distinct but interrelated doctrinal loci: ecclesiology and anthropology.

In the same way the institutional church must "try to mirror the communion and otherness that exists in the triune God," so must the individual "human being as the 'image of God.'"[106] As described by Zizioulas, Orthodox

---

102. Madeleine L'Engle, *Walking On Water: Reflections on Faith and Art* (New York: North Point Press, 1995), 122.
103. John R. W. Stott, *Understanding Christ: An Enquiry into the Theology of Prepositions* (Grand Rapids: Zondervan, 1981), 143.
104. Mark Lewis Taylor, *Remembering Esperanza: A Cultural-Political Theology for North American Praxis* (Minneapolis: Fortress, 2006), 20.
105. See Emmanuel Levinas, *Totality and Infinity: An Essay on Exteriority*, trans. Alphonso Lingis (Pittsburgh: Duquesne University Press, 1969).
106. John D. Zizioulas, *Communion and Otherness: Further Studies in Personhood and the Church*, ed. Paul McPartlan (London: T. & T. Clark, 2006), 4–5.

ecclesiology and anthropology both arise from the doctrine of the Trinity and what it reveals about God as both wholly other and intrinsically relational, as "expressed through the unbreakable *koinonia* [fellowship] that exists between three persons."[107] Inevitably, this focus on Trinitarian theology leads to a *theologia crucis* ("theology of the cross"), for unless "we sacrifice our own will and subject it to the will of the other, repeating in ourselves what our Lord did in Gethsemane in relation to the will of his Father, we cannot reflect properly in history the communion and otherness that we see in the triune God."[108]

In other words, the way of christopraxis—through which we most fully engage in communion with God and with our neighbor—leads to our becoming servant to the other. Christ, in accepting the sinner, did not identify the other "by his or her qualities, but by the sheer fact that he or she is, and is *himself* or *herself*. We cannot discriminate between those who are and those who are not 'worthy' of our acceptance. This is what the Christological model of communion with the other requires."[109] Informed by the Trinitarian theology of the Eastern Fathers, especially the Cappadocians, Zizioulas articulates an embodied theological anthropology that fully embraces the other: "There is no way to God which does not pass through the human being, as there is no way for God's love to reach each of us except through the love of human beings."[110]

The startling consequence of the narrative woven by Eastern Orthodoxy is that a different ethos is demanded beyond mere moralism, an ethos that calls for the full acceptance of the other *as other* rather than perpetuating exclusion, or at best, mere tolerance of the other. In patristic theology, what it means to be human is understood as gift with the proper human response thanksgiving, for we are creatures made in the image and likeness of God, created for communion with God, a *telos* fully realized by Christ, who reveals what it means to be truly human. An ethos grounded in Christ's own life and ministry "does not allow for the acceptance or the rejection of the other on the basis of his or her qualities, *natural or moral*. Everyone's otherness and uniqueness is to be respected on the simple basis of each person's ontological particularity and integrity."[111] Aristotle Papanikolaou reflects on the ethical and political consequences of this Orthodox christocentric anthropology:

> The restoration to the likeness, however, is not to become again like Adam, but to become like Christ, the Son of the Father, who

---

107. Zizioulas, *Communion and Otherness*, 5.
108. Zizioulas, *Communion and Otherness*, 5
109. Zizioulas, *Communion and Otherness*, 6.
110. Zizioulas, *Communion and Otherness*, 78.
111. Zizioulas, *Communion and Otherness*, 86 (emphasis added).

makes possible this restoration. To participate in divine-human communion, which is to iconize God's very being, is to image Christ, who is the image of the Father. This manifestation of the likeness after the Fall is available to all humans without any discrimination, since "there is no longer Jew or Greek, there is no longer slave or free, there is no longer male or female; for all of you are one in Christ" (Gal 3:28).[112]

Orthodox theology emphasizes that human dignity originates in divine grace and, more importantly, that God has always acted toward humanity from this basic assumption about the inherent worth of all human beings. According to Papanikolaou, Zizioulas's theology of personhood elucidates how our communion with God is not dependent on any particular relationship we establish with God; rather, our "irreducible uniqueness" is manifest in our being called by God, who embraces our otherness fully by calling us to communion: "God does not love us *because*; God simply loves us, and it is in this love that we discover and, hence, are constituted as irreducibly unique, as dignified."[113] The theological fragments explored in this book, like these ecclesiological and anthropological insights recovered from Eastern Orthodoxy, are not offered in defense of the church—an institution that many feel does not deserve defending—but in the small hope that they can help others engage Christian beliefs in a more existentially meaningful and personal way, by offering an articulation of the Christian faith rooted in the freedom, compassion, and justice of Jesus Christ.

---

112. Aristotle Papanikolaou, "Dignity: An Orthodox Perspective," in *Value and Vulnerability: An Interfaith Dialogue on Human Dignity*, ed. Matthew R. Petrusek and Jonathan Rothchild (South Bend, IN: University of Notre Dame Press, 2020), 273.

113. Papanikolaou, "Dignity," 282.

3

The Myth of the Free Market

Those who neglect religion in their analyses of contemporary affairs do so at great peril.[1]

The United Nations defines *absolute poverty* as severe deprivation of basic human needs, including food, safe drinking water, sanitation facilities, health, shelter, education, and information. It depends not only on income but also on access to services. Simply put, absolute poverty is a condition in which income is insufficient to provide the basic necessities of life.[2] Since its inception, liberation theology has struggled to "keep human life human"[3] by defending "the rights of the poor and oppressed according to the gospel commandment, urging our governments and upper classes to eliminate anything which might destroy social peace: injustice, inertia, venality, insensibility."[4] In the 1960s the majority of Latin Americans were, for the most part, struggling for basic subsistence, while the people of the First World, even those considered "poor"

---

1. Peter L. Berger, "The Desecularization of the World: A Global Overview," in *The Desecularization of the World: Resurgent Religion and World Politics*, ed. Peter L. Berger (Grand Rapids: Eerdmans, 1999), 18.
2. See the 1995 UN Copenhagen World Summit for Social Development agreements and final documents: https://www.un.org/development/desa/dspd/world-summit-for-social-development-1995.html.
3. Rubem Alves, *A Theology of Human Hope* (St. Meinrad, IN: Abbey Press, 1969), 53.
4. From the final documents of the 1968 meeting of the Latin American Episcopal Council (CELAM) in Medellín, Colombia, published in *Liberation Theology: A Documentary History*, edited with introductions, commentary, and translations by Alfred T. Hennelly (Maryknoll, NY: Orbis Books, 1990), 112.

by the standards of industrialized nations, had access to the basic necessities for sustaining life. This prophetic cry from the poor of Latin America reflected their daily struggle for survival, which *necessitated* a theology of liberation—to paraphrase Gustavo Gutiérrez—because the oldest, most persistent challenge to the church in Latin America has always been, "How do we convey to the poor that God loves them?"[5]

At the 2001 annual meeting of the American Academy of Religion in Denver, Colorado, a panel marking the thirtieth anniversary of the publication of Gustavo Gutiérrez's *A Theology of Liberation* (1971) included theologians James H. Cone, Letty Russell, Kwok Pui Lan, and Orlando Espín alongside Gutiérrez. Together they reflected on the future of liberation theology after the collapse of the Soviet Union, considering Francis Fukuyama's bold claim that with the end of the cold war, Western-style liberal democracy and the capitalist market became hegemonic, thus signaling the end of history in a Hegelian sense.[6] Given the collapse of Soviet communism, is there a viable future for liberation theology at "the end of history"? In his response, Gutiérrez proclaimed, "[S]o long as the material conditions exist that give rise to dehumanizing poverty and perpetuate a culture of death, there will be a need for a theology of liberation, whether we call it that or not."[7]

This chapter seeks to create a conversational space to unravel the moral complexities of political and economic matters by theological means. A liberationist understanding of politics centers on power: *Who has it, who wields it, and to what end?* In the increasingly secularized public square, the liberationist church is countercultural, resisting oppression and defending human dignity, even while recognizing that the institutional church has often served the oppressors rather than the oppressed. Because liberation theology is guided by the biblical teachings and practices of Jesus, its moral praxis and political activism seek to embody the humility and compassion of Jesus. Accordingly, the work of liberation is grounded in the shared hope that through communal action, Christians can make a radical break with the political and economic status quo to bring about profound social change.

---

5. See Gustavo Gutiérrez, *We Drink from Our Own Wells: The Spiritual Journey of a People*, annotated repr. ed. (Maryknoll, NY: Orbis Books, 2003), 28.

6. See Francis Fukuyama, *The End of History and the Last Man* (New York: Free Press, 1992). Fukuyama writes, "What we may be witnessing is not just the end of the Cold War, or the passing of a particular period of postwar history, but the end of history as such: that is, the end point of mankind's ideological evolution and the universalization of Western liberal democracy as the final form of human government" (4).

7. From personal notes taken by the author, who attended Gutiérrez's plenary address, "Liberation Theology and the Twenty-First Century: Celebrating Past, Present, and Future," during the 2001 annual meeting of the American Academy of Religion on Monday, November 19, 2001, 7:00 p.m., at the Colorado Conference Center.

The good news is that the share of the world's population living in absolute poverty has decreased dramatically, from 36 percent in 1990 to 10 percent in 2015, which suggests the United Nations goal of ending absolute poverty is within reach.[8] The bad news is that one out of five children continue to live in absolute poverty, and that the COVID-19 global pandemic has pushed an additional 70 million people into absolute poverty with no clear end in sight.[9] Furthermore, an estimated 4 billion people (55 percent of the world's population) remain highly vulnerable, living without a network of social protection, so the gains made toward eradicating poverty could easily unravel with the prolongation of the global pandemic (or another economic crisis of similar proportion, like the current war in Ukraine).[10] While the United States experienced a series of policy blunders early in the battle against the pandemic, its wealth and resources allowed it to weather the storm better than most nations.[11] Nevertheless, even within the US the most vulnerable populations—the working poor, the elderly, Blacks and Latino/as—were most negatively impacted by the economic instability caused by the pandemic.[12] This suggests that on a global scale the most vulnerable, especially those without adequate access to vaccination, in places like Asia and sub-Saharan Africa, will bear the brunt of the economic downturn caused by the global pandemic, negating many of the gains in the battle to eliminate extreme poverty.

A Christian understanding of these economic realities must be framed by what Jesus teaches about wealth and its impact on communal life, affirming the inherent dignity of every human life as image of God (Gen. 1:26–28; Matt. 25:31–46), while recognizing the intrinsic tension between the kingdom of God and *mammon* (the Aramaic word for riches or wealth): "No one can serve two masters; for a slave will either hate the one and love the other, or be devoted to the one and despise the other. You cannot serve God and wealth" (Matt. 6:24; Luke 16:13). The created universe is inherently good, a gift of God grounded

---

8. See the United Nations fact page, "Global Issues: Ending Poverty." https://www.un.org/en/global-issues/ending-poverty.

9. United Nations fact page, "Global Issues: Ending Poverty."

10. Olivier Knox with Caroline Anders, "Fuel, Food, Finance: Brace for Impact from Russia's Ukraine War," *Washington Post* (April 21, 2022). https://www.washingtonpost.com/politics/2022/04/21/fuel-food-finance-brace-impact-russias-ukraine-war/.

11. Kat Devlin, Moira Fagan, and Aidan Connaughton, "Global Views of How U.S. Has Handled Pandemic Have Improved, but Few Say It's Done a Good Job," Pew Research Center, June 10, 2021, https://www.pewresearch.org/fact-tank/2021/06/10/global-views-of-how-u-s-has-handled-pandemic-have-improved-but-few-say-its-done-a-good-job/.

12. Jevay Grooms, Alberto Ortega, and Joaquin Alfredo-Angel Rubalcaba, "The COVID-19 Public Health and Economic Crises Leave Vulnerable Populations Exposed," Brookings Institution (August 13, 2020). https://www.brookings.edu/blog/up-front/2020/08/13/the-covid-19-public-health-and-economic-crises-leave-vulnerable-populations-exposed/.

in an act of love, so this world and all its trappings—including wealth—are not to be despised or avoided but loved in their proper proportion.

Without question, a central aspect of the Christian story is its accounting of sin and fallenness and the consequent realization that the world we inhabit is radically distorted by greed, violence, and injustice: "For what will it profit them to gain the whole world and forfeit their life?" (Mark 8:36). The sense that the world is not as it ought to be—that our relationship with God our creator is broken and by extension our relations with one another are also broken—underlies the guiding Christian ethos to resist and oppose all attacks on the inherent dignity of persons and the intrinsic goodness of God's creation. The heart of Christian teaching—"For God so loved the world that he gave his only Son, so that everyone who believes in him may not perish but may have eternal life" (John 3:16)—says that Christ suffered for the world, not just so individual souls can be redeemed, but "in hope that the creation itself will be set free from its bondage to decay and will obtain the freedom of the glory of the children of God" (Rom. 8:20–21). Economic activity is judged and valued within this broader soteriological narrative, with the understanding that from a Christian point of view the primary goal of economic life is the creation of wealth in order to meet the economic needs of every member of society without ravaging the creation. So economic systems and institutions exist to serve this common good and are deemed failures when they do not provide the material well-being and survival of *all* life.

Pope Francis, the first Latin American pope and a friend and supporter of liberation theologians, describes the church's ministry in these terms: "we must accompany people, and we must heal their wounds."[13] Recognizing the church's limited resources when addressing the enormity of human suffering, Francis compares the church to a field hospital during wartime:

> I see clearly that the thing the church needs most today is the ability to heal wounds and to warm the hearts of the faithful; it needs nearness, proximity. I see the church as a field hospital after battle. It is useless to ask a seriously injured person if he has high cholesterol and about the level of his blood sugars! You have to heal his wounds. Then we can talk about everything else. Heal the wounds, heal the wounds. . . . And you have to start from the ground up.
>
> The church sometimes has locked itself up in small things, in small-minded rules. The most important thing is the first

---

13. Antonio Spadaro, S.J., "A Big Heart Open to God: An Interview with Pope Francis," *America: The Jesuit Review*, September 30, 2013. https://www.americamagazine.org/faith/2013/09/30/big-heart-open-god-interview-pope-francis.

proclamation: Jesus Christ has saved you. And the ministers of the church must be ministers of mercy above all.[14]

Embracing Pope Francis's image of the church as field hospital, with its ministries of compassion a form of triage, the liberationist call to work together to make life "more human" becomes an entry point for discussing economic realities from a Christian perspective.

THREE PERSPECTIVES ON RELIGION AND ECONOMICS

The modern era gave rise to three competing stories about the relationship of religion to economics: (1) the classical articulation of capitalism by Adam Smith (1723–1790), which seeks to understand the underlying principles of economic relations, including religion, as a part of human nature; (2) the materialist argument of Karl Marx (1818–1883), that "man makes religion; religion does not make man," thus dismissing religion as "the sigh of the oppressed creature" and the "opium of the people";[15] and (3) the sociological analysis of Max Weber (1864–1920), adopted by the "Chicago School,"[16] which ultimately "sees religion as a subjective want that functions by market forces and that can best be understood as a consumer commodity."[17] Despite their differences, these economic worldviews share a methodological failure to treat religion qua religion, attempting instead to explain the human religious impulse in terms of some other, supposedly "rational" explanatory framework. Thus all three approaches are manifestations of the Enlightenment's reductionist and secularizing metanarrative, fundamentally at odds with any view that accepts the divine as an agent in human history.

Classical capitalism, as articulated by Adam Smith, might have been born within the cultural context of Scottish Calvinism, but its analysis of economic relations is decidedly nontheological. Admittedly, Smith presumes a Calvinist theological framework when accounting for humanity's inherently fallen state, and acknowledges a natural religious impulse similar to John Calvin's

---

14. Spadaro, "A Big Heart."
15. Karl Marx, *Critique of Hegel's 'Philosophy of Right,'* trans. Annette Jolin and Joseph O'Malley (Cambridge: Cambridge University Press, 1970), 131.
16. The Chicago school of economics is a neoclassical school of economic thought associated with the work of several faculty members in the economics department at the University of Chicago, most notably Milton Friedman and George Stigler. See Daniel J. Hammond and Claire H. Hammond, eds., *Making Chicago Price Theory: Friedman-Stigler Correspondence 1945–1957* (London and New York: Routledge, 2006).
17. Max L. Stackhouse, *God and Globalization*, vol. 4, *Globalization and Grace* (New York: Continuum, 2007), 5.

argument in the opening chapter of the *Institutes of the Christian Religion* (1559): "But every part of nature, when attentively surveyed, equally demonstrates the providential care of its Author, and we may admire the wisdom and goodness of God even in the weakness and folly of men."[18] This echoes Calvin's assessment of humanity created in the image of God with an innate knowledge of divinity clouded by humanity's sinful fall from grace: "There is within the human mind, and indeed by natural instinct, an awareness of divinity. This we take to be beyond controversy," while at the same time, "we see that many, after they have become hardened in insolent and habitual sinning, furiously repel all remembrance of God."[19] Yet, when Smith accounts for the role of religion within his economic theory, it is almost an afterthought.

Adam Smith is considered the father of modern capitalism, with economic thinkers from Karl Marx to John Maynard Keynes engaging his ideas, even as they move beyond them. As an Enlightenment philosopher, Smith was critical, if not downright skeptical, of religious dogma, seeking instead to ground his understanding of economic forces on reason. Here we find similarities to the thought of John Locke, who justified private ownership of property via an appeal to natural reason:

> God, who hath given the world to men in common, hath also given them reason to make use of it to the best advantage of life and convenience. The earth and all that is therein is given to men for the support and comfort of their being. And though all the fruits it naturally produces, and beasts it feeds, belong to mankind in common, as they are produced by the spontaneous hand of nature, and no body has originally a private dominion exclusive of the rest of mankind in any of them, as they are thus in their natural state, yet being given for the use of men, there must of necessity be a means to appropriate them some way or other before they can be of any use, or at all beneficial, to any particular man. The fruit or venison which nourishes the wild Indian, who knows no enclosure, and is still a tenant in common, must be his, and so his—i.e., a part of him, that another can no longer have any right to it before it can do him any good for the support of his life.[20]

Foundational to this modern way of thinking is the core belief that every person is by nature an autonomous individual who belongs only to oneself, so no one else can claim ownership over their body or the work of their hands: "For this labour being the unquestionable property of the labourer, no man but he

---

18. Adam Smith, *The Theory of Moral Sentiments*, repr. (Mineola, NY: Dover, 2006), 106.
19. John Calvin, *Institutes of the Christian Religion*, vol. 1, ed. John T. McNeill, trans. Ford Lewis Battles (Louisville, KY: Westminster John Knox, 2006), 43, 48 (1.3.1, 1.4.2).
20. John Locke, *Locke's Two Treatises of Government*, critical ed., ed. Peter Laslett, repr. (Cambridge: Cambridge University Press, 1967), 304.

can have a right to what that is once joined to, at least where there is enough, and as good left in common for others."[21] Not just because Locke's conception of human autonomy and property rights allowed for the possibility of slavery—Locke owned stock in slave trading companies like the Lords Proprietors of the Carolinas, where slavery was constitutionally permitted and landowners rewarded with one hundred and fifty acres of land for every slave imported to the North American colony[22]—a Christian theological anthropology is clearly at odds with the modern notion of individual autonomy: "Or do you not know that your body is a temple of the Holy Spirit within you, which you have from God, and that you are not your own? For you were bought with a price" (1 Cor. 6:19–20).

These words from the apostle Paul underlie John Calvin's mistrust of reason and led him to question the very idea of human autonomy:

> If we, then, are not our own but the Lord's, it is clear what error we must flee, and whither we must direct all the acts of our life. We are not our own: let not our reason nor our will, therefore, sway our plans and deeds. . . . We are not our own: in so far as we can, let us forget ourselves and all that is ours. Conversely, we are God's: let us therefore live for Him and die for Him. We are God's: let His wisdom and will therefore rule all our actions. We are God's: let all the parts of our life accordingly strive toward Him as our only lawful goal.[23]

By contrast, Adam Smith's arguments, despite displaying great familiarity with the development of capitalism within Scottish Protestantism, intentionally sought to provide a "natural" explanation for economic forces, while avoiding the dogmatic claims of theology. Smith's accounts of the division of labor, free trade, self-interest in exchange, and limits on government intervention provide a cohesive moral vision of the world that calls for the abolition of monopolies, encourages international trade and cooperation, and supports public funding for education for the sake of the common good. Yet his ideas are not always compatible with a distinctly Christian understanding of the human, due to his inadequate treatment of sin and evil.

The discipline of economics is interconnected with moral philosophy in very important ways. Adam Smith, while remembered primarily as the father of modern economics, held the chair of moral philosophy at the University of

---

21. Locke, *Locke's Two Treatises*, 304.
22. William Uzgallis, "John Locke, Racism, Slavery, and Indian Lands," in *The Oxford Handbook of Philosophy and Race*, ed. Naomi Zack (Oxford: Oxford University Press, 2017), 21–30.
23. John Calvin, *Institutes of the Christian Religion*, vol. 2, ed. John T. McNeill, trans. Ford Lewis Battles (Louisville, KY: Westminster John Knox, 2006), 690 (3.7.1).

Glasgow and argued in *The Theory of Moral Sentiments* (1759) that the market is a moral space that can serve as a moral teacher. As Smith notes, human beings care about the well-being and opinions of others: "However selfish soever man may be supposed, there are evidently some principles in his nature, which interests him in the fortune of others, and render their happiness necessary to him, though he derives nothing from it except the pleasure of seeing it."[24] In other words, human beings are moral animals *naturally* capable of acting altruistically.

Yet, dig deeper, and it becomes evident that for Smith acting morally is grounded in basic self-interest: "It is not from the benevolence of the butcher, the brewer, or the baker, that we expect our dinner, but from their regard to their own interest. We address ourselves, not to their humanity but to their self-love, and never talk to them of our own necessities but of their advantages."[25] Accordingly, he develops a theory of economic justice that assumes the market operates the same way, so that the notion of a common good is undergirded by our individual desire for profitability. Admittedly, Smith was critical of selfishness, and his moral philosophy commended self-control: "every man is, no doubt, by nature, first and principally recommended to his own care; and he is fitter to take care of himself than any other person, it is fit and right that it should be so."[26]

Unfortunately, Smith was also a firm believer in an unfettered free market and condemned any external or governmental regulation of trade, arguing that in the end the market punishes those who abuse the system. Which is why he encouraged free trade between nations and called for the natural flow of goods and services as dictated by supply and demand: "Again, by prohibiting the exportation of goods to foreign markets, the industry of the country is greatly discouraged. It is a very great motive to industry, that people have it in their power to exchange the produce of their labour for what they please, and wherever there is any restraint on people in this respect, they will not be so vigorous in improving manufactures."[27] The natural forces of the market determine and shape market morality, so Smith assumes it is in every participant's self-interest to engage in business practices that are mutually beneficial:

> The absurdity of these regulations will appear on the least reflection. All commerce that is carried on betwixt any two countries must necessarily be advantageous to both. The very intention of

---

24. Smith, *The Theory of Moral Sentiments*, 3.
25. Adam Smith, *The Wealth of Nations*, ed. Edwin Cannan (New York: Random House, 1994), 15.
26. Smith, *The Theory of Moral Sentiments*, 82.
27. Adam Smith, *Lectures on Justice, Police, Revenue and Arms: Delivered in the University of Glasgow*, ed. Edwin Cannan (Oxford: Clarendon, 1896), 205.

commerce is to exchange your own commodities for others which you think will be more convenient for you. When two men trade between themselves it is undoubtedly for the advantage of both. The one has perhaps more of one species of commodities than he has occasion for, he therefore exchanges a certain quantity of it with the other, for another commodity that will be more useful to him. The other agrees to the bargain on the same account, and in this manner the mutual commerce is advantageous to both. The case is exactly the same betwixt any two nations.[28]

Smith's naive trust of the free market does not adequately account for human avarice, but more germane to a contemporary conversation, the market economy has shifted from the manufacture and sale of goods to a finance-driven economy, where profit is generated "through the trading of financial instruments themselves," and markets are easily manipulated in order to inflate the value of financial assets like stocks by uncoupling the value of said asset "from underlying fundamentals just to the degree that expectations about the behavior of other investors are what is fueling demand for it."[29] In other words, whether a company makes profits and pays out dividends to investors is irrelevant to the company's value on the financial markets, where investors gamble on the behavior of other investors while companies—once historically defined by the production of goods and services—must themselves trade these financial instruments as protection from fluctuations in the market.

This does not mean that finance is completely severed from the production of goods and services. Rather, the market for financial instruments has supplanted Smith's law of supply and demand (which fostered mutual profitability in fair market exchanges), creating a "relentless drive toward maximum profitability—not just earnings sufficient to pay one's workers and overhead costs with enough left over to ensure necessary future investment in equipment, but maximally efficient use of as few workers as possible with minimal unnecessary expenditures."[30]

Aristotle in *The Politics* believed that trading for profit encourages greed and the exploitation of others:

> There are two sorts of wealth-getting, as I have said; one is a part of household management, the other is retail trade: the former necessary and honorable, while that which consists in exchange is justly censured; for it is unnatural, and a mode by which men gain from one another. The most hated sort, and with the greatest

---

28. Smith, *Lectures on Justice*, 204.
29. Kathryn Tanner, *Christianity and the New Spirit of Capitalism* (New Haven, CT: Yale University Press, 2020), 14, 15.
30. Tanner, *Christianity and the New Spirit of Capitalism*, 20.

reason, is usury, which makes a gain out of money itself, and not from the natural object of it. For money was intended to be used in exchange, but not to increase at interest. And this term interest, which means the birth of money from money, is applied to the breeding of money because the offspring resembles the parent. Wherefore of any modes of getting wealth this is the most unnatural.[31]

A kindred wisdom is found in the New Testament and held by Christian thought well into the modern era: "the love of money is a root of all kinds of evil, and in their eagerness to be rich some have wandered away from the faith and pierced themselves with many pains" (1 Tim. 6:10). As evidenced by the 2008 subprime mortgage crisis that triggered a global recession, unregulated trade in repackaged subprime mortgages with high interest payments (which generate higher yields for investors), with little regard for the actual housing market, proved a recipe for disaster. With US home prices declining steeply after peaking in mid-2006, it became more difficult for borrowers to refinance their loans; as adjustable-rate mortgages began to reset at higher interest rates (causing higher monthly payments), mortgage delinquencies and foreclosures increased.[32] A major factor in this crisis was the predatory and fraudulent lending practices by banks and other lenders, discrediting Smith's core belief that the market is self-correcting and moral, and always working to the mutual advantage of all trade partners: "Lenders made loans that they knew borrowers could not afford and that could cause massive losses to investors in mortgage securities."[33]

On the thirtieth anniversary of Karl Marx's death, Vladimir Ilyich Lenin argued that Marxism represented a new, more advanced synthesis of modern thought: "The Marxist doctrine is omnipotent because it is true. It is comprehensive and harmonious and provides men with an integral world outlook irreconcilable with any form of superstition, reaction, or defense of bourgeois oppression."[34] Karl Marx's synthesis of German idealism, British economic theory, and egalitarian French politics most fully embodied the Enlightenment's "turn to the subject," by viewing all aspects of human culture

---

31. Aristotle, *The Politics*, trans. Benjamin Jowett (Kitchener, ON: Batoche Books, 1999), 17 (Bk. I.x).

32. John V. Duca, Federal Reserve Bank of Dallas, "Subprime Mortgage Crisis: 2007–2010," Federal Reserve History (November 22, 2013). https://www.federalreservehistory.org/essays/subprime-mortgage-crisis.

33. "The Financial Crisis Inquiry Report," Financial Crisis Inquiry Commission, Washington, DC: Government Printing Office (January 25, 2011), xxii. https://www.govinfo.gov/content/pkg/GPO-FCIC/pdf/GPO-FCIC.pdf.

34. Vladimir Ilyich Lenin, *The Three Sources and Three Component Parts of Marxism*, 3rd ed. (Moscow: Progress Publishers, 1969), 5.

and society as originating in the fulfillment of human (material) needs while pursuing liberation from what Immanuel Kant called humanity's "self-incurred tutelage."[35]

Arguably, the history of the twentieth century cannot be written without reference to Karl Marx, as ideologues ranging from fascists to socialists to anarchists have borrowed from his thought, while in the United States political conservatives opposed all policies that in any way touched on Marxism or leaned toward socialism. Consequently, the stereotype that "democratic socialism is hopelessly un-American" has prevailed, despite the impact Christian socialism has had in the development of American progressive politics, from the social gospel to the Catholic Worker Movement to the rise of Black liberation theology.[36] After World War II, theologians across the religious spectrum—Catholic, Protestant, Jewish, Islamic, Buddhist, Hindu, and so on—began to employ Marxist social analysis in critiquing their own faith traditions, while articulating a postcolonial response to the subjugating theories of so-called "liberal" development theory.[37] Thus, while still a product of the Western Enlightenment, Marx became a vehicle of political liberation for formerly colonized nations intent on tearing down the yoke of Western imperialism.

If Adam Smith's narrative views human nature as basically altruistic—the market forces of supply and demand working to ensure the mutual benefit of trade partners for the long-term benefit of the market itself—the story Marx writes about humankind presumes a material struggle for survival in which the powerful structure society for their own benefit and well-being at the expense of the poor and powerless. Accordingly, Marx reduces all human experience to a history of class struggle:

> Freeman and slave, patrician and plebeian, lord and serf, guild-master and journeyman, in a word, oppressor and oppressed stood in constant opposition to one another, carried on an uninterrupted, now hidden, now open fight, a fight that each time ended either in

---

35. Immanuel Kant, "What Is Enlightenment?," in *Foundations of the Metaphysics of Morals* and *What Is Enlightenment?*, trans. Lewis White Beck (New York: Macmillan, 1959), 85.

36. See Gary Dorrien, *American Democratic Socialism: History, Politics, Religion, and Theory* (New Haven, CT: Yale University Press, 2021), ix.

37. For an introductory survey of liberation theologies within global Christianity, see Deane W. Ferm, *Third World Liberation Theologies: An Introductory Survey* (Maryknoll, NY: Orbis Books, 1986) and *Third World Liberation Theologies: A Reader*, 2nd ed. (Maryknoll, NY: Orbis Books, 1986). For a survey of liberation theologies across the world's religions, see Miguel A. De La Torre, ed., *The Hope of Liberation in World Religions* (Waco, TX: Baylor University Press, 2008).

a revolutionary reconstitution of society at large, or in the common ruin of the contending classes.[38]

Marx's economic interpretation of history, materialist and historicist, analyzed four central aspects of human experience: (1) the material reality in which people live, (2) the organization of social relations, (3) the value of historical context for understanding economic development, and (4) the impact these factors have on political praxis. While Marx identified transitional stages from primitive communism to feudalism, from capitalism to communism, he did not see these stages as progressive steps every culture needed to progress through. Still, he believed that the historical unfolding of the class struggle was an inevitable process of social evolution moving toward communism and away from private property, as evidenced by the modern stratification into two opposing classes: "Our epoch, the epoch of the bourgeoisie, possesses, however, this distinctive feature: it has simplified the class antagonisms: Society as a whole is more and more splitting up into two great hostile camps, into two great classes directly facing each other: Bourgeoisie and Proletariat."[39] While human liberation is the ultimate end of Marx's view of history, his analysis provides a history of human exploitation at the hands of the Enlightenment's grand narrative, which has reduced human beings to mere objects controlled by instrumental reason intent on minimizing costs and maximizing efficiency and profits.

The human condition is thus defined by alienation. The source of this alienation is the loss of subjectivity and autonomy by human beings, who are treated as objects within a political economy controlled by the very few (for their personal gain) to the detriment of the common good: "These labourers, who must sell themselves piece-meal, are a commodity. . . . Owing to the extensive use of machinery and to the division of labour, the work of the proletarians has lost all individual character, and consequently, all charm for the workman. He becomes an appendage of the machine."[40] The market grows to meet the never ending demand for more markets in which to sell until it evolves into a world market in the thrall of unchecked consumption, transforming human cultures by reducing them to production and consumption:

> Modern industry has converted the little workshop of the patriarchal master into the great factory of the industrial capitalist. Masses of labourers, crowded into the factory, are organised like soldiers. . . . Not only are they slaves of the bourgeois class, and of the bourgeois

---

38. Karl Marx and Friedrich Engels, "Manifesto of the Communist Party," in *The Marx-Engels Reader*, 2nd ed. (New York: W. W. Norton, 1978), 473–74.
39. Marx and Engels, "Manifesto," 474.
40. Marx and Engels, "Manifesto," 479.

State; they are daily and hourly enslaved by the machine, by the over-looker, and, above all, by the individual bourgeois manufacturer himself.[41]

Every story needs a villain. For Marx, there is no greater villain than the bourgeoisie, personified by the industrial capitalist who owns the capital for investing, the means of production, and for all intents and purposes, the laborers themselves. Yet Marx compares the capitalist to a "sorcerer, who is no longer able to control the powers of the nether world whom he has called up by his spells."[42] In the end, the forces of production and consumption will devour the bourgeoisie, as they consume everything else in their path, by conscientizing the working class—the proletarians—forging them into a political class organized to eventually and inevitably overturn the bourgeoisie: "What the bourgeoisie, therefore, produces, above all, is its own grave-diggers. Its fall and the victory of the proletariat are equally inevitable."[43]

If the bourgeoisie are the villains in Marx's story, the proletariat are its heroes. Marx's stages in the development of political economy can be viewed as a coming to consciousness of the proletarian class, defined not as the working class, but as the excluded class without property or political representation. Accordingly, the proletarian movement is not a minority movement seeking liberation from a dominant political majority, but a majority movement of the world's poor and oppressed, inevitably coming to the realization that they are subjugated and dehumanized by a vulnerable minority:

> All previous historical movements were movements of minorities, or in the interests of minorities. The proletarian movement is the self-conscious, independent movement of the immense majority, in the interests of the immense majority. The proletariat, the lowest of stratum of our present society, cannot stir, cannot raise itself up, without the whole superincumbent strata of official society being sprung into the air.[44]

The proletariat movement is revolutionary insofar as it cannot work toward the interests of the "immense majority" without first overturning the political and economic structures that keep the proletariat class excluded and exploited. Transcending a society built on the antagonism of class struggle begins with a violent revolution, as the laborer class, cognizant that "instead of rising with the progress of industry, [it] sinks deeper and deeper below the

---

41. Marx and Engels, "Manifesto," 479.
42. Marx and Engels, "Manifesto," 478.
43. Marx and Engels, "Manifesto," 483.
44. Marx and Engels, "Manifesto," 482.

conditions of existence," organizes and cooperates to replace the bourgeoisie, because it "is unfit any longer to be the ruling class in society, and to impose its conditions of existence upon society as over-riding law."[45] Ultimately, the proletariat class evolves into the communist movement, a political economy beyond binary oppositions, in order to build a society without class struggle, where the exploitation of the many by the few is eliminated via the abolition of private property.

Karl Marx makes this process seem not only inevitable, but relatively painless. In a few words he glosses over the fact that for the proletariat to overthrow the bourgeoisie, and to replace the current social order with a classless society, involves a lot of intentional violence and loss of human life:

> Of course, in the beginning, this cannot be effected except by means of despotic inroads on the rights of property, and on the conditions of bourgeois production; by means of measures, therefore, which appear economically insufficient and untenable, but which, in the course of the movement, outstrip themselves, necessitate further inroads upon the old social order, and are unavoidable as a means of entirely revolutionising the mode of production.[46]

Many Christians are offended by the hostile atheism of Marxism, which sees religion as one of the traditional ideas propping up the bourgeoisie that must be overcome and left behind in the new world order. Against the accusation that communism "abolishes all religion, and all morality," Marx responds, "The history of all past society has consisted in the development of class antagonisms, antagonisms that assumed different forms at different epochs. . . . The Communist revolution is the most radical rupture with traditional property relations; no wonder that its development involves the most radical rupture with traditional ideas."[47] God and religion included. Religion is "the opium" that keeps humanity satisfied in its enslavement, making the abolition of religion necessary: "The critique of religion disillusions man so that he will think, act, and fashion his reality as a man who has lost his illusions and regained his reason."[48] Despite this explicit attack on religion, however, it is Marx's uncritical acceptance of political violence that distances him most from the Christian tradition and the Jesus of the Sermon on the Mount.

In fairness to Marx, Engels, and even Lenin, violence is not the only path to bringing about the communist revolution, but it is a central feature in the writings of the mature Marx— *Capital: A Critique of Political Economy* (1847) and

---

45. Marx and Engels, "Manifesto,", 483.
46. Marx and Engels, "Manifesto," 490.
47. Marx and Engels, "Manifesto," 489–90.
48. Marx, *Critique of Hegel's 'Philosophy of Right,'* 132.

Manifesto of the Communist Party (1848)—where it seems a fundamental and necessary feature of his political system. Marx was clear that in some countries, given certain requisite social conditions, nonviolent revolution was possible, and he names the United States and Great Britain specifically. Yet Lenin, by the time he was writing on Marxism, concluded the conditions that had made Marx treat England and the United States as exceptions to violent revolution no longer existed.[49] Regardless, it is widely agreed that according to Marx existing social, political, and economic systems can change only through revolutionary means and that the overthrow of the existing social order will involve political violence.

By contrast, Jesus' teachings on violence seem to contradict Marx's acceptance and use of political violence. Marx is encouraging his followers to engage in violence as an instrument of social change: "The Communists disdain to conceal their views and aims. They openly declare that their ends can be attained only by the forcible overthrow of all existing social conditions. Let the ruling classes tremble at a Communist revolution. The proletarians have nothing to lose but their chains. They have a world to win."[50] This is incongruous with Jesus' command to renounce violence:

> "You have heard that it was said, 'An eye for an eye and a tooth for a tooth.' But I say to you, Do not resist an evildoer. But if anyone strikes you on the right cheek, turn to him the other also; and if anyone wants to sue you and take your coat, give your cloak as well; and if anyone forces you to go one mile, go also the second mile. Give to everyone who begs from you, and do not refuse anyone who wants to borrow from you." (Matt. 5:38–42).

While violence seems an inescapable aspect of the human condition—there is a rich and vibrant tradition of Christian justification of violence in self-defense or for the sake of liberation from extreme tyranny—the Christian life is characterized by a divine preference for nonviolence over against violence.[51] The Marxist revolution seems to privilege revolutionary violence as the moral high ground, with little regard for the human cost of said violence.

Granted, unlike Adam Smith, Karl Marx's atheistic materialist philosophy contains a secularized "doctrine of sin," insofar as the rise of the bourgeois class and the invention of private property caused humanity's current "fallen" condition. Unfortunately, Marx's soteriological vision—the abolition of

---

49. See Vladimir Ilyich Lenin, *The State and Revolution*, ed. Janet B. Kopito, repr. (New York: Dover, 2021), 39.
50. Marx and Engels, "Manifesto," 500.
51. See Rubén Rosario Rodríguez, *Christian Martyrdom and Political Violence: A Comparative Theology with Judaism and Islam* (Cambridge: Cambridge University Press, 2017), 35–82, 170–220.

private property and the rise of a truly egalitarian classless society—in actual historical praxis seems inseparable from authoritarian and genocidal political solutions. To be fair, recent history has seen a rise in authoritarian political practices within so-called neoliberal democracies, as "cuts to social and welfare spending . . . after the global financial crisis, coupled with more policing, the increasing criminalisation of poverty and demonisation of council estates, are symptoms of a shift to authoritarian neoliberalism by the state."[52] Many of the world's leading democratic capitalist economies, from the United States to India to Brazil, have seen a rise in right-wing populism that could be described as neofascism.[53] In the US, the Capitol uprising of January 6, 2021, woke the nation to the more authoritarian tendencies of American conservatism: "The Jan. 6 insurrection at the Capitol gave the country a striking wake-up call to the alarming rise in undemocratic behavior on the right side of the political aisle."[54]

Nevertheless, there is a long-standing critique of Marxism from anarchism, dating back to the struggle between Marx and Bakunin for control of the International Workingmen's Association. Bakunin believed Marxist regimes would inevitably lead to "nothing but the highly despotic government of the masses by a new and very small aristocracy."[55] The historical evidence supports this assessment, from the strong-arm tactics of the former Soviet Union and its allied Eastern Bloc nations (1922–1991), to the genocidal Cultural Revolution in Chinese Communism (1966–1976), to the various authoritarian socialist regimes in Latin America, Africa, and Asia. Add to this Marx and Engels's rationalization for the use of "despotic" political violence to bring about the "forcible overthrow" of bourgeois capitalism, and Marxism contains an unresolved contradiction between its democratic aspirations and its violent praxis of liberation that is also at odds with the moral vision articulated by Jesus.

If Adam Smith argued that production and trade are natural to the human condition and beneficial for all, and Karl Marx responded that private property is the root cause of exploitation and subjugation of the many by the few,

52. Malte Laub, "The Rise of 'Authoritarian Neoliberalism' and Its Impact on Communities," King's College London (July 29, 2021). https://www.kcl.ac.uk/news/study-sheds-light-on-austerity-and-growing-sense-of-fear-in-communities.
53. See Anthony Robert Pahnke and Marcelo Milan, "The Brazilian Crisis and the New Authoritarianism," *Monthly Review* (June 1, 2020). https://monthlyreview.org/2020/06/01/the-brazilian-crisis-and-the-new-authoritarianism/. Also see Kamalakar Duvvuru, "Is India Displaying Signs of Neo-fascism?," *Monthly Review* (July 31, 2019). https://mronline.org/2019/07/31/is-india-displaying-signs-of-neo-fascism/.
54. Cameron Easley, "U.S. Conservatives Are Uniquely Inclined toward Right-Wing Authoritarianism Compared to Western Peers," *Morning Consult* (June 28, 2021). https://morningconsult.com/2021/06/28/global-right-wing-authoritarian-test/.
55. Mikhail Aleksandrovich Bakunin, *Bakunin: Statism and Anarchy*, ed. and trans. Marshall Shatz (Cambridge: Cambridge University Press, 1990), 178.

then Max Weber's chief insight is to diagnose the unnaturalness of capitalism as the massive acquisition of wealth as an end in itself. There is a widely held assumption that Weber's main contribution to the study of capitalism is his analysis of the Protestant work ethic as a primary factor in the development of Western capitalism. This is both a simplification and an exaggeration, easily refuted by Weber's own words:

> We have no intention whatever of maintaining such a foolish and doctrinaire thesis as that the spirit of capitalism . . . could only have arisen as the result of certain effects of the Reformation, or even that capitalism as an economic system is a creation of the Reformation. . . . On the contrary, we only wish to ascertain whether and to what extent religious forces have taken part in the qualitative formation and the quantitative expansion of that spirit over the world.[56]

Max Stackhouse (1935–2016) praises Weber for recognizing, unlike Smith and Marx, who subsume religion under other more primary causal phenomena, "religion as an independent variable that shapes culture" and believing that "cultural factors and interests interact with material interests to shape economies,"[57] even as he critiques Weber's understanding of Christianity: "Capitalist forms of production and trade were more fully developed in some monastic centers and in both Italian and Germanic cities before the Protestant Ethic than he acknowledges."[58]

As Anthony Giddens notes in his introduction to *The Protestant Ethic and the Spirit of Capitalism*, Weber's analysis of Protestantism is but "a fragment" of a larger study of world religions that included "ancient Judaism, Hinduism and Buddhism, and Confucianism (Weber also planned, but did not complete, a full-scale study of Islam)" as part of an integrated study analyzing "divergent modes of the rationalization of culture, and as attempts to trace out the significance of such divergencies for socio-economic development."[59] Therefore, Weber's most important contribution is the insight that motivated his examination of religion as an independent contributing factor in the development of capitalism; the unnatural—even pathological—character of modern capitalism:

> Man is dominated by the making of money, by acquisition as the ultimate purpose of his life. Economic acquisition is no longer subordinated to man as the means for the satisfaction of his material

---

56. Max Weber, *The Protestant Ethic and the Spirit of Capitalism*, trans. Talcott Parsons (New York: Charles Scribner's Sons, 1958), 91.
57. Stackhouse, *God and Globalization*, 30.
58. Stackhouse, *God and Globalization*, 30.
59. Weber, *The Protestant Ethic and the Spirit of Capitalism*, 5.

> needs. This reversal of what we should call the natural relationship, so irrational from a naïve point of view, is evidently as definitely a leading principle of capitalism as it is foreign to all peoples not under capitalistic influence.[60]

In other words, contrary to Adam Smith, Weber recognizes there is something wrong with the spirit of modern capitalism, insofar as it is fixated on the accumulation of wealth for its own sake above all else ("no longer subordinated to man as the means for the satisfaction of his material needs"), yet Weber does not embrace Karl Marx's monological explanation for the class struggle and the inevitable proletariat revolution. Weber, arguably the most influential post-Marxist economic thinker, articulated a distinctive genealogy of modern capitalism that rejected Marx's crude economic materialism. Still, as Weber concludes, "it is, of course, not my aim to substitute for a one-sided materialistic an equally one-sided spiritualistic causal interpretation of culture and history."[61] While affirming the role of religion in cultural formation, Weber is still part of the same Enlightenment project that seeks a rational—and by extension, secular—understanding of human socioeconomic practices.

Weber views history as a dialectical process of disenchantment and reenchantment: the cultural disenchantment that displaced polytheistic worldviews gave rise to monotheistic religions. During the Enlightenment a process of disenchantment motivated by scientific advances led to the view that monotheistic religions are irrational and ought to be set aside by the modern secular world, which Nietzsche termed the "death of God."[62]

Yet rather than witnessing the triumph of rationality over religion, we are witnessing the reenchantment of long dead ways of viewing and interpreting the world, many irrational and superstitious, leading to an increased fragmentation rather than a unifying rationality: "Many old gods ascend from their graves; they are disenchanted and hence take the form of impersonal forces. They strive to gain power over our lives and again they resume their eternal struggle with one another."[63] Weber's diagnosis of modernity is concerned about the contradiction contained within the Enlightenment grand narrative: while a more rational and scientific understanding of human social structures ought (in theory) to advance human freedom, the modern age is also characterized by an ever-increasing loss of freedom resulting from the use of technology to increase production and make distribution more efficient. In the end,

---

60. Weber, *The Protestant Ethic and the Spirit of Capitalism*, 53.
61. Weber, *The Protestant Ethic and the Spirit of Capitalism*, 183.
62. See Friedrich Nietzsche, *The Gay Science: With a Prelude in German Rhymes and an Appendix of Songs*, trans. Walter Kaufmann (New York: Vintage, 1974), 181.
63. Max Weber, "Science as a Vocation," in *From Max Weber: Essays in Sociology*, trans. and ed. H. H. Gerth and C. Wright Mills (London and New York: Routledge, 2009), 149.

Marx is correct that workers become "cogs in the machine," while Weber laments they are caught in an "iron cage" of their own making:

> No one knows who will live in this cage in the future, or whether at the end of this tremendous development entirely new prophets will arise, or there will be a great rebirth of old ideas and ideals, or, if neither, mechanized petrification, embellished with a sort of convulsive self-importance. For of the last stage of this cultural development, it might well be truly said: "Specialists without spirit, sensualists without heart; this nullity imagines that it has achieved a level of civilization never before achieved."[64]

According to Weber, the modern human lives "as did the ancients when their world was not yet disenchanted of its gods and demons," but rather than appeasing old gods through acts of ritual sacrifice, the modern individual must make a choice concerning which modern "god" to embrace:

> What man will take upon himself the attempt to "refute scientifically" the ethic of the Sermon on the Mount? For instance, the sentence, "resist no evil," or the image of turning the other cheek? And yet it is clear, in mundane perspective, that this is an ethic of undignified conduct; one has to choose between the religious dignity which this ethic confers and the dignity of manly conduct which preaches something quite different; "resist evil— lest you be co-responsible for an overpowering evil." According to our ultimate standpoint, the one is the devil and the other the God, and the individual has to decide which is God for him and which is the devil. And so it goes throughout all the orders of life.[65]

Even as he examined how the religious impulse, specifically the Reformed/Calvinist doctrine of vocation, led the pious to submit all spheres of human existence in service to God, Weber noted that this pious behavior soon became severed from the accompanying Christian ethos of loving the neighbor. John Calvin offers a theological vision that values production and trade as divine callings, even as it orders them in service to the greater social good:

> We are here briefly taught that a just and well-regulated government will be distinguished for maintaining the rights of the poor and afflicted . . . for those who are exposed an easy prey to the cruelty and wrongs of the rich have no less need of the assistance and protection of magistrates than the sick have of the aid of the physician. Were the truth deeply fixed in the minds of kings and other

---

64. Weber, *The Protestant Ethic and the Spirit of Capitalism*, 182.
65. Weber, "Science as a Vocation," 148.

judges, that they are appointed to be the guardians of the poor, and that a special part of this duty lies in resisting the wrongs which are done to them, and in repressing all unrighteous violence, perfect righteousness would become triumphant through the whole world.[66]

Ultimately, ascetic Protestantism was replaced by Enlightenment optimism, but without the opiate of religion disenchantment with modern capitalism seems inevitable:

> Economic ethics arose against the background of the ascetic ideal; now it has been stripped of its religious import. It was possible for the working class to accept its lot as long as the promise of eternal happiness could be held out to it. When this consolation fell away it was inevitable that those strains and stresses should appear in economic society which since have grown so rapidly.[67]

In the end, Weber does not offer a solution to the malady he diagnoses in modern capitalism, but while he is impressed by the power of capitalism to create, he is also aware of its power to destroy and concludes *The Protestant Ethic and the Spirit of Capitalism* on an apocalyptic tone: "The Puritan wanted to work in a calling; we are forced to do so. For when asceticism was carried out of monastic cells into everyday life, and began to dominate worldly morality, it did its part in building the tremendous cosmos of the modern economic order."[68] Unfortunately, cut off from its spiritual moorings and subverted by a technologically driven instrumental reason, the spirit of capitalism swallows all—"not only those directly concerned with economic acquisition"—trapping them in an iron cage of production, consumption, and acquisition until "the last ton of fossilized coal is burnt."[69]

THE NEW SPIRIT OF CAPITALISM

This book assumes human beings are defined by the stories they tell. Cultural shifts and historical epochs mark the eclipsing of one dominant narrative by

---

66. John Calvin, *Calvin's Commentaries*, vol. 5, reprint of the Edinburgh edition, various editors and translators (Grand Rapids: Baker Book House, 2003), 332.
67. Max Weber, *General Economic History*, trans. Frank H. Knight (Mineola, NY: Dover, 2003), 369.
68. Weber, *The Protestant Ethic and the Spirit of Capitalism*, 181.
69. Weber, *The Protestant Ethic and the Spirit of Capitalism*, 181.

another; and yet, as Derrida opined, past narratives do not completely fade from memory but continue to haunt our collective imagination.[70] At the heart of Kathryn Tanner's challenging and insightful book *Christianity and the New Spirit of Capitalism* (2019) is a struggle between three competing narratives: (1) the story of capitalism replacing Christianity as the West's foundational narrative, which Max Weber argued cannot be told without recounting the story of Protestantism; (2) the story of finance-dominated capitalism cannibalizing Western capitalism to create an unsustainable and dystopian zero-sum game that even threatens planetary survival; and (3) the still small voice (1 Kgs. 19:12) that constitutes Tanner's carefully crafted tale of a world not governed by the reductionist and ultimately inhuman language of exchange markets, profit-driven schemes, and the constant commodification of human labor.

Tanner's book, which grew out of the 2017 Gifford Lectures at the University of Edinburgh, grants Max Weber's central thesis that religious beliefs and economic behavior are interconnected, yet argues that capitalism has morphed into something Weber might no longer recognize, let alone condone. Tanner analyzes and critiques finance-dominated capitalism for fostering a totalitarian ethos among its labor force "to ensure not just maximum intensity of effort but maximum intensity of commitment to such effort."[71]

Tanner argues that the very logic of capitalism—in which hard work is compensated with good pay and benefits in an effort to engender company loyalty and long-term mutuality—has been inverted by investor demands to maximize profits, which prevent companies from rewarding hard work. As a result, new management practices have evolved that intentionally create worker insecurity since, from the perspective of shareholders, equitable wages and benefits packages threaten profit margins. Finance-driven capitalism perpetuates itself and fosters worker insecurity by encouraging excessive consumer spending and perpetual indebtedness. This insecurity creates an unhealthy bond and dependency between the worker desperate to survive and the employer willing to exploit and gain from such desperation. When "there are no other viable ways of making a living," fear, not equitable wages, becomes the primary means of inducing worker compliance.[72]

---

70. See Jacques Derrida, *Specters of Marx: The State of the Debt, the Work of Mourning, and the New International*, trans. Peggy Kamuf (New York and London: Routledge, 1994).
71. Tanner, *Christianity and the New Spirit of Capitalism*, 64.
72. Tanner, *Christianity and the New Spirit of Capitalism*, 65.

In a move that echoes and resonates with John Milbank's critique of modernism, Tanner's *Christianity and the New Spirit of Capitalism* describes two competing metaphysical systems, one in which the market stands absolute and becomes both object of devotion and unquestioned determinant of human behavior, and the other the biblical worldview, whose God "is a jealous God" (Exod. 34:14) who will not tolerate divided loyalties and demands utter devotion. For "Christian commitment to God is not to be exhibited in only those spheres of life specifically dedicated to it but should make itself felt throughout the whole of one's life."[73] Ironically, as Tanner notes, Christianity and finance-dominated capitalism share many similarities in their demand for total devotion from adherents while employing disciplinary practices that focus and direct followers' lives as part of an ongoing lifelong project. Yet the "mechanisms employed within Christianity to assure wholehearted commitment to God run radically contrary to those used by finance-dominated capitalism to induce total compliance."[74] In other words, in order to trap the laborer in a vicious cycle of self-improvement (defined as financial security), capitalism, especially finance-dominated capitalism, employs the language and practices of Christian spirituality—self-denial and self-sacrifice—without an adequate accounting of human sinfulness or divine grace.

For example, the market dangles the carrot of higher salaries for those with a university degree while burdening the labor force under crippling student loan debt, thereby creating a dependency to one's employer which the employer then exploits by cultivating worker insecurity, demanding greater devotion and increased productivity without increased compensation. As the laborer journeys through life the debt continues to grow—a car loan in order to secure reliable transportation to and from work, a mortgage in order to project the image of maturity and success that will hopefully lead to greater professional advancement—and still more discipline and self-control is demanded, but the god of the market is ravenous and never satisfied, so in the end there is no genuine loyalty, only fearful compliance. From a Christian theological perspective, the market is a false god whose allure and attraction fades. Rescuing the hapless human laborer from this reductionist and ultimately self-destructive devotion demands conversion, and by conversion Tanner means, at the very least, a radical discontinuity between our past and our future, always cognizant that "God is the one who bridges the difference."[75]

---

73. Tanner, *Christianity and the New Spirit of Capitalism*, 87.
74. Tanner, *Christianity and the New Spirit of Capitalism*, 87
75. Tanner, *Christianity and the New Spirit of Capitalism*, 62.

No matter how economists finesse their arguments, capitalism remains inherently self-centered and individualistic, while Christianity is inherently other-centered, given that dependence on God entails interdependence with others. According to the theological anthropology of Orthodox theologian John D. Zizioulas, "there is no way for God's love to reach each of us except through the love of human beings."[76] However, the value of the cooperative religious project does not stand or fall on our ability to cooperate, but rests solely on the fact that it is God's project. Unlike the social forms that constitute capitalism, the communal life of the church as the body of Christ *includes* the individual effort to conform to God's will *but does not depend* on these efforts for success, since the "God who stands outside those human relations is in this sense entering into those relations to do the coordination of them, behind their backs and independently of their own intentions."[77]

Modern secularized thought cringes at the notion of an external divine agent guiding human behavior behind the scenes, yet uncritically embraces the supposedly uncontrollable and absolute deterministic forces of the market. Tanner slowly builds up her argument, presenting two competing and contrasting gods who each make absolute demands, yet demonstrating how the old story of human sinfulness overcome by divine grace ultimately presents a more attractive alternative for humanity, because unlike capitalism, the Christian project calls believers to set aside any attachment that displaces God as object of devotion. Following conversion, the drive for power, money, status, security, and all the other forces of neoliberalism that perpetuate lifelong indentured servitude to the market lose their hold over the Christian believer, since "value does not enter the world through us, by virtue of mixing our labor with it," because "God created them for no purpose or end other than to be the reflections of God's glory."[78] In other words, the Christian response to the ever-present commodification of human labor in modern capitalism is to embrace and affirm a theological anthropology that rejects instrumental reason, grounded in our dependence on God and our inherent dignity as creatures made in the image of God.

In the end, Tanner's tale is not new, but neither is it an attempt to resurrect the dead letter of Christendom. Rather, it is a cautious, critical retrieval of Christian resources for articulating an alternative to the dominant narrative of capitalism, in which the god of the markets is contrasted to the biblical God, who presents humanity with a radically different lifestyle and accompanying

---

76. John D. Zizioulas, *Communion and Otherness: Further Studies in Personhood and the Church*, ed. Paul McPartlan (London: T. & T. Clark, 2006), 78.
77. Tanner, *Christianity and the New Spirit of Capitalism*, 214.
78. Tanner, *Christianity and the New Spirit of Capitalism*, 208.

set of practices. Instead of viewing human beings as autonomous, isolated individuals in constant competition with one another, the Christian God stands outside of us, yet "becomes the basis of a common vision and desire. The community here is intense. People are united, that is, in ways that overcome all division."[79]

At its core Christianity is radically opposed to capitalism, especially its more predatory finance-dominated form, because it is an inherently cooperative project involving the self, the other, and God. The economist will object that profit-driven enterprises depend upon mutually beneficial cooperation and argue that the logic of exchange can serve as the basis for community. The theologian responds that there is a crucial difference between *ecclesia* ("gathering of those summoned") and association ("a group of people organized for a joint purpose"), namely, the identity of the one doing the summoning (God) and the nature of the joint purpose (the kingdom of God).

In *Christianity and the New Spirit of Capitalism*, Tanner challenges readers to embrace what amounts to an "anti-work ethic," rejecting authoritarian and coercive projects that promise social transformation (i.e., political revolution), while encouraging readers to abandon the enslaving god of finance-dominated capitalism through an ethics of self-transformation. A transcendent power grounds and enables this transformative ethic "that has been felt in the past and is still here, no deferred utopia . . . but already at work in the present, with a voice whose force has yet to be extinguished."[80] Tanner's project is not trying to revive the Christian orthodoxy of ages past, nor does she propose imposing a new theological totalitarianism; rather, she gives voice to certain time-proven Christian truths that can provide a locus of critical resistance against the seemingly unstoppable forces of free-market capitalism. It takes an act of faith to leave behind our many false idols, but the good news undergirding Tanner's narrative is the language of grace: God is already at work in countless imperceptible ways to entice us toward conversion. "Let anyone with ears listen!" (Matt. 13:9).

A Christian theological anthropology counters the anthropology of production that dominates finance-driven capitalism by defining the human in terms of an incarnational Christology, in which Jesus reveals the image of redeemed and reconciled humanity: "In virtue of being one with the Word, the humanity that the divine image assumes is itself healed and elevated, shaped

---

79. Tanner, *Christianity and the New Spirit of Capitalism*, 218.
80. Tanner, *Christianity and the New Spirit of Capitalism*, 219.

and re-formed according to the character of the Word itself with which the humanity of Jesus has been united. In Christ, human nature, in short, is itself re-fashioned in the divine image so as to become humanely perfect."[81] The Christian story provides a glimpse of an alternative way of living in community, in which "Christ's human life is the primary witness to what God's being one with the human should mean for human life."[82] Christian eschatological hope extends this redemption and reconciliation to the organizational structures of society itself.

Thus, rather than compete with modern capitalism, Tanner embraces "history's apparent losers" in much the same way Dietrich Bonhoeffer's theology of the cross embraced the underside of history. The implication is not to rebuild society and the market economy along more Christian lines, but to reject the market itself: "I am not suggesting that the Christian account of the future I have just developed provides an alternative model . . . as if the character of those markets could be improved, for example, if Christians themselves acted differently within them."[83] Rather, "I am suggesting . . . that the financial approach to the future is part of the present world to be left behind, a world to be repudiated in all the very basic ways it counsels people to relate to themselves and others, in favor of a whole new world to come that will be as different from this world as possible."[84]

Kathryn Tanner offers a fragment—an eschatological glimpse—of an alternative Christian lifestyle, instead of a detailed plan for rebuilding society in the image of Christ. Why? Because to undertake such a project would mean engaging modern capitalism by employing the instrumentalist reasoning of modern capitalism, which treats fellow human beings as means to an end, as objects to be controlled and manipulated. God, as demonstrated by the incarnation, does not seek an instrumental relationship with humanity but desires instead full communion. God does not violate our inherent dignity, yet makes it known that being human implies more than bodily or volitional autonomy.

---

81. Kathryn Tanner, *Christ the Key* (Cambridge: Cambridge University Press, 2010), 17.
82. Tanner, *Christianity and the New Spirit of Capitalism*, 211.
83. Tanner, *Christianity and the New Spirit of Capitalism*, 165.
84. Tanner, *Christianity and the New Spirit of Capitalism*, 166.

As members of this one body, we become sacramental signs of Christ's transformative grace for one another without replacing Christ's mediating role or contributing in any salvific way to the transformation of others. In other words, "Christ's influence remains irreplaceable, but upon his death his very own influence is conveyed through other human beings who form a community of life with him . . . humans who are dead to themselves in that they now live his very life, their own lives being fundamentally remade insofar as they become an extension of his."[85] As the apostle Paul exhorts, "How can we who died to sin go on living in it? Do you not know that all of us who have been baptized into Christ Jesus were baptized into his death? Therefore we have been buried with him by baptism into death, so that, just as Christ was raised from the dead by the glory of the Father, so we too might walk in newness of life" (Rom. 6:2–4).

The Christian communal project differs from modern capitalism in that the success of the project does not depend on the performance and achievements of the human agents involved. This does not mean that as members of the body of Christ we do not put forth our best effort, but merely recognizes that as flawed and sinful human beings the body of Christ thrives *despite* our best effort: "Their good effect on others . . . an unintended consequence of horribly flawed efforts to lead a Christian life."[86] As Tanner contends, capitalism fails to understand that Christianity is a cooperative project carried out by faithful disciples whose success does not depend on the quality of Christian cooperative activity—the body of Christ continues even when Christians are unable to cooperate—because it is a community called into being and enabled by a divine act.

A FRAGMENT OF THEOLOGY: FRANCIS OF ASSISI AND THE SPIRIT OF LIBERATION

Jorge Mario Bergoglio was named pope on March 13, 2013. This marked several firsts in the history of the papacy: (1) the first Latin American pope selected by a papal conclave, (2) the first member of the Society of Jesus named pope, (3) the first pope to reside in the *Domus Sanctae Marthae* guesthouse instead of the papal apartments in the apostolic palace used by previous popes, and (4) the first pope to choose Francis as his papal name, in honor of Francis of Assisi. Together these four distinctions reveal important similarities

---

85. Tanner, *Christianity and the New Spirit of Capitalism*, 211.
86. Tanner, *Christianity and the New Spirit of Capitalism*, 213.

between Pope Francis and the saint who inspired his papal name and provide insight into the importance of Francis of Assisi as a guidepost or marker for the pilgrim church in the twenty-first century.

Francis of Assisi (c. 1181–1226) is rarely described as a political and social reformer. The saint's commitment to evangelical poverty is often reduced to a spiritual detachment from the things of the world, with little mention made of the root causes of poverty or the Christian's role in eliminating poverty. Consequently, most believers picture Francis as the harmless lover of nature—witness the statuary adorning many gardens—rather than Francis the disturbing advocate of voluntary poverty. Even Leonardo Boff (1938–), a noted Brazilian liberation theologian who left the priesthood and the Franciscan order after being silenced by Rome, wrote an analysis of the life and ministry of Francis from the perspective of liberation theology in which he said that "to look for social liberation in Saint Francis, within present-day schemes of society or liberation, means to fail to find any parallel."[87] Thus, even while acknowledging Francis's importance as a protoliberationist, Boff cautions great care must be taken to read Francis in his medieval context: "One must place Francis within his time. In the medieval world, religion dominated everything; it organized all of society. Although it did not stop being the ultimate, economics is interpreted from theology and religion."[88] At the same time, Boff is concerned that romantic idealizations of Francis will negate the radical nature of his critique of wealth, as in the analysis by Franciscan Heribert Roggen, who declares, "We do not find in Francis any social concern; he did not want to change anything, he did not challenge anyone, nor was he against anything."[89]

In the Middle Ages, Christian care of the poor centered around two social practices: (1) begging and almsgiving, and (2) public hospitals.[90] Begging was the primary way in which the poor were assisted, and almsgiving was a significant component of personal *and* public piety within the sacramental system of salvation, since beggars were regarded as holy persons in the medieval theology of almsgiving, in which the almsgiver sees "the face of Christ

---

87. Leonardo Boff, *Francis of Assisi: A Model for Human Liberation*, trans. John W. Diercksmeier (Maryknoll, NY: Orbis Books, 2006), 79.

88. Boff, *Francis of Assisi*, 78–79.

89. See H. Roggen, "¿Hizo Francisco una opción de clase?," in *Selecciones de Teología* 3 (1974): 287–95. Cited in Boff, *Francis of Assisi*, 78.

90. See Elaine Clark, "Institutional and Legal Responses to Begging in Medieval England," *Social Science History* 26, no. 3 (Fall 2002): 447–73; Maureen Flynn, *Sacred Charity: Confraternities and Social Welfare in Spain, 1400–1700* (London: Macmillan, 1989); and Donald J. Kagay and Theresa M. Vann, eds., *On the Social Origins of Medieval Institutions: Essays in Honor of Joseph F. O'Callaghan* (Leiden: E. J. Brill, 1998).

in the beggar."[91] Despite theological support for begging, and the rise of the mendicant orders that incorporated begging into their ascetic rule, begging eventually became a public nuisance and a criminal enterprise in many cities. Most European cities of the late Middle Ages began to look for alternatives to begging and almsgiving as the primary means of caring for the poor, leading to the creation of public hospitals.

Unlike hospitals in the modern age, hospitals in the late medieval period did not just provide care for the sick but were more like comprehensive social welfare institutions providing general care for the poor through various ministries of "hospitality." Some hospitals were large and cared for hundreds of guests, but most were small, private residences bequeathed by a wealthy patron at death for the purpose of caring for the poor: "In this house would live a priest, who would say masses for the souls of the dead donors and direct the activities of the hospital with the assistance of one or two servants."[92] A dozen or so people in need—elderly widows, orphans, men physically unable to work—would also live in the house. This practice eventually spread to all the major cities of Europe so that by the time of the Protestant Reformation, "most municipalities depended on a combination of regulated begging and hospitals to meet the needs of their poor."[93]

With the rapid growth of cities in the fifteenth century, these efforts proved insufficient to meet the needs of the poor, as evidenced by a 1531 imperial edict from the Holy Roman emperor, Charles V, implementing reform of poor relief practices in the Low Countries, based on municipal reforms successfully implemented in Catholic cities like Mons and Ypres.[94] These reforms emphasized a move toward lay control of social welfare ministries and more prudent financial administration, often calling on prominent business leaders to administer hospitals, as opposed to the previous practice of having clergy—without business training or acumen—manage poor relief.

Boff contends that in this medieval context, Francis's embracing of evangelical poverty was an inherently political practice with widespread repercussions beyond his personal spiritual journey, because "Francis made, without any doubt, an option for the poor."[95] Clearly influenced by a Marxist reading of history, Boff argues that Francis lived during a time of transition for feudalism, "because its rule is threatened by the emerging merchant means of

---

91. Robert M. Kingdon, "Calvinism and Social Welfare," *Calvin Theological Journal* 17 (1982): 213.
92. Kingdon, "Calvinism and Social Welfare," 213.
93. Kingdon, "Calvinism and Social Welfare," 213.
94. Robert M. Kingdon, "Social Welfare in Calvin's Geneva," *American Historical Review* 76, no. 1 (February 1971): 50.
95. Boff, *Francis of Assisi*, 79.

production of the common bourgeoisie," and Francis reflected "the crisis of the times and gives to it his personal version of the possible ways."[96] Marxist rhetoric aside, the political dimensions of Francis's option for voluntary poverty become more evident once he is located within the long Christian tradition of apostolic poverty, itself grounded in the praxis of Christ himself as encountered in the Gospels. Thomas Aquinas, responding to critics who argued Christ ought not have chosen a life of poverty, replied, "Humility is not much to be praised in one who is poor of necessity. But in one who, like Christ, is poor willingly, poverty itself is a sign of very great humility."[97] Christianity has historically and consistently combated certain popular perceptions of wealth, especially the desire and acquisition of great wealth.

No passage in the Gospels better encapsulates this tension than the encounter between Jesus and the rich ruler who asked Jesus, "Good Teacher, what must I do to inherit eternal life?" (Luke 18:18). The ruler in the story is turned away with a harsh rebuke from Jesus, "How hard it is for those who have wealth to enter the kingdom of God! Indeed, it is easier for a camel to go through the eye of a needle than for someone who is rich to enter the kingdom of God" (Luke 18:24–25). Jesus was harsh with the ruler because Jesus quickly became aware of the hold wealth and all its trappings had on the man's life. First, Jesus was suspicious when the ruler began their conversation by calling him "Good Teacher": "Why do you call me good? No one is good but God alone" (v. 19). Then, after Jesus delineates for him what the Law commands, the ruler responds, "I have kept all these since my youth" (v. 21). It is at that point that Jesus tells him: "There is still one thing lacking. Sell all that you own and distribute the money to the poor, and you will have treasure in heaven; then come, follow me" (v. 22). The ruler heard this and became sad, because he was very rich and personally unable to voluntarily give up his wealth (v. 23). Unlike Francis, the ruler could not embrace evangelical poverty.

Yet we ought not be too harsh with the rich ruler. After all, the idea of voluntary poverty cuts against the grain of modern capitalism: "Voluntary poverty in itself is despised, as a proof of foolishness; involuntary as a proof of incompetency."[98] In other words, according to the capitalist anthropology of production, an involuntary fall into poverty is a moral failure, while the conscious decision to embrace poverty is nonsensical.

---

96. Boff, *Francis of Assisi*, 79.

97. Thomas Aquinas, *The "Summa Theologica" of St. Thomas Aquinas, Part 3*, literally translated by the Fathers of the English Dominican Province (New York: Benziger Brothers, 1914), 198 (III, Q. 40, Art. 3).

98. Albert R. Bandini, "St. Francis and the Ideal of Poverty," *The American Ecclesiastical Review* 75 (1926): 352.

Still, there are some liberationists who contend giving away all one's wealth—and the social power wealth represents—is counterproductive. Let me explain. At an academic conference hosted by Princeton Theological Seminary I had the privilege of having breakfast with Gustavo Gutiérrez. Soon the conversation turned to the work I was doing with US university students who undertook a two-month immersion experience in a Christian base community outside of Managua, Nicaragua. When I told Gutiérrez about one student who gave up his wealth and privilege to stay in Nicaragua to live and work among the poor of Ciudad Sandino, the kindly priest responded, "Great. Just what Latin America needs: one more poor person." Over breakfast he then explained that my students need to realize that their wealth and privilege are gifts from God that ought to be used in solidarity with the poor to transform the social realities that cause and perpetuate poverty. Voluntary poverty, despite romantic visions of a stark-naked Francis giving all his clothes to a beggar, is best understood as solidarity with the poor by employing the resources at one's disposal to humanize and liberate. When done properly, a life in political and economic solidarity with the poor is just as foolish from the perspective of modern capitalism.

As Boff writes, seen "from the point of view of a system that defines what is possible and what is not, what is sensible and what is not, the path of Francis seems like foolishness."[99] Francis rejected the trappings of wealth and the social relations and practices this entailed during his day and age, in order to live a life of simple obedience and service. This put him in direct conflict with the prevailing social mores, embodied in the dispute with his father, "who went to the consuls of Assisi to force Francis to return the money that he had distributed among the poor."[100] Appearing before the consuls and magistrates of the city, Francis proclaimed, "By the grace of God I am free and I am not obligated to obey the consuls, because I am a servant of the Most High God," to which the consul declared, in response to the father's request, "Seeing that your son is in the service of God, it is not up to us to judge him."[101]

Such behavior is likely to land one in legal trouble today, yet it provides an insight into the relationship between spiritual and temporal powers in medieval Europe. To those who argue Francis's commitment to evangelical poverty lacked a social-political dimension, I observe that Francis was aware of the power wielded by consuls and magistrates, and he was in the habit of

---

99. Boff, *Francis of Assisi*, 82.
100. Boff, *Francis of Assisi*, 82.
101. Boff, *Francis of Assisi*, 82. Boff here cites and translates the Latin text of *The Legend of St. Francis by the Three Companions*. For a published English translation of this text, see *The Legend of St. Francis*, trans. Emma Gurney Salter (London: J. M. Dent & Sons, 1926).

employing the authority that came with his religious vocation to offer guidance and advice to the rulers of Assisi:

> Brother Francis, your little and looked-down-upon servant in the Lord God, wishes health and peace to all mayors and consuls, magistrates and governors throughout the world and to all others to whom these words may come.
>
> Reflect and see that the day of death is approaching [Gen. 47:29]. With all possible respect, therefore, I beg you not to forget the Lord because of this world's cares and preoccupations and not to turn away from His commandments, for all those who leave Him in oblivion and turn away from His commandments are cursed [Ps. 119:21; Vulgate, Ps. 118:21] and will be left in oblivion [Ezek. 33:13] by Him.
>
> When the day of death does come, everything they think they have shall be taken from them [Matt. 13:12]. The wiser and more powerful they may have been in this world, the greater will be the punishment they will endure in hell [Wis. 6:7].
>
> Therefore I strongly advise you, my Lords, to put aside all care and preoccupation and receive the most holy Body and Blood of our Lord Jesus Christ with fervor in holy remembrance of Him. May you foster such honor to the Lord among the people entrusted to you that every evening an announcement may be made by a messenger or some other sign that praise and thanksgiving may be given by all people to the all-powerful Lord God.[102]

This suggests that Francis employed his social and political power to encourage social transformation for the benefit of the poor and marginalized, and while he voluntarily gave up personal wealth, he was keenly aware of the role wealth plays in addressing poverty. Here he stands in good company, insofar as the argument can be made that Jesus in the Gospels regularly interacted with the rich and powerful—figures like Nicodemus, a Pharisee and member of the Sanhedrin (John 3:1–21; 7:50–51; 19:39–42), Joseph of Arimathea (John 19:39–42), and Joanna, the wife of Herod's steward Chuza (Luke 8:3), who financially supported Jesus' ministry—even as he lived a life in solidarity with the poor: "Foxes have holes, and birds of the air have nests; but the Son of Man has nowhere to lay his head" (Matt. 8:20).

---

102. Saint Francis, "A Letter to the Rulers of the Peoples (1220)," in *Francis of Assisi—The Saint: Early Documents*, vol. 1, trans. Regis J. Armstrong, ed. Regis J. Armstrong, OFM Cap.; J. A. Wayne Hellmann, OFM Conv.; William J. Short, OFM (New York: New City Press, 1999), 58. A copy of this letter was discovered by Luke Wadding in the *De origine seraphicae religionis franciscanae* of Francisco Gonzaga, General Minister from 1579 to 1587. According to Gonzaga, John Parenti, the first Provincial Minister of Spain, brought a copy of this letter to Spain.

Accordingly, Leonardo Boff interprets Francis's commitment to evangelical poverty as "a liberating vision," even though he "did not point out to his followers any specific apostolic activity. He did not build hospitals, leper colonies, or other assistance works, because he did not see the poor primarily as objects of aid. To be poor like the poor is superseded by being with the poor in deep solidarity."[103] Francis becomes a model of Christian resistance to the new spirit of capitalism, not by proposing a new social project to remake the world in a more Christlike image, but by embodying a spirituality of solidarity focused on preserving the inherent dignity of the neighbor in need above all else—the antithesis of the ethos of acquisition.

In Boff's analysis, Francis represented a radical critique of the dominant culture of medieval Christianity, "including the forces of clericalism and paternalism and legalism," but rather than advocate a cooperative social and political project, Francis's commitment to liberation "appeared more in his embodiment of an alternative way of life than through an attempt to transform existing structures of power."[104] This open-ended but pastorally focused vision to live in solidarity with the poor illumines the ministry of Pope Francis, who chooses to share power (for example, by naming women, lay and religious, to positions of leadership within the Vatican), who works to build up the church, even as he criticizes it, and who always acts from fraternal love toward all of creation.

Francis of Assisi inspired Pope Francis to write *Laudato Si'* (2015), in which the pope critiques consumerism and irresponsible economic development, laments environmental degradation and global warming, and calls all people of the world to take "swift and unified global action" to reverse these trends. Pope Francis praises the saint whose "response to the world around him was so much more than intellectual appreciation or economic calculus, for to him each and every creature was a sister united to him by bonds of affection. That is why he felt called to care for all that exists."[105] This in turn led to Pope Francis's most comprehensive statement on political and economic solidarity with the poor, *Fratelli tutti* (2020), guided by how "Saint Francis expressed the essence of a fraternal openness that allows us to acknowledge, appreciate and love each person, regardless of physical proximity, regardless of where he or she was born or lives," because wherever Francis went, "he sowed seeds of peace and walked alongside the poor, the abandoned, the infirm and the

---

103. Boff, *Francis of Assisi*, 84.
104. Brian Hamilton, "The Politics of Poverty: A Contribution to a Franciscan Political Theology," *Journal of the Society of Christian Ethics* 35, no. 1 (Spring/Summer 2015): 34.
105. Pope Francis, "Encyclical Letter *Laudato Si'* of the Holy Father Francis on Care for Our Common Home" (May 24, 2015), §11. https://www.vatican.va/content/francesco/en/encyclicals/documents/papa-francesco_20150524_enciclica-laudato-si.html.

outcast, the least of his brothers and sisters."[106] In his 2020 encyclical letter Pope Francis envisions a global community without borders, lamenting the fact that "in today's world, the sense of belonging to a single human family is fading, and the dream of working together for justice and peace seems an outdated utopia" (§30). Furthermore, he chastises the growing tendency among the world's wealthier nations to treat human life as disposable: "Some parts of our human family, it appears, can be readily sacrificed for the sake of others" (§18); and he is troubled that, "in practice, human rights are not equal for all" (§22). Accordingly, Pope Francis insists that any viable solutions to the problems of violence, climate change, and economic disparity must confront the breakdown of the common good afflicting the international community by including a "shared roadmap" toward globalization and progress that includes *all* the world's nations, not just the rich.

Leonardo Boff reminds us that the Christian life "is understood by Francis as a 'passing through the world' as a pilgrim and a stranger, without any stability."[107] The legacy we as Christians leave behind cannot be measured by acquisitions or political victories. Therefore, the church ought not engage in the practices of modern capitalism but should live in solidarity with the poor. In the words of Pope Francis, the church becomes a field hospital after a battle, and the mission of the church simply to heal. Our guiding virtue? Doing everything in our power to keep human life human.

---

106. Pope Francis, "Encyclical Letter *Fratelli Tutti* of the Holy Father Francis on Fraternity and Social Friendship" (October 3, 2020), §§1–2. https://www.vatican.va/content/francesco/en/encyclicals/documents/papa-francesco_20201003_enciclica-fratelli-tutti.html.

107. Boff, *Francis of Assisi*, 90.

4

The Myth of Human Uniqueness[1]

> I have given the evidence to the best of my ability; and we must acknowledge, as it seems to me, that man with all his noble qualities, with sympathy which feels for the most debased, with benevolence which extends not only to other men but to the humblest living creature, with his god-like intellect which has penetrated into the movements and constitution of the solar system—with all these exalted powers—Man still bears in his bodily frame the indelible stamp of his lowly origin.[2]

Some years back a colleague in the department of biology at Saint Louis University approached me—a theologian—for advice on how to better communicate with students from conservative Christian backgrounds preparing for careers in medicine or the life sciences. Her problem was with students who dogmatically rejected evolution because it contradicted their core beliefs. She

---

1. Thank you to Prof. Mohamed Noor, PhD, Dean of Natural Sciences and a professor in the biology department at Duke University, for his critical feedback and invaluable advice in regard to this chapter. Dr. Noor is a noted evolutionary geneticist who was one of the first scientists to demonstrate speciation by reinforcement, that is, as a result of natural selection mating preferences diverge against harmful hybridization and reduce gene flow between species. Currently, his research team is focusing on understanding variation in recombination rate within and between species, and its impact on DNA sequence variation. See https://scholars.duke.edu/person/noor.

2. Charles Darwin, *The Descent of Man, and Selection in Relation to Sex* (1871), in *From So Simple a Beginning: The Four Great Books of Charles Darwin*, ed. with intro. by Edward O. Wilson (New York: W. W. Norton, 2006), 1248.

wanted them to succeed but was having a difficult time convincing these students that the insights of evolutionary theory are foundational for a career in the life sciences. For far too long combat and confrontation has characterized the discourse between religion and science, with fundamentalist Christianity on one side and some form of scientism on the other.[3]

While Saint Louis University draws students from a wide range of backgrounds, many of our students (especially those from rural Missouri) represent religious traditions resistant to—if not downright dismissive of—evolutionary science. In order to adequately prepare these students for careers in medicine, bioengineering, pharmaceutical research, or other aspects of the life sciences, it is crucial that educators overcome religious objections to evolutionary theory without undermining or dismissing students' spiritual convictions. My colleague in biology and I envisioned a mutually beneficial conversation between religion and the natural sciences that would model greater acceptance and cooperation from both sides.

Unfortunately, 163 years after the publication of Charles Darwin's *On the Origin of Species* (1859), many Christians still seek "refuge in pre-Darwinian understandings" rather than engage evolutionary science with enough seriousness to facilitate multidisciplinary cooperation on fundamental philosophical questions about the human condition.[4] These Christians either embrace fideism by refusing to submit their core religious beliefs to rational scrutiny, or satisfy themselves with the truism that science and religion seek to answer different questions through divergent means.[5] Granting that the natural sciences

---

3. Christian fundamentalism is a modern religious movement, most often linked to British and American Protestantism but not confined to any single denomination, known for emphasizing biblical literalism, biblical infallibility, and biblical inerrancy. For a history and analysis of the impact of Christian fundamentalism in the US, see George M. Marsden, *Fundamentalism and American Culture* (New York: Oxford University Press, 2006). Conversely, scientism can be described as a fundamentalism of science too narrowly conceived. Understood as the belief that science and the scientific method are the only objective and reliable means by which people determine normative and epistemological values, scientism lacks a healthy respect for science, its methods, and its goals, while marginalizing religion and morality. For a discussion of the problems with popular forms of scientism, see J. P. Moreland, *Scientism and Secularism: Learning to Respond to a Dangerous Ideology* (Wheaton, IL: Crossway, 2018), and Jeroen de Ridder, Rik Peels, and Rene van Woudenberg, eds., *Scientism: Prospects and Problems* (Oxford: Oxford University Press, 2018).

4. John F. Haught, *Making Sense of Evolution: Darwin, God, and the Drama of Life* (Louisville, KY: Westminster John Knox, 2010), xvii.

5. See Stephen Jay Gould, "Nonoverlapping Magisteria," *Natural History* 106 (1997): 16–22, and *Rocks of Ages: Science and Religion in the Fullness of Life* (New York: Ballantine, 1999). Gould's concept of "nonoverlapping magisteria" views religious and scientific worldviews as distinct forms of rationality seeking answers to very different questions. Science seeks to understand the empirical realm: "what is the universe made of (fact) and why does it work this way (theory)," whereas religion "extends over questions of ultimate meaning and moral value" (Gould, *Rocks of Ages*, 6).

and theology are disparate academic disciplines, each with its own methodology, areas of study and investigational goals, recent efforts by both scientists and theologians have fostered an interdisciplinary space in which the possibility of methodological overlap can lead to mutually enriching conversation. To get there, however, certain tensions must be resolved, including misunderstandings about the Christian belief in human uniqueness.

The assumption that humanity occupies a special place in the natural order as creatures made in the image of God was undermined by the publication of Darwin's *On the Origin of Species* (1859), considered by some "the greatest scientific book of all time."[6] The book's narrative contradicts the theological account of human uniqueness in which humankind is the "image of God," a "little lower than God," with dominion over "the beasts of the field, the birds of the air, and the fish of the sea" (Gen. 1:26–28; Ps. 8:5–8). As a natural philosopher, Darwin sought an explanation for the origin of life and its differentiation into millions of distinct species that accepted the "lowly origin" of humanity as part of the evolutionary descent from the first simplest organisms.

Methodologically committed to a "natural" explanation, Darwin rejected the very notion of a guiding hand or intelligence directing this process, but still needed to identify the mechanism by which life could adapt and modify itself to produce such diversity. His solution was elegant in its simplicity and has stood the test of time as a rational and verifiable explanation for the complex natural processes that enable organisms to adapt and evolve over time. Darwin, inspired by his experiences breeding pigeons, drew upon his knowledge of "artificial" selection to develop his theory of evolution by means of "natural" selection. Darwin was attempting to describe a blind, undirected, natural process:

> As man can produce and certainly has produced a great result by his methodical and unconscious means of selection, what may not nature effect? Man can act only on external and visible characters: nature cares nothing for appearances, except insofar as they may be useful to any being. She can act on every internal organ, on every shade of constitutional difference, on the whole machinery of life. Man selects only for his own good; Nature only for that of the being which she tends.[7]

---

6. From Edward O. Wilson's introduction to *On the Origin of Species*, in *From So Simple a Beginning*, 437.

7. Darwin, *On the Origin of Species*, in *From So Simple a Beginning*, 503.

Furthermore, given that artificial breeding programs are designed to meet human needs, Darwin argued that the process of natural selection is in the long run more efficient and beneficial to the well-being of a species.[8]

Through the preservation of favorable traits resulting from the natural competition of courtship, alongside the introduction of naturally occurring random mutations, Darwin counters the dominant view of his day that believed each species was independently created as they exist today. Instead, Darwin demonstrated how each species alive today descended from other species. By reflecting on "the mutual affinities of organic beings, on their embryological relations, their geographical distribution, geological succession, and other such facts," he set out to demonstrate "how the innumerable species inhabiting this world had been modified, so as to acquire that perfection of structure and coadaptation which most justly excites our admiration."[9] The mechanism by which these processes occur, independent of any guiding intelligence or predetermined end, is natural selection. The struggle for survival impacts which members of a species live to reproduce and pass down those traits that made them better adapted for survival:

> As many more individuals of each species are born than can possibly survive; and as, consequently, there is a frequently recurring struggle for existence, it follows that any being, if it vary however slightly in any manner profitable to itself, under the complex and sometimes varying conditions of life, will have a better chance of surviving, and thus be *naturally selected*. From the strong principle of inheritance, any selected variety will tend to propagate its new and modified form.[10]

From the point of view of the survival of a species, natural selection greatly increases the chances of adaptation and survival, compared to human breeding efforts through artificial selection, because the latter emphasize only those traits the breeder deems beneficial for his or her purposes. Human breeders, whether driven by compassion or some other, altruistic impulse, also lack the harsh and impersonal hand nature's crucible employs in the struggle for life.

The struggle for survival is central to the process of natural selection, which is why organisms tend to produce more offspring than eventually survive, and why those best adapted for survival live long enough to pass their traits to their

---

8. For a fascinating look at a well-documented breeding experiment with silver foxes in the former Soviet Union that accelerated speciation, see Lee Alan Dugatkin and Lyudmila Trut, *How to Tame a Fox (and Build a Dog): Visionary Scientists and a Siberian Tale of Jump-Started Evolution*, repr. ed. (Chicago: University of Chicago Press, 2019).

9. Darwin, *On the Origin of Species*, 450.

10. Darwin, *On the Origin of Species*, 451 (emphasis in the original).

offspring. Another argument in favor of natural selection over against artificial selection is that animal husbandry as a human practice dates back only tens of thousands of years, whereas natural selection is dated by geological epochs covering millions—even hundreds of millions—of years:

> [The breeder] does not allow the most vigorous males to struggle for the females. He does not rigidly destroy all inferior animals, but protects during each varying season, as far as lies in his power, all his productions. . . . Under nature, the slightest difference of structure or constitution may well turn the nicely-balanced scale in the struggle for life, and so be preserved. How fleeting are the wishes and efforts of man! How short his time! And consequently how poor will his products be, compared with those accumulated by nature during whole geological periods.[11]

Despite our close genetic proximity to other animal life, we are—for the moment—the only species that continues to refine its natural ability to shape habitats for maximal survival to such a degree that we are affecting evolutionary processes themselves, as evidenced by humanity's impact on global climate change.[12] A theological defense of human uniqueness acknowledges and embraces the human capacity to transform nature on a broad scale in order to find positive solutions for adverse and destructive climate change by encouraging more meaningful dialogue and cooperation between religious beliefs and the natural sciences. Can Christianity continue to affirm human uniqueness in light of the claims of evolutionary theory that all animal life—including human beings—is descended from a common ancestor? Can a Darwinian account of human descent coexist alongside the deeply held belief that humankind has a sacred origin?

DARWINISM AND THE DOCTRINE OF CREATION

The Christian doctrine of creation is derived from the biblical literature and its interpretation by patristic, medieval, and Reformation theologians like Augustine of Hippo, Thomas Aquinas, and John Calvin. Unlike biblical Judaism in the Hebrew Bible, which conceived of creation as God ordering a preexisting chaos,[13] the New Testament texts favor the notion of *creatio ex*

---

11. Darwin, *On the Origin of Species*, 503.
12. Ecosystem engineers, like beavers, can shape the environment for maximal survival, but nowhere near the extent humanity has been able to impact climate change on a global scale.
13. See Karl Löning and Erich Zenger, *To Begin With, God Created . . . : Biblical Theologies of Creation*, trans. Omar Kaste (Collegeville, MN: Liturgical Press, 2000); Bernhard W.

nihilo ("creation out of nothing").[14] Consequently, certain aspects of God's character are emphasized in the development of early Christian thought: God's transcendence, God's omnipotence, God's eternal existence, and God's unbound freedom. Furthermore, many Christians read the Hebrew Bible through a christocentric lens, firm in the belief that Jesus played a central role in primal creation: "It is the memory of Jesus' mighty works in the world that spurred the development of the doctrine of his agency in creation."[15]

As the early church came to terms with the divinity of the Christ, it began to apply key Old Testament texts that exhibited these four divine attributes to Jesus: "Before the mountains were brought forth, or ever you had formed the earth and the world, from everlasting to everlasting you are God" (Ps. 90:2). It is a small conceptual leap from this to the prologue to John's Gospel: "In the beginning was the Word, and the Word was with God, and the Word was God. He was in the beginning with God. All things came into being through him, and without him not one thing came into being" (John 1:1–3). Divine transcendence is emphasized to such a degree that even in the act of divine revelation God remains eternal mystery: "For my thoughts are not your thoughts, nor are your ways my ways, says the LORD. For as the heavens are higher than the earth, so are my ways higher than your ways and my thoughts than your thoughts" (Isa. 55:8–9). Thus, not only does God create out of nothing, but God also maintains the creation and directs its every move: "But the LORD is the true God; he is the living God and the everlasting King. At his wrath the earth quakes, and the nations cannot endure his indignation" (Jer. 10:10). Accordingly, in coming to terms with Jesus' earthly ministry, the New Testament authors came to identify Jesus as the "Son of the Most High God" (Mark 5:7), and many of the miracles performed by Jesus reinforce the notion that Jesus has dominion over the creation: "He woke up and rebuked the wind, and said to the sea, 'Peace! Be still!' Then the wind ceased, and there was a dead calm" (Mark 4:39).

Anderson, *Creation in the Old Testament* (Minneapolis: Fortress, 1984) and *Creation versus Chaos: The Reinterpretation of Mythical Symbolism in the Bible*, repr. ed. (Eugene, OR: Wipf & Stock, 2005); Terence E. Fretheim, *God and World in the Old Testament: A Relational Theology of Creation* (Nashville: Abingdon, 2010); David T. Tsumura, *The Earth and the Waters in Genesis 1 and 2: A Linguistic Investigation* (Sheffield, UK: Sheffield Academic, 1989).

14. See Gerhard May, *Creatio ex Nihilo: The Doctrine of 'Creation out of Nothing' in Early Christian Thought* (Edinburgh: T. & T. Clark, 1995); Sean M. McDonough, *Christ as Creator: Origins of a New Testament Doctrine* (Oxford: Oxford University Press, 2009); Gary A. Anderson and Markus N. A. Bockmuehl, eds., *Creation ex nihilo: Origins, Development, Contemporary Challenges* (Notre Dame, IN: University of Notre Dame Press, 2018); Paul M. Blowers, *Drama of the Divine Economy: Creator and Creation in Early Christian Theology and Piety* (Oxford: Oxford University Press, 2012).

15. McDonough, *Christ as Creator*, 25.

This understanding of God as transcendent, omnipotent, eternal, and unbound comes into conflict with Darwinian evolution. As the transcendent and all-powerful Creator who authored the very laws of nature that science is trying to understand, God is beyond scientific analysis and observation. If created reality is contingent on the divine will, human observers can only describe what is, not postulate a better (more efficient?) creation. Still, as previously noted, one major tension between Darwinian evolution and the Christian belief in a benevolent and all-powerful God is the problem of innocent suffering and evil.[16] Natural selection as described by Charles Darwin is a slow process involving much suffering and death, leading some to describe natural selection as "wasteful."[17] Here the term "wasteful" is employed to describe the great loss of life that accompanies natural selection, which contributed to Darwin eventually rejecting belief in a good and loving God, as he confessed in a letter to his friend and supporter Asa Gray, a Harvard biologist and practicing Christian: "I cannot see, as plainly as others do, and as I should wish to do, evidence of design and beneficence on all sides of us. There seems to be too much misery in the world."[18]

Is Charles Darwin's theory of evolution fundamentally incompatible with the Christian belief in a divine Creator? Arguably, when Darwin wrote and published *On the Origin of Species*, he could be described as a deist, insofar as he rejected divine revelation and supranatural agency in everyday life but maintained a very high regard for the beauty and magnificence of nature in all its complexity, remaining open to the possibility of a Creator who authored the underlying laws of nature. Without compromising his belief that science seeks natural explanations for the workings of creation, Darwin seems to suggest such complexity is not accidental: "The whole history of the world, as at present known, although of a length quite incomprehensible by us, will hereafter be recognized as a mere fragment of time, compared with the ages which have elapsed since the first creature, the progenitor of innumerable extinct and living descendants, was created."[19]

---

16. Darwin's theory of natural selection emphasized struggle and competition over limited resources in general. However, as Dr. Mohamed Noor notes, natural selection does not "require" suffering and death. In natural selection, one type can simply be better than the other at reproduction. For instance, if type A produces one offspring (consistently), and type B produces two offspring (consistently), eventually virtually all individuals will be type B, but it doesn't necessarily mean type A ones were dying or suffering; they simply were less efficient at reproduction.
17. Denis R. Alexander, "Creation and Evolution," in *The Blackwell Companion to Science and Christianity*, ed. J. B. Stump and Alan G. Padgett (Malden, MA: Wiley-Blackwell, 2012), 238.
18. Charles Darwin, letter to Asa Gray, dated May 22, 1860, published by the University of Cambridge as part of the Darwin Correspondence Project, "Letter no. 2814." https://www.darwinproject.ac.uk/letter/DCP-LETT-2814.xml.
19. Darwin, *On the Origin of Species*, 759.

Some of Darwin's language even echoes the Genesis creation story (Gen. 2:7) as he acknowledges someone or something breathed life into the first simple organism: "Therefore I should infer from this analogy that probably all organic beings which have ever lived on this earth have descended from some primordial form, into which life was first breathed."[20] In other words, the Creator who ordered the universe according to eternal and unchanging laws, established the processes of natural selection and evolution by which the natural order continues to create itself free from divine interference. Without espousing Christian dogma about the nature and character of God, Darwin affirms belief in an originating act by a divine hand. He then concludes *On the Origin of Species* by acknowledging that from this first act of breathing life into the simplest organism, the divinely ordered laws of nature give rise to higher orders of animals—even human life—via a natural process that might appear random and blind to the suffering it causes but is in fact awe-inspiring in scope:

> Thus, from the war of nature, from famine and death, the most exalted object which we are capable of conceiving, namely, the production of the higher animals, directly follows. There is grandeur in this view of life, with its several powers, having been originally breathed into a few forms or into one; and that, whilst this planet has gone cycling on according to the fixed law of gravity, from so simple a beginning endless forms most beautiful and most wonderful have been, and are being evolved.[21]

As a theory, evolution does not (cannot) disprove the existence of God. It simply refutes William Paley's argument from design as a means of explaining the complexity of organic life by positing a naturalistic explanation for how those complex organic structures that suggest an intelligent designer came to be *without necessitating* God's continuing involvement in the world (Providence). Still, by the end of his life Darwin had moved away from even this minimally deist conception of God.

Yet, despite popular mythmaking by Richard Dawkins and other figures associated with the "new atheism," that Darwin not only abandoned the Christian faith but became an atheist,[22] evidence suggests that while he no longer believed in the God of the Bible and Christian tradition, Darwin remained receptive to some of the arguments of natural theology. Dawkins contends

---

20. Darwin, *On the Origin of Species*, 756.
21. Darwin, *On the Origin of Species*, 760.
22. See Richard Dawkins, *The God Delusion* (Boston: Houghton Mifflin., 2006); Sam Harris, *The End of Faith: Religion, Terror, and the Future of Reason* (New York: W. W. Norton, 2005); and Daniel C. Dennett, *Breaking the Spell: Religion as a Natural Phenomenon* (New York: Penguin, 2006).

that "Darwin made it possible to be an intellectually fulfilled atheist,"[23] yet to the end of his life Charles Darwin insisted one could be both "an ardent theist and an evolutionist."[24] In the same letter, Darwin goes on to say, "I have never been an atheist in the sense of denying the existence of a God—I think that generally (and more and more so as I grow older) but not always, that an agnostic would be the most correct description of my state of mind."[25]

There is no clear statement of Darwin's religious sympathies. Descended from religious freethinkers, we know he was a devout Anglican during his time as a student at Cambridge and that his father (Robert Darwin, himself a Unitarian) wanted Charles to be ordained an Anglican priest. But by the time he published *On the Origin of Species* (1859) Darwin's views were more in line with a nonbiblical deism, and late in life he acknowledged his own religious agnosticism. Furthermore, Darwin was keenly aware that his changing views on religion would distress his wife Emma, as evidenced by this letter from her to Charles prior to their marriage, in which she expresses concerns that his scientific endeavors would create distance between them:

> When I am with you I think all melancholy thoughts keep out of my head but since you are gone some sad ones have forced themselves in, of fear that our opinions on the most important subject should differ widely. My reason tells me that honest & conscientious doubts cannot be a sin, but I feel it would be a painful void between us. I thank you from my heart for your openness with me & I should dread the feeling that you were concealing your opinions from the fear of giving me pain. It is perhaps foolish of me to say this much but my own dear Charley we now do belong to each other & I cannot help being open with you. Will you do me a favour? yes, I am sure you will, it is to read our Saviour's farewell discourse to his disciples which begins at the end of the 13th Chap of John. It is so full of love to them & devotion & every beautiful feeling. It is the part of the New Testament I love best. This is a whim of mine it would give me great pleasure, though I can hardly tell why I don't wish you to give me your opinion about it.[26]

---

23. Richard Dawkins, *The Blind Watchmaker: Why the Evidence of Evolution Reveals a Universe without Design*, repr. (New York: W. W. Norton, 1996), 6.

24. Letter to John Fordyce from Charles Darwin, dated May 7, 1879, Darwin Correspondence Project, "Letter no. 12041." https://www.darwinproject.ac.uk/letter/DCP-LETT-12041.xml.

25. Letter to John Fordyce.

26. Letter to Charles Darwin from his fiancée Emma Wedgwood, dated November 21–22, 1838, Darwin Correspondence Project, "Letter no. 441." https://www.darwinproject.ac.uk/letter/DCP-LETT-441.xml.

Though Darwin affirms one can believe in God and in evolution at the same time, inconsistencies between theistic claims and the evidence of natural science contributed to his departure from orthodox Christianity into eventual agnosticism. In the same letter to Harvard botanist Asa Gray where Darwin contends that the vast amount of suffering and death that characterizes natural selection undermines evidence of design in nature, Darwin also rejects belief in the goodness of God, because "I cannot persuade myself that a beneficent and omnipotent God would have designedly created the *Ichneumonidae* [parasitic wasps] with the express intention of their feeding within the living bodies of caterpillars."[27] Nevertheless, Darwin's agnosticism cannot be blamed on his scientific commitments alone—since, as he argues at different points throughout his life, they are not incompatible with theistic belief: "[I see] no good reason why the views given in this volume should shock the religious feelings of anyone."[28]

One factor in Darwin's loss of faith that resonates with the Millennial and Gen Z generations concerns his moral repugnance at the judgmental and exclusionary nature of Christian belief. Two deaths loom large over the life of Charles Darwin: that of his father, physician Robert Darwin (1766–1848), and that of his beloved youngest daughter Annie (1841–1851), within a few of years of each other. When his father, a Unitarian freethinker like his grandfather Erasmus Darwin (1731–1802), died, Charles Darwin confronted the hatefulness of the Christian doctrine of hell. He railed against what he called the "damnable doctrine" that teaches sinners that those who die outside the church's orthodoxy—be they unbelievers or unorthodox thinkers who reject aspects of Christian doctrine (like his father)—are condemned to eternal suffering after death:

> I gradually came to disbelieve in Christianity as a divine revelation. . . . But I was very unwilling to give up my belief; I feel sure of this for I can well remember often and often inventing day-dreams of old letters between distinguished Romans and manuscripts being discovered at Pompeii or elsewhere which confirmed in the most striking manner all that was written in the Gospels. But I found it more and more difficult, with free scope given to my imagination, to invent evidence which would suffice to convince me. Thus disbelief crept over me at a very slow rate, but was at last complete. The rate was so slow that I felt no distress, and have never since doubted even for a single second that my conclusion was correct. I can hardly see how anyone ought to

---

27. Darwin, letter to Asa Gray.
28. Darwin, *The Origin of Species: 150th Anniversary Edition* (New York: Signet Classics, 2003), 452.

wish Christianity to be true; for if so the plain language of the text seems to show that the men who do not believe, and this would include my father, brother, and almost all my best friends, will be everlastingly punished.

And this is a damnable doctrine.[29]

Tellingly, Darwin's wife Emma redacted this passage in his autobiography and instructed his publisher to remove the sections she had marked with these comments: "I should dislike the passage in brackets to be published. It seems to me raw. Nothing can be said too severe upon the doctrine of everlasting punishment for disbelief—but very few now would call that 'Christianity' (tho' the words are there)."[30] Yet, despite employing language that describes "losing" his faith, Darwin is mostly objecting to Christian orthodox teachings about eternal damnation, which, as Emma Darwin points out, are contested within Christianity itself.[31] In other words, Darwin is not rejecting theistic belief in general, which he defends elsewhere.

Yet, if his coming to terms with this "damnable doctrine" following his father's death caused him to sever his commitment to Christianity, the death of his youngest daughter at the age of ten from tuberculosis undermined his belief in a benevolent and loving God in a more fundamental way, even if he still left the door open to a theoretical belief in a Creator who established the laws of nature. Though he did not write extensively about this loss, it is evident from his correspondence that her death greatly affected his physical and mental health, and the memorial he wrote for her hints at the depth of his suffering: "We have lost the joy of the Household, and the solace of our old age—she must have known how we loved her; oh that she could now know how deeply, how tenderly we do still and shall ever love her dear joyous face. Blessings on her."[32] It has been argued that Darwin's alienation from God had less to do with his commitment to natural selection and evolution than his rejection of a morally repugnant judgmental Christianity that would condemn good and kind persons to hell, that Darwin did not reject God so much as the kind of God espoused by the orthodox Christianity of his day and

---

29. Charles Darwin, "Autobiography of Charles Darwin," in *The Works of Charles Darwin*, vol. 29, ed. Paul H. Barrett and R. B. Freeman (London: Routledge, 2016), 119.

30. Darwin, "Autobiography," 119n8.

31. As evidenced, for example, by the current debate on universal salvation between David Bentley Hart and Michael McClymond. See David Bentley Hart, *That All Shall Be Saved: Heaven, Hell, and Universal Salvation* (New Haven, CT: Yale University Press, 2019); and Michael J. McClymond, *The Devil's Redemption: A New History and Interpretation of Christian Universalism*, 2 vols. (Grand Rapids: Baker Academic, 2018).

32. Charles Darwin, "Charles Darwin's Memorial of Anne Elizabeth Darwin," Darwin Correspondence Project (April 30, 1851). https://www.darwinproject.ac.uk/people/about-darwin/family-life/death-anne-elizabeth-darwin.

age.³³ Coupled with the death of Annie, and the pious assertions that often accompany such a loss ("it is God's will," "her suffering has ended"), "the tragedy of her innocent suffering and his loss muted any attraction he might have had for a caring, beneficent God."³⁴

While there is much ambiguity concerning Darwin's religious beliefs, it becomes clear that he wanted nothing to do with a God who would allow the death of an innocent child or condemn a good man like his father to eternal suffering. Yet, there is nothing in Darwin's understanding of natural selection and evolution that necessarily contradicts belief in God—or that requires abandoning belief in the goodness of God.

John Polkinghorne (1930–2021), a theoretical physicist, Anglican priest, and theologian, confronted the argument that the "wastefulness" of natural selection undermines belief in a good and loving God with the counterargument that the long and slow process of evolution, which admittedly entails much death and suffering, can actually be interpreted as a compassionate act of God's design whose established laws help species better adapt to their environment, such that "from so simple a beginning endless forms most beautiful and most wonderful have been, and are being, evolved."³⁵

Polkinghorne devoted a lifetime to making belief in God both reasonable and compatible with science by articulating a natural theology, far removed from Paley's "divine watchmaker" argument, that nevertheless encourages human consciousness to reflect on the Creator. Unlike Paley, who found direct evidence of divine agency in the world, Polkinghorne acknowledged that in the modern era we must be contented with "general hints of the divine presence."³⁶ Still, modern science has identified two areas where such hints are most evident:

> One is the vast cosmos itself, with its fifteen-billion-year history of evolving development following the big bang. The other is the "thinking reed" of humanity, so insignificant in physical scale but, as Pascal said, superior to all the stars because it alone knows them and itself. The universe and the means by which that universe has become marvellously self-aware—these are the centres of our enquiry.³⁷

---

33. See Ronald L. Numbers, *Galileo Goes to Jail and Other Myths about Science and Religion*, repr. ed. (Cambridge, MA: Harvard University Press, 2010), 146–47.
34. Elizabeth A. Johnson, *Ask the Beasts: Darwin and the God of Love* (London: Bloomsbury, 2014), 39.
35. Darwin, *On the Origin of Species*, 760.
36. John Polkinghorne, *Belief in God in an Age of Science* (New Haven, CT: Yale University Press, 1998), 1.
37. Polkinghorne, *Belief in God*, 1–2.

By looking at creation at both the macro and micro levels, Polkinghorne accentuates a truism of contemporary science: "The essence of evolutionary process, whether cosmic or terrestrial, is an interplay between two contrasting tendencies that in a slogan way may be called 'chance and necessity.'"[38] When applied to biological evolution, this tension between chance and necessity renders the suffering and death characteristic of natural selection meaningful in a way that can overcome Darwin's doubts about a beneficent God, because it is from this very randomness that evolutionary change arises: "A world that was pure chance would be too haphazard for anything new to be able to persist in it. A world that was pure necessity would be too rigid for anything to be possible beyond endless rearrangements of already existing structures."[39] In natural selection, "If there were no genetic mutations (sheer necessity), there would be no new species. If there were endless genetic mutations (sheer chance), there would be no stable species on which natural selection could act."[40] Thus, without postulating a God who directly intervenes and directs every aspect of evolutionary development, Polkinghorne preserves theistic belief within a Darwinian framework:

> While the exact details of what has emerged in the course of cosmic history was not fixed from the start, nevertheless the presence of the deep potentiality built into the given fabric of created nature, of the kind that anthropic fine-tuning implies, indicates the universe to be a world of purposed fertility. Five-fingered homo sapiens was not decreed from the beginning, but it seems no accident that some form of self-conscious life has evolved.[41]

Polkinghorne responds to a major critique of theology, the problem of innocent suffering—"theodicy's struggle to understand the presence of disease and disaster in a world claimed to be the creation of a loving and powerful God"—with a scientific argument.[42] In other words, as science continues to gain a deeper understanding of the complexities of biological evolution—especially something as unpredictable as genetic mutation—it becomes evident that what "happens in nature cannot arbitrarily be torn apart and decomposed into parts that are good and parts that are bad, so that a benevolent Creator could readily have retained the good and eliminated the bad."[43]

---

38. John Polkinghorne, *Theology in the Context of Science* (New Haven, CT: Yale University Press, 2009), 108.
39. Polkinghorne, *Theology in the Context of Science*, 108.
40. Polkinghorne, *Theology in the Context of Science*, 108–9.
41. Polkinghorne, *Theology in the Context of Science*, 110.
42. Polkinghorne, *Theology in the Context of Science*, 111.
43. Polkinghorne, *Theology in the Context of Science*, 111.

In other words, it is not that God acts malevolently or is powerless to eliminate unwanted suffering, but as the Anthropic Cosmological Principle has demonstrated, the physical structures of the universe needed for the evolution of organic (carbon-based) life are so rigid and complex that

> this stellar alchemy takes over ten billion years to complete. Hence, for there to be enough time to construct the constituents of living beings, the Universe must be at least ten billion years old and therefore, as a consequence of its expansion, at least ten billion light years in extent. We should not be surprised to observe that the Universe is so large. No astronomer could exist in one that was significantly smaller. The Universe needs to be as big as it is in order to evolve just a single carbon-based life-form.[44]

According to Polkinghorne, *if* the universe is created by God, *if* God acts in accord with the divine nature, and *if* natural selection is the process by which God intends organic life to evolve and attain its highest perfection, *then* the suffering and death that accompanies biological evolution of necessity constitutes the most efficient and compassionate pathway to evolving higher order animals. Analogous to the free-will defense in theodicy that explains the existence of moral evil by affirming human free will (who wants a God who is little more than a cosmic tyrant pulling our strings?), Polkinghorne responds to Darwin's assertion that the sheer volume of suffering and death that accompanies natural selection contradicts belief in a benevolent God by arguing that an undirected and natural process entails genetic mutation (chance) as "the engine driving biological evolution."[45] Consequently, "The agonizing fact of cancer is not gratuitous, something that a Creator who was a bit more competent, or a bit less callous, could easily have avoided. It is the *necessary* cost of a world in which creatures make themselves."[46] By recalling Blaise Pascal's assessment of humanity's place in the universe, "A human being is only a reed, the weakest in nature, but he is a thinking reed,"[47] Polkinghorne affirms human uniqueness without contradicting natural selection, confident that "only a universe to whose physical fabric the free-process defence applied could give rise to beings to whom the free-will defence applies."[48]

---

44. John D. Barrow and Frank J. Tipler, *The Anthropic Cosmological Principle* (Oxford: Oxford University Press, 1986), 3.
45. Polkinghorne, *Theology in the Context of Science*, 111.
46. Polkinghorne, *Theology in the Context of Science*, 111 (emphasis added).
47. Blaise Pascal, *Pensées and Other Writings*, trans. Honor Levi (Oxford: Oxford University Press, 1999), 72 (¶231).
48. Polkinghorne, *Theology in the Context of Science*, 113.

THEISTIC RESPONSES TO DARWINISM

In a famous speech at Oxford in 1864, Benjamin Disraeli addressed the unsettling evolutionary theories being advanced by Charles Darwin: "The question is this—Is man an ape or an angel? My Lord, I am on the side of the angels. I repudiate with indignation and abhorrence the contrary view, which is, I believe, contrary to the conscience of mankind."[49] The popular imagination became outraged by Darwin's claims that human beings were descended from lower animals, which meant that as primates humans were most likely descended from a primitive (now extinct) species of monkey: "Man is descended from some lower form, notwithstanding that connecting-links have not hitherto been discovered."[50] The details proved even more unsettling: "The early progenitors of man were no doubt once covered with hair, both sexes having beards; their ears were pointed and capable of movement; and their bodies were provided with a tail."[51] Yet Darwin seemed aware of the impact his work was having on the general public, so he cautioned readers that this primordial ancestor was quite removed and different from any currently existing lower primate: "But we must not fall into the error of supposing that the early progenitor of the whole simian stock, including man, was identical with, or even closely resembled, any existing ape or monkey."[52]

In the United States, the 1925 Scopes "Monkey Trial" distorted the reception of Darwinian evolution, setting the stage for the still ongoing conflict between Christian fundamentalism and modern science.[53] Yet in the decades after the publication of *On the Origin of Species* in 1859, the reception of Darwin's ideas remained mixed, with some religious thinkers supporting the theory of natural selection, and others forcefully opposing evolution as dangerous to theistic belief. No stronger statement exists of the compatibility of Christian faith with Darwinian evolution than the funeral sermon for Charles Darwin preached by Harvey Goodwin, bishop of Carlisle, in Westminster Abbey on Sunday, May 1, 1882:

> I think that the interment of the remains of Mr. Darwin in Westminster Abbey is in accordance with the judgement of the wisest of his countrymen. It would have been an unfortunate thing if it had

---

49. William Flavelle Monypenny and George Earle Buckle, *The Life of Benjamin Disraeli; Earl of Beaconsfield*, vol. 4 (London: John Murray, 1916), 374.
50. Darwin, *The Descent of Man*, 882.
51. Darwin, *The Descent of Man*, 894.
52. Darwin, *The Descent of Man*, 890.
53. See Edward J. Larson, *Summer for the Gods: The Scopes Trial and America's Continuing Debate over Science and Religion* (New York: Basic Books, 2020).

been opposed or if he himself or those dearest to him had recognized an incompatibility between the results of his scientific studies and the solemn committal with prayer and thanksgiving to the ground of the mortal material frame that had done its work. . . . I believe that such intellects as those which were given to Newton and to Darwin, were given for the purpose of being applied to the examination of the universe which God who gave intellect created and made. But if I am told that because Newton discovered gravitation, therefore I can dispense with the Apostles' Creed, or that, having got the works of Darwin, I may leave my Bible, I reject the conclusion, not only as illogical and monstrous, but as contradicting a voice within me which has as much right to be heard as my logical understanding.[54]

Following the publication of *On the Origin of Species*, several leading liberal theologians including the Reverend Baden Powell, an Anglican priest and the Savilian Chair of Geometry at Oxford University, published a collection of essays defending Darwin's work. The more orthodox Bishop Samuel Wilberforce (1805–1873), who published an anonymous negative review of Darwin's book, criticized Darwin primarily on scientific grounds—not theological reasons—by citing respected scientists who also opposed the theory of evolution. This led to the now infamous encounter between Bishop Wilberforce and one of Darwin's staunchest defenders, his friend Thomas Henry Huxley (1825–1895), at the Oxford University Museum of Natural History on June 30, 1860.

Ostensibly the meeting's focal point was a lecture by New York University professor John William Draper (1811–1882) on Charles Darwin's views on the evolution of organisms. Though no transcript of the proceedings exists, the event is mostly remembered for a spontaneous exchange between Wilberforce and Huxley in which Wilberforce supposedly asked Huxley whether it was through his grandfather or his grandmother that he claimed descent from a monkey. Ornithologist Sir Alfred Newton (1829–1907) described the events in a letter to his brother:

> Referring to what Huxley had said two days before, about after all its not signifying to him whether he was descended from a Gorilla or not, the Bp. chafed him and asked whether he had a preference for the descent being on the father's side or the mother's side? This gave Huxley the opportunity of saying that he would sooner claim kindred with an Ape than with a man like the Bp. who made so ill a use of his wonderful speaking powers to try and burke [avoid], by a display of authority, a free discussion on what was, or was not,

---

54. Hardwicke Drummond Rawnsley, *Harvey Goodwin, Bishop of Carlisle: A Biographical Memoir* (London: John Murray, 1896), 223–24.

a matter of truth, and reminded him that on questions of physical science 'authority' had always been bowled out by investigation, as witness astronomy and geology. A lot of people afterwards spoke ... the feeling of the meeting was very much against the Bp.[55]

Published reports suggest the meeting was a major victory for Darwin and his supporters, but it is inaccurate to portray the Oxford gathering as a clash between religion and science, given the fact that many of the members of the British Science Association were themselves Christian clergy. In fact, opening remarks by the president of the Association explicitly expressed compatibility between religion and science: "Let us ever apply ourselves to the task, feeling assured that the more we thus exercise, and by exercising improve our intellectual faculties, the more worthy shall we be, the better shall we be fitted to come nearer to our God."[56]

Charles Darwin worried the publication of his book would create a public outcry, and the clash between Wilberforce and Huxley certainly confirmed his worst fears, but overall, Darwin's theory of natural selection was welcomed by scientists and religious thinkers alike. It is important to remember that in 1860, Darwin's theory was one of many competing for scientific and popular acceptance, since "there were other mechanisms of evolution that had credibility at the time."[57] Today, Darwin's theory of biological evolution by means of the naturalistic and material mechanism called natural selection represents scientific orthodoxy, its widespread acceptance due to the theory's "considerable explanatory force, a point recognized by many at the time, even those who were anxious about the implications of his ideas for the place of humanity within nature."[58] Despite representing a major conceptual leap, however, Darwin's naturalistic explanation for biological evolution still had one major obstacle to overcome: "How did nature 'remember' and 'transmit' these new developments? What mechanism could be proposed by which these new developments could be passed on to future generations?"[59]

Only after Augustinian monk Gregor Mendel (1822–1884) published the results of his experiments on patterns of inheritance in the hybridization of pea plants and proposed a theory of particulate inheritance, "in which

---

55. A. F. R. Wollaston, *Life of Alfred Newton: Late Professor of Comparative Anatomy, Cambridge University 1866–1907, with a Preface by Sir Archibald Geikie OM* (New York: Dutton, 1921), 118–20.
56. J. Vernon Jensen, "Return to the Wilberforce-Huxley Debate," *British Journal for the History of Science* 21, no. 2 (June 1988): 179.
57. Peter J. Bowler, "Christian Responses to Darwinism in the Late Nineteenth Century," in *The Blackwell Companion to Science and Christianity*, 37.
58. Alister E. McGrath, *A Fine-Tuned Universe: The Quest for God in Science and Theology* (Louisville, KY: Westminster John Knox, 2009), 172.
59. McGrath, *A Fine-Tuned Universe*, 172.

characteristics were determined by discrete units of inheritance that were passed intact from one generation to the next," did Darwin's theory "suddenly became much more plausible."[60] While the exact structure of DNA was not critical for understanding the hereditary mechanism of evolution, the introduction of critical models by Ronald Fisher and other contemporaries (Sewall Wright, J. B. S. Haldane) in the 1920s and 1930s joined the Darwinian process of natural selection with Mendel's concept of discrete hereditary factors (eventually called "genes") to give rise to the modern "neo-Darwinian" synthesis.[61] Today we know, according to the double-helix model of Watson and Crick (1953),[62] that DNA replicates by "acting as a template for RNA, which in turn acts as a template for proteins. . . . It is the sequence of these base pairs which determines the genetic information transmitted."[63] Given Darwin's foundational assumption—that chance in the form of random genetic mutations, alongside competitive sexual selection, provide the driving mechanism of evolution—it is understood that some of these mutations will have positive survival value and those organisms with "these favorable mutations should have relative advantage in survival and reproduction, and they will tend to pass their characteristics on to their descendants."[64]

This investigation assumes that the natural sciences and theology are both human pursuits in search of answers to discrete questions about the universe that over the centuries have intersected and interacted. American physicist Ian Barbour (1923–2013), in his 1990 Gifford Lectures at the University of Aberdeen, identified four ways science and religion have tended to engage one another: conflict, independence, dialogue, and integration.[65] Many assume that the age of science has superseded the age of faith, and mistakenly accept conflict as the only accurate way of describing the relationship between Christian belief and the natural sciences: "It is, of course, widely believed that science and religion are in conflict. Many people, indeed, suppose that this battle has already been won—that science has in some sense 'disproved' religion."[66]

As demonstrated in the previous discussion on the compatibility of theism with evolutionary theory, *conflict* need not be the inevitable conclusion to the

---

60. McGrath, *A Fine-Tuned Universe*, 173.
61. See Richard C. Lewontin, "Theoretical Population Genetics in the Evolutionary Synthesis," in *The Evolutionary Synthesis: Perspectives on the Unification of Biology*, rev. ed. (Cambridge, MA: Harvard University Press, 1998), 58–68.
62. Francis H. C. Crick and James D. Watson, "Molecular Structure of Nucleic Acids: A Structure for Deoxyribose Nucleic Acid," *Nature* 171 (1953): 737–38.
63. McGrath, *A Fine-Tuned Universe*, 175.
64. McGrath, *A Fine-Tuned Universe*, 175.
65. Ian G. Barbour, *Religion and Science: Historical and Contemporary Issues*, rev. and expanded ed. of *Religion in an Age of Science* (San Francisco: HarperSanFrancico, 1997), 77–105.
66. Mary Midgley, *Science as Salvation: A Modern Myth and Its Meaning* (London: Routledge, 1992), 51.

narrative relating theology to science. Rather, Barbour argues this has become the dominant public perception because two schools of thought, one within the sciences and the other within religion, have dominated the discourse: *scientific materialism* and *biblical literalism*. Both assume that conflict is unavoidable and that in the end only one side can be true and victorious.

A contemporary example of scientific materialism at its most virulent is the movement labeled the "new atheism," which views religion as the cause of myriad social problems and seeks to remove religious perspectives from the public discourse. The leading figures of this movement—Richard Dawkins, Sam Harris, Christopher Hitchens, Daniel Dennett—claim Friedrich Nietzsche as an ideological forefather (though Nietzsche might not warmly embrace his stepchildren), insofar as they accept the same basic premise: the religious impulse can be explained by some underlying neurosis or pathology, implying that the religious person needs a cure.[67] As a scientific methodology, this version of scientific materialism is reductionist in nature in its claim that "matter (or matter and energy) is the fundamental reality in the universe," and makes unverifiable metaphysical assertions in its quest for epistemological certainty by seeking "knowledge with a sure foundation."[68] According to this way of thinking, "Science alone is objective, open-minded, universal, cumulative, and progressive. Religious traditions, by contrast, are said to be subjective, closed-minded, parochial, uncritical, and resistant to change."[69] Some, like Daniel Dennett, push the supremacy of scientific materialism over religion to extremes with claims that "we can (in principle!) account for every mental phenomenon using the same physical laws and raw materials that suffice to explain radioactivity, photosynthesis, reproduction, nutrition and growth."[70]

As demonstrated by Thomas Kuhn's work in the philosophy of science—specifically his analysis of "paradigm shifts" in science—science and theology share some conceptual models that lend themselves to dialogue and cooperation between religion and the natural sciences.[71] Furthermore, as Barbour has argued repeatedly, scientific materialism transcends the limits of the scientific method by making bold metaphysical claims like Dennett's cited above, leading him to conclude that "scientific materialism and biblical literalism both represent a *misuse* of science."[72]

---

67. See Friedrich Nietzsche, *On the Genealogy of Morality*, ed. Keith Ansell-Pearson, trans. Carol Diethe (New York: Cambridge University Press, 1994, 2007) and *Beyond Good and Evil: Prelude to a Philosophy of the Future*, ed. and trans. Walter Kaufmann (New York: Vintage, 1989).
68. Barbour, *Religion and Science*, 78.
69. Barbour, *Religion and Science*, 78–79.
70. Daniel Dennett, *Consciousness Explained* (New York: Little Brown, 1991), 33.
71. See Thomas S. Kuhn, *The Structure of Scientific Revolutions*, 50th anniversary ed. (Chicago: University of Chicago Press, 2012), 43–51.
72. Barbour, *Religion and Science*, 78 (emphasis added).

Elizabeth Johnson elaborates on Barbour's critique of scientific materialism:

> To be clear: the integrity of the scientific method requires that it seek natural explanations for what occurs in the natural world. A scientist cannot properly introduce God to account for a phenomenon that is not yet understood. In that sense, scientific method is properly atheistic. The game changes, however, when thinkers allow scientific understanding of the natural world to expand into a metaphysical claim. . . . Whether or not God exists cannot be resolved by scientific method, according to the definition of both God and scientific method. Materialist critics of religion thus step beyond the zone of their own expertise in making philosophical judgments about the non-existence of spiritual or ultimate reality, judgments not warranted by scientific evidence.[73]

Accordingly, theism "is not inherently in conflict with science, but it does conflict with a metaphysics of materialism."[74]

If scientific materialism constitutes one end of the religion-vs.-science conflict, biblical literalism is its opposite. The conflict between Darwinian evolution and Christian fundamentalism centers around a literal reading of the first chapter of the book of Genesis, according to which God created the heavens and the earth—including all plant and animal life—in six calendar days (resting on the seventh!). Ironically, throughout Western history biblical interpretation has been receptive to multiple levels of meaning and a diversity of hermeneutical approaches, including allegorical and mystical readings of texts; but with the rise of Christian fundamentalism in the early twentieth century, the literal interpretation of texts began to predominate. As biblical scholar John Dominic Crossan underscores: "My point, once again, is not that those ancient people told literal stories and we are now smart enough to take them symbolically, but that they told them symbolically and we are now dumb enough to take them literally. They knew what they were doing; we don't."[75]

By forcing a literal reading of the Genesis creation narrative, fundamentalists set up an inflexible and insurmountable conflict with the natural sciences. Today, the view known as "scientific" or "young-earth creationism," which employs a literal reading of biblical history to conclude that the earth is six thousand years old (as opposed to the figure of 4.54 billion years established by radiometric dating), has become the established orthodoxy within Christian fundamentalism, even dictating the natural science curriculum at

---

73. Johnson, *Ask the Beasts*, 8.
74. Barbour, *Religion and Science*, 82.
75. John Dominic Crossan and Richard G. Watts, *Who Is Jesus? Answers to Your Questions about the Historical Jesus* (Louisville, KY: Westminster John Knox, 1996), 79.

Christian colleges like Cedarville University in Ohio, Bob Jones University in South Carolina, and Liberty University in Virginia. This creationist curriculum also impacts private religious schools at the primary and secondary levels, as well as the growing homeschooling market,[76] which now accounts for 5.4 percent of school age children (kindergarten through grade twelve) in the United States.[77]

Christian fundamentalists represent a sizeable portion of the Evangelical Protestant demographic that makes up about 25 percent of the US population.[78] Since the 1980s this demographic has organized politically at the grassroots level to transform local school boards in order to influence public school curriculums—especially science curriculums—to reflect their beliefs.[79] As the battle over school curriculums makes clear, interaction between biblical literalism and scientific materialism is inevitable in our day and age, but conflict need not be the only way for religion and science to interact.

Conflict arises because these two political extremes have taken absolutist positions, refusing to compromise with the other. In Barbour's assessment, scientific materialism is guilty of bad science whose metaphysical claims "have extended scientific concepts beyond their scientific use to support comprehensive *materialistic philosophies*," whereas biblical literalism is guilty of bad theology by insisting "that scripture is inerrant throughout," even as "the Roman Catholic Church and most of the mainline Protestant denominations have held that Scripture is the human witness to the primary revelation."[80] Therefore, it is vital for both science and theology to acknowledge that since contact is inevitable, it is important to explore avenues where these two approaches overlap.

Unfortunately, one very popular response to the dominant view that religion and science are in conflict is to avoid conflict, by insisting that science

---

76. See Joseph Murphy, *Homeschooling in America: Capturing and Assessing the Movement* (New York: Simon & Schuster, 2014). The homeschool movement has been extremely popular among political conservatives, including a marked overlap with Evangelical and fundamentalist Christian conservatives. See Heath Brown, *Homeschooling the Right: How Conservative Education Activism Erodes the State* (New York: Columbia University Press, 2021).

77. Though there was a surge of homeschooling caused by the global coronavirus pandemic, numbers have stabilized and returned to prepandemic levels as schools returned to face-to-face instruction. See "Homeschooled Children and Reasons for Homeschooling," National Center for Education Statistics (May 2022). https://nces.ed.gov/programs/coe/indicator/tgk/homeschooled-children?tid=4.

78. Pew Research Center, "America's Changing Religious Landscape," May 12, 2015, https://www.pewresearch.org/religion/2015/05/12/americas-changing-religious-landscape/.

79. See Melissa M. Deckman, *School Board Battles: The Christian Right in Local Politics* (Washington, DC: Georgetown University Press, 2004); and Angus M. Gunn, *Intelligent Design and Fundamentalist Opposition to Evolution* (Jefferson, NC: McFarland & Co., 2015).

80. Barbour, *Religion and Science*, 82 (emphasis in the original), 83–84.

and religion can exist independently of one another. The view that *independence* best describes the relationship of faith to science has proponents in both camps. The most influential scientific voice advocating independence is the late Stephen Jay Gould (1941–2002), a Harvard paleontologist, evolutionary biologist, and historian of science, who advocated for independence as a way of resolving the conflict between religion and science by arguing that science and religion never come into conflict, because they are investigating wholly different areas of human experience. Science studies the world according to a methodology that seeks material and mechanistic explanations for natural phenomena, while religion is seeking answers to questions of ultimate meaning. Each of these discrete areas of study, which Gould termed "magisteria," represents "a domain where one form of teaching holds the appropriate tools for meaningful discourse and resolution."[81] According to Gould's idea of "non-overlapping magisteria" (NOMA), there can be no conflict between science and religion, because each discipline is dedicated to its own separate magisterium, with science dedicated to "the empirical realm: what the Universe is made of (fact) and why does it work in this way (theory)," while the "magisterium of religion extends over questions of ultimate meaning and moral value."[82]

Within the religious realm, there exists a similar tendency to emphasize the divergence between science and religion via an approach called fideism, or the belief that faith is independent of reason, so the claims of theology need not be verified or submitted to rational verification. The term "fideism," coined in the nineteenth century and attributed to the French Protestant theologian Louis Auguste Sabatier (1839–1901), is often used to describe the philosophical theology of Søren Kierkegaard (1813–1855), but the approach has roots in the patristic theologian Tertullian (ca.160–230 CE), who asked the loaded rhetorical question, "What indeed has Athens [philosophy] to do with Jerusalem [theology]?"[83] Ultimately, like Gould, with his concept of NOMA, the fideist believes that reason cannot prove (or disprove) the claims of religion, so believers ought only rely upon their subjective religious experience (faith).

Still, as the French Enlightenment philosopher Blaise Pascal (1623–1662) cautioned, "If we submit everything to reason, our religion will contain nothing mysterious or supernatural. If we shock the principles of reason, our religion will be absurd and ridiculous."[84] Hardline fideists, especially within US Evangelicalism, acknowledge no overlap between religion and science, while

---

81. Gould, *Rocks of Ages*, 5.
82. Gould, *Rocks of Ages*, 6.
83. See Eric Osborn, *Tertullian, First Theologian of the West* (Cambridge: Cambridge University Press, 2003), 45.
84. Pascal, *Pensées and Other Writings*, 60 (¶204).

Pascal's intellectual heirs defend faith by setting *limits* on human reason without completely rejecting it: "Reason's last step is to recognize that there is an infinite number of things which surpass it. It is simply feeble if it does not go as far as realizing that."[85] Either way, much like Gould's nonoverlapping magisteria, Christian fideism avoids direct and meaningful exchange with science. Given the ongoing conflicts between religion and science in the public discourse, avoidance and independence fail to provide satisfactory solutions.

So, Ian Barbour advocates for some form of *dialogue* between religion and science. Dialogue assumes some degree of overlap, even as it acknowledges differences between religion and science, on the assumption that science, like religion, asks foundational ontological questions. As the continuing relevance of natural theology demonstrates, the "orderliness and intelligibility of the universe" leads science to ask questions about the nature of reality; science, in turn, "cannot answer these questions on the basis of science alone, so dialogue with religion is necessary."[86] Were science to acknowledge that it "does raise these wider questions," then perhaps the scientific establishment would become "more open to religious answers."[87] Like the model of independence, Barbour's model of dialogue understands that religion and science are distinct investigational disciplines, but remains open to the possibility of the two learning from one another: "While they cannot answer each other's proper questions, a sharing of insights from one field to another may enrich or even correct each other."[88]

Here the example cited in the previous section of this chapter, where John Polkinghorne, a theologian and physicist, responds to the Darwinian criticism that natural selection erodes belief in the goodness of God, proves instructive. Polkinghorne develops an argument that draws both from Christian theology about the nature of God and from the role of genetic mutations in animal speciation, to argue for the compatibility of natural selection with belief in a loving God: "A creation in which creatures make themselves can rightly be seen as a greater good than a ready-made world would have been, but it has a necessary cost."[89] That cost is the possibility of genetic mutations—necessary for biological evolution—becoming malignant and causing suffering and death. While humans like to think that (had we been in charge of creation), "we would have done it better," science "shows us that this is just not possible."[90]

---

85. Pascal, *Pensées and Other Writings*, 62 (¶220).
86. Nathan J. Hallanger, "Ian G. Barbour," in *The Blackwell Companion to Science and Christianity*, 606.
87. Barbour, *Religion and Science*, 91.
88. Johnson, *Ask the Beasts*, 9–10.
89. John Polkinghorne and Nicholas Beale, *Questions of Truth: Fifty-one Responses to Questions about God, Science, and Belief* (Louisville, KY: Westminster John Knox, 2009), 16.
90. Polkinghorne and Beale, *Questions of Truth*, 16.

A dialogical approach understands that "if there are some points of contact between particular doctrines and particular scientific theories," as suggested by Polkinghorne's scientific explanation for the problem of innocent suffering, then "there is in principle the possibility of significant doctrinal development and reformulation" resulting from Christian theology's engagement of the natural sciences.[91]

According to Barbour, while dialogue is preferred over conflict and independence, *integration* is the ideal model for understanding the relationship between religion and science. Unlike dialogue, which finds common ground by appealing to those aspects of the natural order in which religion and science overlap, integration probes "the relationships between theological doctrines and particular scientific theories."[92] Integration moves beyond dialogue to explore the ways in which the content of each distinct area of knowledge can inform and contribute to the other, seeking a "deep synthesis of scientific ideas with religious belief."[93]

Barbour then identifies three distinct attempts at integration: natural theology, a theology of nature, and a systematic synthesis. By *natural theology* Barbour means a post-Darwinian reimagining of natural theology that "starts from scientific data on which we might expect agreement despite cultural and religious differences," with the goal of overcoming "obstacles to belief by showing that the idea of a Designer is as reasonable as alternative interpretive proposals."[94] In contrast, a *theology of nature* does not start from scientific facts or principles but from within a particular "religious tradition based on religious experience and historical revelation," seeking meaningful dialogue with science by recognizing that "some traditional doctrines need to be reformulated in the light of current science."[95]

Barbour's own approach to integration sought to articulate a theology of nature through the *systematic synthesis* of science and religion via process philosophy and theology by embracing foundational concepts from both evolutionary science and Christian doctrine:

> I am in basic agreement with the "Theology of Nature" position, coupled with a cautious use of process philosophy. Too much reliance on science in natural theology can lead to the neglect of the areas of experience that I consider most important religiously. As I see it, the center of the Christian life is an experience of reorientation, the healing of our brokenness in new wholeness, and

91. Barbour, *Religion and Science*, 93.
92. Barbour, *Religion and Science*, 98.
93. Johnson, *Asks the Beasts*, 10.
94. Barbour, *Religion and Science*, 100.
95. Barbour, *Religion and Science*, 100.

the expression of a new relationship to God and to the neighbor. Existentialists and linguistic analysts rightly point to the primacy of personal and social life in religion, and neo-orthodoxy rightly says that for the Christian community it is in response to the person of Christ that our lives can be changed. But the centrality of redemption need not lead us to belittle creation, for our personal and social lives are intimately bound to the rest of the created order. We are redeemed in and with the world, not from the world. Part of our task, then, is to articulate a theology of nature, for which we will have to draw from both religious and scientific sources.[96]

One of the advantages Barbour sees in employing a process philosophy is its openness to a broader ecological perspective that emphasizes the value the whole of the created order has in the eyes of the Creator, thereby overcoming some of the more anthropocentric theologies that have emphasized humankind's dominion over the Creation (Gen. 1:26; 2:15) and in doing so have enabled material exploitation and environmental degradation. Without downplaying human uniqueness within the created order—believers ought to show concern for all forms of life while prioritizing higher-order life (life demonstrating sentience and self-conscious behavior)—Barbour envisions a theological worldview that respects and protects all of nature as "the scene of God's continuing activity."[97]

In *Ask the Beasts: Darwin and the God of Love* (2014), a thoughtful theological engagement of Darwinian evolution, Elizabeth Johnson praises Barbour's fourfold typology and echoes his concern and commitment to a theology encompassing all life, not just human life:

> If human beings were to wake up to the grandeur of the living world, fall in love with life, and change their behavior to protect it, much of the dying-off could be slowly brought under control. But in our day the dire situation appears to be accelerating, with humanity's rapacious habits driving species to extinction faster than new species are able to evolve. The tree of life is thinning out.[98]

While appreciative of Barbour's dialogical and integrative approaches, Johnson recommends a fifth model for relating religion and science, *practical cooperation*, motivated by a deep need to reverse environmental degradation: "Using scientific knowledge about growing ecological distress, many theologians have been working on the recovery of biblical and theological themes

---

96. Barbour, *Religion and Science*, 195.
97. Ian G. Barbour, *Nature, Human Nature, and God* (Minneapolis: Fortress, 2002), 131–32.
98. Johnson, *Ask the Beasts*, 253.

that give strong support to an ethic of environmental care."[99] While Christian theologians have been urging religious communities to take up the mantle of environmentalism since the 1970s,[100] the move toward practical cooperation between religion and science accelerated in 1990 when a group of "prominent scientists led by atheist Carl Sagan issued a public statement appealing to religious groups to join in preserving and cherishing the earth."[101]

There is something to this call for practical cooperation considering the extreme environmental crisis facing the planet. Especially since, aside from Sagan's statement, the work of dialogue and integration between religion and science has been done primarily by Christian scientists and/or Christian theologians, with very few contributions originating from the more traditionally atheistic scientific side of the aisle.[102] Given the urgency and need for a concerted and united effort to reverse climate change, many scientists who would not otherwise seek meaningful engagements with theological perspectives share Carl Sagan's desire for practical cooperation, setting aside past conflicts for the sake of a better future for the environment:

> As scientists, many of us have had profound experiences of awe and reverence before the universe. We understand that what is regarded as sacred is more likely to be treated with care and respect. Our planetary home should be so regarded. Efforts to safeguard and cherish the environment need to be infused with a

---

99. Johnson, *Ask the Beasts*, 11.
100. For some examples, see Glenn C. Stone, ed., *A New Ethic for a New Earth* (New York: Friendship Press, 1971); Larry L. Rasmussen, "The Future Isn't What It Used to Be: 'Limits to Growth' and Christian Ethics," *Lutheran Quarterly* 27, no. 2 (1975): 101–11, and *Earth-Honoring Faith: Religious Ethics in a New Key* (Oxford: Oxford University Press, 2015); Rosemary Radford Ruether, "The Biblical Vision of the Ecological Crisis," *Christian Century* 95, no. 38 (1975): 1129–32, and *Gaia and God: An Ecofeminist Theology of Earth Healing* (New York: HarperCollins, 1994); Ian G. Barbour, "An Ecological Ethic," *Christian Century* 87 (1970): 1180–84, and *Technology, Environment, and Human Values* (New York: Praeger, 1980); Sallie McFague, *The Body of God: An Ecological Theology* (Minneapolis: Fortress, 1993); John B. Cobb, *Is It Too Late? A Theology of Ecology* (Beverly Hills, CA: Bruce, 1972), and *Sustainability: Economics, Ecology, and Justice*, repr. (Eugene, OR: Wipf & Stock, 2007); Irene Diamond and Gloria Feman Orenstein, eds., *Reweaving the World: The Emergence of Ecofeminism* (San Francisco: Sierra Club Books, 1990); Rosemary Radford Ruether, ed., *Women Healing Earth: Third World Women on Ecology, Feminism, and Religion* (Maryknoll, NY: Orbis Books, 1996); and Catherine Keller, *Political Theology of the Earth: Our Planetary Emergency and the Struggle for a New Public* (New York: Columbia University Press, 2018), and *Facing Apocalypse: Climate, Democracy and Other Last Chances* (Maryknoll, NY: Orbis Books, 2021).
101. Johnson, *Ask the Beasts*, 11.
102. One notable exception is the work of astrophysicist and self-described atheist Adam Frank, a popularizer of science who regularly contributes to National Public Radio's *All Things Considered* as well as its *Cosmos and Culture Blog*, who has written about the sense of awe and wonder that motivates both scientific and theological speculation. See Adam Frank, *The Constant Fire: Beyond the Science vs. Religion Debate* (Berkeley: University of California Press, 2009).

vision of the sacred. At the same time, a much wider and deeper understanding of science and technology is needed. If we do not understand the problem, it is unlikely we will be able to fix it. Thus, there is a vital role for both religion and science.[103]

This book emphasizes and values the impact of narratives—especially theological narratives—on human cultural projects. Our moment in time, described as postmodern by some, is distinguished by political, cultural, and religious pluralism—so much so, that many now question their foundational narratives and find themselves lost amid a sea of clashing story fragments. The environmental crisis has forced scientists and theologians to question their own foundational narratives. Science can no longer advocate technological advancement without accounting for the environmental cost, and Christianity has begun to deconstruct those theologies that granted humanity unchecked dominion over creation. They both acknowledge how these entrenched narratives have contributed to the destruction of the planet and ultimately see the importance of weaving a new narrative—ideally one marked by dialogue and cooperation. The ecotheology movement, and in particular ecofeminism, represents a fragment of theology that can enable believers to map a new path—in conversation with scientists and nonbelievers—that can provide hope in a seemingly hopeless situation.

A FRAGMENT OF THEOLOGY: THE HOPE OF ECOFEMINIST THEOLOGY

This chapter has argued that despite the popular perception that science and religion are always in conflict, scientists and theologians have fostered an interdisciplinary space in which conceptual overlap leads to mutually beneficial conversation and practical cooperation on pressing concerns like climate change. Without denying humanity's place within the Darwinian tree of life, this chapter has advocated a revised conception of human uniqueness that does not reinforce outdated and dangerous theologies of dominion but opens new vistas for human moral responsibility amid the impending ecological collapse. In other words, the very complex evolutionary processes that produced humankind as organisms capable of self-awareness, of understanding and predicting complex events, and of reflective decision-making and goal-directed action, also mark humans as distinct from other life on the planet. Thus,

---

103. Carl Sagan, "An Open Letter to the Religious Community," presented at the Global Forum of Spiritual and Parliamentary Leaders Conference in Moscow, Russia (January 1990). http://earthrenewal.org/open_letter_to_the_religious_.htm.

despite our common descent, humans are—for the moment at least—the *only* species capable of altering its natural habitat to such a degree that it is affecting long-term evolutionary processes themselves, as evidenced by humanity's impact on global climate change. Ecotheologies challenge humankind to acknowledge and embrace its capacity to transform nature on a broad scale in order to find positive solutions for adverse and destructive climate change by encouraging more meaningful dialogue and cooperation between religious beliefs and the natural sciences.

For generations, scientists and ecologically minded theologians have been warning about the impending environmental collapse. As Carl Sagan's open letter acknowledged, "Some of the short-term mitigations of these dangers such as greater energy efficiency, rapid banning of chlorofluorocarbons or modest reductions in nuclear arsenals are comparatively easy and at some level are already underway."[104] The real concern, however, is that the type of long-lasting change needed to reverse climate change will inevitably "encounter widespread inertia, denial and resistance," especially as humanity tries to wean itself "from fossil fuels to a nonpolluting energy economy."[105] Consequently, among voices that have been leading the charge for years, even decades, we are hearing panic:

> Time, our time, the time of human civilization, appears to be running out. The science of climate has been unhysterically, relentlessly, increasingly signaling: not that time *will* run out but that *if* we stay on the present course . . . we had a fighting chance of changing course within the narrow window of time that climate change allots. After the political shift, however, the window seemed to be slamming shut. Not on all of life, not on the earth, not necessarily even on our species. But on historic human civilization as it flows into its future. Yet it is precisely so-called civilization that had brought us to this moment of self-contradiction.[106]

Leaders of the world's religions recognize the gravity of this historic self-contradiction and unequivocally concede that human activity is negatively affecting biological processes and environmental systems, even to the point of destruction on a global scale. In 1989, prior to Carl Sagan's appeal to religious communities, Patriarch Dimitrios I of the Greek Orthodox Church issued a statement advocating concern for the environment: "The abuse by contemporary man of his privileged position in creation and of the Creator's order to

---

104. Sagan, "An Open Letter to the Religious Community."
105. Sagan, "An Open Letter to the Religious Community."
106. Catherine Keller, *Political Theology of the Earth: Our Planetary Emergency and the Struggle for a New Public* (New York: Columbia University Press, 2018), 1–2.

him 'to have dominion over the earth' (Genesis 1:28) has already led the world to the edge of apocalyptic self-destruction, either in the form of natural pollution which is dangerous for all living beings, or in the form of the extinction of many species of the animal and plant world, or in other forms."[107] Pope Francis, in his encyclical letter *Laudato Si'* (2015), makes one of the strongest ecclesial statements on ecological responsibility to date, acknowledging "the harm we have inflicted on her [Mother Earth] by our irresponsible use and abuse of the goods with which God has endowed her."[108] Similar statements have been made by many Christian communions,[109] as well as all the major religions of the world including Islam,[110] Judaism,[111] Buddhism,[112] and Hinduism.[113]

Sadly, as Brazilian liberation theologian Ivone Gebara (1944–) discerns, when religion attempts to embrace biodiversity, especially within Christianity, it often encounters "great resistance on the part of the representatives of the dominant patriarchal theological traditions and is quickly repudiated

---

107. Ecumenical Patriarch Dimitrios, Archbishop of Constantinople and New Rome, "Encyclical Letter on the Day of Protection of the Environment" (September 1, 1989). https://www.orth-transfiguration.org/wp-content/uploads/2016/05/Lecture_HAH-1989-Patr.-Dimitrios-on-Day-of-Prayer-for-Envir.pdf.

108. Pope Francis, "Encyclical Letter *Laudato Si'* of the Holy Father Francis on Care for Our Common Home" (May 24, 2015), §2. https://www.vatican.va/content/francesco/en/encyclicals/documents/papa-francesco_20150524_enciclica-laudato-si.html.

109. For example, see "Affirmation of Creation," Presbyterian Church (U.S.A.), 222nd General Assembly (June 22, 2016). https://ncse.ngo/presbyterian-church-usa; "An Evangelical Declaration on the Care of Creation," Evangelical Environmental Network (1994). https://creationcare.org/what-we-do/an-evangelical-declaration-on-the-care-of-creation.html; "AME Church Climate Change Resolution," African Methodist Episcopal Church (July 2016). http://www.ame-church.com/wp-content/uploads/2016/07/AME-Climate-Change-Resolution.pdf; and "A Pastoral Message on Climate Change" from the Anglican Church of Canada, the Episcopal Church, the Evangelical Lutheran Church in America, and the Evangelical Lutheran Church in Canada (September 19, 2014). https://www.episcopalchurch.org/publicaffairs/a-pastoral-message-on-climate-change/.

110. See "Islamic Declaration on Global Climate Change," International Islamic Climate Change Symposium, Istanbul, Turkey (August 17–18, 2015). https://www.ifees.org.uk/about/islamicdeclaration/.

111. See "Statement by Israel Orthodox Rabbis on the Climate Crisis," Jewish Climate Initiative and The Interfaith Center for Sustainable Development. https://www.jewishecoseminars.com/statement-by-israel-orthodox-rabbis-on-the-climate-crisis/; also "'Elijah's Covenant'—New Rabbinic Statement on the Climate Crisis," The Shalom Center (January 1, 2020). https://theshalomcenter.org/content/elijahs-covenant-new-rabbinic-statement-climate-crisis.

112. See "The Time to Act Is Now: A Buddhist Declaration on Climate Change," Buddhist Climate Project (May 14, 2015). https://fore.yale.edu/files/buddhist_climate_change_statement_5-14-15.pdf; and "Buddhist Climate Change Statement to World Leaders," Global Buddhist Climate Change Collective (October 29, 2015). https://plumvillage.org/articles/buddhist-climate-change-statement-to-world-leaders-2015/.

113. See "Hindu Declaration on Climate Change," Parliament of the World's Religions, Melbourne, Australia (December 8, 2009). https://hinduclimatedeclaration2015.org/english.

as unorthodox, that is to say, not conforming with traditional theological thought."[114]

Ecofeminism represents the "radicalization that takes place as ecological consciousness is incorporated into feminist theology," which begins with the deconstruction and reconstruction of "the cosmological framework out of which the Christian worldview grew from its ancient roots in the Hebrew and Greek worlds."[115] Feminist theologians like Rosemary Radford Ruether and Elisabeth Schüssler Fiorenza contend that the Genesis creation story lacked an "explicit mandate for the domination of some humans over others, as male over female, or master over slave." They see Genesis as the "basis for an egalitarian view of all humans as equal in God's image in later Christian movements that sought to dismantle slavery and sexism."[116] The narrative of feminist theology challenges patriarchal theologies by emphasizing the radically inclusive character of the earliest Christian communities, while recognizing that as Christianity became co-opted by the surrounding culture of patriarchy, the more radical and egalitarian interpretations of the earliest Christ movements became muted. Against this gradual assimilation, feminist theology affirms the equality of all humans as image of God.

Ivone Gebara's vision of ecofeminism builds upon this fundamental assertion to critique the complicity of Christian patriarchal theologies "in the persistent domination of women and the unchecked exploitation of natural resources," arguing that not enough has been done to address the role of Christian colonialism in "the destruction of indigenous divinities" by denying "other religious rapprochements" their due as "equally truthful," and ignoring the important role indigenous and African religious narratives can play in fostering an "egalitarian and solidary dialogue."[117] Consequently, ecofeminist theology embraces the apophatic critique of false idols, "the *via negativa*—devoted path of the ancient mystics—that is to say, what we can no longer say about God based on our personal and communitarian experience."[118]

---

114. Ivone Gebara, *Intuiciones ecofeministas: Ensayo para repensar el conocimiento y la religión*, trans. Graciela Pujol (Madrid: Editorial Tratto, 2000), 133 (all translations from the Spanish my own).

115. Rosemary Radford Ruether, "Ecofeminism—The Challenge to Theology," *Deportate, esuli, profughe: Rivista telematica di studi sulla memoria femminile*, no. 20 (2012): 27.

116. Ruether, "Ecofeminism," 25. See Elisabeth Schüssler Fiorenza, *In Memory of Her: A Feminist Theological Reconstruction of Christian Origins*, rev. and annotated (New York: Crossroad, 1994), 63.

117. Gebara, *Intuiciones ecofeministas*, 28.

118. Gebara, *Intuiciones ecofeministas*, 134.

The Myth of Human Uniqueness 131

One of the divine attributes ecofeminism cannot continue to affirm, based in part on knowledge from the ecological sciences, is the "image of the patriarchal God as dominating nature," with "nature in submission to God, which then God hands over to the man so that he can subdue nature under his proper dominion."[119] According to this dominion theology,

> The male human is the preferred one among all God's creatures, the one who is most fully image of God, the one closest to his creator. This led to the development within Christianity of an anthropocentric and androcentric spirituality centered almost exclusively on the human male. Nature, other living beings, and the complex biological web in which we live, were all placed in service to maleness.[120]

As pioneering feminist theologian Mary Daly (1928–2010) stated so succinctly in *Beyond God the Father* (1973), "if God is male, then the male is God."[121]

Ivone Gebara has articulated a Trinitarian theology that rejects the human-centered and male-centered theologies of domination, attributing this androcentrism to the almost exclusive use of images of God as father and king with Christ as his son, offering in its place a "sustaining matrix of immanent relationality."[122] Accordingly, "Gebara sees the Trinity not as a separate, self-enclosed relation of two divine males with each other, mediated by the Spirit, but rather as the symbolic expression of the basic dynamic of life itself as a process of vital interrelational creativity."[123] Christologically, the focus is not on Christ as king, but Christ as the incarnation of this life-affirming divine relationality: "if Jesus reveals God, the God he reveals is not the split off, dominating Logos of immortalized male sovereignty, but the Holy Wisdom of mutual self-giving and life-sustaining love."[124] This divine relationality, unlike patriarchal visions of an aloof king on his throne who is sovereign over all of Creation, offers a reconstruction of the Trinitarian God as transcendent yet everywhere immanent: "Transcendence is that feeling of always belonging to something greater—much greater—whose full breadth we barely know and are unable to express. . . . [T]he human experience of transcendence is also the experience of beauty, the majesty of nature, and all its relationships and interdependencies."[125]

---

119. Gebara, *Intuiciones ecofeministas*, 135.
120. Gebara, *Intuiciones ecofeministas*, 135.
121. Mary Daly, *Beyond God the Father: Toward a Philosophy of Women's Liberation* (Boston: Beacon, 1993), 19.
122. Ruether, "Ecofeminism," 30.
123. Ruether, "Ecofeminism," 30.
124. Ruether, "Ecofeminism," 31.
125. Gebara, *Intuiciones ecofeministas*, 136.

Within this Trinitarian reconstruction of the doctrine of God, Gebara finds ample room for the insights and knowledge provided by the natural sciences: "All life from the evolution of the galaxies to the dynamics of the self manifests the presence of God as sustaining Wisdom of creation."[126] Yet Gebara is not satisfied with an abstract relationality. Given that divine transcendence is incarnated in human form in the Christ, through whom God welcomes all of humanity into the divine interrelationality, God's preferential option for the poor becomes a *necessary* lens through which to see God in the world.

For Gebara, the exploitation of the world's poor is indivisible from the exploitation of nature, as verified by the fact that "the dispossessed, like all marginalized groups and persons, reveal better than others the contradictory and destructive character of our actions. It is among the poor and in the ecosystems where they are found that today we see the most obvious signals of this destruction, the fruits of human action."[127] God's preferential option for the poor as articulated by liberation theologians "seeks to correct the destructive option for the rich at the expense of the wellbeing of the whole community of life. The ethic of preferential option for the poor calls us to feed and nurture the child of the poor dying from malnutrition and unclean water and rectify the conditions that are causing this untimely death, while the ethic of sustainability calls us to help the mother of this child limit her childbearing."[128] This preferential option leads to a life lived in solidarity with the victims of technocratic capitalism, which, as Catherine Keller contends, stands in opposition to a global commons: "Neoliberalism treats the multiple self-organizing ecologies of the earth—geological, biological, climatic—as externalities irrelevant to its own organization of the world. This world scheme with its extractions, exploitations, and extinctions ignores the fragilities of the world *in which the most vulnerable* but soon the all of us will be in peril."[129]

But such solidarity must be nurtured and disseminated, which entails overturning and transcending the entrenched narratives of patriarchal dominion theology, finance-driven capitalism, and scientific materialism, by articulating a different, more inclusive vision of the common good: "This option is a cultivated condition, a chosen lifestyle, a faith option insofar as it constitutes struggling on behalf of the most vulnerable, the victims of exclusionary systems whose numbers increase daily. This entails rejecting all sexist and racist ideologies originating from totalitarian regimes that seek to protect an elite group to the detriment of those considered impure, useless, marginalized."[130]

---

126. Ruether, "Ecofeminism," 32.
127. Gebara, *Intuiciones ecofeministas*, 142.
128. Ruether, "Ecofeminism," 33.
129. Keller, *Political Theology of the Earth*, 35 (emphasis added).
130. Gebara, *Intuiciones ecofeministas*, 142.

In *Light of the Stars: Alien Worlds and the Fate of the Earth* (2018), astrophysicist Adam Frank also identifies the need for a new narrative about humanity's place in the universe that affirms human uniqueness while embracing humanity's interdependence with the planet earth and its ecosystems. Frank's central insight, drawn from the relatively new field of astrobiology,[131] resonates with the deep interrelationality sought by ecofeminism: "The evolution of the planet and its life cannot be separated. That is what our science has shown us. Earth and its life must be thought of as a whole that 'coevolves' together."[132] Science and religion are in agreement about the global environmental crisis, given Adam Frank's sympathy with what Catherine Keller has described as our moment of self-contradiction:

> Two decades into the twenty-first century, we find ourselves facing the existential challenge of creating a sustainable version of human civilization. The scale of human activities is pushing hard on the tightly linked planetary systems that make up Earth's climate. As the planet begins to move off into a different climate state, our project of civilization will, at the very least, find itself under stress. At worst, Earth's changes may make our project impossible to maintain.[133]

Frank is not a naive idealist, instead making claims within the limits of the available data. Therefore, he is critical of environmentalists who think we can eliminate humanity's carbon footprint: "There is nothing wrong with such a goal, but the message often gets mangled in public debate from 'less impact' into 'no impact.' If we take the astrobiological view and start thinking like a planet, we see there's no such thing as 'no impact.'"[134]

Frank proposes a complex thought experiment—a multidisciplinary exercise in civilization building—that will "require input from fields as diverse as atmospheric science, geology, energy science, and ecology. To create realistic models, we'll have to get the physics, chemistry, planetary science, and ecological interactions right in terms of what we build into the models."[135] His experiment yielded three distinct trajectories: (1) Civilizations "die off," meaning that as they use their energy resources, their populations grow beyond

---

131. Astrobiology is a multidisciplinary scientific field of study concerned with the origins, early evolution, distribution, and future of life in the universe. It primarily investigates the material conditions and contingent events necessary for life to arise in the universe, and to a lesser extent considers the question of extraterrestrial life. See David C. Catling, *Astrobiology: A Very Short Introduction* (Oxford: Oxford University Press, 2013).
132. Adam Frank, *Light of the Stars: Alien Worlds and the Fate of the Earth* (New York: W. W. Norton, 2018), 13.
133. Frank, *Light of the Stars*, 125.
134. Frank, *Light of the Stars*, 137.
135. Frank, *Light of the Stars*, 141.

what the environment can sustain. (2) Civilizations reach a "soft landing," meaning that as the population grows and the planetary system changes due to increased energy consumption, the civilizations make the necessary changes by switching to a low-impact energy source to reach a sustainable ecological equilibrium. (3) There is a "full-blown collapse," wherein a civilization grows so fast and impacts the planetary ecosystem so drastically that it leads to a massive extinction.

While Adam Frank grants that scientific models are not reality, he contends carefully constructed models are more than mere fictions; by relying on known natural laws applied on a planetary scale, astrobiologists are able to predict possible outcomes with reliable precision. Given enough civilizational models accounting for a wide range of possible natural and artificial conditions, scientists are able to "ask what explicitly led some civilizations to achieve planetary sustainability and others to collapse. Like a doctor looking for a cure by studying the most pathological cases of a disease, we can see what common factors drove the civilizations that died to their fate. The models will have a lot to teach us that we can't see now with the tunnel vision of just our planet and just our own uncertain future."[136]

Frank's thought experiment shares a major conceptual overlap with ecofeminism: the realization that we cannot continue to treat human civilizations and technologies as distinct or removed from nature. The rise and fall of human civilizations are a natural part of the planet's evolutionary history, where every "civilization must be seen as a new form of biospheric activity arising within a planet's history of transformation and evolutionary innovation"; as we direct our knowledge and resources to the question of ecological sustainability, our civilization must "enter into a long, cooperative relationship" with our planet or risk extinction.[137]

Maintaining a theological perspective while in deep conversation with the natural sciences allows believers to keep hope alive in the face of possible environmental collapse, not because God will bend the laws of nature to save us from our own selfish and reckless behavior, but because a proper understanding of God's magnitude—much like the grandness of nature—leads to the realization that our ultimate hope lies not with "political parties, labor unions, governments, churches, science," for "they do not have the last word on the meaning of life."[138] Rather, to say "God" is to affirm "a thousand paths, a thousand wagers, a thousand hopes, a thousand screams and a thousand silences."[139] The image of God as immanent in every facet of creation—the

---

136. Frank, *Light of the Stars*, 148.
137. Frank, *Light of the Stars*, 156.
138. Gebara, *Intuiciones ecofeministas*, 147.
139. Gebara, *Intuiciones ecofeministas*, 147

God who makes a preferential option for the poor and disenfranchised—keeps hope alive, because hope arises where God wills and not where we expect or desire it. A scientific understanding of our finiteness is not cause for despair but helps us realize our role in the bigger picture. In the words of Ivone Gebara:

> There will always be a tomorrow, even though I myself personally might not be here, although I never had children nor even planted a tree. "God is my hope" means there is a place for my personal responsibility within the historical process. But this process is much grander and more complex than my simple analysis: it involves a thousand and one actors, and I cannot maintain the pretense that my analysis is the only one, or even the best one.[140]

---

140. Gebara, *Intuiciones ecofeministas*, 147–48.

5

The Myth of Political Sovereignty

> The main reason religion needs to be privatized is that, in political discussion with those outside the relevant religious community, it is a conversation stopper.[1]

> Speaking civically, today we need to cultivate the public discourse of religious citizens, not further constrain it.[2]

It is shortsighted to presume that political theology began in the twentieth century in reaction to Carl Schmitt, an intellectual defender of political dictatorship and a Nazi sympathizer. A generation after World War II, theologians Jürgen Moltmann, Dorothee Sölle, and Johann Baptist Metz articulated what became known as the new political theology, an explicitly Christian and European response to the horrors of the Holocaust—especially Christian complicity and culpability for the Holocaust—in critical conversation with the Jewish thinker Richard L. Rubenstein, whose groundbreaking work, *After Auschwitz: Radical Theology and Contemporary Judaism* (1966), set the agenda for post-Holocaust theology.[3] Among their goals was countering Schmitt's

---

1. Richard Rorty, "Religion as Conversation-Stopper," in *Philosophy and Social Hope* (New York: Penguin, 1999), 171.
2. Charles Mathewes, *A Theology of Public Life* (Cambridge: Cambridge University Press, 2007), 7–8.
3. Richard L. Rubenstein, *After Auschwitz: Radical Theology and Contemporary Judaism* (Indianapolis: Bobbs-Merrill, 1966).

controversial essay fetishizing totalitarianism, "Politische Theologie" (1922), which argued that divine sovereignty has been replaced by the secularized and absolute "sovereignty of the modern state."[4]

As theologian and ethicist Gary Dorrien has opined, "Political theology needs a better genealogy than the Carl Schmitt story it usually tells."[5] The narrative of political theology is further complicated by the fact that while the Holocaust marked the first time Europe had confronted "the targeted, systematic killing of a group of civilians," the victims of European colonization in Africa, Asia, and Latin America had a very different opinion of European Christianity: "Twenty years after the Jewish Holocaust, Europe was abuzz with talk and images of other holocausts, and other forms of violence against marginalized communities. In Vietnam, Africa, Latin America, and elsewhere, Europeans and Americans were committing mass murder. It was now clear that the Nazi era had not been anomalous."[6] The rise of neofascist populism in the United States, shrouded with the aura of religious nationalism, highlights the importance of articulating a better genealogical narrative for political theology.

Philosopher Alasdair MacIntyre, in his landmark book *After Virtue* (1981), describes the current era as a new Dark Ages and the state of political discourse today as "civil war carried on by other means."[7] Sadly, the events at the US Capitol on January 6, 2021, only confirm this analysis. While MacIntyre offers a road map for achieving common moral discourse, he concludes *After Virtue* with the troubling and enigmatic declaration that the most viable alternative for peaceful coexistence entails retreat into small intentional communities of shared belief: "We are waiting not for a Godot, but for another—doubtless very different—St. Benedict."[8] Motivating MacIntyre's seemingly sectarian solution is the desire to preserve Christian identity against the forces of secularism in much the same way Benedict, through the influence of his monastic rule, helped Europe reemerge from barbarism after the fall of the Roman Empire.

Unfortunately, MacIntyre's critical insight has been co-opted by Christian Evangelicalism, specifically Rod Dreher's plea for Christians to embrace the

---

4. Carl Schmitt, *Political Theology: Four Chapters on the Concept of Sovereignty*, trans. George Schwab, repr. (Chicago: University of Chicago Press, 2005), 38.

5. Gary Dorrien, *Imagining Democratic Socialism: Political Theology, Marxism, and Social Democracy* (New Haven, CT: Yale University Press, 2019), 2.

6. Vincent Lloyd, "Christian Responses to the Holocaust: Political Theology in Europe," in *T. & T. Clark Handbook of Political Theology*, ed. Rubén Rosario Rodríguez (London: T. & T. Clark, 2019), 17.

7. Alasdair MacIntyre, *After Virtue: A Study in Moral Theory*, 2nd ed. (Notre Dame, IN: University of Notre Dame Press, 1984), 253.

8. MacIntyre, *After Virtue*, 263.

"Benedict Option" by withdrawing from the culture in imitation of sixth-century monk Benedict, who established cloistered religious communities across Europe while the Roman Empire collapsed all around them.[9]

Thankfully, not all conservative Christians agree with Dreher's sectarian solution. David Brooks, conservative political commentator for the *New York Times* who describes himself as "a wandering Jew and a confused Christian,"[10] reacted strongly to Dreher's book: "The right response to the moment is not the Benedict Option, it is Orthodox Pluralism. It is to surrender to some orthodoxy that will overthrow the superficial obsessions of the self and put one's life in contact with a transcendent ideal."[11] According to Brooks, Dreher's solution is not the integrated monasticism of Benedict (who sought to preserve culture), but the failure of religious orthodoxy to engage pluralism (by cutting itself off from culture). In other words, Dreher's sectarian purism fails because it attempts to trap God in a box, since it "can't tolerate difference because it can't humbly accept the mystery of truth."[12] While introducing religion into the political conversation can get messy, politicians continue to cite Scripture when courting religious voters and theological (or pseudotheological) arguments abound in the public discourse. Therefore, political theology ought to be part of our civic discourse; an open and respectful dialogue about the role of theological convictions in public life can only improve the quality of our life together in the *polis*.

Theologian and ethicist Charles Mathewes agrees: "Speaking civically, today we need to cultivate the public discourse of religious citizens, not further constrain it."[13] According to Mathewes, concrete political ends ought not to be the main motivation for Christians entering the public arena; rather, "Christians should be interested in thinking about public life, not just for their fates as citizens, but also for their fates as Christians."[14] Mathewes makes a compelling case for a politically engaged Christianity because he understands public life as a form of Christian spiritual discipline: "[M]y goal is not to use faith to support our democratic culture, but the reverse, and more—to use our civic interactions with one another to deepen faith."[15] While speaking from within the Western democratic context, Mathewes is clear that Christians

---

9. See Rod Dreher, *The Benedict Option: A Strategy for Christians in a Post-Christian Nation* (New York: Penguin, 2017).
10. Peter Wehner, "David Brooks's Journey toward Faith," *Atlantic* (May 7, 2019). https://www.theatlantic.com/ideas/archive/2019/05/second-mountain-brooks-discusses-his-faith/588766/.
11. David Brooks, "The Benedict Option," *New York Times* (March 14, 2017), A23.
12. Brooks, "The Benedict Option."
13. Mathewes, *A Theology of Public Life*, 7–8.
14. Mathewes, *A Theology of Public Life*, 24.
15. Mathewes, *A Theology of Public Life*, 23.

living under absolute monarchies or even totalitarian regimes can live out their Christian faith in public just as well as under a liberal democracy; in other words, he is not concerned with propping up any one political system over against another:

> Democracy is not the "ideal" institutional state of Christian believers. Political life in the world has no "ideal" state. . . . Democracy is not our divine destiny, and heaven is not a New England town meeting. Christians have survived many different political structures during the world. Good Christians live as subjects of the tyrannical autocracies of East and Central Asia, in the oligarchic kleptocracies of the Middle East, in the semi-democracies of Latin America, even in the completely "stateless" conditions across much of Africa. Public life can occur (imagine!) even where democracy is not.[16]

So how does civic duty deepen Christian commitment? Because Christian life together—as a community of faith *in* the world—is not that of sectarian isolation but of going out into the world to "make disciples of all nations" (Matt. 28:19). Therefore, engaging "others is not simply an optional extra on this account; reaching out to others is in a fundamental way just what it is to live a properly nourishing human life."[17]

Simply put, to live one's religion in public—regardless of the political system one inhabits as a Christian—is an inherent part of the Christian call. Unfortunately, what "has actually happened in the last few decades is that those religious voices attuned to the complexity of religion in public life have effectively ceded the rhetorical high ground of thick discourse to extremist and often reactionary (whether right-wing or left-wing) voices. Culture, like nature, abhors a vacuum, and bad theology drives out good."[18]

The widespread popularity of the QAnon conspiracy among white Evangelical Christians drives this point home. QAnon is more than a fringe political movement. It has embraced the tradition of American exceptionalism, it borrows language and imagery from the Bible, and its followers exhibit cultlike devotion. In effect, QAnon presents itself as a white Christian political theology whose goal—captured in Donald Trump's 2016 campaign slogan—is to make America great again *for white people*: "For white Christian nationalists, taking back the country is about more than just political power. They see themselves as faithful patriots fulfilling the American Founders' covenant with

---

16. Mathewes, *A Theology of Public Life*, 23.
17. Mathewes, *A Theology of Public Life*, 129.
18. Mathewes, *A Theology of Public Life*, 7.

God."[19] On the surface, QAnon is a "baseless conspiracy theory, which imagines Trump in a battle with a cabal of deep-state saboteurs who worship Satan and traffic children for sex."[20] But what began as speculation on a single fringe internet message board became a national obsession that tripled in popularity during the COVID-19 pandemic. In 2020, QAnon conspiracies even spread to Canada and Europe, with German neo-Nazis hopeful that Trump would lead an army to restore the Reich.[21]

Eighty-one percent of white Evangelicals and 60 percent of white Catholics voted for Donald Trump in 2016.[22] In Charlottesville, Virginia, the weekend of August 11–12, 2017, several hundred white nationalists from all over the nation descended on the small college town for a "Unite the Right" rally. Ostensibly a protest concerning the removal of a Confederate monument to Robert E. Lee, the rally was also a calculated move to draw national media attention to the various factions comprising the Alt-Right, in a concerted effort to move from the internet fringes of US politics into the Trump-era mainstream. Instead of immediately repudiating the heinous acts of white nationalism in Charlottesville, President Trump claimed there were "very fine people on both sides," and that the mob chanting hateful racist propaganda included "a lot of people in that group that were there to innocently protest and very legally protest."[23] On January 6, 2021, these same so-called "fringe" groups took part—in much greater numbers—in an armed assault on the US Capitol. QAnon believers documented their activities on January 6 on social media, proud of the "starring role they had played in battling their hero's enemies," confident that Q would one day "be in every history book."[24]

In the aftermath of the Capitol riot, many Evangelical Christians still support Trump, fueling "Trump's baseless allegations of widespread voter

---

19. Lauren R. Kerby, "White Christian Nationalists Want More Than Just Political Power," *Atlantic* (January 15, 2021). https://www.theatlantic.com/ideas/archive/2021/01/white-evangelicals-fixation-on-washington-dc/617690/.

20. Drew Harwell, Isaac Stanley-Becker, Razzan Nakhlawi, and Craig Timberg, "QAnon Reshaped Trump's Party and Radicalized Believers: The Capitol Siege May Just Be the Start," *Washington Post* (January 13, 2021). https://www.washingtonpost.com/technology/2021/01/13/qanon-capitol-siege-trump/.

21. Katrin Bennhold, "QAnon Is Thriving in Germany. The Extreme Right Is Delighted," *New York Times* (October 11, 2020). https://www.nytimes.com/2020/10/11/world/europe/qanon-is-thriving-in-germany-the-extreme-right-is-delighted.html.

22. Jessica Martínez and Gregory A. Smith, "How the Faithful Voted: A Preliminary 2016 Analysis," Pew Research Center, November 9, 2016, https://www.pewresearch.org/fact-tank/2016/11/09/how-the-faithful-voted-a-preliminary-2016-analysis/.

23. Glenn Thrush and Maggie Haberman, "Giving White Nationalists an Unequivocal Boost," *New York Times* (August 16, 2017), A1.

24. Harwell, Stanley-Becker, Nakhlawi, and Timberg, "QAnon Reshaped Trump's Party and Radicalized Believers."

fraud."[25] For them, Trump is a savior. In the words of presidential advisor Kellyanne Conway, Trump was the "most pro-life president in history,"[26] a belief that proved well-founded, given the recent decision to overturn *Roe v. Wade* by a US Supreme Court that included three Trump-appointed justices.[27] The revelations witnessed on January 6, 2021, confirm what many on the left have worried about for years: there is a push by many loosely connected popular organizations to impose Christian theocracy on the nation. Most alarming, these Christian groups in the name of Christ are proclaiming a white racist nationalism that seeks to dominate women, marginalize non-Christian perspectives, and at its most rotten core, eliminate the racially other.

As scholars of religion begin to unravel what has happened to American Christianity, hoping to diagnose, treat, and if necessary, amputate the more cancerous parts of this populist form of American religion, the "silent majority" that elected Donald Trump in 2016 remains an emboldened white supremacist political movement with deep pockets and nationwide organization. As many political pundits have noted, striking down legalized abortion is only the first step in a carefully crafted strategy to roll back advances in civil rights like affirmative action and voter protection laws.[28] According to Charles Mathewes's analysis, the "shunning of religious rhetoric in public" by more liberal to centrist believers "has permitted, and perhaps encouraged, the rising prominence of more strident and intolerant voices in public speech."[29] This shift in US politics, elevating and celebrating "whiteness," as if white people were a repressed minority that had suffered generations of oppression and were now being delivered from captivity—an integral part of the QAnon mythos—should prompt bold theological responses from the church.

Whatever genealogical narrative one embraces to account for the revival of political theology, the fact remains a great many political theologies abound

---

25. Rick Jervis, Marc Ramirez, and Romina Ruiz-Goiriena, "'No Regrets': Evangelicals and Other Faith Leaders Still Support Trump after Deadly US Capitol Attack," *USA Today* (January 12, 2021). https://www.usatoday.com/story/news/nation/2021/01/12/evangelicals-donald-trump-capitol-riot-voter-fraud/6644005002/.

26. Elizabeth Dias, Annie Karni, and Sabrina Tavernise, "Trump Tells Anti-Abortion Marchers, 'Unborn Children Have Never Had a Stronger Defender in the White House,'" *New York Times* (January 24, 2020). https://www.nytimes.com/2020/01/24/us/politics/trump-abortion-march-life.html.

27. Adam Liptak, "In 6-to-3 Ruling, Supreme Court Ends Nearly 50 Years of Abortion Rights," *New York Times* (June 24, 2022). https://www.nytimes.com/2022/06/24/us/roe-wade-overturned-supreme-court.html.

28. David Leonhardt, "What's Next for the Supreme Court? Five Republican-Appointed Justices Are Ambitious and Impatient to Change American Law," *The New York Times* (June 27, 2022). https://www.nytimes.com/2022/06/27/briefing/supreme-court-abortion.html.

29. Mathewes, *A Theology of Public Life*, 6–7.

The Myth of Political Sovereignty

that differ in local flavor and context, especially in relation to a particular people's cultural and historical experiences; differ on how they adapt and employ the theological resources of their distinctive faith tradition in the public arena; and differ on how faith communities relate in general with the state as the locus of political life. Consequently, it is a mistake to think of "political theology" as a single approach to theological reasoning.

To that end, someone like Charles Mathewes is not interested in articulating yet another political theology so much as he seeks to articulate a theology of the political that asks the question, "How does our love of the world lead to love of God?"[30] By employing an Augustinian ontology of grace, Mathewes does not see the world as instrumental to our salvation. Instead he celebrates the world as the unfolding of divine love; our Christian "life in the world" is realized when we affirm God's world as a "work of love."[31] Accordingly, in a pluralistic society it is important to nurture love for the other *as* other: "To do better, we need a more complex picture of the self, one that depicts the self as always already involved in dialogue."[32] Within this wide and varied mosaic, however, what distinguishes "political theology" from other types of theological discourse is conscious reflection on the nature of the relationship between the (often secular) state and the communities of faith living under the authority of that state.

If we grant that anarchy (the complete breakdown of governance or any form of external control on human freedom) is one extreme and totalitarianism (absolute governmental control of every facet of human life) the other, we can agree that everything in between these two poles can be categorized as some form of political discourse. We must also recognize that there is no *one* Christian way of relating the church to the state—or to the secular culture, for that matter. Therefore, when balancing the biblical demand for the rule of law, "Let every person be subject to the governing authorities" (Rom. 13:1), with the apostle Peter's exhortation, "We must obey God rather than any human authority" (Acts 5:29), we ought to recall Reformation theologian John Calvin's guiding paradigm:

> In that obedience which we have shown to be due the authority of rulers, we are always to make this exception, indeed, to observe it as primary, that such obedience is never to lead us away from obedience to him, to whose will the desires of all kings ought to

---

30. Mathewes, *A Theology of Public Life*, 84.
31. Mathewes, *A Theology of Public Life*, 84.
32. Mathewes, *A Theology of Public Life*, 127.

be subject, to whose decrees all their commands ought to yield, to whose majesty their scepters ought to be submitted.[33]

In other words, the Word of God supersedes all human authority when that authority demands an act of obedience contrary to what God commands.

If, as Charles Mathewes asserts, tolerance of pluralism serves as a guiding axiom for a Christian political theology, then a second principle is the shared belief that through communal action citizens can make a radical break with the entrenched status quo to bring about positive social transformation. Liberation theology, arguably one of the most significant and influential theological movements of the last fifty years, emphasizes political praxis. Its impact has altered the canon of theological education in universities and seminaries, changed the language of authoritative ecclesial statements, and even crossed over into popular culture. From the liberationist perspective, the church is confronted with an existential decision, and liberation theology insists it must choose sides.

Although the phrase "preferential option for the poor" was not officially endorsed by any magisterial document until the third Latin American Episcopal Council (CELAM), held in Puebla, Mexico, in 1979, Gustavo Gutiérrez reminds us that at the 1968 meeting of CELAM in Medellín, Colombia, the final documents called for the church to give "preference to the poorest and most needy sectors and to those segregated for any cause whatsoever."[34] At Medellín the bishops made a preferential option for the poor, unequivocally stating "that poverty expresses solidarity with the oppressed and a protest against oppression," so that instead of "talking about the Church of the poor, we must be a poor Church."[35]

As Cuban-born theological ethicist Miguel A. De La Torre has noted, given liberation theology's troubled relationship with modern liberalism, capitalism, and its political defenders, "We are left asking if capitalism and Christianity are compatible or irreconcilable."[36] To which Gutiérrez responds that for a church without "a real commitment against exploitation and alienation and for a society of solidarity and justice, the eucharistic celebration is an empty

---

33. John Calvin, *Institutes of the Christian Religion*, vol. 2, ed. John T. McNeill, trans. Ford Lewis Battles (Louisville, KY: Westminster John Knox, 2006), 1520 (4.20.32).

34. Gustavo Gutiérrez, *A Theology of Liberation: History, Politics and Salvation*, rev. ed., ed. and trans. Sister Caridad Inda and John Eagleson (Maryknoll, NY: Orbis Books, 1988), xxv. Gutiérrez here cites paragraph 9 of the "Document on the Poverty of the Church" from the Medellín conference. See Alfred T. Hennelly, ed., *Liberation Theology: A Documentary History* (Maryknoll, NY: Orbis Books, 1990), 114–19.

35. Gutiérrez, *A Theology of Liberation*, 70.

36. Miguel A. De La Torre, *The Politics of Jesús: A Hispanic Political Theology* (Lanham, MD: Rowman & Littlefield, 2015), 5.

action, lacking any genuine endorsement by those who participate in it."[37] A church guided by God's preferential option has no choice but to divest itself from the centers of political and economic power and put its social weight behind concrete social transformation on the side of the poor and oppressed, and "the groups that control economic and political power will not forgive the Church for this."[38]

Unfortunately, the arc of modern politics tilts toward authoritarian encroachment on democratic freedoms, forever haunted by the specter of Carl Schmitt's fetishizing of totalitarian power, contributing to what many view as the breakdown of the modern, liberal, and democratic order. By emphasizing the role of political solidarity through the preferential option for the poor, a liberationist political theology makes an intentional act of political activism on behalf of the marginalized and oppressed, not only by giving voice to the voiceless, but by actively working to preserve the political agency of the disenfranchised. This political act remains authentic so long as it stays grounded in the academic theologian's organic interactions with marginalized communities.

Nichole M. Flores's *The Aesthetics of Solidarity: Our Lady of Guadalupe and American Democracy* (2021), an explicitly liberationist political theology, levels a theological critique of modern democratic liberalism and its institutions for empowering antidemocratic, capitalistic oligarchies while also perpetuating white supremacy. While originating within "the political concerns of the Chicanx Catholic community," Flores articulates a "political theology of Guadalupe and Juan Diego [that] asserts the necessity of interpreting particular religious symbols within the common life of democracy and of identifying and rectifying the enduring inequalities that hinder the cultivation of a thriving democracy."[39]

THEOPOETICS AS POLITICAL ACTIVISM

Latino/a theology in the United States stands under the umbrella of liberation theology, deeply indebted to both Catholic and Protestant Latin American liberation theologians like Gustavo Gutiérrez, Jon Sobrino, Ivone Gebara, Rubem Alves, Elsa Támez, and José Miguez Bonino, but articulating a distinctive response to the dominant Euro-American theological discourse. In the late 1960s, influenced by the hard-fought political gains of the civil rights

---

37. Gutiérrez, *A Theology of Liberation*, 150.
38. Gutiérrez, *A Theology of Liberation*, 151.
39. Nichole M. Flores, *The Aesthetics of Solidarity: Our Lady of Guadalupe and American Democracy* (Washington, DC: Georgetown University Press, 2021), 43.

movement, the United States witnessed the birth of multiple political identity movements by previously marginalized populations. The church-born civil rights movement yielded the more radical Black power movement, which rose to prominence alongside second-wave feminism, the Chicano movement, and the campaign for gay rights set off by the Stonewall uprising. The 1970s proved a decade of internal debate, cautious cooperation, and political advocacy by various minority groups seeking recognition, while struggling for political representation and power in a nation that had previously denied their voices in the political arena while also trying to erase their contributions from the nation's collective history.

From this fertile soil of racial pride and identity politics in the late 1970s arose the theological movement collectively labeled "Latino/a theology" in the 1980s, with roots in the work of the Mexican-American Cultural Center, established by Virgilio Elizondo in 1972, and the work of Cuban-born Methodist historian and theologian Justo L. González, who founded the first academic journal of Latino/a theology in 1980, *Apuntes: Reflexiones Teológicas Desde el Contexto Hispano-Latino*, in cooperation with the Mexican American Program of Perkins School of Theology at Southern Methodist University. Both men had direct links to events in Latin America in the 1960s and 1970s, as González was unable to return to his native Cuba after the revolution, and Elizondo had attended the 1968 conference of Latin American bishops in Medellín, Colombia, as part of an effort by the Archdiocese of San Antonio to connect with Hispanic Catholics.

Located within the Western Christian tradition, US Latino/a theology nonetheless emerged as a critique from the margins, questioning dominant forms of Christianity. González contends that whatever form Latino/a theology takes, there is within its discourse an implied critique of modernity: "We are those whom modernity colonized, those whom the colonial powers saw as objects of modernization, those whose metanarratives were assaulted and suppressed in the name of the great modern metanarrative. We are those who must still believe in the metanarrative that justice shall prevail and the crooked will be made straight."[40] The experience of marginalization has led Latino/a theologians to build coalitions and work in solidarity to articulate a collaborative, ecumenical, and multicultural theology. This movement, called *teología en conjunto* ("theology done jointly"), models an inclusive discursive methodology found in many Latino/a church communities. It is characterized by the gathering together of theologians, pastors, and lay people in ecumenical

---

40. Justo L. González, "Metamodern Aliens in Postmodern Jerusalem," in *Hispanic/Latino Theology: Challenge and Promise*, ed. Ada María Isasi-Díaz and Fernando F. Segovia (Minneapolis: Fortress, 1996), 347.

cooperation to reflect on the beliefs and practices of the people they serve, producing a theology that truly belongs to, and is validated by, the people.[41]

A common theme in Latino/a theologizing is popular religion, the concrete religious practices of the people of God, arising independently of church teaching and discipline and often in resistance to the institutional church. Latino/a Christianity is indelibly shaped by the Iberian Catholic conquest of the New World in the fifteenth and sixteenth centuries. Therefore, an important resource for understanding Latino/a Christianity is the syncretistic religious practices of the people of Latin America that combine the Christian symbols and rituals of the Iberian Catholic conquerors with indigenous forms of spirituality and the religions of African slaves. In great part because of the attention given to popular religion as a distinct source for theology, Latino/a theologians critically engage those academic disciplines that facilitate and inform the study of popular religious practices, such as ethnography (Ada María Isasi-Díaz), political science (Gastón Espinosa), sociology (Milagros Peña), and philosophical hermeneutics (Orlando O. Espín).

While it would be a mistake to reduce Christ to culture, it is equally problematic to remove Christ from culture.[42] Catholic theologian Orlando O. Espín affirms the necessity of Christ revealed *through* culture: "All human reality is historical *and* cultural. All that is human and all who are human occur and live always within culture, and cannot ever be a-cultural. Culture, therefore, is a context we cannot avoid or even imagine to escape. We are only and always in culture."[43] Despite the proliferation of contextual theologies in the

---

41. This movement was born through the collaborative efforts of US Latino/a theologians in professional organizations like *La Comunidad* of Hispanic American Scholars of Theology and Religion (American Academy of Religion), the Academy of Catholic Hispanic Theologians in the United States (ACHTUS), *Asociacion para la Educacion Teológica Hispana* (AETH), and the Hispanic Theological Initiative (HTI). *Teología en conjunto* (also called *teología de conjunto*) was the theme of a major conference sponsored by ACHTUS called *Somos un Pueblo* ("We Are a People") held at Emory University in June 1990, resulting in the publication of a highly influential collection of essays, *We Are a People!*, ed. Roberto S. Goizueta (Minneapolis: Fortress, 1992). In 1995 a group of Protestant Latino/a theologians, pastors, teachers, and students gathered at Princeton Theological Seminary; the proceedings were published in the volume *Teología en Conjunto: A Collaborative Hispanic Protestant Theology*, ed. José David Rodríguez and Loida I. Martell-Otero (Louisville, KY: Westminster John Knox, 1997). The spirit of *teología en conjunto* is perhaps best embodied in the ecumenical cooperation of the Hispanic Summer Program (HSP), an annual intensive summer workshop where Latino/a students, pastors, lay persons, and professors of theology and religion gather at different member institutions to reflect theologically on the challenges facing the Latino/a church.

42. See H. Richard Niebuhr, *Christ and Culture* (New York: Harper Torchbooks, 1951), for a classic paradigm of the various ways in which Christianity responds and interacts with culture: Christ against culture, Christ of culture, Christ above culture, Christ and culture in paradox, and Christ transforming culture.

43. Orlando O. Espín, *Idol and Grace: On Traditioning and Subversive Hope* (Maryknoll, NY: Orbis Books, 2014), 44.

late twentieth and early twenty-first centuries, dominant theologies within the academy and the church refuse to acknowledge that the human experience of God, and consequent interpretations of that experience, always occurs within a *particular* cultural context. According to Espín, theology needs to account for the role of culture even in the very composition, redaction, and canonization of the Bible itself: "It is in this diverse and inescapable context of cultures, of history, of experience (of God's self-revelation and self-donation), of hope, and of faith, that the texts of the New Testament were written, collected, and trusted as hermeneutical response of the People to God's revelation."[44] Due to this emphasis on culture, the lived experiences of the people, their faith, their liturgy, and their social praxis become rich sources for theological reflection, for it is through such communal experiences that God is encountered and within which all theologians must struggle to understand the mystery of God. In the work of Nichole Flores, the story of Guadalupe and Juan Diego—often retold through the lens of contemporary experience as in the play *The Miracle at Tepeyac* (1975) by Anthony J. Garcia—energizes and focuses the struggles and aspirations of all Chicanos and Chicanas.[45]

While Orlando Espín's body of work represents a more thorough and systematic analysis of popular Catholicism, popular religious practices prove an even more important theological source for Ada María Isasi-Díaz (1943–2012), given her focus on the daily struggle for survival of Latina women. Isasi-Díaz contends that the resources for liberating praxis are found in the community's traditions and religious beliefs; however, popular religious practices do not gain their authority through any official recognition by the magisterium of the Roman Catholic Church, but only insofar as they contribute to the community's historical liberation. In her own words, "Hispanic women's experience and our struggle for survival, not the Bible, are the source of our theology and the starting point for how we should interpret, appropriate, and use the Bible."[46] While most Latino/a theologies preference a "canon within the canon," the theology of Ada María Isasi-Díaz subsumes the authority of the canon under the rubric of liberation: "From the start we can say that a *mujerista* biblical hermeneutic submits the Bible to a Latinas' liberative canon. This means that the Bible is to be accepted as part of divine revelation and becomes authoritative for us only insofar as it contributes to our struggle for liberation."[47]

---

44. Espín, *Idol and Grace*, 19.
45. See Flores, *The Aesthetics of Solidarity*, 19.
46. Ada María Isasi-Díaz, *Mujerista Theology: A Theology for the Twenty-First Century* (Maryknoll, NY: Orbis Books, 1996), 149.
47. Isasi-Díaz, *Mujerista Theology*, 150.

For that reason, Isasi-Díaz views divine revelation as ongoing, not "completed and closed when the canon of Christianity was determined," taking place "through the faith and religiosity of the poor and oppressed of this world."[48] Accordingly, the praxis of liberation embodied in the popular faith of marginalized peoples becomes the very basis upon which to select a canon. Nichole Flores values the emphasis on the everyday spirituality and praxis of Latina women by Ada María Isasi-Díaz because it integrates the human thirst for spiritual transcendence with the *practical* demands of social justice work. Citing Isasi-Díaz, Flores links the aesthetic spirituality of Latina experience that thirsts for transcendent beauty amid the daily struggle for survival with the political praxis of revolution: "My own relationship with the divine finds expression walking picket lines more than in kneeling; in seeking ways to be involved with the work of reconciliation more than in fasting and mortifying the flesh; in striving to be passionately involved with others more than in seeking to be attached from human love."[49]

Nevertheless, despite this emphasis on liberative praxis, US Latino/a theology has come under criticism for abandoning Marxian conceptions of political praxis in favor of more aesthetic categories. Granted, by focusing on the "liberative dimensions of everyday forms of aesthetic and cultural production (*lo cotidiano*)," US Latino/a theologians "have explored the potential life-giving aspects of Latino popular religion, a topic that several early Latin American theologians dismissed."[50] Yet, by "turning to cultural and aesthetic categories, US Latino/a theologians may often risk losing ties with the ethical and political dimension of faith practice," abandoning the preferential option for the poor in favor of a "preferential option for culture."[51] As one critic has argued, "Aesthetics looms large in U.S. Latina/o theology. Yet lurking behind the beautiful is the monstrosity of marginalized and oppressed people which for the most part U.S. Hispanic theology has chosen to idealize."[52] Ivan Petrella, commenting on developments within US Latina feminist theology, argues this aesthetic turn relegates "liberation from poverty and social injustice to an afterthought. What really has priority is the inclusion of Latinas in the

---

48. Ada María Isasi-Díaz, "Preoccupations, Themes, and Proposals of Mujerista Theology," in *The Ties That Bind: African American and Hispanic American/Latino/a Theologies in Dialogue*, ed. Anthony B. Pinn and Benjamin Valentin (New York: Continuum, 2001), 137–38.

49. Flores, *The Aesthetics of Solidarity*, 132–33. For the original, see Ada María Isasi-Díaz, *La Lucha Continues: Mujerista Theology* (Maryknoll, NY: Orbis Books, 2004), 29.

50. Christopher D. Tirres, *The Aesthetics and Ethics of Faith: A Dialogue Between Liberationist and Pragmatic Thought* (Oxford: Oxford University Press, 2014), 6.

51. Tirres, *The Aesthetics and Ethics of Faith*, 7.

52. Manuel Mejido, "A Critique of the 'Aesthetic Turn' in U.S. Hispanic Theology: A Dialogue with Roberto Goizueta and the Positing of a New Paradigm," *Journal of Hispanic/Latino Theology* 8, no. 3 (February 2001): 18.

United States' mainstream."[53] The work of Nichole M. Flores, greatly influenced by the theopoetics of an earlier generation of US Latino/a theologians like Roberto S. Goizueta and Alejandro García-Rivera,[54] rejects this simplistic binary in order to argue that a lived faith rooted in the cultural identity and religious aesthetics of the local community is better suited to promote civic activism that contributes to concrete social change than Latin American understandings of liberation as political revolution.

According to Flores, for solidarity to move from mere intellectual assent to engaged activism requires a holistic view of human beings as interdependent, as contrasted to the modern conception of the autonomous self. In effect, the guiding anthropology of modern democratic liberalism can be summed up as "enlightened self-interest," which creates obstacles when trying to build community in a pluralistic context. When Flores applies the preferential option for the poor to the question of fostering solidarity with the marginalized and politically disenfranchised, she argues that "lifting up the lowly is a crucial principle for an aesthetics of the common good, a common good that supplants a project of 'oneness' with 'wholeness' and allows distinct identities to be stitched together to cultivate solidarity."[55]

To that end, she employs the insights of US Latino/a theology and Catholic social teaching to emphasize "the inherently relational character of human beings by virtue of our creation in the image of a Trinitarian God (*imago Trinitatis*)," over against "excessively individualistic accounts of anthropology."[56] While a Latino/a theological anthropology favors the "thick notion of familial belonging that is prominently featured in Latine cultures," this resonates with the "emphasis on human relationality expressed in Catholic theological ethics."[57] Answering those critics who question the aesthetic turn in US Latino/a theology—especially the muting of social justice praxis—Flores acknowledges that Latino/a theology "has often struggled to convey the individual dignity of particular members of the community," and tolerated the "subordination of vulnerable individuals (women, children, LGBTQ folx, persons with disabilities) within Latine families."[58]

---

53. Ivan Petrella, *The Future of Liberation Theology: An Argument and Manifesto*, reprint (London: Routledge, 2014), 134.

54. See Roberto S. Goizueta, *Caminemos Con Jesús: Toward a Hispanic/Latino Theology of Accompaniment* (Maryknoll, NY: Orbis Books, 1999) and *Christ Our Companion: Toward a Theological Aesthetics of Liberation* (Maryknoll, NY: Orbis Books, 2009); Alejandro García-Rivera, *The Community of the Beautiful: A Theological Aesthetics* (Collegeville, MN: Liturgical Press, 1999).

55. Flores, *The Aesthetics of Solidarity*, 106.

56. Flores, *The Aesthetics of Solidarity*, 107.

57. Flores, *The Aesthetics of Solidarity*, 107.

58. Flores, *The Aesthetics of Solidarity*, 107–8.

Nevertheless, Latino/a culture's emphasis on relationality grounded in familial relationships, in conjunction with the "just" relationality articulated by Catholic social teaching, corrects the potential for perpetuating patterns of abuse within families, making it imperative for Latino/a theology to always protect the most vulnerable members of the community by valuing their incarnate particularity as "other" rather than forcing all members into the same mold.

Flores diagnoses the civil discourse in our increasingly oligarchic democracy, mired as it is in the bog of late-stage capitalism, and concludes the United States suffers from a bad case of "consumptive solidarity" and prescribes "aesthetic solidarity" as the cure. Solidarity is crucial for promoting human flourishing and building the common good. Unfortunately, as the critics of US Latino/a theology make clear, aesthetic categories do not necessarily lead down the path of social justice.

The prototypical example of consumptive solidarity given by Flores is the type of communal cohesiveness on display at the 2017 Unite the Right Rally in Charlottesville, Virginia. Yes, it is solidarity of a sort, but not one that promotes justice as it fosters community. Rather, consumptive solidarity builds community by catering to the most base and hateful prejudices to build a "virtual" community around that hate, not in the pursuit of the common good—that which unites—but in the pursuit of dividing the culture according to some hierarchy that benefits one group at the expense of the other. The rally in Charlottesville brought together a wide range of white supremacist hate groups, employing "signs and symbols associated with racial and religious violence to construct a community united by racial hatred," demonstrating how an "aesthetic solidarity unhinged from a conception of justice" quickly degenerates into inhumane social practices.[59] US Latino/a theology, despite its emphasis on shared aesthetic categories, engenders solidarity because it remains linked to a guiding social ethic, God's preferential option for the poor, which promotes the common good by creating structures that protect and ensure the full participation of the most marginalized and powerless members of society.

Flores recognizes that consumptive solidarity poses an almost insurmountable challenge to the project of aesthetic solidarity, in great part because we live in a culture in which we are constantly bombarded by disembodied images, removed from all meaningful context, then encouraged to build our individual and collective identities from this wide array of options—like items

---

59. Flores, *The Aesthetics of Solidarity*, 137.

on an à la carte menu. The modern conception of freedom is built on freedom of choice, so the idea that the collective common good has a right to impinge on the individual's freedom is seriously undermined. Consequently, as "consumers" we are confronted with aesthetic choices that are "abstracted, disembodied, and disconnected from the realities of human suffering," and which fail to "foster concrete political solidarity."[60] So even when media images are intended to create political solidarity—think of the image of George Floyd, an African American man choked to death by white police officer Derek Chauvin—because the overriding conception of the self is that of an isolated individual exercising absolute freedom of choice, solidarity gets reduced to a shallow and transitory statement without generating "the kinds of exchanges that build relationships and affirm mutual personhood."[61]

Aesthetic solidarity, in contrast, is always highly contextualized, immersed in real-world concrete relationships of mutuality, and informed by a social justice ethic that always strives to build the common good. In that way, the aesthetic experiences that bring people together—for example, the narrative of Guadalupe and Juan Diego—are always directed and focused beyond the desires of self toward the greater common good, ultimately grounded in a transcendent experience of the divine that affirms a view of the human as deeply interconnected and interdependent.

More to the point, the encounter with the other is transformative for both the self and the society: "When Juan Diego first approaches Guadalupe, he views himself as one of the lowest of society," yet his "aesthetic encounter with Guadalupe serves as a turning point in his self-understanding as a dignified human being."[62] This transformative affirmation of one's inherent dignity, grounded in the belief that all humankind is created in the image of God (Gen. 1:26–27), inevitably leads to the affirmation of the other as other and also serves as the foundation for an aesthetic solidarity that leads to engaged political praxis and positive social change for the good of all. Here Flores once again links the aesthetic turn in US Latino/a theology to the rich tradition of Catholic social teaching as articulated by Pope Francis: "Faith in Christ brings salvation because in him our lives become radically open to a love that precedes us, a love that transforms us from within, acting in us and through us."[63]

---

60. Flores, *The Aesthetics of Solidarity*, 139.
61. Flores, *The Aesthetics of Solidarity*, 139.
62. Flores, *The Aesthetics of Solidarity*, 142.
63. Pope Francis, Encyclical Letter *Lumen Fidei* ("The Light of Faith") (June 29, 2013), §20. https://www.vatican.va/content/francesco/en/encyclicals/documents/papa-francesco_20130629_enciclica-lumen-fidei.html.

NEOLIBERALISM'S FALSE NARRATIVE

Democratic liberalism stands or falls on the notion of rule by consent of the governed, the promise of greater democratic freedoms, and the principle that the rule of law limits government's encroachment on the freedom of the individual. Yet events during the first two decades of the twenty-first century raise questions about the efficacy of the liberal experiment, given the rise of authoritarian regimes, the spread of state-sponsored terrorism, and the impingement on civil liberties in the name of national security. Even philosopher Francis Fukuyama, who declared victory for the "liberal idea" after the collapse of Soviet communism in 1991, recognizes that while "democratic ideas undermined the legitimacy of communist regimes around the world, democracy itself has had tremendous difficulties in establishing itself."[64]

Nevertheless, while cognizant that emerging nationalisms often undermine liberal democracy following the collapse of authoritarian states, Fukuyama takes a long view of history and cautions that we "should be careful to distinguish transitional conditions from permanent ones."[65] Fukuyama remains optimistic, pointing to the established track record of liberal democracies in Europe and North America as evidence for the lasting power of the liberal idea to adapt, change, and innovate, while also recognizing that liberalism can exist outside of democratic structures, even granting it "is possible for a country to be liberal without being particularly democratic."[66] He defines political liberalism as "a rule of law that recognizes certain individual rights or freedoms from government control."

Then, drawing upon Lord Bryce's classical definition of liberalism, he identifies three fundamental rights: *civil rights* (freedom from government control of one's person and property), *religious rights* (freedom from government control of religious expression and practice), and *political rights* (freedom from government interference in all else that does not directly pertain to the common good, including but not limited to free speech, freedom of the press, and the right to assembly).[67] Democracy he defines as "the right held universally by all citizens to have a share of political power, that is, the right of all citizens to vote and participate in politics."[68] While the right to share and participate in political power is fundamental within liberal democracies, Fukuyama acknowledges the possibility of regimes that allow democratic participation yet restrict individual freedoms, for example, the Islamic Republic of Iran,

---

64. Francis Fukuyama, *The End of History and the Last Man* (New York: Free Press, 1992), 36.
65. Fukuyama, *The End of History*, 37.
66. Fukuyama, *The End of History*, 43–44.
67. Fukuyama, *The End of History*, 42–43.
68. Fukuyama, *The End of History*, 43.

and liberal states that limit democratic participation through the manipulation of the electoral system by a ruling elite, like Brazil, India, and arguably the United States.

At stake is "the degree of openness permitted in political debate, and the basket of rights that societies are willing to distribute among their members."[69] Whether individual states live up to the ideals of liberalism and democracy, that which defines democratic liberalism is the extent to which individual rights are protected from government intrusion and the level of political agency granted its citizens. Michael Freeden questions Fukuyama's claim that the liberal idea has triumphed, and is troubled by the rise of neoliberalism, which he defines in terms of economic freedom from government regulation, to "maintain and develop the economic power inherent in capitalist production and transactions, to open up new areas for investment, and to benefit from the plethora of goods available for consumption."[70] Rather than emphasizing autonomy and self-rule, neoliberalism views the world "as an immense and potentially unencumbered global market, in which the exchange of goods for profit overrides other aspects of cross-national relations," and thus it is willing to "subordinate social, political, and cultural spheres to a professed self-regulating economic market."[71] Given its support of free-market capitalism, Freeden finds much common ground between neoliberalism (as embodied by Bill Clinton's and Barack Obama's presidencies, for example) and neoconservatism (as embodied by the presidency of George W. Bush, political thinkers like Fukuyama, and think tanks like the RAND Corporation), and argues that the liberal commitment to individual freedom has been subsumed by the capitalist desire for increased wealth to such a degree that "governments themselves are predominantly recast as investors and facilitators of trade, rather than deliverers of welfare or social justice."[72] Fukuyama agrees with this assessment, recasting economic liberalism as one of the fundamental rights of private (property-owning) citizens by arguing that "liberalism is the recognition of the right of free economic activity and economic exchange based on private property and markets," and states "that protect such economic rights we will consider liberal; those that are opposed or base themselves on other principles (such as 'economic justice') will not qualify."[73]

Nick Hanauer, entrepreneur and venture capitalist, is both a staunch defender of capitalism and a vocal critic of neoliberalism:

---

69. Michael Freeden, *Liberalism: A Very Short Introduction* (Oxford: Oxford University Press, 2015), 6.
70. Freeden, *Liberalism*, 109.
71. Freeden, *Liberalism*, 109.
72. Freeden, *Liberalism*, 110.
73. Fukuyama, *The End of History and the Last Man*, 44.

> Many economists would have you believe that their field is an objective science. I disagree, and I think that it is equally a tool that humans use to enforce and encode our social and moral preferences and prejudices about status and power, which is why plutocrats like me have always needed to find persuasive stories to tell everyone else about why our relative positions are morally righteous and good for everyone: like, we are indispensable, the job creators, and you are not; like, tax cuts for us create growth, but investments in you will balloon our debt and bankrupt our great country; that we matter; that you don't. For thousands of years, these stories were called divine right. Today, we have trickle-down economics. How obviously, transparently self-serving all of this is.[74]

Hanauer wants a better narrative for capitalism, because he believes the fundamental drive of capitalism works: "We have centuries of evidence now that capitalist economies do better at delivering high standards of living to their citizens than do economies run by communist, authoritarian, or other nonmarket systems."[75] Hanauer pushes back on the economic orthodoxies of both the left and the right, "Traditional economic orthodoxy assumes that markets are efficient, people are rational, and economies naturally move to an optimal state. But we now understand that markets can be far from efficient, people are not always rational, and the economy is a complex, dynamic, evolutionary problem-solving system—more like an interdependent ecosystem than an efficient machine."[76] The stubborn persistence of economists who continue to view economic narratives as objective facts, working according to immutable laws of nature (Adam Smith), fails to adequately account for the irrational and self-centered core of neoliberalism: "This new perspective also makes obvious why both the laissez-faire policies of the far right and the statism of the far left fail. Policies that provide opportunities for all citizens to fulfill their potential, and investments that enable them to expand their potential, are the surest ways to animate prosperity and growth."[77]

In other words, like astrophysicist Adam Frank and ecofeminist Ivone Gebara, venture capitalist Nick Hanauer longs for a new narrative that affirms the interconnectedness of all humans to one another and to the planet itself. Over against neoliberalism, Hanauer speaks out against plutocracy (while identifying as a plutocrat), challenging the United States to "have the courage to enact

---

74. Nick Hanauer, "Beware, Fellow Plutocrats, the Pitchforks Are Coming," TED Talks (August 12, 2014). https://www.ted.com/talks/nick_hanauer_beware_fellow_plutocrats_the _pitchforks_are_coming/transcript.
75. Nick Hanauer and Eric Beinhocker, "Capitalism Redefined," *Democracy: A Journal of Ideas* 31 (Winter 2014). https://democracyjournal.org/magazine/31/capitalism-redefined/.
76. Hanauer and Beinhocker, "Capitalism Redefined."
77. Hanauer and Beinhocker, "Capitalism Redefined."

policies that are good for capitalism broadly, not policies that benefit a few capitalists narrowly."[78]

In her analysis and critique of liberalism, Nichole Flores focuses on the contributions of John Rawls (1921–2002), whose political philosophy defined liberalism in the twentieth century, and Martha Nussbaum (1947–), in many ways Rawls's successor to the title of most influential and recognized American political philosopher. What they have in common is a general disregard for religious particularity in the public discourse: "One struggles to imagine how Nussbaum might conceive of acceptable engagement of Our Lady of Guadalupe and associated justice claims within a liberal framework."[79] Despite having Reformed theological roots, the Rawlsian project is ultimately pragmatic and secular, if not outright atheistic in its methodology. As I have argued elsewhere,[80] modern thought, including modern political liberalism, establishes itself first and foremost by emancipating itself from biblical and ecclesial authority. In *A Theory of Justice* (1971), Rawls was trying to articulate a model of distributive justice, the socially just distribution of goods in a society, not based on the relative merits (or failings) of the individual:

> Perhaps some will think that the person with greater natural endowments deserves those assets and the superior character that made their development possible. Because he is more worthy in this sense, he deserves the greater advantages that he could achieve with them. This view, however, is surely incorrect. It seems to be one of the fixed points of our considered judgments that no one deserves his place in the distribution of native endowments, any more than one deserves one's initial starting place in society.[81]

Behind Rawls's anti-Pelagian language is a desire for *impartiality* in moral reasoning,[82] a hallmark of modernism, which seeks to mimic the objectivity of the scientific method in all things. Yet, unlike more foundationalist modern thinkers, Rawls's pragmatic approach does not try to build an overarching metanarrative but contents itself with "provisional" fixed points. In other words, the goal of political philosophy is to reach rationally defensible conclu-

---

78. Hanauer and Beinhocker, "Capitalism Redefined."
79. Flores, *The Aesthetics of Solidarity*, 10.
80. Rubén Rosario Rodríguez, *Dogmatics after Babel: Beyond the Theologies of Word and Culture* (Louisville, KY: Westminster John Knox, 2018), 1–33.
81. John Rawls, *A Theory of Justice* (Oxford: Oxford University Press, 1971), 103–4.
82. See Eric Nelson, *The Theology of Liberalism: Political Philosophy and the Justice of God* (Cambridge, MA: Belknap Press, 2019). Nelson's analysis of John Rawls's political philosophy argues that an embrace of a secularized Pelagianism marked a major turning point in the development of modern liberal political philosophy, and that a shift in the thought of the later Rawls from Pelagianism to anti-Pelagianism reveals an irreconcilable contradiction in Rawls's moral philosophy.

sions about how best to organize our political life, with the understanding that philosophy approximates "reflective equilibrium" without ever achieving perfect equilibrium. By this standard, there is no privileged set of beliefs in political discourse; all beliefs are rational judgments that ought to remain open ended and always subject to revision in search of the ever-elusive greater overall coherence. But as Flores demonstrates, Rawls stipulates that "citizens must justify their political decisions to each other using publicly available language, values, and standards."[83] If Rawls's insistence on a "public" standard of reason excludes religious discourse, then "religious symbols such as Our Lady of Guadalupe confound it."[84]

Flores notes that feminist philosophy "has critiqued Rawls's prioritization of objectivity, arguing that the false universalization of thought and rationality exalts the subjectivity of those with power while relegating less-powerful people and groups to social, political, economic, and sexual margins."[85] Rawls argues that we need to foster objectivity in moral decision-making, especially toward ourselves and our personal motivations, which is why we "need a conception [of justice] that enables us to envision our objective from afar."[86] But as Flores has convincingly demonstrated, this detached perspective—which excludes the "interested" and "partial" arguments of a prophetic theology of liberation from the public discourse—neglects the very real suffering of persecuted peoples and invalidates their struggles for liberation. "How would such knowledge of the world account for the ongoing agony of Black deaths at the hands of police?" Without concrete and direct experience of the "particular history of policing as it relates to slavery, Reconstruction, Jim Crow, school-to-prison pipelines, and other patterns of discrimination that undermine the stable basic structures that Rawls seeks," this demand for "objectivity" in moral reasoning "renders invisible countless aspects of human identity, experience, and relationship that are, in fact, crucial to pursuing stable principles of justice."[87]

Having exposed the limits of Rawls's political philosophy as a vehicle for fostering a sense of justice that "engenders a commitment to the project of justice,"[88] Flores acknowledges that "Nussbaum's liberal aesthetics improve on Rawls's mechanisms for engaging religious particularity in society and offer a corrective to his prohibitive demands for strict impartiality and public reason."[89] Nevertheless, by emphasizing universal human rights—which, as

---

83. Flores, *The Aesthetics of Solidarity*, 57.
84. Flores, *The Aesthetics of Solidarity*, 59.
85. Flores, *The Aesthetics of Solidarity*, 65.
86. Rawls, *A Theory of Justice*, 22.
87. Flores, *The Aesthetics of Solidarity*, 55.
88. Flores, *The Aesthetics of Solidarity*, 55.
89. Flores, *The Aesthetics of Solidarity*, 77.

Flores notes, many critics have argued are far from "being accepted as some cross-cultural invariant"—Martha Nussbaum is guilty of the same objectifying tendency as Rawls.[90] This, in turn, contributes to an uncritically accepted ethnocentrism in Nussbaum's thought, as evidenced by the "Western assumptions latent in Nussbaum's universal claims concerning human flourishing."[91]

Most telling, the Black Lives Matter movement "presents a significant challenge to Nussbaum's account of political emotions. Specifically, her account does not allow a place for public expression of emotions associated with experiences of racial injustice, including anger."[92] Like Rawls, Nussbaum wants to subsume particular religious expressions to the standard of universal "public" reason, offering a reinterpretation of Dr. Martin Luther King's "I Have a Dream" speech (1963) as a model for "appropriate" civil discourse denuded of all its prophetic indignation and anger. Nussbaum grants that symbols "sometimes come out of a religious tradition, but they can be appropriated into the general language of a society without being exclusionary," pointing to King's use of the Hebrew prophets "as a kind of civic poetry" in service to an inclusive liberal pluralism.[93]

The problem with this assertion, as Jeffrey Stout, John Milbank, and others have argued, is that such a narrow conception of public reason excludes religious voices from the public discourse and restricts the participation of religious believers in democratic processes. In other words, the secularized public square of modern liberalism championed by Rawls and Nussbaum is inherently antidemocratic, because it limits the freedom of religious expression guaranteed by the Bill of Rights of the US Constitution.

A FRAGMENT OF THEOLOGY: WALTER WINK'S THIRD WAY

For a certain generation of seminarians, Walter Wink (1935–2012)—a biblical scholar, theologian, and activist who taught at Union Theological Seminary and Auburn Theological Seminary in New York—embodied the best of progressive Protestantism. Known for his acclaimed trilogy on "the principalities and powers," *Naming the Powers: The Language of Power in the New Testament* (1984), *Unmasking the Powers: The Invisible Forces that Determine Human Existence* (1986), and *Engaging the Powers: Discernment and Resistance in a World of Domination* (1992),

---

90. Flores, *The Aesthetics of Solidarity*, 79.
91. Flores, *The Aesthetics of Solidarity*, 81.
92. Flores, *The Aesthetics of Solidarity*, 90.
93. Martha C. Nussbaum, *Political Emotions: Why Love Matters for Justice* (Cambridge, MA: Belknap Press, 2013), 388.

Wink was an outspoken critic of the US war in Vietnam and was awarded a Peace Fellowship from the US Institute of Peace to complete the final volume of his trilogy. In the third and final volume, *Engaging the Powers*, he relates the New Testament concept of "principalities and powers" to the concrete reality of evil in the world today, examining the question, "How can we oppose evil without creating new evils and being made evil ourselves?"[94] In the letter to the Ephesians, the apostle Paul compares the powers of this world—princes and governments—to cosmic forces bent not only on earthly domination but spiritual desolation: "For our struggle is not against enemies of blood and flesh, but against the rulers, against the authorities, against the cosmic powers of this present darkness, against the spiritual forces of evil in the heavenly places" (Eph. 6:12–13). Such powers can appear unstoppable, but as Christians, Wink argues, we are called to resist them. The question at stake in Wink's body of work is, How ought we to resist?

Twice in *Engaging the Powers*, Wink cites Friedrich Nietzsche, one of the harshest yet most insightful critics of Christianity, who cautioned, "Whoever fights monsters should see to it that in the process he does not become a monster," and "And when you look long into an abyss, the abyss also looks into you."[95] Wink employs Nietzsche as a warning to Christians that while there is no question we are called to resist the forces of evil in the world, how we go about resisting determines whether or not we ourselves contribute to the world's evil. Ultimately, Wink is committed to *nonviolent resistance*, and even his strongest supporters admit that in the end his hermeneutical gymnastics—in the service of this ethical commitment to nonviolence—are not always *true to the text*, even if they remain faithful to the *spirit* of Jesus' Sermon on the Mount.

As a divinity student at Union Theological Seminary in New York in the early 1990s, I had the benefit of knowing and working with Walter Wink, though I never had the chance to study with him. As one of two student coordinators for the Union soup kitchen, housed in the basement of Broadway Presbyterian Church (my home church), I got to know him over a three-year period, during which time he would faithfully bring volunteers once a month from his church. Over the routine tasks of chopping vegetables, setting tables, and washing dishes we had some fascinating and deep conversations that I wish I could recall with greater detail. Nevertheless, a conviction I carry with me to this day in both my preaching and my academic work—which I owe to my time with Walter Wink—is to interpret the whole of the Christian tradition through the lens of the Sermon on the Mount.

---

94. Walter Wink, *Engaging the Powers: Discernment and Resistance in a World of Domination*, 25th anniversary edition (Minneapolis: Fortress, 2017), 1.

95. Wink, *Engaging the Powers*, 209, 415.

Rawls might say I am too personally invested in Wink's project and lack the adequate critical distance, but I am not troubled by the supposed exegetical weaknesses supporting Wink's central argument. As theological ethicist Scott Paeth has argued, rather than offering a historical-critical analysis, Wink's Powers Trilogy offers a *theological* interpretation of the Sermon on the Mount; so instead of being an example of "bad" exegesis, Wink ought to be read and valued as an excellent example of constructive biblical theology.[96] Fellow ethicist Kevin Carnahan questions Wink's interpretation and challenges the assertion that Jesus teaches nonviolent resistance in the Sermon on the Mount.[97] Carnahan argues that Wink's analysis would receive a failing grade in a class on the historical-critical analysis of the New Testament, and the fact that Wink's model of nonviolent resistance is good ethics cannot overcome bad exegesis.

Carnahan is correct that Walter Wink interprets the Jesus of the Sermon on the Mount "as a very early, long misunderstood, architect of the kind of nonviolent resistance carried out by Martin Luther King, Jr."[98] But that does not necessarily invalidate Wink's interpretation of the ethos Jesus articulates in the Sermon on the Mount. Let me explain. Jesus never explicitly condemned slavery in the New Testament. In fact, a compelling argument can be made that there were no first-century abolitionists, so Jesus can be excused for not having spoken directly against the institution of slavery. Nevertheless, there is no question from a Christian theological and ethical standpoint that slavery is contrary to the will of God as revealed in the life and ministry of Jesus of Nazareth, which led directly to the explicitly abolitionist doctrine of Gregory of Nyssa (ca. 335–ca. 395 CE) preserved in Nyssa's fourth homily on the book of Ecclesiastes.[99]

As David Bentley Hart has noted, "No other ancient text still known to us—Christian, Jewish, or Pagan—contains so fierce, unequivocal, and indignant a condemnation of the institution of slavery."[100] The dearth of abolitionist writings "in an age when an economy sustained otherwise than by chattel slavery was all but unimaginable, the question of abolition was simply never

---

96. Scott Paeth, "Walter Wink, the Powers, and the Sermon on the Mount," Political Theology Network (October 28, 2021). https://politicaltheology.com/walter-wink-the-powers-and-the-sermon-on-the-mount/.

97. Kevin Carnahan, "Jesus Did Not Teach Nonviolent Resistance in the Sermon on the Mount," Political Theology Network (October 14, 2021). https://politicaltheology.com/jesus-did-not-teach-nonviolent-resistance-in-the-sermon-on-the-mount/.

98. Carnahan, "Jesus Did Not Teach Nonviolent Resistance."

99. See Gregory of Nyssa, *In Ecclesiasten homiliae*, in *Gregorii Nysseni Opera*, ed. Werner Jaeger, Friedrich Müller, et al. (Leiden: E. J. Brill, 1958), 5:334–52.

100. David Bentley Hart, "The 'Whole Humanity': Gregory of Nyssa's Critique of Slavery in Light of His Eschatology," *Scottish Journal of Theology* 54, no. 1 (2001): 51.

raised, and so the apparent uniqueness of Gregory's sermon is, in one sense, entirely unsurprising."[101] What is surprising, at least to me as a liberation theologian, is how long after the death and resurrection of Christ it took for the abolitionist argument to be made.

The fact that Jesus addressed the political realm indirectly—most often using parables requiring analysis and interpretation—means that discerning Jesus' ethical command in new situations carries a certain level of risk and ambiguity.[102] Even for a political theology of liberation, the historical Jesus known primarily through the canonical Gospels must stand as a primary source. Given the necessity of employing historical-critical methods, no subject creates greater hermeneutical frustration for contemporary emancipatory theologies than the Gospels' tacit acceptance and toleration of slavery. The Bible condoned slavery and the treatment of slaves as property to be bought and sold like cattle; no amount of hermeneutical trickery can conceal this. The Torah declares as lawful to own aliens residing in Israel as well those enslaved through military conquest: "These you may treat as slaves, but as for your fellow Israelites, no one shall rule over the other with harshness" (Lev. 25:46). Even when the Torah provides legal protections for slaves and resident aliens (Exod. 20:10; Deut. 5:14–15), slaves remain subject to treatment no Israelite would tolerate. Nearer the time of Jesus, the intertestamental book of Sirach even provides practical advice for the treatment of slaves, reflecting a complete lack of theological resistance to the practice of slavery:

> Fodder and a stick and burdens for a donkey; bread and discipline and work for a slave. Set your slave to work, and you will find rest; leave his hands idle, and he will seek liberty. Yoke and thong will bow the neck, and for a wicked slave there are racks and tortures. Put him to work, in order that he may not be idle, for idleness teaches much evil. Set him to work, as is fitting for him, and if he does not obey, make his fetters heavy. (Sir. 33:25–30a)

Therefore, it is not surprising that Jesus employed the term "slave" (*doulos/ doule*) in his preaching, "No slave can serve two masters" (Luke 16:13), and often illustrated his stories by referencing the institution of slavery (Luke 12:42–46; 14:16–24; 15:22), revealing a more than passing familiarity with the everyday lives of slaves. This does not mean Jesus condoned slavery, but did Jesus ever question the morality of slavery?

In the Gospel of Luke, Jesus begins his earthly mission citing Isaiah's prophecy "to proclaim release to the captives" and "to let the oppressed go free"

---

101. Hart, "The 'Whole Humanity,'" 51–52.
102. For a fuller treatment of this topic, see Rubén Rosario Rodríguez, *Racism and God-Talk: A Latino/a Perspective* (New York: New York University Press, 2008), 141–49.

(Luke 4:18), a not-so-veiled reference to the exodus. The book of the prophet Isaiah explicitly links the work of liberation to the *ruach YHWH* ("spirit of the Lord GOD," NRSV) in Isaiah 61:1. Jesus, "filled with the power of the Spirit" (Luke 4:14), quotes this passage when he preaches his first sermon in Nazareth, only to receive a rather hostile reception (Luke 4:28). Why? Surely not for advocating release to the captives, since deliverance from Egyptian slavery was the chief narrative of biblical Judaism. Thus these words would have been received as good news by Jesus' first-century Jewish audience: "Today this scripture has been fulfilled in your hearing" (Luke 4:21).

The source of their anger is the fact that Jesus extends God's justice and mercy to Gentiles:

> "Truly I tell you, no prophet is accepted in the prophet's hometown. But the truth is, there were many widows in Israel in the time of Elijah, when the heaven was shut up three years and six months, and there was a severe famine over all the land; yet Elijah was sent to none of them except to a widow at Zarephath in Sidon. There were also many lepers in Israel in the time of the prophet Elisha, and none of them was cleansed except Naaman the Syrian." (Luke 4:24–27)

In both instances Jesus references Hebrew prophets sent by God to minister to the needs of Gentiles. By framing his sermon with the good news of liberation to the captives, then extending that grace to Gentiles, Jesus not only articulates God's judgment against slavery, but he also explicitly condemns the Torah practice of enslaving foreigners. As Nyssa so astutely stated some centuries later, "You have divided human nature between slavery and mastery and have made it at once slave to itself and master over itself."[103] The argument implied in Jesus' first sermon is made explicit in the homily of Nyssa, who decried slavery as an affront to the *imago Dei*, voicing the strongest condemnation of slavery among the ancient church fathers, by arguing that if we respected the image of God in one another, "poverty would no longer afflict humankind, slavery no longer debase it, shame would no longer distress it, for all things would be common to all."[104]

Paul, like Jesus, does not explicitly condemn slavery or call for the abolition of slavery, yet his use of slavery as a metaphor for humankind's relationship to God builds upon Jesus' own, in order to eliminate differences between free and slave within Christian communities. In Christ Jesus—that is, between

---

103. Hart, "The 'Whole Humanity,'" 53, citing Gregory of Nyssa, *In Ecclesiasten homiliae*, 335.
104. Justo L. González, *Faith and Wealth: A History of Early Christian Ideas on the Origin, Significance, and Use of Money*, repr. ed, (New York: Harper & Row, 1990), 180. González is here paraphrasing from Gregory of Nyssa's fourth homily on Ecclesiastes.

fellow Christians—there is neither slave nor free (Gal. 3:27–28; Col. 3:11). So, while slaves are told to "obey your earthly masters with fear and trembling, in singleness of heart, as you obey Christ" (Eph. 6:5), masters are also cautioned to "do the same to them [slaves]. Stop threatening them, for you know that both of you have the same Master in heaven, and with him there is no partiality" (Eph. 6:9).

Paul's teaching on slavery, however, is not limited to the metaphoric. In the letter to Philemon, a friend and fellow convert, Paul returns Philemon's runaway slave, Onesimus (who has also converted to Christianity), with the instruction to welcome him "no longer as a slave but more than a slave, a beloved brother" (Phlm. 16). In this passage Paul explicitly distinguishes metaphoric from literal, exhorting Philemon to receive Onesimus as a beloved brother both in the "flesh" and "in the Lord," then drives the point home by writing, "Confident of your obedience, I am writing to you, knowing that you will do even more than I say" (v. 21). That this letter survived, was duplicated, and widely dispersed—despite the pervasiveness of slavery in first-century Mediterranean culture—reflects its importance for the earliest Christian communities. In David Bentley Hart's reading of Nyssa, we are encouraged to take Paul's exhortation literally that Philemon is to receive Onesimus as a brother in Christ and no longer a slave because "for now, in the between times, the mystical body of Christ, the church, is the only visible form of that redeemed nature."[105]

I return to Kevin Carnahan's critique of Walter Wink, namely, the assertion that Wink's interpretation of nonviolent resistance in the Sermon on the Mount rests on bad exegesis. According to Carnahan, Wink cannot overcome the critique that *antistēnai*, where it reads, "But I say to you: Do not resist an evildoer. But if anyone strikes you on the right cheek, turn the other also" (Matt. 5:39), means "resist" not "resist violently." Carnahan asserts that, while Wink demonstrates the term is often used to describe acts of martial resistance, he fails to provide a single instance in the ancient literature where it is used solely as "resist violently."

In other words, for Carnahan, the message of Jesus' Sermon on the Mount, when he commands to "turn the other cheek," to "give your coat as well," and "go also the second mile," suggests very literally that Jesus is opposed to all forms of resistance—violent or otherwise. To be clear, Carnahan values the moral argument Wink makes, and believes there are good reasons for Christians to embrace Wink's vision of nonviolent resistance in the style of King and Gandhi, but he thinks it weakens Wink's position to base his existential

---

105. Hart, "The 'Whole Humanity,'" 61.

commitment to nonviolent resistance on the argument that Jesus teaches this form of resistance in the Sermon on the Mount.

Walter Wink recognizes that the "critical issue is the meaning of *antistēnai*," and affirms that most translators interpret it as "do not resist" in a general sense, but in the context of the Sermon on the Mount, where Jesus has offered multiple examples of "aggressive nonviolent actions," it does not make sense to translate *antistēnai* as "resist not."[106] The crux of what Wink argues is Jesus' "third way"—an alternative to both violent resistance and passivity—hinges on how one interprets the three acts Wink describes as "aggressive nonviolent actions." Wink makes much of the fact that Jesus commands us to turn the other cheek when we have been struck on the right cheek: "The only way one could naturally strike the right cheek with the right hand would be with the back of the right hand. We are dealing here with insult, not a fistfight. The intention is clearly not to injure but to humiliate."[107] By turning the other cheek, the offended party is asking to be struck with an open-hand slap instead of a backhand slap, "the usual way of admonishing inferiors"—not an act of violent retaliation, but neither an act of passive submission.[108] Jesus' third way is to offer nonviolent resistance by demanding to be treated with dignity—to be treated as an equal by demanding to be struck with an open-hand slap, which "robs the oppressor of the power to humiliate."[109]

This leads Wink to conclude that Jesus "abhors both passivity and violence"; that Jesus drew from "the history of his own people's struggles" to resist the oppressor without resorting to the oppressor's violent ways; and that he discovers a way of "lifting up the lowly" (Flores) that preserves their dignity through a political act of solidarity: "Jesus here reveals a way of fighting evil with all one's power but without being transformed into the very evil we fight. It is a way of not becoming what we hate. Do not counter evil in kind—this insight is the distilled essence, stated with sublime simplicity, of the experience of those Jews who had, in Jesus' very lifetime, so courageously and effectively practiced nonviolent direct action against Rome."[110]

Kevin Carnahan's objections, especially his reliance on historical-critical methods for reading and interpreting the New Testament, resemble John Rawls's call for objectivity and detachment in moral reasoning. In other words, when we limit our understanding of the term *antistēnai* to how it is used

---

106. Walter Wink, "Neither Passivity nor Violence: Jesus' Third Way (Matt. 5:38–44 par.)," in *The Love of Enemy and Nonretaliation in the New Testament*, ed. Willard M. Swartley (Louisville, KY: Westminster John Knox, 1992), 113.
 107. Wink, "Neither Passivity nor Violence," 105.
 108. Wink, "Neither Passivity nor Violence," 105.
 109. Wink, "Neither Passivity nor Violence," 105.
 110. Wink, "Neither Passivity nor Violence," 117.

literally in extant ancient texts—most of which were written by the Roman oppressors—we fail to hear in the text the experience of the oppressed community. Wink is not reading a modern agenda into the text. Rather, he is allowing the text to speak by not letting this one term keep us from seeing the bigger picture, which is Jesus' narration of three acts of nonviolent resistance by Jews under repressive Roman rule. Based on this experience, Wink is saying that we then ought to read the commandment not to resist (*antistēnai*) as *not to resist violently*.

As this book has stated again and again, there are no objective and unmediated commands from God, but only human interpretations of divine commands, seen through the eyes of our own cultural and individual subjectivity. By paying attention to the biblical theme of God's preferential option for the poor and oppressed, we can, at the very least, affirm that God values the dignity of every human being and thus would not command actions that demean, exploit, or destroy another human being. If as Nichole Flores has argued, lifting up the lowly is an essential component of an aesthetics of solidarity, then Walter Wink's third way becomes a powerful tool for engaged political praxis grounded in a Christian ethic of compassion.

6

The Myth of Christian Uniqueness

> Christians should deal with the fact of pluralism in our modern world. One of the most important questions for Christians today is not only what we think of other faiths, but how we understand our own faith, for this perception will certainly shape all of our relationships.[1]

Not only is Christian theology characterized by a growing doctrinal diversity, but Christianity also exists in a religiously pluralistic cultural context where engagement and interaction with other faiths is unavoidable. One way of preventing the church's limited and all-too-human perspective from becoming a false idol is by undertaking the task of critical reflection of Christian beliefs and practices in mutually enriching dialogue with other religions. Sadly, in an age when Christianity has begun to celebrate its own diversity, Thatamanil raises an obvious question: "Why is religious diversity routinely perceived to be different from other modes of diversity?"[2] Can Christian voices accommodate religious pluralism? Or has the Christian narrative—at least in the US context—become so entwined with the dominant culture it is no longer distinguishable from the myth of American exceptionalism?

Comparative theology affirms a wide range of theological voices, on the premise that we can know God better by studying traditions in their

---

1. S. Mark Heim, *Is Christ the Only Way? Christian Faith in a Pluralistic World* (Valley Forge, PA: Judson, 1985), 9.
2. John J. Thatamanil, *Circling the Elephant: A Comparative Theology of Religious Diversity* (New York: Fordham University Press, 2020), 3.

particularity *while* asserting that no single theological interpretation of divine revelation can claim absolute authority. An exercise in comparative theology is risky. The possibility of giving offense is high, the analysis of traditions other than one's own is inevitably thin, and there is always the risk of essentializing other traditions into static representations unrecognizable to that religion's practitioners. Knowing the limitations that hinder a study of this type, it is still worth pursuing, precisely because there is so much hesitation about entering the deep waters of comparative theology—hesitation to have one's doctrinal commitments questioned, challenged, and even changed. Ironically, this hesitation ignores the fact that historically, theology "has always been an inherently comparative discipline. Major developments within the theological systems of communities of faith frequently grow out of at least implicit comparisons among systems of thought or doctrinal options presented by those communities as they define themselves."[3]

Take, for example, the revival of Aristotelian thought during the medieval period, facilitated by Islam's translation of long-lost philosophical texts from Arabic to Latin during the Islamic Golden Age (eighth to fourteenth centuries CE). This cultural exchange serves as a prime example of this kind of comparative dialogue and interaction between Jewish, Christian, and Muslim thinkers: "Thomas Aquinas' evaluation of important features in the thought of major Jewish and Muslim thinkers, for example, certainly moves in that direction, even when Thomas ends up passing a negative judgment."[4]

Given the impact of Aristotle on all three Abrahamic religions, as evidenced by the magisterial works of Samuel Ibn Tibbon (ca. 1150–ca. 1230 CE), Maimonides/Moses ben Maimon (1138–1204 CE), and Gersonides/Levi ben Gershom (1288–1344 CE) within Judaism,[5] Albertus Magnus (ca. 1200–1280 CE) and Thomas Aquinas (1225–1274 CE) within Christianity,[6] and Ibn Sina (ca. 980–1037 CE), al-Ghazali (ca. 1058–1111 CE), and Ibn Rushd

---

3. John Renard, "Comparative Theology: Definition and Method," *Religious Studies and Theology* 17, no. 1 (1998): 3.

4. Renard, "Comparative Theology," 3.

5. See *Samuel Ibn Tibbon's Commentary on Ecclesiastes: The Book of the Soul of Man*, ed. and trans. James T. Robinson (Heidelberg, Germany: Mohr Siebeck, 2007); Moses Maimonides, *The Guide for the Perplexed*, ed. and trans. Michael Friedländer (New York: Dover, 1956); Levi ben Gershom, *Commentary on Song of Songs*, ed. and trans. Menachem Kellner (New Haven, CT: Yale University Press, 1998).

6. See Albertus, *On the Body of the Lord*, trans. Albert Marie Surmanski (Washington, DC: Catholic University of America Press, 2017); Thomas Aquinas, *Summa Theologiae: A Concise Translation*, ed. Timothy McDermott, repr. ed. (Notre Dame, IN: Christian Classics, 1991) and *Summa Contra Gentiles. Book One: God*, ed. and trans. Anton Charles Pegis (Notre Dame, IN: University of Notre Dame Press, 1975).

(1126–1198 CE) within Islam,⁷ the Aristotelian concept of natural law seems an obvious starting point for a comparative study of Jewish, Christian, and Muslim theologies. However, the path of natural theology—while well suited to a comparative study—is an artificial and external starting point reflective of a dominant Eurocentric perspective, rather than communicating the true scriptural foundations of all three Abrahamic (non-European) religions.

The dialogue and cooperation among the Abrahamic religions on the Iberian peninsula during the medieval period exemplifies the reliance on Aristotelian thought for navigating religious differences. However, medieval Spain was unique insofar as it was the only region of Europe where Jews, Christians, and Muslims lived and worked side by side, often in relative peace and harmony, though such harmony ought not to be romanticized or exaggerated.⁸ Thus, despite a period of *convivencia* ("coexistence") among the diverse peoples, languages, cultures, and religions of medieval Spain, whose extraordinary mingling produced a distinctive civilization in terms of art, architecture, music, science, and literature, this brief interregnum was followed by the extreme intolerance of the *Reconquista* ("to reconquer") culminating in the end of Muslim rule in 1492 and characterized by the racist ideology of *limpieza de sangre* ("cleansing" or "purity of blood"), leading to the forced conversion or expulsion of Muslims and Jews.⁹ As historian David Nirenberg has argued, the intolerance and persecution that characterized relations among the Abrahamic religions in medieval Europe is complicated and cannot be reduced to a simple binary between harmonious coexistence and outright civilizational conflict,¹⁰ but demands that scholars navigate the

---

7. Ibn Sina, *Ibn Sina's Remarks and Admonitions: Physics and Metaphysics; An Analysis and Annotated Translation*, trans. Shams C. Inati (New York: Columbia University Press, 2014); Al Ghazali, *The Incoherence of The Philosophers (Tahāfut al-Falāsifah): A Parallel English-Arabic Text*, trans. Michael E. Marmura, rev. ed. (Salt Lake City, UT: Brigham Young University Press, 2000); Ibn Rushd, *Ibn Rushd's Metaphysics: A Translation with Introduction of Ibn Rushd's Commentary on Aristotle's Metaphysics, Book Lām*, ed. and trans. Charles F. Genequand (Leiden: E. J. Brill, 1986).

8. See María Rosa Menocal, *The Ornament of the World: How Muslims, Jews, and Christians Created a Culture of Tolerance in Medieval Spain* (New York: Little, Brown, 2002).

9. See Matthew Carr, *Blood and Faith: The Purging of Muslim Spain* (New York: New Press, 2009), and Benzion Netanyahu, *The Origins of the Inquisition in Fifteenth-Century Spain* (New York: Random House, 1995).

10. See Samuel P. Huntington, *The Clash of Civilizations and the Remaking of World Order* (New York: Simon & Schuster, 1996). A highly popular text with undue influence on US foreign policy, Huntington's views have contributed to increased discrimination against Muslims and the conflation of Islam with terrorism, on the dubious premise that "civilizational" conflicts are particularly pervasive between "Muslim and non-Muslim peoples" (255).

thick reality that Jews, Christians, and Muslims "loved, tolerated, massacred, and expelled each other—all in the name of God."[11]

Accordingly, in my own work I explore a more organic starting point for comparative theology: sacred Scripture.[12] Scripture as a vessel of divine revelation is considered the most reliable source of knowledge of God by believers within all three Abrahamic religions. An analysis of how religious communities read one another's sacred texts brings to light an often ignored, yet potentially instructive, methodology for comparative theology.

The Scriptural Reasoning (SR) movement is an evolving interdisciplinary practice among Jews, Christians, and Muslims committed to reading each other's sacred Scriptures (Tanakh, New Testament, and Qur'an) together, in order to draw upon each tradition's wisdom to better understand and engage a range of contemporary situations and issues.[13] While scriptural reasoning has been labeled a postliberal theological project, insofar as it embraces George Lindbeck's hermeneutical insight that every religion has a distinctive "grammar" embedded in its own culture and practices, best understood within that particular religion's own internal logic,[14] elsewhere I have argued that Lindbeck's ultimate intent was to break through religion's internal monologue in order to foster genuine conversation and cooperation across religious traditions.[15]

---

11. David Nirenberg, *Neighboring Faiths: Christianity, Islam, and Judaism in the Middle Ages and Today* (Chicago: University of Chicago Press, 2014), 3.

12. See Rubén Rosario Rodríguez, *Dogmatics after Babel* (Louisville, KY: Westminster John Knox, 2018), 147–67. In this chapter I make the argument, through a comparative study of conceptions of Spirit in the sacred Scriptures of all three Abrahamic religions, that Judaism, Christianity, and Islam contain a similar notion of Spirit as the divine manifestation in acts of liberation that preserve human dignity and reveal an indispensable aspect of God's true nature. Also see Rosario Rodríguez, *Christian Martyrdom and Political Violence* (Cambridge: Cambridge University Press, 2017), 221–38. There I explore a Trinitarian framework for a comparative theology in conversation with Judaism and Islam by employing the patristic concept of *perichoresis* (literally "rotation" or "going around," the term is used to describe the relationship of the three persons of the triune God to one another) to understand how God can accommodate others—including different religions—into God's life without ceasing to be God, thereby providing the basis for a Christian doctrine of religious pluralism.

13. See *The Promise of Scriptural Reasoning*, ed. David F. Ford and C. C. Pecknold (Malden, MA: Blackwell, 2006); Wesley Wildman, *Religious Philosophy as Multidisciplinary Comparative Inquiry: Envisioning a Future for the Philosophy of Religion* (Albany: SUNY Press, 2010); David F. Ford, "An Interfaith Wisdom: Scriptural Reasoning between Jews, Christians and Muslims," *Modern Theology* 22, no. 3 (2006): 345–66; Steven Kepnes, "A Handbook for Scriptural Reasoning," *Modern Theology* 22, no. 3 (2006): 367–83; and Marianne Moyaert, "Scriptural Reasoning as Inter-Religious Dialogue," in *The Wiley-Blackwell Companion to Inter-Religious Dialogue*, ed. Catherine Cornille (Malden, MA: Wiley-Blackwell, 2013), 64–86.

14. See George A. Lindbeck, *The Nature of Doctrine: Religion and Theology in a Postliberal Age*, 25th anniversary ed. (Louisville, KY: Westminster John Knox, 2009).

15. See Rosario Rodríguez, *Dogmatics after Babel*, 20–31.

Given increased efforts among the Abrahamic religions to foster cooperation and establish common ground amid increased political tensions—even armed conflict—it is important to affirm that each tradition's distinctive grammar contributes something unique to the public discourse.[16] While focusing on each tradition's distinctive theological "grammar" might sound counterintuitive, a comparative theology grounded in the practice of scriptural reasoning helps identify that which *distinguishes* each Abrahamic tradition, while also establishing *shared loci* for dialogue and cooperation.

John Renard, a historian of medieval Islam, labels this model of comparative theology the intertextual approach, wherein "theologians of one tradition engage the scriptures or theological texts of another directly."[17] Admittedly, this kind of direct engagement can degenerate into polemics, yet intertextual study of another tradition's sacred Scriptures "can also yield signs of serious theological engagement beyond the needs of apologetics."[18] Comparative theology is defined in diverse ways but always distinguished by a methodological commitment to the thoughtful engagement of other religious traditions. It is differentiated from, though related to, the theology of religions, what John Thatamanil prefers to call theologies of religious diversity (TRD), broadly understood as reflection on the reality of other religions in light of the particular claims of one's faith.[19]

In other words, the theology-of-religions approach views the reality of religious pluralism as a challenge to the internal coherence of exclusivist theological claims and attempts to account for the reality of religious pluralism through internal theological rationalization. Although Thatamanil is more optimistic about the possibilities within Christian theologies of religious diversity for fostering interreligious learning, in the end we both agree that without engaging in comparative theology it is unlikely for Christian theology to affirm truth, especially salvific truth, in other religious traditions.

Comparative theology reflects on God (Ultimate Reality) from an explicitly pluralistic perspective. Recognizing that many belief systems are not theistic, this book continues to employ the term "comparative theology" because it is widely accepted as "any explicitly intellectual interpretation of a religious tradition that affords a central place to the fact of religious pluralism in the

---

16. See Miroslav Volf, *Allah: A Christian Response* (New York: HarperOne, 2011) and *Do We Worship the Same God? Jews, Christians, and Muslims in Dialogue*, ed. Miroslav Volf (Grand Rapids: Eerdmans, 2012).
17. Renard, "Comparative Theology: Definition and Method," 9.
18. Renard, "Comparative Theology: Definition and Method," 9.
19. See Thatamanil, *Circling the Elephant*, 12.

tradition's self-interpretation."[20] Operating under the assumption that so long as a belief system addresses the universal concerns of the human condition (suffering, sin, evil, death, etc.), articulates some path to ultimate transformation (enlightenment, salvation, liberation, fulfillment, etc.), and does this by relating its own understanding of ultimate reality to that of other traditions in dialogical relationship, it operates as a comparative theology. Comparative theology also affirms the particularity of different religions. Accordingly, comparative theology does not set out to undermine the foundational truth claims of traditional theologies—such as the uniqueness of Christ in the doctrine of the incarnation or the Qur'an's affirmation that "there is no god save the one God" (Sura 5:73)[21]—but aims instead for a deeper understanding of God by studying other traditions in their concreteness.

Such an approach is inherently pluralistic, affirming that no single tradition can claim absolute authority concerning knowledge of God and demanding a methodological humility that recognizes all "that is true and holy" in other religions.[22] In other words, a normative assumption of comparative theology is that all theology is inherently hermeneutical and that a primary task of theologians is to interpret the truth claims of a religious tradition for a particular time and place. Thus comparative theology is a constructive endeavor, grounded in a particular confessional tradition, yet engaged in deep comparative analysis with other religions, going beyond a simple comparison of doctrines toward a critical reconstruction of one's own doctrines as a direct result of this comparative work.

From a Muslim perspective, there is solid scriptural foundation for the type of comparative dialogue this chapter advocates: "And dispute not with the People of the Book, save in the most virtuous manner, unless it be with those of them who have done wrong. And say, 'We believe in that which was sent down unto us and was sent down unto you; our God and your God are one, and unto Him are we submitters'" (Sura 29:46). Within the Qur'an one finds a high degree of tolerance and peaceful coexistence between the three Abrahamic religions during Islam's first century:

---

20. David Tracy, "Comparative Theology," in *The Encyclopedia of Religion*, ed. Mircea Eliade (New York: Macmillan, 1987), 14:447.

21. *The Study Quran: A New Translation and Commentary*, Seyyed Hossein Nasr, editor-in-chief; Caner K. Dagli, Maria Massi Dakake, and Joseph E. B. Lumbard, gen. eds.; Mohammed Rustom, asst. ed. (New York: HarperOne, 2015). Unless otherwise noted, all citations from the Qur'an are from this translation.

22. Pope Paul VI, "*Nostra Aetate*: Declaration on the Relation of the Church to Non-Christian Religions," Second Vatican Council (October 28, 1965). https://www.vatican.va/archive/hist_councils/ii_vatican_council/documents/vat-ii_decl_19651028_nostra-aetate_en.html.

> Permission is granted to those who are fought, because they have been wronged—and truly God is able to help them—who were expelled from their homes without right, only for saying, "Our Lord is God." Were it not for God's repelling people, some by means of others, monasteries, churches, synagogues, and mosques, wherein God's Name is mentioned much, would have been destroyed. And God will surely help those who help Him—truly God is Strong, Mighty. (Sura 22:39–40)

The Qur'an even acknowledges the Tanakh and the New Testament as genuine sources of divine revelation, while questioning Jewish and Christian interpretations of the revelation contained in these Scriptures:

> And they say, "Be Jews or Christians and you shall be rightly guided." Say, "Rather, [ours is] the creed of Abraham, a *hanif*, and he was not of the idolaters." Say, "We believe in God, and in that which was sent down unto us, and in that which was sent down unto Abraham, Ishmael, Isaac, Jacob, and the Tribes, and in what Moses and Jesus were given, and in what the prophets were given from their Lord. We make no distinction among any of them, and unto Him we submit." (Sura 2:135–136)

Furthermore, the Qur'an tolerates some religious pluralism without demanding conversion to Islam, so long as there is agreement of inner submission to the one God: "Truly those who believe, and those who are Jews, and the Christians, and the Sabeans—whosoever believes in God and the Last Day and works righteousness shall have their reward with their Lord. No fear shall come upon them, nor shall they grieve" (Sura 2:62). Admittedly, though there is but one God, who is the source of all revelation, in Islamic practice the Qur'an supersedes the earlier Scriptures insofar as these earlier traditions perpetuate certain errors about the nature of God and God's revelation. Nevertheless, the phrase "People of the Book" in the Qur'an serves as a unifying idea for reading the sacred Scriptures of Judaism, Christianity, and Islam, insofar as it refers to "the spiritual and physical descendants of the monotheistic faith of Abraham, whose faith is basic to all our faiths, and whose faith, as the Qur'an says, predates the Torah and the Gospel."[23]

Since Judaism and Christianity predate Islam, neither the Hebrew Bible nor the Christian New Testament contains an authoritative statement identifying its God with the God of the Qur'an. Still, the earliest Christians were Jews, whose primary Scripture was the Hebrew Bible. These early Christians,

---

23. Mahmoud Ayoub, "The Need for Harmony and Collaboration between Muslims and Christians," in *A Muslim View of Christianity: Essays on Dialogue by Mahmoud Ayoub*, ed. Irfan A. Omar (Maryknoll, NY: Orbis Books, 2007), 13.

while eventually expelled for heresy, worshiped in the synagogue and the temple in Jerusalem and saw no conflict between the God of Abraham, Moses, and the prophets and the God revealed in the life, ministry, death, and resurrection of Jesus of Nazareth, whose words and deeds they interpreted through the lens of the Hebrew Bible.

Therefore, despite a long and troubled history of Christian anti-Semitism, the argument can be made that rabbinic Judaism and Christianity are distinct but related religions emerging from the fertile soil of biblical Judaism. Jewish scholar Daniel Boyarin understands rabbinic Judaism and Christianity "as points on a continuum—many gradations that provided social and cultural mobility from one end of the spectrum to the other," and argues that a comparative analysis of early Jewish and Christian practices demonstrates that "there was much more contact between the Rabbis and the Christians long after these contacts are held to have ceased."[24]

Today, despite continuing tensions between all three Abrahamic religions—complicated by multiple geopolitical factors—there exists genuine commitment to dialogue and cooperation among the leaders and practitioners of Judaism, Christianity, and Islam. The "Dabru Emet" (2000) statement, a Jewish document acknowledging recent conciliatory statements from the Christian churches, begins with this unequivocal proposition: "Jews and Christians worship the same God."[25] This statement, along with the similar proclamation by Muslim leaders from around the world, "A Common Word between Us and You" (2007),[26] validates the belief that despite differences in theology and worship, Judaism, Christianity, and Islam believe and worship the same God. These scholarly statements are indicative of widely held opinions across the three Abrahamic religions, as demonstrated by the growing number of signatories and endorsements from within Judaism, Christianity, and Islam.

Validating the work of the Scriptural Reasoning movement, both statements conclude that it is through the mutual love of God and love of neighbor articulated in the sacred Scriptures of all three religions that genuine interfaith cooperation can take place: "Although justice and peace are finally God's, our joint efforts, together with those of other faith communities, will help bring the kingdom of God for which we hope and long. Separately and together, we

---

24. Daniel Boyarin, *Dying for God: Martyrdom and the Making of Christianity and Judaism* (Stanford, CA: Stanford University Press, 1999), 8, 19.

25. National Jewish Scholars Project, "Dabru Emet: A Jewish Statement on Christians and Christianity," Jewish Christian Relations: Insights and Issues in Ongoing Jewish-Christian Dialogue (July 2002). https://www.jcrelations.net/article/dabru-emet-a-jewish-statement-on-christians-and-christianity.pdf.

26. The Royal Aal al-Bayt Institute for Islamic Thought, "The ACW Letter: A Common Word between Us and You," Jordan (2007). http://www.acommonword.com/the-acw-document/.

must work to bring justice and peace to our world. In this enterprise, we are guided by the vision of the prophets of Israel" ("Dabru Emet"). And according to "A Common Word," while "Islam and Christianity are obviously different religions—and whilst there is no minimising some of their formal differences—it is clear that the Two Greatest Commandments are an area of common ground and a link between the Qur'an, the Torah and the New Testament."

The approach of Scriptural Reasoning as a model for interfaith dialogue is distinguished by small gatherings of Jews, Christians, and Muslims who come together to read each other's sacred Scriptures. The "practice convenes conversations around texts that stand at the center of these three Abrahamic religious traditions, and thus brings particular religious points of view into engagement with one another, without the dynamics of dialogue eroding or dissolving such differences."[27] Admittedly, this model of comparative theology has come under criticism for glossing over doctrinal differences for the sake of interfaith harmony: "If all religions were to drop their most fundamental unique insights into the nature of reality so as not to cause offence to those who had different views, interreligious dialogue would cease!"[28] Others see the movement as an offshoot of postliberal theology (George Lindbeck) that "eschews liberal attempts to speak to audiences beyond its hermeneutic base in Scripture" while standing within the tradition of American pragmatism (John Dewey, Richard Rorty, Jeffrey Stout).[29] To suggest that postliberal theology, at least as conceived by George Lindbeck in *The Nature of Doctrine* (1984), deliberately avoids speaking to "audiences beyond its hermeneutic base in scripture" misrepresents Lindbeck's project.

First, Lindbeck's presentation of the cultural-linguistic analysis of religion, a widespread social-science approach to the study of religion, is a constructive proposal about the nature of human religions as shared conceptual frameworks that facilitate interreligious dialogue, not a myopic point of view that "merely reflect[s] back the horizons of the community . . . in self-affirmation."[30] Second, as a model intended to foster ecumenical and interfaith dialogue, Lindbeck's postliberal theology does not advocate a more divided sectarian reality.

---

27. Darren Sarisky, "Religious Commitment in Scriptural Reasoning: A Critical Engagement with Gavin D'Costa's 'Catholics Reading the Scripture of Other Religions,'" *Modern Theology* 36, no. 2 (April 2020): 318–19.

28. Gavin D'Costa, "The Trinity in Interreligious Dialogues," in *The Oxford Handbook of the Trinity*, ed. Gilles Emery and Matthew Levering (Oxford: Oxford University Press, 2011), 576. Also see Jon D. Levenson, "How Not to Conduct Jewish-Christian Dialogue," *Commentary* 112, no. 5 (December 2001): 31–37.

29. Gary Slater, "Scriptural Reasoning and the Ethics of Public Discourse," *American Journal of Theology and Philosophy* 38, nos. 2–3 (May-September 2017): 123.

30. Anthony C. Thiselton, *New Horizons in Hermeneutics: The Theory and Practice of Transforming Biblical Reading* (Grand Rapids: Zondervan, 1992), 410.

Rather, it ought to be seen as embracing religious difference and encouraging conversation among the world's religions: "In short, while a cultural-linguistic approach does not issue a blanket endorsement of the enthusiasm and warm fellow-feelings that can be easily promoted in an experiential-expressive context, it does not exclude the development of powerful theological rationales for sober and practically efficacious commitment to interreligious discussion and cooperation."[31]

In Jewish, Christian, and Muslim thought, articulating a comparative theology through the process of scriptural reasoning uncovers shared themes among the three Abrahamic religions. Such topoi prove reliable and trustworthy *because* they originate in sacred Scripture, the primary source of divine revelation. The hypothesis presented here—arguing for revelational coherence across the three Abrahamic traditions—might sometimes rest on strained textual readings, but only from necessity, to move the discipline of theology out from behind confessional walls. Recognizing that all our theological and ethical systems are socially constructed, religious traditions cannot keep asserting that their point of view is a direct, unmediated revelation from God, while avoiding the scrutiny of rational critique. Belief in one God necessarily implies one of two things: either affirming that the God of Judaism, Christianity, and Islam is one and the same God, or a dangerous return to labeling one another idolaters and infidels and then using coercion to convert or silence opponents. A guiding axiom of this investigation is the belief that the latter option is no longer tenable because it is inconsistent with belief in the one true God—the God of love and compassion revealed in the sacred Scriptures of Judaism, Christianity, and Islam.

It is more productive to engage in comparative theological discourse where there already exist multiple shared norms, as is the case with the three Abrahamic religions and their desire to establish social and economic justice. As articulated in the "Dabru Emet" statement, working toward justice and peace in cooperation with other faith communities "will help bring the kingdom of God for which we hope and long," which "A Common Word" says provides "an area of common ground and a link between the Qur'an, the Torah and the New Testament." The recognition that faith leads to concrete moral action is shared by all three Abrahamic religions and finds its genesis in the religion of the Hebrew Bible, especially the admonitions of the prophets, who equated genuine worship of YHWH with maintaining just social relations: "What does the LORD require of you but to do justice, and to love kindness, and to walk humbly with your God?" (Mic. 6:8).

---

31. Lindbeck, *The Nature of Doctrine*, 41.

The biblical witness, originating in the Hebrew Bible but encompassing the Christian New Testament and the Muslim Qur'an, views creation as an act of divine grace that values humanity as creatures intended to live in covenant with God. As an act of grace, the gift of life is unmerited; the value of humanity as God's creatures is thus independent of our physical and mental abilities or current social status. Theologically speaking, the value and dignity of every human life originates in the act of creation and can never be lost or taken away. Accordingly, this foundational fact prescribes how humankind, as image and likeness of God, must treat one another.

While many theologians and ethicists have emphasized God's work of historical liberation, as in the exodus narrative, or the divine imperative for justice, as in the prophetic and Deuteronomic traditions, another constant theme found in the scriptural testimony about the one true God is God's abounding compassion. Consistently, this compassion manifests in love toward the enemy, whether in YHWH's rebuke of the prophet Jonah for desiring the death of all Nineveh's inhabitants (Jonah 4:11), despite Jonah's knowing that God is "a gracious God and merciful, slow to anger, and abounding in steadfast love, and ready to relent from punishing" (Jonah 4:2), in Christ's commands to love the enemy and turn the other cheek (Matt. 5:39, 44), or in the instruction of Allah (who is called "the Compassionate, the Merciful") to treat others as you would your closest kin: "O you who believe! Be steadfast for God, bearing witness to justice, and let not hatred for a people lead you to be unjust. Be just; that is nearest to reverence. And reverence God. Surely God is aware of whatsoever you do" (Sura 5:8).

It is God's desire that humans live in peace with one another, and that God's justice as revealed in the sacred Scriptures—Tanakh, New Testament, or Qur'an—guide and instruct all human relations. These sustained biblical themes of liberation, justice, and compassion are sufficient to put into practice an interpretive norm for negotiating religious differences that engenders respect and tolerance without resorting to violence. Despite differences of interpretation as to how God's justice is defined and applied in all circumstances, even within the same confessional tradition, the sacred texts of all three Abrahamic religions are clear that God prefers life over death, justice over injustice, peace over strife, nonviolence over violence.

PACHYDERM PERAMBULATIONS

A comparative theology between the Abrahamic traditions is facilitated by the simple fact that it begins with shared cultural, linguistic, and even doctrinal norms. The kind of work John Thatamanil undertakes proves a bigger challenge. In *Circling the Elephant* (2020), Thatamanil embraces religious pluralism, affirms religious particularity, and celebrates—citing Abraham Joshua Heschel—that religious diversity is the will of God.[32] In other words, if the ultimate end of theology is to know the mystery of God better, then this mystery is not known by reducing all belief into a singular creed, but by encountering the divine in all its varied glory. This explains the central metaphor of Thatamanil's book, the admittedly overused Indian parable of the blind men and the elephant, often attributed to the Buddha (fifth century BCE) and found in Buddhist, Jain, and Hindu teaching.[33] Acknowledging that the allegory is problematic for a variety of reasons (especially in its depiction of blindness), Thatamanil still contends it a fruitful parable that enables the theologian to imagine diversity as a virtue.

The parable has been dismissed by some for implying that the sighted king has a superior vantage point from which to interpret the limited perspective of each blind man. As Thatamanil notes, this assumption—that one human being can see the whole of reality, while others have only limited perspectives—is particularly problematic when trying to employ the parable as a framework for discussing religious pluralism. Not only does the story privilege the abled, but it also reinforces troubling cultural hierarchies (e.g., the king representing the voice of wisdom). Nevertheless, a careful reading of the allegory supports the claim that the king is not asserting a superior vantage point, merely reinforcing the need for *all* religious traditions to acknowledge they have something to learn from the religious other, even when that other makes seemingly incompatible claims. As the story is preserved in Theravada Buddhism (the oldest school of Buddhist thought), the king reveals only part of the elephant to each blind man:

> To some of the blind people he presented the head of the elephant, saying, "This is an elephant." To some he presented an ear of the elephant, saying, "This is an elephant." To some he presented a tusk . . . the body . . . the foot . . . the hindquarters . . . the tail . . . the tuft at the end of the tail, saying, "This is an elephant."[34]

---

32. See Thatamanil, *Circling the Elephant*, 1.
33. The version I am familiar with can be found in the Pāli Canon, the standard collection of Scriptures in the Theravada Buddhist tradition, Buddhism's oldest existing school. See *Udana and the Itivuttaka: Two Classics from the Pali Canon*, ed. John D. Ireland, repr. ed. (Kandy, Sri Lanka: Buddhist Publication Society, 2007), 81–84.
34. *Udana and the Itivuttaka*, 83.

In the parable, the king *intentionally* keeps the whole of the elephant away from the blind men's touch, to produce multiple descriptions for the sake of a pedagogical point:

> Those blind people who had been shown the head of the elephant replied, "An elephant, your majesty, is just like a water jar." Those blind people who had been shown the ear of the elephant replied, "An elephant, your majesty, is just like a winnowing basket." Those blind people who had been shown the tusk of the elephant replied, "An elephant, your majesty, is just like a ploughshare." Those blind people who had been shown the trunk replied, "An elephant, your majesty, is just like a plough pole." Those blind people who had been shown . . . [etc., etc.][35]

According to this canonical version, the parable ends with wise words from the Buddha: "Some recluses and brahmins, so called, are deeply attached to their own views; People who see only one side of things engage in quarrels and disputes."[36] Understood as instruction on the limits of human points of view and the need to learn from the perspective of others, the parable reinforces that all religious views speak from a distinct location while also affirming its views as true, even if only partially so. As John Thatamanil contends, many interpretations of the story of the blind men and the elephant fail to recognize a central point of the parable, "namely, that each blindfolded person has true, albeit partial, knowledge of the elephant."[37]

John Thatamanil wrestles with the parable of the blind men and the elephant, despite its shortcomings, because it supports the goals of the comparative theologian by (1) affirming the limited vantage point of *every* religious tradition; (2) recognizing the truth (even if partial) in each religious tradition; (3) inviting all religious traditions to exercise humility, since no tradition can claim to have exhaustive knowledge of divine reality; and (4) acknowledging how divine self-revelation preserves the mystery of God by granting genuine, albeit partial, knowledge. Given that all religious perspectives are inherently shortsighted, that God reveals God's self in all religions, and that no single religious tradition can provide complete knowledge of the mysterious and infinite God, spiritual wisdom demands a certain kind of methodological humility and accompanying discursive practices that celebrate and embrace the religious other: "there is considerable promise in learning to think about

---

35. *Udana and the Itivuttaka*, 83.
36. *Udana and the Itivuttaka*, 84.
37. Thatamanil, *Circling the Elephant*, 8.

ultimate reality by way of conversation with other blindfolded persons, other valid, albeit partial, perspectives on ultimate reality."[38]

Thatamanil describes his contribution to comparative theology as "a *Christian* exercise in pachyderm perambulation," recognizing that we all inhabit our own limited religious point of view but affirming the need to undertake the journey around the elephant in interreligious cooperation for maximal understanding.[39] Yes, as a work of Christian theology, we "walk around the elephant with the guidance of others and learn from them . . . I see now that others' judgments are also warranted."[40] Growing in the realization that other descriptions of the elephant are themselves truthful and also originate from God, believers can affirm their version of ultimate reality as truth even if only partial truth open to the possibility that other versions of ultimate reality can correct and improve their own.[41]

The heart of *Circling the Elephant* is chapter 7, where Thatamanil offers a comparative and constructive exercise in trinitarian theology in dialogue with Hinduism and Buddhism. Secure in the knowledge that "my neighbors can often see me not only better than I can myself, but they are sometimes in a position to discern the limitations of my seeing,"[42] Thatamanil develops a pluralistic and inclusive theology of religious diversity that helps comprehend Christian trinitarian claims through an engagement of non-Christian religious traditions.

Accordingly, comparative theology embraces both religious particularity and religious pluralism, while defending a conception of religious truth that does not demand consensus but learns to embrace dissensus. Rather than exposing some epistemological shortcoming in comparative approaches, this tolerance of uncertainty in religious knowing originates in the very nature of God: "Ultimate reality is understood differently across traditions because these differences are rooted in the divine life itself."[43]

THE TRINITY AND RELIGIOUS PLURALISM

Theology is reflection on and speech about the unfathomable mystery (Gk. *mystērion*, meaning "a hidden or secret thing") we call God. As rational creatures we have a desire to know God, so we strive to understand this mystery.

---

38. Thatamanil, *Circling the Elephant*, 11.
39. Thatamanil, *Circling the Elephant*, 11 (emphasis in the original).
40. Thatamanil, *Circling the Elephant*, 11, 12.
41. See Thatamanil, *Circling the Elephant*, 12.
42. Thatamanil, *Circling the Elephant*, 12.
43. Thatamanil, *Circling the Elephant*, 18.

Yet, despite all our efforts, God's infinite mystery eludes us. Nevertheless, Christian theology does not speak about God in vague generalities, but dares speak concretely about God based on what is revealed in the sacred Scriptures of the Christian faith (the Hebrew Bible and the New Testament). Confronted by the mystery of a God who remains hidden—even in the act of divine self-revelation—Christian theology employs the doctrine of the Trinity to put into words the mystery of God's grace as revealed in the Christ who is present in the world by the power of the Holy Spirit. In other words, Christianity's distinctive grammar is inherently Trinitarian.

As with all theological constructs, Trinitarian doctrine proves inadequate at communicating the fullness of God, yet has become an integral part of the ecumenical creeds of the church because it has been deemed an appropriate—if, in the final analysis, incomplete—understanding of God as revealed and encountered in the Bible. The earliest Christian literature, the letters of Paul, employ explicitly Trinitarian liturgical language (2 Cor. 13:13), and Paul asserts that salvation for all people—Jew and Gentile—somehow involves all three members of the divine Trinity (Eph. 2:18). The concrete and particularly "Christian" way of speaking about the one true God references God the Father, Creator and sovereign over all creation; Jesus the Son, the Christ (Gk. *christos*, Hebrew *mashia*, meaning "anointed" or "anointed one") of God through whom sinful humanity is redeemed before God; and the Holy Spirit (Gk. *pneumatos hagiou*), by whose efforts God's revelation is received and the true God known (Mark 1:10; Matt. 3:16–17; Matt. 28:19; 1 John 5:7). At Jesus' baptism we encounter all three members of the Trinity at one time (Mark 1:9–11); before ascending to heaven Jesus explicitly commands his disciples to baptize in the name of the Father, the Son, and the Holy Spirit (Matt. 28:19); and John's Gospel also speaks of divine agency in terms of Father, Son, and Holy Spirit (John 14:26; 15:26; 16:13). As early as the second century, theologians like Irenaeus of Lyons (ca. 130–ca. 200 CE) employed Trinitarian language in presenting the *regula fidei* ("rule of faith") that undergirds the church's early creeds and preserves the preaching of the apostles that would eventually become canonized in Scripture:

> And this is the drawing-up of our faith, the foundation of the building and the consolidation of a way of life. God, the Father, uncreated, beyond grasp, invisible, one God the maker of all; all this is the first and foremost article of our faith. But the second article is the Word of God, the Son of God, Christ Jesus our Lord, who was shown forth by the prophets according to the design of their prophecy and according to the manner in which the Father disposed; and through Him were made all things whatsoever. . . . And the third article is the Holy Spirit, though whom the prophets

prophesied and the patriarchs were taught about God . . . and who in the end of times has been poured forth in a new manner upon humanity over all the earth renewing [humanity] to God.[44]

At first glance, it seems counterproductive to focus on the distinctly *Christian* language of God that accompanies these Trinitarian affirmations when articulating a comparative theology in conversation with Judaism and Islam. The religion of ancient Israel professed a radical monotheism: "Hear, O Israel: The LORD is our God, the LORD alone. You shall love the LORD your God with all your heart, and with all your soul, and with all your might" (Deut. 6:4–5). Rabbinic Judaism cites the authority of Moses Maimonides (1138–1204 CE) in condemning Trinitarian language for God: "Those who believe that God is One, and that He has many attributes, declare the unity with their lips, and assume plurality in their thoughts. This is like the doctrine of the Christians, who say that He is one and He is three, and that the three are one."[45] The Qur'an also questions Christianity's commitment to monotheism, considering its confessional statements about the divinity of Christ and the Trinitarian nature of God: "Say, 'He, God, is One, God, the Eternally Sufficient unto Himself, He begets not; nor was He begotten. And none is like unto Him'" (Sura 112:1–4). Without question, Judaism, Christianity, and Islam have serious disagreements over the nature of God. Yet, as theologian Robert Jenson has reasoned, the narrative contained in the Bible affirms that "God is whoever raised Jesus from the dead, having before raised Israel from Egypt."[46] Therefore, even though Christian "trinitarianism is commonly thought to depart from Israel's interpretation of God," Jenson argues the church proclaimed the doctrine of the Trinity in an effort to explain how and why the God of Israel "has prior to the general resurrection raised one of his servants from the dead."[47]

John Thatamanil stands within a Trinitarian revival of Christian advocates of religious pluralism like S. Mark Heim, Gavin D'Costa, and Raimundo Panikkar, who employ the doctrine of the Trinity to promote an inclusivist or pluralist position. According to Heim, the doctrine of the Trinity cultivates humility among Christian theologians by reminding them that the "fullness of God's mystery is never grasped by us. It is hidden in the Father and source,

---

44. St. Irenaeus, "Proof of the Apostolic Preaching," trans. Joseph P. Smith, vol. 16, *Ancient Christian Writers: The Works of the Fathers in Translation* (Westminster, MD: Newman Press, 1952), 51.

45. Moses Maimonides, *The Guide for the Perplexed*, rev. ed., trans. M. Friedländer (New York: Dover, 2000), 1:50, 68.

46. Robert W. Jenson, *Systematic Theology*, vol. 1, *The Triune God* (Oxford: Oxford University Press, 1997), 63.

47. Jenson, *Systematic Theology*, 63.

overflows in Christ beyond the measure of our means to receive it, and is continually active in all of creation through the Spirit."[48] Echoing Jenson, Heim also locates the earliest Christians within Judaism, worshiping the God of Israel while trying to make sense of what God is doing in the person of Jesus: "The Trinity is Christianity's 'pluralistic theology.' Its basis was set by the disciples' conviction that their encounter with Jesus could be correlated with the encounter with Israel's one God and with the new life they experienced within and among themselves as a result of Jesus."[49]

Thus, while Trinitarian language often obscures and confuses, it "tells us something true about God and also embodies the pattern of Christian conviction and experience."[50] Trinitarian theology affirms that the God of Israel is none other than who God is revealed to be in Christ and the Holy Spirit. Though the Latin terms "Trinity," "person," and "substance" were first used by the North African theologian Tertullian (ca. 160–ca. 225 CE), the naming of God as triune is part of the conceptual framework of the New Testament: "Baptismal and eucharistic invocation of the triune name, 'Father, Son, and Holy Spirit,' and prayer in the defining Christian pattern, to the Father with the Son in the Spirit, were the substance of the church's worshiping from the beginning."[51] The basic Trinitarian orthodoxy achieved at the Council of Constantinople (381 CE) states that God exists as three persons in one nature (*mia ousia, treis hypostaseis*): the one God exists as Father, Son, Spirit. Still, the Cappadocian fathers insisted that God is never fully comprehended by human reason or language; at most, theology can speak about what God is for us in the economy of salvation (Gk. *oikonomia*, meaning "household management")—to speak about the mystery of God is possible because of God's self-revelation—but such God-talk is at best analogical. The economy discloses *that* and *how* God is but not the fullness of *what* God is.

Thatamanil agrees that "the trinity is a natural Christian way to speak about diversity in the divine life," and "by acknowledging distinction within the divine life, Christians can account for substantial differences among the world's religions."[52] Yet he is also worried that Christians will employ Trinitarian doctrine as yet another form of Christian exclusivism.

Consequently, Christian pluralists must avoid presenting the Trinity as a "universal solution to questions of religious diversity."[53] Therefore, Christian

---

48. S. Mark Heim, *Salvations: Truth and Difference in Religion* (Maryknoll, NY: Orbis Books, 1995), 167.
49. S. Mark Heim, *The Depth of the Riches: A Trinitarian Theology of Religious Ends* (Grand Rapids: Eerdmans, 2001), 133.
50. Heim, *The Depth of the Riches*, 131.
51. Robert Jenson, "Jesus in the Trinity," *Pro Ecclesia* 8, no. 3 (Summer 1999): 310.
52. Thatamanil, *Circling the Elephant*, 214, 215.
53. Thatamanil, *Circling the Elephant*, 215.

theologians must resist "the temptation to assert that whereas other traditions offer a monolithic account of divine life, Christian trinitarianism, by contrast, is encompassing and polyphonic; Christians see the whole whereas others see only in part."[54]

Accordingly, Thatamanil encourages and seeks mutuality in comparative discourse and challenges Christian theologies of religious pluralism to approach other traditions with a willingness to think doctrines anew, even the Trinity. To that end, Thatamanil undertakes a comparative theology with Hinduism and Buddhism that reimagines the divine life. Thatamanil achieves this by approaching the Trinity as "a question and a problem rather than as a transparent dogmatic dictum."[55]

Before espousing any one intra-Christian Trinitarian formulation over another, a genuinely comparative theology uses the diversity within the divine life that Trinitarian doctrine attempts to capture as a *starting point* for theological reflection in conversation with other religions. John Thatamanil identifies precedents for this within Christian theology, specifically the Augustinian tradition of *vestigio trinitatis* ("traces of the Trinity"). He also suggests that the Christian tradition has already employed Trinitarian doctrine as a means of navigating religious pluralism, invoking Gregory of Nyssa (ca. 335–ca. 395 CE).[56]

Finally, Thatamanil encourages Christians to expose central doctrines like the Trinity to interreligious scrutiny in an act of "spiritual vulnerability," asserting that it is only through this kind of encounter with the religious other—in which we open our core beliefs to correction from non-Christian sources—that we can "be fully and truly Christian."[57] To that end, Thatamanil engages in reflection on divine plurality through a Trinitarian framework that is not explicitly Christian, but draws upon the vestiges of Trinitarian thought in non-Christian religions, in this case Hindu and Buddhist traditions, to conceptualize divinity, or ultimately reality, as relationality. Or, as Thatamanil so eloquently states, "This is just one Christian theologian's venture at redescribing the elephant after a series of forays into Buddhist and Hindu traditions."[58]

Returning to the central image of the blind men and the elephant, Thatamanil proceeds like a naturalist observing and recording all he encounters, but instead of describing flora and fauna in exhaustive detail he describes human experiences that disclose the trinitarian structure of reality itself. If, as Christianity asserts, ultimate reality is disclosed via Trinitarian

---

54. Thatamanil, *Circling the Elephant*, 215.
55. Thatamanil, *Circling the Elephant*, 216.
56. See Thatamanil, *Circling the Elephant*, 216.
57. Thatamanil, *Circling the Elephant*, 217.
58. Thatamanil, *Circling the Elephant*, 220.

relationships inherent to the divine nature, evidence of this Trinity ought to be available to human experience and traces found within the natural order itself.

Thatamanil tests this hypothesis via an admittedly selective phenomenological reading of Hindu, Christian, and Buddhist traditions and what they have to say about divinity. Beginning with a pervasive existential question about the nature of reality—"Why is there something rather than nothing?"—Thatamanil reflects on being and God as the ground of being to identify two affirmations made by both the Hindu and Buddhist traditions that resonate with Western Christian ontology: "Anything that is, exists because either it has a share in being-itself or because it just is being itself, which is divine."[59] The second affirmation incorporates humanity and human experience within the divine life itself: "our awareness of being, indeed awareness itself, is itself also divine."[60]

Building on a phenomenological description that transcends confessional particularity, Thatamanil affirms being as an aspect of divine reality, then identifies being with the first person of the Trinity (God the Father), not as other Christian theologians have done by appealing to Christian sources, but through a reading of the Upanishads and the Advaita Vedanta. In Hinduism, *Brahman* refers to the ultimate reality underlying all phenomena, describing the infinite and eternal truth that does not change, yet is the cause of all changes.[61]

Thatamanil is indebted to Sankara, who understood Brahman as being, with all reality merely a transformation of Brahman itself: "Just as clay pots, jars, cups, and the like are ultimately nothing but modifications of one lump of clay, so the world is ultimately nothing but Brahman. The world emerges from undifferentiated being-itself, and that is Brahman."[62] At the same time, Brahman is also always unchangeable and immutable, the ground of all being. Accordingly, the human experience of Brahman contains within it two conflicting realities held in tension, wherein we experience reality as contingent, in flux, and transitory, while always aware of the ever-present and unchanging reality of being itself.

This Hindu philosophical tradition shares conceptual and experiential commonalities with Western metaphysics, as made evident by the ancient Greek schools of thought identified earlier in the book as the Heraclitian, which viewed ultimate reality as always in change, and the Platonic, which viewed ultimate reality as immutable and unchanging. The inherent tension between these two phenomenological "intuitions" persists, even with the

---

59. Thatamanil, *Circling the Elephant*, 224.
60. Thatamanil, *Circling the Elephant*, 224.
61. See Jeaneane D. Fowler, *Perspectives of Reality: An Introduction to the Philosophy of Hinduism* (Brighton, UK: Sussex Academic Press, 2002), 49–55, 246–48, 252–55.
62. Thatamanil, *Circling the Elephant*, 224–25.

rise of the scientific method and antimetaphysical thinking, as evidenced by John Polkinghorne's claim that modern science can be viewed as an interplay between chance and necessity, reflecting the same underlying tension Thatamanil identifies in Brahman between the unchangeable immutability of Brahman as the ground of all being and the human experience of the impermanence of all beings-in-the world as differentiations within Brahman.

Thatamanil's interpretation of the Advaita Vedanta intersects my own work—and complements the goals of a comparative theology—in emphasizing Sankara's assertion that "Brahman is ineffable and beyond language and thought."[63] Granted, Brahman as described in Sankara's reading of the Upanishads differs greatly from classical theism, yet in emphasizing Brahman as the ground of being, the Advaita Vedanta school of Hindu thought shares much with the speculative theology and philosophy of influential thinkers within the Abrahamic traditions like Pseudo-Dionysius, Thomas Aquinas, Ibn Sina, Moses Maimonides, Martin Luther, Søren Kierkegaard, Martin Buber, Bernard Lonergan, Paul Tillich, and David Tracy.

According to Thatamanil, Sankara recognizes that even to speak about differentiation and singularity within Brahman reflects the perspective of the subjective self as locus of consciousness, since "to name Brahman as ground . . . is not the final truth about Brahman."[64] Here there are similarities with the critique of classical theism of Paul Tillich, who contends that even in revelation God remains mystery:

> Revelation is the manifestation of what concerns us ultimately. The mystery which is revealed is of ultimate concern to us because it is the ground of our being. In the history of religion revelatory events always have been described as shaking, transforming, demanding, significant in an ultimate way. They derive from divine sources, from the power of that which is holy and which therefore has an unconditional claim on us. Only that mystery which is of ultimate concern for us appears in revelation.[65]

According to Sankara, human beings are the locus of Brahman, yet Brahman is forever beyond our full comprehension or even our capacity to adequately name; thus it always remains unknowable mystery: "Language inevitably breaks down because even a discourse of Brahman as being is rooted in the character of Brahman as source of being to beings. That is why Sankara's discourse takes, in the final analysis, an apophatic turn."[66] The

---

63. Thatamanil, *Circling the Elephant*, 226.
64. Thatamanil, *Circling the Elephant*, 227.
65. Paul Tillich, *Systematic Theology* (Chicago: University of Chicago Press, 1951), 1:110.
66. Thatamanil, *Circling the Elephant*, 227.

lesson to be learned from Sankara is that rather than drawing our attention to the human particularity within which Brahman is embodied—or dare I say, incarnated?—he guides his students by asserting the path of wisdom lies in focusing on being itself rather than on the *particular* and *individualized* being of things.

John Thatamanil then argues that the question of being and ultimate reality as the ground of being also preoccupies Buddhist thought, especially the Tibetan Buddhist traditions that debate the meaning of emptiness (*sunyata*) in deciding whether ultimate reality is foundational or relational. While Thatamanil recognizes many Buddhists will be uncomfortable with his analysis of these debates, as in the comparison of the Western apophatic tradition with the Hindu Advaita Vedanta school, Thatamanil concludes that many Buddhist traditions share a similar intuition about the nature of reality as containing an inherent and unresolvable tension. Thatamanil suggests that within Buddhism there is warrant for the claim that the Buddha-self is analogous to Brahman insofar as the Buddha-nature is the source of all experience.[67]

While Paul Tillich remains trapped within many of the conceptual constraints of classical theism—for example, despite arguing that it is more accurate to say God does not exist insofar as God is not one being among others but is the ground of all being, he then asserts that "the relation of the ground of revelation to those who receive revelation can be conceived *only* in personal categories; for that which is the ultimate concern of a person cannot be less than a person although it can be and must be more than personality"[68]—Thatamanil nevertheless argues that Tillich's critique of classical theism serves as the best bridge for a Christian engagement of Hindu and Buddhist traditions. While Thatamanil dismisses Tillich's insistence that divinity (ultimate concern, ground of being) be conceived *only* in personal categories (e.g., I-Thou relationships), he contends that Tillich's critique of Christian theism resonates with both Hindu and Buddhist traditions. Tillich acknowledges that the language of personality leads Christian thought to conceive of God/Ultimate Reality as a being among beings, or as first cause in a very long chain of causal relations, so he employs the language of "ground of being" as a corrective, for "the ground of revelation is neither a cause which keeps itself at a distance from revelatory effect nor a substance which effuses itself into the effect, but rather the mystery which appears in revelation and which remains a mystery in its appearance."[69]

---

67. See Thatamanil, *Circling the Elephant*, 231. Thatamanil cites the work of Dolpopa (1292–1361 CE), referenced in Douglas Duckworth, *Mipam on Buddha-Nature: The Ground of the Nying-ma Tradition* (Albany: SUNY Press, 2008), 59.
68. Tillich, *Systematic Theology*, 1:156.
69. Tillich, *Systematic Theology*, 1:156.

At the same time, Tillich defends the objective reality of the revelatory event, despite its inherently intersubjective character: "Revelation always is a subjective and an objective event in strict interdependence. Someone is grasped by the manifestation of the mystery; this is the subjective side of the event. Something occurs through which the mystery of revelation grasps someone; this is the objective side. These two sides cannot be separated. If nothing happens objectively, nothing is revealed."[70] According to Thatamanil, this interdependence is so entwined with the conception of divinity as ground of being that Tillich's theology comes quite close to the nondualism of both Hindu and Buddhist tradition. Paul Tillich embraces the open-ended and provisional status of all dogmatic claims, which is why he prefers symbolic and mythical language as the medium for communicating divine revelation: "Nothing less than symbols and myths can express our ultimate concern."[71]

For Tillich, myth and symbol are the proper medium for faith because human language fails to adequately represent our ultimate concern and ground of all being. This impacts Trinitarian thought by blurring the distinction between creaturely existence and God as ground of being, since all relationships exist within and participate in the divine life: "All relations are present beyond the distinctions between potentiality and actuality. But they are not the relations of the divine life with something else. They are the inner relations of the divine life."[72] Echoing the transpersonal accounts of ultimate reality in Buddhism and Hinduism, Tillich concludes that the Christian "doctrine of creation affirms that God is the creative ground of everything in every moment. In this sense there is no creaturely independence from which an external relation between God and the creature could be derived."[73]

The path of comparative theology is always in progress and open ended, its task never completed. Returning to the central metaphor of his book, John Thatamanil reminds the reader that "if the elephant itself stands in for the infinite, how could we ever complete the circle, that circle whose center is everywhere and whose circumference is nowhere?"[74] Therefore, if the object of theological reflection is infinite mystery, there is no destination apart from the journey itself. Divine self-revelation "stands in interdependence with our searching, the seeker and the sought so bound together that we might even imagine that not just knowledge of the elephant but the elephant herself grows as we seek and know her."[75]

---

70. Tillich, *Systematic Theology*, 1:111.
71. Paul Tillich, *Dynamics of Faith*, repr. (Grand Rapids: Zondervan, 2001), 53.
72. Tillich, *Systematic Theology*, 1:271.
73. Tillich, *Systematic Theology*, 1:271.
74. Thatamanil, *Circling the Elephant*, 249.
75. Thatamanil, *Circling the Elephant*, 249.

Thatamanil's book, *Circling the Elephant*, ought to be read as a sustained argument against religious insularism and dogmatic exclusivism. Yet, rather than leading to a muddled pluralism or contentious relativism, Thatamanil argues for doctrinal polyphony by appealing to the Trinitarian mystery that understands divinity as relationality, not only within the intra-Trinitarian relations, but also in the economy of salvation where humanity—in Christ—participates in the divine life. The patristic concept of *perichoresis* used to describe the interrelationships between each person of the triune God as oneness in differentiation, is extended to the fellowship of the Christian community via the mediating grace of Jesus Christ: "As you, Father, are in me and I am in you, may they also be in us, so that the world may believe that you have sent me" (John 17:21). What results is a conception of God that can accommodate other persons into the divine life without undermining God-ness. Both Eastern and Western Christianity agree that God is not known because God can be "objectified" by human cognitive powers. Rather, we know God because God grants believers what they cannot attain on their own: knowledge of God made possible by God's grace enabling human participation in the divine reality through communion with God, the Father, Son, and Holy Spirit.

John Thatamanil pushes this Trinitarian paradigm to encompass all of humanity, not just confessing Christians, based on Christian doctrine about the primacy of love, which demands vulnerability and openness to the other—even the religious other: "If I am to move ever more fully into the divine life, I must move toward my neighbor in receptivity and love. No pilgrimage to God apart from a pilgrimage toward the holiness of my neighbor."[76] In concrete terms, God's gift of participation in the triune life is not random but purposeful. God lives with us in order that we may live with God. Consequently, to know God means knowing God's will for us, which implies that how we as a Christian community (*koinōnia*) order our life is not left to chance.

Mohandas Gandhi, who read Jesus' Sermon on the Mount daily, considered Jesus a *satyagrahi* (someone who practices nonviolent resistance). Gandhi, in turn, influenced Martin Luther King Jr.'s nonviolent resistance, demonstrating how Christians gain a better understanding of Christ from their engagement with Hinduism. Accordingly, "Jesus's death on the cross cannot be severed from his preaching and teaching of enemy love. . . . Christians are now called to follow Jesus the satyagrahi."[77] Because the elephant transcends all efforts to know the elephant, we benefit from circling the elephant in dialogue and cooperation with others, for in knowing how the other names the

---

76. Thatamanil, *Circling the Elephant*, 251.
77. Thatamanil, *Circling the Elephant*, 253.

elephant, we not only gain additional truth, but also enrich the understanding of our own tradition by seeing it anew from the perspective of the other.

A FRAGMENT OF THEOLOGY: THE NEGATIVE WAY OF PSEUDO-DIONYSIUS

While there is a tendency to describe spirituality as the human desire to seek God, the Christian tradition speaks unequivocally when it says we come to know God because God first seeks us: "But the LORD God called to the man, and said to him, 'Where are you?'" (Gen. 3:9); "For the Son of Man came to seek out and to save the lost" (Luke 19:10); "The Lord is not slow about his promise, as some think of slowness, but is patient with you, not wanting any to perish, but all to come to repentance" (2 Pet. 3:9); "Work out your own salvation with fear and trembling; for it is God who is at work in you, enabling you both to will and to work for his good pleasure" (Phil. 2:12b–13). Consequently, God is a mystery that is known—but never *fully* known.

The great sages of Christianity value humility above all else, and caution against making sweeping authoritative statements when describing the ineffable mystery of God. Yet, even saying, "God is ineffable," creates a contradiction, since that which is ineffable cannot be spoken. Therefore, Augustine advised, "This contradiction is to be passed over in silence rather than resolved verbally. For God, although nothing worthy may be spoken of him, has accepted the tribute of human voice and wished us to take joy in praising him with our words."[78]

Philosopher and closeted mystic Ludwig Wittgenstein articulated a similar sentiment in the enigmatic closing words of his *Tractatus Logico-Philosophicus* (1921): "What we cannot speak about we must pass over in silence."[79] Earlier in the same volume Wittgenstein writes, "It is not how things are in the world that is mystical, but that it exists."[80] Wittgenstein's primary goal in the *Tractatus* is to mark the limits of human language and thought as a strategy for resolving philosophical problems, but a secondary and equally important goal is to help us see how little is gained by reducing knowledge to that which is linguistically "meaningful." A generous reading of Wittgenstein suggests that he did not dismiss religious claims as nonsensical. Rather, he argued that human beings are burdened with questions about transcendence and spirituality that cannot

---

78. Augustine of Hippo, *On Christian Doctrine*, trans. D. W. Robertson Jr. (New York: Macmillan, 1958), 11.
79. Ludwig Wittgenstein, *Tractatus Logico-Philosophicus*, trans. D. F. Spears and B. F. McGuinness, repr. (London: Routledge Classics, 2001), 89.
80. Wittgenstein, *Tractatus Logico-Philosophicus*, 88.

be resolved by empirical science. For Wittgenstein, "Christianity is not a doctrine, not, I mean, a theory about what has happened and will happen to the human soul, but a description of something that actually takes place in human life."[81] Wittgenstein recognized that faith "could only be (something like) passionately committing oneself to a system of co-ordinates," which, "although it's belief, it is really a way of living, or a way of judging life."[82] Which is why Paul Tillich's assertion, "God does not exist,"[83] while unsettling to some, is not an affirmation of atheism nor a denial of the reality of God. Echoing the apophatic theology of Pseudo-Dionysius, Tillich claims that "to argue that God exists is to deny him," and concludes that "it is as atheistic to affirm the existence of God as it is to deny it."[84]

It would be a mistake to lump Paul Tillich (1886–1965)—a German Lutheran theologian best known for defying Hitler's rise to power in 1933 (eventually removed from his tenured position by the Nazi regime, forcing his emigration to the United States) and for writing books for general audiences about complex issues of theology and culture, such as *The Courage to Be* (1952) and *Dynamics of Faith* (1957)—with "death of God" theology or even postmodern a/theology.[85] Tillich affirms the reality of God.

He is also not the first Christian theologian to see the necessity of making the claim that God does not "exist." Pseudo-Dionysius, historically identified with Dionysius the Areopagite, a first-century Athenian convert of the apostle Paul (Acts 17:16–34), was a fifth- or sixth-century theologian and Neoplatonic philosopher who wrote under the pseudonym of Dionysius; his theological methodology embraced both cataphatic (positive) and apophatic (negative) approaches that heavily influenced medieval Christianity. Like Tillich, Pseudo-Dionysius insisted that God—while the ground and source of being—is not a being among other beings. Pseudo-Dionysius emphasized the absolute transcendence of God in order to demonstrate the limits of human knowing and to emphasize the dependence of all creation on the Creator by affirming that everything—from the angelic hierarchy of heaven to plants and animals to "soulless and lifeless matter"—exists "because of the Good; through it

---

81. Ludwig Wittgenstein, *Culture and Value*, ed. G. H. von Wright, trans. Peter Winch, repr. of rev. ed. (Chicago: University of Chicago Press, 1984), 28.
82. Wittgenstein, *Culture and Value*, 73.
83. Tillich, *Systematic Theology*, 1:205.
84. Tillich, *Systematic Theology*, 1:205, 237.
85. See Thomas J. J. Altizer and William Hamilton, *Radical Theology and the Death of God* (New York: Penguin, 1966); Gabriel Vahanian, *The Death of God: The Culture of Our Post-Christian Era*, repr. ed. (Eugene, OR: Wipf & Stock, 2009); Mark C. Taylor, *Erring: A Postmodern A/theology* (Chicago: University of Chicago Press, 2013).

they received their state of existence."[86] Thus, while it is proper to speak of God as "being," human language for God—that is, all theology—does not "reveal that being in its transcendence, for this is something beyond words, something unknown and wholly unrevealed," which is why Pseudo-Dionysius characterizes his theological treatise on the divine names as "a hymn of praise for the being-making procession of the absolute divine Source of being into the total domain of being."[87]

In other words, when confronted with the ineffable and infinite source of all being, the most adequate response is either contemplative silence or devout praise, not philosophical babbling, because "the divine name 'Good' tells of all the processions of the universal Cause; it extends to beings and nonbeings and that cause is superior to being and nonbeings."[88] Accordingly, it is accurate to say that God does not "exist," insofar as God is not some individuated being—an object in the world—but is being itself, by which all that exists came to be, yet transcends all that exists: "The name 'Being' extends to all beings which are, and it is beyond them. The name of 'Life' extends to all living things, and yet is beyond them. The name 'Wisdom' reaches out to everything which has to do with understanding, reason, and sense perception and surpasses them all."[89]

Pseudo-Dionysius employs four names (Good, Being, Life, and Wisdom) to delineate what can and cannot be said about the eternal God, always certain to remind the reader that whatever is said of God refers to how God is known by humanity in God's self-revelation and does not (cannot!) capture the fullness of the transcendent God. Thus, the need to balance every positive true proposition about God with its negation, in order to acknowledge that while God provides us with true and reliable knowledge, God remains infinite mystery, and theological knowledge is never comprehensive, only partial, and "in a mirror, dimly" (1 Cor. 13:12). Therefore, when Pseudo-Dionysius affirms the divine transcendence beyond all that exists, it is accurate to say that the concept of "God" necessarily transcends existence, and so in some sense God does *not* exist. Yet it is not his intention to deny the reality of God.

Rather, Pseudo-Dionysius is making an important claim about human knowing and the possibility of speaking about the infinite God. Echoing many of the same tensions about the nature of Being found in both Brahman and the Buddha-nature, Pseudo-Dionysius describes ultimate reality as source and ground of all being: "For God is not some kind of being. No. But in a way that is simple and indefinable he gathers into himself and anticipates every

---

86. Pseudo-Dionysius, "The Divine Names," in *Pseudo-Dionysius: The Complete Works*, trans. Colm Luibheid, ed. and trans. Paul Rorem (New York: Paulist, 1987), IV.2, 73.
87. Pseudo-Dionysius, "The Divine Names," V.1, 96.
88. Pseudo-Dionysius, "The Divine Names," V.1, 96.
89. Pseudo-Dionysius, "The Divine Names," V.1, 96–97.

existence ... for in him and around him all being is and subsists."[90] In distinction from the personalism of classical theism, Pseudo-Dionysius also affirms the transpersonal nature of ultimate reality, like Advaita Vedanta and Tibetan Buddhism: "Being precedes the entities which participate in it. Being in itself is more revered than the being of Life itself and Wisdom itself and Likeness to divinity itself. Whatever beings participate in these things must, before all else, participate in Being. More precisely, those absolute qualities of which things have a share must themselves participate in being itself."[91] Therefore, "He is at rest and astir, is neither resting nor stirring and has neither source, nor middle nor end. He is nothing. He is no thing. The categories of eternity and of time do not apply to him, since he transcends both and transcends whatever lies between them. Eternity itself and beings and the measure of beings and the measured world exist through him and from him."[92]

Neither Pseudo-Dionysius nor Tillich is particularly concerned about the apologetic task of theology. Instead, both theologians are more interested in the mystical dimension of theological work, desiring to know the God beyond epistemology, the God known via the transcendent sacramental encounter, because experiential knowledge is truer to God's very nature. Given that humanity is alienated from God, in great part because of our own misguided desire for absolute freedom (symbolically communicated in the doctrine of fallenness and original sin), rational argumentation cannot satisfactorily overcome epistemological doubt. As Tillich contends, "The question of God is possible because an awareness of God is present in the question of God. The awareness precedes the question. It is not the result of the argument but its presupposition."[93] Whatever else we can say about God, God is "that being which is always present in human awareness," even amid our all-too-human human doubt, since "the Unconditional is the grounding certainty from which all doubt can proceed, but it can never itself be the object of doubt. Therefore the object of religion is not only real, but is also the presupposition of every affirmation of reality."[94]

Consequently, Tillich insists doubt is not the opposite of faith, and does not undermine faith, but is part and parcel of the journey of faith: "The affirmation that Jesus is the Christ is an act of faith and consequently of daring courage. It is not an arbitrary leap into darkness but a decision in which elements of immediate participation and therefore certitude are mixed with elements of strangeness and therefore incertitude and doubt. But doubt is not

---

90. Pseudo-Dionysius, "The Divine Names," V.4, 98.
91. Pseudo-Dionysius, "The Divine Names," V.5, 99.
92. Pseudo-Dionysius, "The Divine Names," V.10, 103.
93. Tillich, *Systematic Theology*, 1:206.
94. Paul Tillich, "The Philosophy of Religion," in *What Is Religion?* ed. James Luther Adams (New York: Harper & Row, 1969), 71.

the opposite of faith; it is an element of faith. Therefore, there is no faith without risk."[95] The theologian is, by definition, a believer. Whether or not the content of the theologian's faith is demonstrably true, the theologian is a person who "acknowledges the content of the theological circle as his ultimate concern. Whether this is true does not depend on the intensity and certitude of faith. . . . Rather, it depends on his being ultimately concerned with the Christian message even if he is sometimes inclined to attack and to reject it."[96]

Pseudo-Dionysius speaks of the "mysterious darkness of unknowing," wherein the believer surrenders will and rationality in contemplative worship as the highest form of knowing God: "renouncing all that the mind may conceive, wrapped entirely in the intangible and the invisible, he belongs to him who is beyond everything. Here, being neither oneself nor someone else, one is supremely united to the completely unknown by an inactivity of all knowledge, and knows beyond the mind by knowing nothing."[97] This mystical union with God is characterized by both a complete absence of speech and a complete absence of rational conceptualization: "If only we lacked sight and knowledge so as to see, so as to know, unseeing and unknowing, that which lies beyond all vision and knowledge."[98] While *cataphatic* theology—positive statements about divine reality—is possible and has its proper place, namely, when explicating divine self-revelation in the Trinitarian economy of salvation, *apophatic* theology—the attempt to know God in terms of what may *not* be said about the infinite God—is methodologically desirable to counteract the hubris of theological traditions that present their subjective and local interpretations as universal and authoritative.

The lesson to be learned from Thatamanil's comparative deep dive with Hinduism and Buddhism is reinforced by Christian theology itself, from Pseudo-Dionysius to Aquinas and from Martin Luther to Paul Tillich, by affirming the absolute transcendence and unknowability of the infinite God. Consequently, the proper attitude for the person of faith seeking to know God more deeply is humility, which manifests itself in an openness to other religious points of view and the desire to sojourn with the other to gain just a little more truth about the infinite goodness. Therefore, John Thatamanil calls for a Christian theology of religious pluralism that honors the infinite transcendence of God, while reinforcing the need for methodological humility in theological construction.

---

95. Paul Tillich, *Systematic Theology* (Chicago: University of Chicago Press, 1957), 2:116–17.
96. Tillich, *Systematic Theology*, 1:10.
97. Pseudo-Dionysius, "The Mystical Theology," in *Pseudo-Dionysius: The Complete Works*, I.3, 137.
98. Pseudo-Dionysius, "The Mystical Theology," II.1, 138.

7

The Myth of Materialism

> The world has proclaimed freedom, particularly of late, and yet what do we see in this freedom of theirs: nothing but servitude and suicide! For the world says: "You have needs, so satisfy them, for you have as much rights as the wealthiest and most highly placed of men. Do not be afraid to satisfy them, but even multiply them"—that is the present-day teaching of the world. In that, too, they see freedom. And what is the result of this right to the multiplication of needs? Among the rich solitariness and spiritual suicide, and among the poor—envy and murder, for while they have been given rights, they have not yet been afforded the means with which to satisfy their needs.[1]

Christianity has a history of conflict and confusion over material existence—and seems especially troubled by matters of the flesh and human embodiment in a material body—which can be traced to the encounter of the Hebraic worldview with Hellenic Platonism. The first major heresy to threaten the unity of the church was Marcionism, a dualistic system of thought originating in the teachings of Marcion of Sinope (ca. 85–ca. 160 CE) who taught that Jesus was sent by the true God, who is distinct from the cruel and vengeful God of Israel, who was responsible for creating the material world (as recounted in

---

1. Fyodor Dostoyevsky, *The Brothers Karamazov*, trans. David McDuff, rev. ed. (London: Penguin, 2003), 406.

the book of Genesis).[2] This rejection of material creation led to the rejection of God's incarnation in Christ, since material "flesh" is evil and has nothing to do with the true God or higher spiritual reality. As a consequence of this spirit-flesh duality, Marcion refused to recognize the Hebrew Scriptures (the Christian Old Testament) as canonical and authoritative for Christian faith. He also rejected the God found therein as a "Demiurge, not the God of love revealed by Christ . . . utterly superseded by the new law proclaimed by the Saviour."[3]

Marcion did not go to the extreme of Valentinian Gnosticism by identifying the Old Testament Demiurge with Satan, and he was even willing to recognize some spiritual merit in the Hebrew Bible, acknowledging that certain divine precepts (the Ten Commandments) contain truth and are perfected and fulfilled by the Christ (Matt. 5:17).[4] Nevertheless, he differentiated between the true God, "who had remained the unknown God until the coming of Jesus," and "the Creator of the universe, [who] was recognized on the basis of creation."[5] Marcion was eventually excommunicated by the church in Rome and then founded his own church, but according to Tertullian (ca. 160–ca. 225 CE) Marcion's biggest impact on Christianity was "the separation of the law and the gospel,"[6] which contributed to the unfortunate persistence of anti-Semitism within Christian thought.[7]

If Marcion tried to sever Hebraic thought from Christian faith, Alexandrian Judaism provides the mediating link between Palestinian Judaism and Greek Neoplatonism, given the importance of the Septuagint (LXX), the Greek translation of the Hebrew Scriptures, and the work of the Jewish mystic, biblical commentator, and philosopher Philo of Alexandria (ca. 30 BCE–ca. 45 CE). Philo, a Platonist, taught that God is utterly transcendent and thus cannot be included under any of the logical categories by which philosophers classify finite beings (an idea later embraced by the Christian Platonist Pseudo-Dionysius). Given this, how does the transcendent God interact with the world? Philo introduces a series of intermediate powers that are distinct from God yet carry out God's will in the world, with the highest of

---

2. See J. N. D. Kelly, *Early Christian Doctrines*, rev. ed. (San Francisco: HarperSanFrancisco, 1978), 52–79; Aloys Grillmeier, *Christ in the Christian Tradition*, vol. 1, *From the Apostolic Age to Chalcedon (451)*, 2nd rev. ed., trans. John Bowden (Atlanta: John Knox, 1975), 3–124.

3. Kelly, *Early Christian Doctrines*, 67.

4. Kelly, *Early Christian Doctrines*, 67.

5. Jaroslav Pelikan, *The Christian Tradition*, vol. 1, *The Emergence of the Catholic Tradition (100–600)* (Chicago: University of Chicago Press, 1971), 74.

6. Tertullian, "Against Marcion," cited in Pelikan, *The Christian Tradition*, 1:72.

7. See Samuel Loncar, "Christianity's Shadow Founder: Marcion, Anti-Judaism, and the Birth of Liberal Protestantism," *The Marginalia Review* (November 19, 2021). https://themarginaliareview.com/christianitys-shadow-founder-marcion-anti-judaism-and-the-birth-of-liberal-protestantism/.

these identified as the *Logos* (Gk. λόγος, meaning "word, speech, or reason"). Arguably, Philo is the first to identify the Logos as an agent of the biblical God in creating the universe, as well as claiming the Logos as the means by which humankind knows the transcendent God, though he is clearly influenced by the Stoic doctrine of the Logos as the universal reason that orders creation. As a student of Scripture, Philo harmonized Platonic philosophy with the Pentateuch, finding in the Bible justification for various Greek philosophical concepts. The Logos, the medium of God's providential activity in the world, is described by Philo as "the captain and steersman of the universe,"[8] so that by contemplating this Logos (the rational ordering of the universe) humankind comes to know the transcendent and infinite God.

In John's Gospel, as well as in second-century Christian apologetics, the Logos became identified with Jesus Christ. Furthermore, by declaring that "the Word became flesh and lived among us" (John 1:14), the "Gospel of John's account of the incarnation places flesh at the center of Christian corporeal imaginaries."[9] Nevertheless, despite this strong affirmation of human fleshliness, there remains within contemporary Christian thought a tendency to bifurcate the world into the spiritual and the material. Within Evangelical Christianity and Pentecostalism, the confusion over our material existence is compounded on the one hand by the prosperity gospel, which equates material well-being and success with spiritual blessing,[10] and on the other by the discomfort with human sexuality manifest as purity culture, which emphasizes sexual abstinence outside of marriage by supposedly maintaining biblical standards of "sexual purity."[11] In other words, many Christians today celebrate and indulge in material culture by viewing material wealth as proof of divine blessing, yet live alienated from their own embodied existence, promulgating a sexual ethic that equates self-worth with virginity and chastity and the physical sexual act with sinfulness.

Ironically, while espousing a body-flesh dualism, Evangelical purity culture—like the prosperity gospel—became enmeshed in the culture of materialism, generating a highly profitable industry selling purity rings, purity pledges (preprinted certificates), purity balls (in place of high school proms),

---

8. Philo of Alexandria, "On the Cherubim," cited in Kelly, *Early Christian Doctrines*, 11.
9. Mayra Rivera, *Poetics of the Flesh* (Durham, NC: Duke University Press, 2015), 17.
10. See Kate Bowler, *Blessed: A History of the American Prosperity Gospel* (Oxford: Oxford University Press, 2018), and Costi W. Hinn, *God, Greed, and the (Prosperity) Gospel: How Truth Overwhelms a Life Built on Lies* (Grand Rapids: Zondervan, 2019).
11. See Emily Joy Allison, *#ChurchToo: How Purity Culture Upholds Abuse and How to Find Healing* (Minneapolis: Broadleaf Books, 2021), and Linda Kay Klein, *Pure: Inside the Evangelical Movement That Shamed a Generation of Young Women and How I Broke Free* (New York: Simon & Schuster, 2019).

and even "purified" knock-off brands of popular clothing lines and fashion jewelry marketed at Evangelical Christians.[12]

Therefore, despite employing rhetoric of being set apart from the mainstream "secular" culture and purified by God, Evangelicalism and Pentecostalism in the United States—at least in terms of material consumption—differ little from the rest of North American Christianity. In polls conducted by the Pew Research Center, 58 percent of respondents who identify as "born again" Christians, be they Evangelical, Pentecostal, or charismatic, list *tithing* (giving at least a tenth of one's income to the church) as "essential for being a good evangelical Christian."[13] Yet, when compared to other Christian groups, Evangelicals, Pentecostals, and charismatics are just as likely to overstate their charitable giving. Across all Protestant denominations, including Evangelicals and Pentecostals, less than 25 percent of church members tithe (give one-tenth of their income), on average Christians give away only 2.5 percent of their income, and 37 percent of regular church attendees don't give any money to the church (these same studies show the gap between actual and perceived giving is even wider among Roman Catholics).[14]

To be fair, statistics show that people of faith in the United States tend to be more giving and charitable than the rest of the population, with Mormons and Evangelicals having the highest rates of charitable giving.[15] But the truth is that Christians in general do not give at the rate they profess to, especially when it comes to tithing. Whatever narratives Christians weave concerning their compassionate care for others, the sad reality is that they too are part of the culture of material consumerism. This raises questions as to whether Christianity can articulate an effective counternarrative to the dominant and overwhelming culture of consumerism and predatory capitalism.

---

12. See Jake Meador, "Purity as Branding in the Evangelical Sub-Culture," in *Mere Orthodoxy: A Christian Review of Ideas* (September 2, 2016). https://mereorthodoxy.com/purity-culture-branding/.

13. Pew Research Center, "Global Survey of Evangelical Leaders: Evangelical Beliefs and Practices," June 22, 2011, https://www.pewresearch.org/religion/2011/06/22/global-survey-beliefs/.

14. See "Church and Religious Charitable Giving Statistics," Nonprofits Source (2022 statistics). https://nonprofitssource.com/online-giving-statistics/church-giving/; Leonardo Blair, "Only 13% of Evangelicals Tithe, Half Give Away Less Than 1% of Income Annually: Study," *The Christian Post* (October 29, 2021). https://www.christianpost.com/news/only-13-of-evangelicals-tithe-study.html; and "Americans Seriously Overestimate Their Own Generosity," Grey Matter Research Consulting (May 25, 2017). https://greymatterresearch.com/generosity/.

15. Karl Zinsmeister, "Less God, Less Giving? Religion and Generosity Feed Each Other in Fascinating Ways," *Philanthropy Magazine* (Winter 2019). https://www.philanthropyroundtable.org/magazine/less-god-less-giving/.

WORD AND FLESH IN THE GOSPEL OF JOHN

In the mid-second century, Bishop Irenaeus of Lyons (ca. 130–ca. 200 CE) waged an intellectual war against Gnosticism over the competing claims each movement made about material existence. For Irenaeus, the affirmation of material existence as something good created by God and part of God's salvific plans had repercussions for both the embodied individual and the broader body politic: "The Gnostic struggle pushed him to distinguish Christianity's way of imagining the body (politic) as tied to Christ's flesh from Gnosticism's vision of the body . . . [with] Christology as the discursive site of negotiating the meaning of material existence."[16]

After a comparative study with the Valentinian *Gospel of Truth* and the "incipiently Gnostic" *Gospel of Thomas*, biblical scholar and commentator Raymond E. Brown (1928–1998) noted that while these same Gnostic ideas permeated the cultural context in which the Gospel of John was written, the canonical Gospel of John is considerably different from these Gnostic contemporaries, and found "the two Gospels far apart."[17] Brown also recognized that Hellenistic thought (Platonism, Stoicism, Philo of Alexandria) and Palestinian Judaism (Hebrew Bible, rabbinic Judaism, Qumran) are equally important sources for understanding John's Gospel. Therefore, contra twentieth-century biblical scholar Rudolf Bultmann, who argued that the Gospel of John is a Gnostic text,[18] I contend that the Gospel of John can be read as a polemic *against* the gnostic dualistic ontology that denigrated the flesh over against the Spirit.

The Gospel of John, while exhibiting some parallels with the Synoptic Gospels (Matthew, Mark, and Luke), is distinguished by a unique tradition recounting a series of miracles performed by Jesus, independent of the Synoptic tradition, that scholars have labeled the Book of Signs (John 1:19–12:50) or the *semeia* source (from the Greek σημεια, meaning "signs" or "miracles"). This collection of stories presents the public ministry of Jesus as a series of miracles intended to demonstrate his divine origin and unique mission. From the wedding at Cana (John 2:1–11) to the feeding of the five thousand (John 6:1–14), to the raising of Lazarus (John 11:1–44), the narrative arc of John's Gospel can be read as a divine celebration of embodied flesh, beginning with the incarnational claim that Jesus is God in the flesh living among us (John 1:14). Therefore, while these miracles are performed by the co-eternal Logos

---

16. J. Kameron Carter, *Race: A Theological Account* (Oxford: Oxford University Press, 2008), 11–12.

17. Raymond E. Brown, *The Gospel according to John (I–XII)*, Anchor Yale Bible Commentaries (New Haven, CT: Yale University Press, 2007), liii.

18. See Rudolf Bultmann, *Primitive Christianity in Its Contemporary Setting*, trans. R. H. Fuller (New York: New American Library, 1974).

of God, it is of utmost importance that the divine Logos *first* becomes flesh—valuing humanity in all its embodied messiness—and performs a series of miracles, each intended to meet some bodily need.

The Gospel of John begins with a prologue that directly invokes the opening verses of the book of Genesis, linking the protagonist of this story, Jesus of Nazareth, with the protagonist of the creation story, YHWH. Genesis begins with the words, "In the beginning when God created the heavens and the earth, the earth was a formless void and darkness covered the face of the deep, while a wind from God swept over the face of the waters" (Gen. 1:1–2), which is echoed in the opening verses of John's Gospel: "In the beginning was the Word, and the Word was with God, and the Word was God. He was in the beginning with God" (John 1:1–2). The author of John's Gospel goes to great lengths to make sure the reader knows that the Word (Logos) was there in the beginning. If there are any questions about the Word's identity, he clears them up for us: "the Word was God" (John 1:1).

Furthermore, this seemingly eternal Word was more than a mere spectator during the act of creation. Just as YHWH calls things into existence merely by speaking (one of the meanings of the Greek word λόγος)—"Then God said, 'Let there be light'; and there was light" (Gen. 1:3)—the Word/Logos is directly connected with YHWH's act of creation in John's Gospel: "All things came into being through him, and without him not one thing came into being. What has come into being in him was life, and the life was the light of all people" (John 1:3–4). In case the reader did not catch the literary allusion concerning the Word as the one who brings forth light, the author punctuates the point one more time: "The light shines in the darkness, and the darkness did not overcome it" (John 1:5).

The author highlights the relationship between the Word and YHWH, uniting them while also differentiating them, revealing the explicitly Trinitarian framework of John's Gospel, where ultimate reality (God) is known as God the Father, God the Son (Logos/Word), and God the Holy Spirit. While the binary of light and darkness suggests gnostic dualism, the proclamation that the Word—as the creator and source of the light—resists and overcomes the darkness communicates that not only is the Word cocreator with the Father, but also that God loves and embraces the material creation. This point is driven home with an explicitly Trinitarian proclamation identifying the divine and coeternal Logos as the Son of God, who was with God the Father at the creation, through whom everything that exists was made; this one has now chosen to dwell among humankind by taking on human flesh (Gk. σάρξ, meaning "body" or "flesh," as in the edible flesh of a piece of fruit): "And the Word became flesh and lived among us, and we have seen his glory, the glory as of a father's only son, full of grace and truth" (John 1:14).

Neither Marcionism nor Valentinian Gnosticism accepted the incarnation of the Son of God, preferring instead a Hellenistic conception of divinity as transcendent, eternal, and unchanging, with the implication that the Word of God was pure Spirit and not flesh. This fueled Irenaeus's theological response to Valentinianism in *Against Heresies* (ca. 180 CE), in which "he articulates one of the most important pre-Nicene accounts of the person and work of Christ, an account that stressed the ongoing significance of Christ's flesh in the work of redemption and constituting Christian identity . . . distinguishing and separating it from the Gnosticism that had come to infect it."[19]

In other words, embodied human existence in the flesh is of such high value and esteem to the eternal and infinite God that God "in Christ Jesus" took on human flesh and dwelt among us:

> who, though he existed in the form of God,
>   did not regard equality with God
>   as something to be exploited,
> but emptied himself,
>   taking the form of a slave,
>   assuming human likeness.
> And being found in human form,
>   he humbled himself
>   and became obedient to the point of death—
>   even death on a cross.
>   (Phil. 2:6–8)

Irenaeus's *Against Heresies* has been described as an early systematic presentation of Christian beliefs, written in response to gnostic heresies within the Christian church. The work is organized according to the "rule of faith" (*regula fidei*), a widely accepted oral tradition that followed a Trinitarian pattern and served as a narrative creed summarizing apostolic teaching (a proto-Apostles' Creed) patterned after several New Testament confessional fragments such as "Jesus is Lord" (Rom. 10:9), Paul's christological hymn in Philippians 2:5–11, and the gospel outline in 1 Corinthians 15:3–9. Irenaeus summarizes the content of the rule of faith under the name of the three-in-one: the one God, Father, the Almighty, maker of heaven and earth; the one Christ Jesus, Son of God, incarnate for human salvation; and the Holy Spirit, who inspired the prophets and now proclaims the *oikonomia* ("household") of God.

At its core, *Against Heresies* tackles the question of how to interpret the Scriptures correctly. The gnostics offer "secret" knowledge, but Irenaeus argues that God's revelation is publicly proclaimed and trustworthy, while gnostic

---

19. Carter, *Race: A Theological Account*, 13.

speculation is suspect, because it has no basis in Scripture or the apostolic tradition. By applying the "rule of faith" when interpreting Scripture—there is one God who alone is Lord, Creator, Father, and sustainer of all—Irenaeus rejects the Marcionite and Valentinian assertion that the God of the Hebrew Bible, who created the material world, is not the true God, and he affirms the Gospel of John's proclamation that God the Father and God the Son are one.

For Irenaeus, the genuine, embodied, and fleshly humanity of Christ is of key soteriological significance. The incarnation is God's means of bringing about the renewal of all creation—especially fallen humanity. Employing the doctrine of recapitulation originating in the Pauline literature (Rom. 3:21–26; 2 Cor. 5:21), Irenaeus concludes that what we lost in Adam—the image and likeness of God—we recover in Christ Jesus. Christ did for us what we could not do for ourselves. Irenaeus distinguishes Christian orthodoxy from the gnostic belief in two gods—the demiurge who created the material world and the true (spiritual) God revealed in Christ—by affirming that the Word of God became flesh (John 1:14), which is why the affirmations that God is the Creator and that God is one became the first article of faith in the earliest creeds: "The glory of the human being is God; in truth, the receptacle of the operation of God and of all God's wisdom and power is the human being."[20]

Given this struggle to differentiate Christian belief from gnostic heresies, it is not surprising to find gnostic themes in the Gospel of John, given its composition in the late first or early second century, at a time when these ideas were being formulated across the Hellenistic world, had influenced Alexandrian Judaism, and could have even impacted the Qumran sect of Palestinian Judaism.[21] However, given the centrality of the incarnation in the Gospel's prologue, these gnostic themes are present in the Gospel of John in order to refute them, while reinforcing the importance of material embodiment in mortal flesh—both in the divine economy of salvation and in terms of human creatureliness.

Therefore, it is not accidental that the seven miracles Jesus performs address some material need of fleshly existence as part of the author's rejection of gnostic dualism. The first "sign" is the wedding at Cana, where, at his mother's insistence, Jesus turns water into wine after the host had run out of wine. Despite Jesus' hesitation—"Woman, what concern is that to you and to me? My hour has not yet come" (John 2:4), suggesting he was not yet

---

20. Irenaeus of Lyon, *Against Heresies* 3.20.3, cited in Ann Donovan, *One Right Reading? A Guide to Irenaeus* (Collegeville, MN: Liturgical Press, 2000), 84–85.

21. See Aldo Magris, "Gnosticism: Gnosticism from Its Origins to the Middle Ages (Further Considerations)," in *Macmillan Encyclopedia of Religion*, ed. Lindsay Jones, 2nd ed. (New York: Macmillan Reference USA, 2004), 3515–16; and Menahem Mansoor, "The Nature of Gnosticism in Qumran," in *The Origins of Gnosticism*, ed. Bianchi (Leiden: E. J. Brill, 1970), 389–400.

ready to reveal his divine nature—he concedes. So in John's account of the life and ministry of Jesus this miracle marks the beginning of Christ's earthly ministry. Then, after ordering the servants to fill six stone jars used for Jewish purification rites (Lev. 11:29–38) with water, he commands them to draw some out. When they do, the water drawn from the jars is turned to wine (John 2:7–8). When the wine is served at the wedding feast, the steward exclaims to the bridegroom with great surprise, "Everyone serves the good wine first, and then the inferior wine after the guests have become drunk. But you have kept the good wine until now" (John 2:10).

By performing this miracle Jesus not only saves the host from embarrassment, but he also enables the wedding feast to continue, ensuring that the host, the bride and bridegroom, and all the guests can celebrate the union of husband and wife without interrupting their drunken revelry. Recalling that marriage is the coming together of two human beings as one flesh (Gen. 2:24; Matt. 19:5; Mark 10:8; Eph. 5:31), the first miracle performed by Jesus not only signals the Messiah's arrival; it also serves to reinforce the antignostic argument that frames the prologue to John's Gospel.

The second "sign" or miracle performed by Jesus also occurs in Cana, when Jesus heals a royal official's son; then the official and his entire household become followers of Jesus (John 4:46–54). Here the divine concern for human flesh is direct and inescapable, as the incarnate Word of God responds to the official's request to heal his sick son by immediately reassuring the father that his son will live (John 4:49–50). Like the second miracle at Cana, the next miracle is also an act of healing; it takes place at the pool of Bethsaida in Jerusalem (John 5:2–9). This miracle is part of a separate subnarrative demonstrating Jesus' divinity by having him perform certain miraculous acts on the Sabbath that only YHWH could accomplish. Raymond Brown writes, "That the violation of the Sabbath is the main theme of the miracle as it is now reported is clear. . . . That Jesus violated the rules of the scribes for the observance of the Sabbath is one of the most certain of all the historical facts about his ministry."[22] Nevertheless, this healing story also fits the antignostic polemic in John's Gospel, insofar as Jesus is responding to a bodily need—the suffering of a man who has been crippled for thirty-eight years. Upon seeing the man, Jesus asks, "Do you want to be made well?," to which the sick man responds, "Sir, I have no one to put me into the pool when the water is stirred up; and while I am making my way, someone else steps down ahead of me" (John 5:6–7). The sick man does not ask for healing directly, merely for help getting into the pool, because it was believed to have healing powers. Jesus tells the man, "Stand up, take your mat and walk" (John 5:8), and immediately

---

22. Brown, *The Gospel according to John (I–XII)*, 210.

the man is healed and able to walk. There is no mention of spiritual salvation. The man is crippled and has suffered for thirty-eight years, yet with a simple verbal command—much like YHWH commanding the light into existence at the moment of creation (Gen. 1:3)—Jesus is able to heal the man.

While the miracle at Cana is attested only by the Gospel of John, the fourth miracle in the "signs" source, the feeding of the five thousand, is the only miracle (apart from the resurrection of Jesus) recorded in all four canonical Gospels (Matt. 14:13–21; Mark 6:31–44; Luke 9:12–17; John 6:1–14). Also known as the miracle of the five loaves and two fish, the Gospel of John claims that Jesus uses five loaves and two fish provided by a young boy to feed a multitude of five thousand people. Afterward, "when they were satisfied," the remaining fragments of the five barley loaves miraculously "filled twelve baskets" (John 6:12–13). It is interesting to note that the crowd has gathered—and continues to follow Jesus—because of the miracles he has performed healing the sick (John 4:46–54; 5:2–9). Jesus might be preaching about spiritual matters, but many who follow him are seeking relief for material needs, and Jesus does not turn them away. Instead—contra Marcion and Valentinus—Jesus provides for their bodily needs (hunger) by making sure the hungry crowd is properly satisfied (John 6:12).

Without question, the feeding of the five thousand makes an intentional eucharistic allusion, recalling the central sacrament of the Christian life, in which the body of Christ—represented by the broken fragments of bread—is gathered together in union with Christ. But this only reinforces the incarnated (fleshly) existence of the Christ, who becomes the bread of life (John 6:35). As the coeternal Word of God, the Christ is a spiritual being, but according to the narrative arc of John's Gospel the spiritual becomes material ("became flesh," John 1:14) in the economy of salvation for the sake of the material ("so that everyone who believes in him may not perish but may have eternal life" John 3:16). As Mayra Rivera summarizes, "not only does the word become flesh, but what became flesh will become spirit."[23]

The next miracle follows closely on the heels of the miracle of the loaves and fish. Jesus flees the crowd for fear they might "take him by force to make him king" and withdraws to a mountaintop to be alone (John 6:15). That evening, his disciples walk down to the lake and board a boat sailing for the city of Capernaum across the Sea of Galilee. It has gotten dark, and they are worried that Jesus has not yet returned when "they saw Jesus walking on the sea and coming near the boat, and they were terrified" (John 6:19).

Like all the miracles contained in the signs source, this story serves as a theophany—a manifestation of God in the world—that emphasizes the

---

23. Rivera, *Poetics of the Flesh*, 21.

otherworldly origin of the Christ. This same theme is found in the Synoptic variants (Mark 6:45–53; Matt. 14:22–34), where Jesus calms the storm, serving as further proof of his divine origin. Some scholars consider verse 20, where Jesus reassures the terrified disciples by saying, "It is I; do not be afraid," an allusion to the divine name spoken to Moses from the burning bush, "I AM WHO I AM" (Exod. 3:13), because the Greek text (*egō eimi*) can be translated "I am." Regardless, what is important in the context of John's antignostic polemic is that Christ, while appearing as an otherworldly divine figure, cares for the disciples and acts to comfort them in their fright.

The sixth miracle is another act of healing. This time Jesus heals a blind man in Jerusalem, which prompts a theological discussion about sin, evil, and innocent suffering. Reflecting a popular though mistaken theological opinion that suffering was punishment for sin (see Job 4:7–9), his disciples ask Jesus, "Rabbi, who sinned, this man or his parents, that he was born blind?" He replies, "Neither this man nor his parents sinned; he was born blind so that God's works might be revealed in him" (John 9:2–3). Once again, a human need (blindness) serves as an occasion to reveal God working in the world through Jesus, called the light of the world (John 9:5), who performs a miraculous healing by mixing some mud with his spittle and anointing the blind man's eyes with it. Jesus then commands the blind man, "Go, wash in the pool of Siloam" (John 9:7); when he returns, he is able to see, to the astonishment of all his neighbors, who know the man was born blind. Interestingly, Irenaeus comments on this passage in *Against Heresies*, noting how Jesus used mud to heal the blind man as a reminder that humankind was created from the earth (Gen. 2:7), thus reinforcing both that God loves embodied humanity (God sent the Messiah for our salvation) and that Jesus was God in human flesh (what better proof than Jesus spitting to make mud?).[24]

The seventh and final miracle before Jesus' passion is the grandest of all: the raising of Lazarus from the dead (John 11:1–44). Keeping with the theme of the signs source material, this miracle is intended to convince people of Jesus' divine nature, confirming he is the Messiah and the Son of God. Ironically, while some who witness this final miracle come to believe in Jesus as Messiah, just as many walk away unconvinced, and some even begin to plot his death (vv. 45–53). Until now, the people Jesus has healed are strangers he encounters while preaching, but Jesus knows and loves Lazarus and his two sisters, Mary and Martha, intimately. Therefore, when Jesus arrives at Lazarus's tomb and sees his sister Mary weeping, he is "greatly disturbed in spirit and deeply moved," and he "began to weep" (vv. 33, 35).

---

24. Irenaeus of Lyon, *Against Heresies* 5.15.2, cited in Brown, *The Gospel according to John (I–XII)*, 372.

Clearly, whatever else can be said about Jesus of Nazareth, the author of the Gospel of John wants his audience to know that Jesus was fully human, living an embodied existence with all its accompanying physical limitations (Jesus experiences hunger and feels pain) and bodily secretions (like spit and tears). Like the other miraculous acts preserved in the Book of Signs, the raising of Lazarus from the tomb stands as proof of Jesus' divinity, while also meeting the ultimate need of embodied human existence. In this instance, not only does Jesus' miracle alleviate the suffering and grief of Mary, Martha, and all their friends and neighbors. It grants life to his friend Lazarus, who has died after a serious illness (vv. 1–3, 17). To drive the point home, we are told that when the tomb was opened, there was "a stench because he has been dead four days" (v. 39). Lazarus is not raised to new life as some kind of insubstantial phantom or as a spiritual being. He is resurrected into his (healed and restored) material body: "The dead man came out, his hands and feet bound with strips of cloth, and his face wrapped in a cloth. Jesus said to them, 'Unbind him, and let him go'" (v. 44).

When Jesus reassures the grieving Mary, he tells her, "Did I not tell you that if you believed, you would see the glory of God?" (v. 40). This final sign, the resurrection of Lazarus, confirms Jesus' identity as Messiah and Son of God, who has come into the world (v. 27) for our sake and for our salvation, while underscoring that salvation comes via God's incarnation in human form. Contrary to Marcionite and Valentinian teaching, Jesus is the eternal Word in human flesh, taking on full humanity—not just the *appearance* of humanity—bringing together the two themes characterizing all seven signs. As a literary passage, the final scene finds completion by setting the stage for Jesus' miracle through the simple act of showing his humanity in the form of sorrow and tears, demonstrating that in Christ spirit and flesh are indivisible and necessary, for it is through the incarnation that God's work of salvation enters the world.

FLESH AND SPIRIT ARE ONE

In *Poetics of the Flesh*, Mayra Rivera writes, "The Christian body has never been one."[25] While her comments can be applied to the historical reality that the church is a broken communion—split along denominational and ideological lines—her comments strike on a more visceral level. Rivera is here concerned not with ecclesial unity but with the competing cultural imaginaries about flesh coexisting within Christian thought. She is particularly concerned with

---

25. Rivera, *Poetics of the Flesh*, 17.

the persistent contradiction over flesh in contemporary forms of Christianity that embrace Christ's bodily incarnation as salvific on the one hand, while demanding a flesh-denying sexual purity on the other, while also deeply entangled in loving the material world and all its comforts and pleasures. As a result of this enduring confusion, Christians have tolerated and allowed untold violence, exploitation, and even enslavement of human flesh to go unchallenged, prompting Rivera's multilayered and complex critique of colonial, racist, and sexist discourses. Furthermore, Rivera does not limit her understanding of flesh to human bodily existence but takes a broader ecological perspective that acknowledges biological diversity and pushes back on the idea of human uniqueness. In the process, she makes a persuasive argument for a radical transformation of Christian perspectives on flesh that emphasize the interconnectedness of all life on the planet.

As Rivera employs the term "flesh," it retains all its christological, incarnational, and eucharistic dimensions, but it also reveals the social and material conditions that impact fleshly existence, in order to ethically confront the real harm done to human bodies. The complexities of bodily existence, much like divine existence, are shrouded in mystery: "Envisioning flesh as a condition of material life implies ineffability. The weaving of flesh precedes the emergence of this body as my own. My body is here, in this world, exposed to it and yet it has traces of a past that is not my own, that I can never know."[26] By giving voice to the ineffability of fleshly existence, Rivera is acknowledging the limits of human knowledge, in order to emphasize the importance of mutuality when bodies encounter and engage one another. She insists that corporeal materiality cannot reduce the embodied other to an object to be controlled and dominated, but challenges us to always interact with "the irreducible otherness in all bodies, the indeterminacy of becoming flesh."[27]

If Pseudo-Dionysius blazed the trail of apophatic theology, Rivera is calling for an apophatic anthropology that views the other as mystery and not an object to be manipulated. This openness to the other as other demands a "new poetics of elemental flesh [that] attends to the broader, complex matrix of relations that ground all life. These relations are not limited to sexual difference; they encompass all materiality—human and nonhuman. Yet this poetics also needs to address the corporeal effects of social differentiations between bodies—including but not limited to sexual difference."[28] Rivera writes with a sense of ethical urgency because she is aware of the real-world suffering afflicting millions of bodies daily, especially those on the underside of history.

26. Rivera, *Poetics of the Flesh*, 104.
27. Rivera, *Poetics of the Flesh*, 105.
28. Rivera, *Poetics of the Flesh*, 109.

She offers a multidisciplinary analysis of flesh drawn from Christian theology, continental philosophy, and political theory that analyzes the concept of flesh in early Christian literature, explores the social-material realities impacting embodied existence, and draws attention to the ways gender and race have become objectified and exploited by different cultural imaginaries, since "social forces affect our bodies in ways that precede and exceed our personal acts."[29] Embodied existence is not experienced the same by all, which might go a long way to explain the persistence of world-denying spiritualities, but the inequities of how different bodies are treated become magnified when considering race and gender: "Race is pinned to the body," asserts Rivera; she then notes how colonial discourses inevitably accentuate the intersectionality of "flesh, race, and sex."[30]

In her analysis of early Christian literature, Mayra Rivera identifies the conflict between the apostle Paul's understanding of flesh and that of John the evangelist. Paul asserts a spirit-flesh dualism even to the point of denying a bodily resurrection (1 Cor. 15:50), while John's Gospel adamantly links salvation to the bodily incarnation of the Christ (John 1:14). Paul contends that while humanity was formed by God from the earth (Gen. 2:7), and inhabits fleshly bodies, his recapitulation soteriology does not accommodate bodily resurrection—or more exactly, a resurrection of the *fleshly* body:

> The first man [Adam] was from the earth, a man of dust; the second man [Jesus] is from heaven. As was the man of dust, so are those who are of the dust; and as is the man of heaven, so are those who are of heaven. Just as we have borne the image of the man of dust, we will also bear the image of the man of heaven. What I am saying, brothers and sisters, is this: flesh and blood cannot inherit the kingdom of God, nor does the perishable inherit the imperishable. (1 Cor. 15:47–50)

Rivera suggests Paul's views of resurrected humanity have been influenced by the Platonism of Philo of Alexandria, for whom "the two creation stories establish a distinction between spiritual and material bodies."[31] For Paul, physical existence precedes spiritual rebirth, so in a very real sense humanity is never fully image of God (Gen. 1:26–27) unless and until it is redeemed by Christ: "So it is with the resurrection of the dead. What is sown is perishable, what is raised is imperishable. It is sown in dishonor, it is raised in glory. It is sown in weakness, it is raised in power. It is sown a physical body, it is raised a spiritual body" (1 Cor. 15:42–44).

---

29. Rivera, *Poetics of the Flesh*, 114.
30. Rivera, *Poetics of the Flesh*, 122, 125.
31. Rivera, *Poetics of the Flesh*, 31.

Rivera is troubled by this spirit-flesh duality, because it cleaves the material from the spiritual, which in turn "affects human inclinations in the world" and opens the door to a devaluing of embodied existence that facilitates the abuse of material bodies.[32] Though Paul's discourse on flesh is the earliest Christian literature on the subject, Paul's dualistic theology of the body does not represent the only Christian theology of the body and ought to be read not as authoritative and absolute, but as in dialogue with other canonical theologies of the body. Rivera argues that the poetics of the Gospel of John offer a more inclusive imaginary for evaluating the relationship between spirit and flesh.

As I have argued above, a central motif of the Gospel of John is the coming together of spirit and flesh in the incarnation of the Word of God. The incarnation "joins the tangible and the intangible. It renders the real world evident and invisible."[33] Without dissolving the differences between spirit and flesh, the Gospel of John makes the case for keeping the two dimensions of human existence in tension, not as contradictory realities but as complementary aspects of finite embodied beings created in the image of the infinite God. Despite the centrality of the incarnation in the Gospel of John—"the Word became flesh" (John 1:14)—and by extension the whole of the New Testament, given parallel passages in the Synoptic Gospels, Rivera is rightly concerned that "it is also easy to lose sight of flesh."[34]

The rise of Marcionism and Valentinianism in the second century validates this concern, as previously discussed, but the biggest struggle in the early church against forces wanting to marginalize flesh, in favor of a highly spiritualized Christology, coalesced around the teachings of Arius (256–336 CE), a fourth-century priest and ascetic whose heretical teaching became one of the chief motivations behind emperor Constantine convening the First Council of Nicaea (325 CE). Arius emphasized the self-subsistence and immutability of God; because God the Father existed prior to the Son, the Son exists because of the Father; therefore, the Son is a creature and not equal with God (albeit the highest of all God's creations). Influenced by Platonism, Arius defended his views by appealing to the absolute transcendence and unknowability of God, while his critics appealed to passages from the New Testament like the christological hymn in Philippians 2:5–11 and the incarnational claim of John's prologue (John 1:14), to demonstrate the widely held belief in the equality of God and Jesus.

Athanasius of Alexandria (ca. 296–373 CE), one of the chief defenders of Trinitarianism over against Arianism, countered Arius by arguing that if Jesus

---

32. Rivera, *Poetics of the Flesh*, 32.
33. Rivera, *Poetics of the Flesh*, 19.
34. Rivera, *Poetics of the Flesh*, 20.

Christ is a creature, then he is unable to save humanity, for only God can save, overcome sin and death, and grant eternal life. Rivera not only draws on the Johannine incarnational Christology; she also links the incarnation of the Word to the divinization (*theosis*) of the flesh in the theology of Athanasius, who declared, "For he was made man that we might be made God."[35] Implied in the Johannine message about the eternal Word become flesh is the good news about human flesh gaining eternal life (John 3:16), because "those born of flesh are being called to be born of spirit."[36]

One major contrast between the Pauline discourse on flesh and that found in the Gospel of John is the rhetorical move by the author of John to link the incarnation with the Eucharist, for it is through the sacrament that spirit transforms flesh: "Flesh, bread, and life are in Jesus and given by him to his followers. In the process the flesh and bread seem to mutate—flesh is bread given, bread is life, wheat dies to gives fruit, and so on. Jesus's followers are in turn transformed by these elements—they come to have life in them."[37] In John's Gospel, following the feeding of the five thousand, there is an obvious eucharistic allusion in which Jesus affirms, "For the bread of God is that which comes down from heaven and gives life to the world" (John 6:33). Jesus then clarifies that he is the bread from heaven: "I am the bread of life" (John 6:35). Recognizing the antignostic rhetoric in John's Gospel as repudiation of the spiritualization of the Christ, Rivera emphasizes the embodied presence of Jesus in a ministry that fulfills the material needs of fleshly human existence: "The claim to be bread comes from the same Jesus who divided and multiplied bread and fish to feed a multitude. Surely, we are expected to interpret the hunger of the multitude and the food given as real."[38]

The exaltation of the flesh through the transforming power of the Spirit serves to counteract the tradition's negligence of marginalized and exploited flesh, by emphasizing the liberative dimension of Jesus' earthly ministry "to give life to those who are excluded."[39] Despite the popularity of more spiritualized Christologies, like the aforementioned Pauline dualistic ontology that elevates spirit above flesh, the Christian tradition has always preserved counternarratives—especially emancipatory counternarratives—that employ Jesus' full humanity as a moral compass for a more politically engaged faith that does not ignore or tolerate any abuse of human flesh—especially the flesh of the racialized and gendered other.

---

35. Athanasius, "On the Incarnation of the Word," in *Christology of the Later Fathers*, ed. Edward Hardy in collaboration with Cyril Richardson (Philadelphia: Westminster, 1954), 107.
  36. Rivera, *Poetics of the Flesh*, 21.
  37. Rivera, *Poetics of the Flesh*, 24.
  38. Rivera, *Poetics of the Flesh*, 22.
  39. Rivera, *Poetics of the Flesh*, 23.

Thus, Rivera can link the protoliberationist sixteenth-century Benedictine friar Bartolomé de las Casas (1484–1566) to the eucharistic theology articulated in the antignostic Gospel of John. The demands of the flesh—in this instance the abused and exploited flesh of the indigenous people of Latin America who had been enslaved by the Catholic conquistadores—were met by the healing salve of the bread of life, but not as a spiritual promise of future eschatological deliverance, but instead, as an act of political resistance by Las Casas intended to bring about the moral conversion of the Spanish conquerors:

> In preparation for saying the Mass, he read in Ecclesiasticus 34, "Bread is the life of the poor." He concluded that the Eucharist could not be offered unless the Amerindians were freed. For the liberationist readers of las Casas, the bread offered in the Eucharist cannot be abstracted from the gifts of the earth and the labor that materializes in the bread.[40]

The ethical urgency driving Rivera's *Poetics of the Flesh* is intensified by this identification of exploited human bodies with the Eucharist. She argues that "an elemental materiality connects the bodies of workers with shared bread, with consecrated bread. These are not arbitrary metaphors—bread is produced by the labor of human hands and the fecundity of the earth."[41] Here Rivera echoes a central point of Gustavo Gutiérrez's *A Theology of Liberation* (1971), that genuine communion cannot take place without "a real commitment against exploitation and alienation," for without this emancipatory dimension, "the Eucharistic celebration is an empty action."[42] Rivera's embrace of the carnal is not made at the expense of the spiritual, but seeks to integrate flesh and spirit into a unified vision of the divine-human encounter that accepts limitation and incompletion as constitutive of the human condition, in which fleshly vulnerability leads to ethical obligation. A poetics of the flesh derived from the Gospel of John's incarnational Christology "leads us to explore the world again in wonder, to describe it faithfully. We pray that our bodies may keep us open to others, to sense the entanglements of our carnal relations."[43]

---

40. Rivera, *Poetics of the Flesh*, 23.
41. Rivera, *Poetics of the Flesh*, 23.
42. Gustavo Gutiérrez, *A Theology of Liberation: History, Politics and Salvation*, rev. ed., ed. and trans. Sister Caridad Inda and John Eagleson (Maryknoll, NY: Orbis Books, 1988), 150.
43. Rivera, *Poetics of the Flesh*, 158.

A FRAGMENT OF THEOLOGY: DISABILITY AND THE BODY OF CHRIST

In the context of late Roman antiquity, one of the ways Christianity differentiated itself from the dominant (pagan) culture was through its treatment of human bodies—especially the bodies of the weak, sick, and disabled—who would have been outcast, left to die, or euthanized. As Brian Brock writes, under Roman rule marked by intermittent persecution, "Christians had repudiated the Greco-Roman view of nonstandard newborns as the work of malevolent supernatural powers by rescuing these babies, a politically subversive act tempting the wrath of angry gods and breaching the law of scarcity."[44] Guided by Jesus' repudiation of the belief that illness or disability was divine punishment—"Neither this man nor his parents sinned; he was born blind so that God's works might be revealed in him" (John 9:3)—Augustine of Hippo (354–430 CE) articulated a theological foundation for viewing disability as part of the human condition and not a deficiency to be "corrected" by the bodily resurrection.

Without neglecting or ignoring Augustine's limitations—for example, he had little sympathy for the plight of women or slaves in his pastoral writings (though he did write "an extended address comforting Christian nuns dealing with the aftermath of rape")[45]—Brock argues he ought to be praised for not universalizing the "hope that God would restore all people to the 'normal' human form by healing all physical disproportions as well as sensory and mental deviations."[46] Jesus' response to the question, "Rabbi, who sinned, this man or his parents, that he was born blind?" (John 9:2), inspired Augustine to come to terms with what he called "strange vocations"—the reality that some people, like the early Christian martyrs, were called to endure suffering, even torture and death, and that the physical scars of that suffering signified their glory and ought not be erased in the afterlife. In like manner, Jesus responds to the question about who is to blame for the man's blindness with the assertion that the man's disability is not divine punishment but an occasion for manifesting the divine. Like Irenaeus refuting Marcionism and Valentinianism, Augustine of Hippo was entangled in a struggle with Manichean dualism and refuted the denigration of the flesh by emphasizing the goodness of the material creation, insisting "that *every* human being in existence is good because they are *created by God exactly as they are*."[47]

---

44. Brian Brock, *Wondrously Wounded: Theology, Disability, and the Body of Christ* (Waco, TX: Baylor University Press, 2019), 29.
  45. Brock, *Wondrously Wounded*, 30.
  46. Brock, *Wondrously Wounded*, 30.
  47. Brock, *Wondrously Wounded*, 16 (emphasis added).

Reflecting on embodied reality as part of God's providential care for the creation, Augustine was troubled by the birth of an "abnormal" child and sought to understand how deformity and disability fit within his belief in a benevolent and all-powerful Creator. As Brock notes, "like everyone else at that time, Augustine of Hippo understood such a birth as a clear departure from the orderly progress of nature."[48] Unlike his contemporaries, Augustine fought the tendency to view such births as divine punishment for sin and, more importantly, argued that every human life—including those born monstrously deformed or cognitively impaired—is image of God (Gen. 1:26–27):

> For God is the Creator of all things: He Himself knows where and when anything should be, or should have been, created; and He knows how to weave the beauty of the whole out of the similarity and diversity of its parts. The man who cannot view the whole is offended by what he takes to be the deformity of a part; but this is because he does not know how it is to be adapted or related to the whole. We know of men who were born with more than five fingers or five toes. This is a trivial thing and not any great divergence from the norm. God forbid, however, that someone who does not know why the Creator has done what He has done should be foolish enough to suppose that God has in such cases erred in allotting the number of human fingers. So, then, even if a greater divergence should occur, He whose work no one may justly condemn knows what He has done.[49]

By refusing to concede that God has erred in allowing such births—for example, where the newborn has a different number of fingers than is the norm—Augustine must then accommodate such births within the divine providence. As part of God's creation every human life is judged good (Gen. 1:31) and intended to be part of the creation; so the challenge for the believer is to understand how and where this particular human life—whatever its physical and/or cognitive challenges—fits into the divine plan, or, in the words of John's Gospel, to contemplate and understand how this life provides an occasion "that God's works might be revealed" (John 9:3).

Not only does Augustine's exploration of disability as "strange vocation" open the door to viewing disabled bodies not as deficient or in need of redemption but as vehicles of divine revelation and thus accepted and valued as they are, but it also leads to a theological anthropology in which no human life, however different, can be discarded or eliminated as less than human:

---

48. Brock, *Wondrously Wounded*, 15.
49. Augustine, *City of God*, 16.8, cited in Brock, *Wondrously Wounded*, 16.

> Who could call to mind all the human infants who have been born very unlike those who were most certainly their parents? It cannot be denied, however, that these derive their origin from that one man, Adam; and the same is therefore true of all those races which, by reason of their bodily differences, are said to have deviated from the usual pattern of nature exhibited by most—indeed by almost the whole—of mankind. If these races are included in the definition of "human," that is, if they are rational and mortal animals, then it must be admitted that they trace their lineage from that same one man, the first father of all mankind.[50]

Like the martyrs, Jesus endured torture and abuse that left his body deformed and disabled before he was crucified (John 19), and it is important that when Thomas encountered the risen Christ, he verified the bodily resurrection by placing his hands in Jesus' wounds (John 20:19–31). In other words, the resurrected body retains its "imperfections," validating fleshly existence and what is experienced and endured by our material bodies. If the spirit and flesh coexist in material bodies, as the persistent narrative of John's Gospel contends, then the scars and distinguishing particularities that mark *my* embodied existence matter to God and have a place in the church as the body of Christ and in eternal life.

Once again, the eucharistic dimensions of Christ's incarnation stand as a hermeneutical key for interpreting our human existence, and with it the affirmation that God values human bodies in their particularity and not as an idealized abstraction. When the community gathers around the communion table, we not only celebrate our union with Christ, but we also celebrate our union with one another *as* the body of Christ, where each member is valued and contributes for the edification of the whole body:

> The members of the body that seem to be weaker are indispensable, and those members of the body that we think less honorable we clothe with greater honor, and our less respectable members are treated with greater respect; whereas our more respectable members do not need this. But God has so arranged the body, giving the greater honor to the inferior member, that there may be no dissension within the body, but the members may have the same care for one another. If one member suffers, all suffer together with it; if one member is honored, all rejoice together with it. (1 Cor. 12:22–26)

---

50. Augustine, *City of God*, 16.8, cited in Brock, *Wondrously Wounded*, 16.

Concluding Unscientific Postscript

> We're in the world, not against it. It doesn't work to try to stand outside things and run them, that way. It just doesn't work, it goes against life. There is a way but you have to follow it. The world is, no matter how we think it ought to be. You have to be with it. You have to let it be.[1]

Ursula K. Le Guin's dystopian novella *The Lathe of Heaven* (1971) introduces the reader to a mild-mannered sad sack named George Orr—an allusion to the author of the classic dystopian novel *Nineteen Eighty-Four* (1949), George Orwell—who discovers he has the Godlike power to alter reality in his dreams. Being a generally caring and compassionate human being, George realizes no single person ought to have such absolute power and attempts to control his powers by taking drugs to avoid entering the dream-state caused by deep REM sleep. Living in a highly regulated dystopian future, George is eventually caught falsifying prescriptions and overdosing on drugs and is sentenced to rehabilitative psychotherapy, where he meets Dr. William Haber, a sleep-disorder specialist who at first does not believe George's claims, but eventually comes to accept George's powers before then attempting to control them.

Dr. Haber is an ambitious man motivated by benevolent ideals, but as he manipulates George's dreamworld for the supposed betterment of society, he also maneuvers himself into positions of greater and greater power, until

---

1. Ursula K. Le Guin, *The Lathe of Heaven*, repr. ed. (New York: Simon & Schuster, 2008), 140.

his ambition supersedes his ethics. Inevitably, every one of his attempts to improve the world creates unintended—and horrific—consequences, like the time Haber commands George to dream of a world without hunger and overpopulation and George dreams of a plague that wipes out most of the world's population. Seeking to end food shortages, George dreams into existence an even more dystopian future where euthanasia is performed on anyone with a terminal illness. To bring about peace on Earth and an end to war, George dreams of an alien invasion from outer space that unites the world. To end racial and ethnic conflict, George dreams that all humans have always been gray skinned but in doing so erases the African American woman he loves from the new continuity. The tragedy at the heart of Le Guin's story is that George remembers every alternate timeline, so he experiences each loss personally, which is slowly driving him insane: "You're a psychiatrist. Don't you see that I'm going to pieces?"[2]

Dr. Haber is not a megalomaniacal tyrant—he truly believes he is acting benevolently by controlling George's dreams—but the more he attempts to control reality, the greater the harm caused by the unintended consequences. Haber's attempt to solve racism comes at the expense of racial, ethnic, and cultural diversity, forever changing the natural order by turning humanity into something it was never meant to be. George is not alone against Dr. Haber, as the aforementioned woman he falls in love with is a lawyer assigned to his case. She too believes and accepts George's frightful dream powers and tries to help free him from Dr. Haber's control by implanting a countersuggestion through hypnosis. Unlike Dr. Haber, however, she is aware of the frightful responsibility she has undertaken by trying to control George's dreams, which in turn leads George to reflect on Dr. Haber's abuse of power: "It's not right to play God with masses of people. . . . Just believing you're right and your motives are good isn't enough."[3]

Le Guin's speculative fiction serves as a parable about the dangers of power and humanity's tendency to want to control others. Dr. Haber is a case study on the consequences of absolute power corrupting absolutely, while the unimposing George Orr stands as a model of spiritual resignation, given his realization that as human beings it is sometimes better to set aside our utopian dreams and accept the world as it is. Despite the best of intentions, our vision of how the world ought to be can quickly become someone else's dystopian

---

2. Le Guin, *The Lathe of Heaven*, 88.
3. Le Guin, *The Lathe of Heaven*, 155.

nightmare. Therefore, there is wisdom in resisting the urge to remake the world in our own image.

The core message of my book is simple: religion ought not to be confused with God. Today, American Christianity is in crisis, because if current trends continue, by the year 2050 Christians will constitute less than half of the US population.[4] As demonstrated by the decline in membership across all denominations, but most recently seen in the mass exodus of Millennials and Gen Z youth from white Evangelicalism in the US, the rise of the religious Nones is a reaction to certain triumphalist theologies that have sought to impose a rigid doctrinal orthodoxy upon all Christian believers. Not only is such dogmatic totalitarianism idolatrous—usurping God by elevating a *human* theological construct to divine status—by insisting that its view is universal and absolute. Such dogmatism is blinded to the ongoing activity of God's Spirit in the world. Much like the blind men in the Buddhist parable, such dogmatists refuse to recognize that their religion—a local and contextual view of divine reality—is but one perspective among many others of an infinite goodness and truth that can never be fully "captured" by any single ideology, religious confession, or philosophical school of thought.

A friend and colleague raised this objection to my preferring a Heraclitian worldview over a Platonic worldview in developing this book's argument: "If all our theologizing is a Heraclitian flux, then wouldn't this make every one of our theological utterances the creature of a moment? Not lasting for a century or a generation, nor even a decade, year, month, day, or hour, but only for a moment . . . like a little puff of smoke?" His reaction reflects the human desire for certainty amid the radical plurality of the cosmos, but as with many Christian apologists, he makes the mistake of assuming God-talk is a zero-sum game.

I am not interested in all-or-nothing arguments. It is ridiculous to assume that simply because I deny and reject the Platonic demand for a single, universal, and unchanging conception of truth, I am then unable to make *any* true statements—especially about God. We are self-reflective beings made in the image of God, with memory, history, and culture, so our predicate statements are not leaves in the wind but simply attempts to be as exact as humanly possible when talking about the infinite God, fully cognizant that we speak from a particular time and place in history, reflecting a concrete and singular point of view within a fixed horizon. It is sinful to assume

---

4. Stephanie Kramer and Conrad Hackett, "Modeling the Future of Religion in America," Pew Research Center, September 13, 2022, https://www.pewresearch.org/religion/2022/09/13/modeling-the-future-of-religion-in-america/.

our theological claims carry the weight of divine command, given we lack God's infinite perspective and are unable to transcend our given horizons. We do not know all, have not experienced all, therefore cannot speak for or about all.

As Bruce McCormack concludes in *The Humility of the Eternal Son* (2021), divine hiddenness "is a function of the modality of divine self-revelation. It is objective. It is no longer a conception that results from a human act of 'locating' the being of God just beyond the limits of human knowing as established by some philosophical epistemology or another, or simply by means of an agnostic gesture and accompanied by protestations of respect for 'mystery.'"[5] That is to say, theology does not suddenly become silent when human knowing fails. Rather, as Pseudo-Dionysius has taught us, worshipful contemplative silence is the most appropriate response when confronted with divine self-revelation, which conceals as well as discloses: "Against such false humility stands the true humility that acknowledges that the Revealer is fully revealed—and is fully hidden at the same time—and both as a consequence of [God's] own revelatory activity."[6] To speak of divine mystery is not a failure of human cognition, but an insight into the infinite majesty that is the ground of all being we call God. Therefore, if the eternal Logos willingly surrenders divinity in humility and obedience (Phil. 2:5–11), thereby inverting the world's conceptions of power and glory, we who bend our knees and confess with our tongues that "Jesus Christ is Lord" ought to set aside our misguided desire for theological supremacy.

At the same time, I share my colleague's concern that the rush to deconstruct the Christian faith has undermined our ability to speak meaningfully about God. While the rise of the Nones has yielded many projects *deconstructing* the Christian faith, such projects have little to say to those still attracted to the life and ministry of Jesus, seeking to remain his followers in a fractured world. This book offers a theological vision that takes the incomplete nature of revelation seriously, accepting the fact that even in revelation God remains infinite mystery and that fragments of truth are often all we have, in order to map a path for *reconstructing* the Christian faith for the third millennium.

Guided by the liberationist claim that God is found wherever the work of human liberation happens—succinctly condensed by Rubem Alves's foundational question, "What does it take to make and keep life human in the world?"[7]—I have argued that one time-tested path to spiritual reconstruction

---

5. Bruce Lindley McCormack, *The Humility of the Eternal Son: Reformed Kenoticism and the Repair of Chalcedon* (Cambridge: Cambridge University Press, 2021), 272–73.
6. McCormack, *The Humility of the Eternal Son*, 273.
7. Rubem Alves, *A Theology of Human Hope* (St. Meinrad, IN: Abbey Press, 1969), 53.

inevitably and concretely involves believers in historical struggles for justice. This book is an invitation to those Nones on the journey to authentic selfhood still seeking the truth of God to reconsider Christian resources—often little more than fragments of theology—confident that the living God transcends all religions and trusting that God's infinite grace can heal all wounds . . . even those caused by persons and institutions acting in the name of God.

Bibliography

"A Pastoral Message on Climate Change." Anglican Church of Canada, Episcopal Church, Evangelical Lutheran Church in America, and the Evangelical Lutheran Church in Canada, September 19, 2014. https://www.episcopalchurch.org/publicaffairs/a-pastoral-message-on-climate-change/.

Abrams, Amanda. "How Raleigh's John Pavlovitz Went from Fired Megachurch Pastor to Rising Star of the Religious Left." *INDYweek*, November 22, 2017. https://indyweek.com/news/raleigh-s-john-pavlovitz-went-fired-megachurch-pastor-rising-star-religious-left/.

"Affirmation of Creation." Presbyterian Church (U.S.A.), 222nd General Assembly, June 22, 2016. https://ncse.ngo/presbyterian-church-usa.

Albertus. *On the Body of the Lord*. Translated by Albert Marie Surmanski. Washington, DC: Catholic University of America Press, 2017.

Al Ghazali. *The Incoherence of The Philosophers (Tahāfut al-Falāsifah): A Parallel English-Arabic Text*. Translated by Michael E. Marmura. Revised edition. Salt Lake City: Brigham Young University Press, 2000.

Alexander, Denis R. "Creation and Evolution." In *The Blackwell Companion to Science and Christianity*, edited by J. B. Stump and Alan G. Padgett, 233–45. Malden, MA: Wiley-Blackwell, 2012.

Allen, Diogenes. *Christian Belief in a Postmodern World: The Full Wealth of Conviction*. Louisville, KY: Westminster John Knox, 1989.

Allison, Emily Joy. *#ChurchToo: How Purity Culture Upholds Abuse and How to Find Healing*. Minneapolis: Broadleaf Books, 2021.

Altizer, Thomas J. J. *The New Gospel of Christian Atheism*. Aurora, CO: Davies Group, 2002.

Altizer, Thomas J. J., and William Hamilton, *Radical Theology and the Death of God*. New York: Penguin, 1966.

Alves, Rubem. "Dietrich Bonhoeffer: Teólogo da Vida." *CEI Suplemento* 22 (1970): 1–4.

———. *Protestantism and Repression: A Brazilian Case Study*. Translated by John Drury. Reprint edition. Eugene, OR: Wipf & Stock, 2007.

———. *A Theology of Human Hope*. Meinrad, IN: Abbey Press, 1969.

"AME Church Climate Change Resolution." African Methodist Episcopal Church, July 2016. http://www.ame-church.com/wp-content/uploads/2016/07/AME-Climate-Change-Resolution.pdf.

"Americans Seriously Overestimate Their Own Generosity." Grey Matter Research Consulting, May 25, 2017. https://greymatterresearch.com/generosity/.

"An Evangelical Declaration on the Care of Creation." Evangelical Environmental Network, 1994. https://creationcare.org/what-we-do/an-evangelical-declaration-on-the-care-of-creation.html.

Anderson, Bernhard W. *Creation in the Old Testament*. Minneapolis: Fortress Press, 1984.

———. *Creation versus Chaos: The Reinterpretation of Mythical Symbolism in the Bible*. Reprint edition. Eugene, OR: Wipf & Stock, 2005.

Anderson, Gary A., and Markus N. A. Bockmuehl, eds. *Creation ex nihilo: Origins, Development, Contemporary Challenges*. Notre Dame, IN: University of Notre Dame Press, 2018.

Aristotle. *The Politics*. Translated by Benjamin Jowett. Kitchener, ON: Batoche Books, 1999.

Asad, Talal. *Formations of the Secular: Christianity, Islam, Modernity*. Stanford, CA: Stanford University Press, 2003.

Athanasius. "On the Incarnation of the Word." In *Christology of the Later Fathers*, edited by Edward Hardy and Cyril Richardson. Philadelphia: Westminster, 1954.

Augustine of Hippo. *On Christian Doctrine*. Translated by D. W. Robertson Jr. New York: Macmillan, 1958.

Ayoub, Mahmoud. "The Need for Harmony and Collaboration between Muslims and Christians." In *A Muslim View of Christianity: Essays on Dialogue by Mahmoud Ayoub*, edited by Irfan A. Omar, 9–16. Maryknoll, NY: Orbis Books, 2007.

Bakunin, Mikhail Aleksandrovich. *Bakunin: Statism and Anarchy*. Edited and translated by Marshall Shatz. Cambridge: Cambridge University Press, 1990.

Bandini, Albert R. "St. Francis and the Ideal of Poverty." *American Ecclesiastical Review* 75 (1926).

Barbour, Ian G. "An Ecological Ethic." *Christian Century* 87 (1970): 1180–84.

———. *Nature, Human Nature, and God*. Minneapolis: Fortress, 2002.

———. *Religion and Science: Historical and Contemporary Issues*. San Francisco: HarperSanFrancisco, 1997.

———. *Technology, Environment, and Human Values*. New York: Praeger, 1980.

Barrow, John D., and Frank J. Tipler. *The Anthropic Cosmological Principle*. Oxford: Oxford University Press, 1986.

Barry, John M. *Roger Williams and the Creation of the American Soul: Church, State, and the Birth of Liberty*. New York: Penguin, 2012.

Barth, Karl. *Church Dogmatics*. Edited by G. W. Bromiley and T. F. Torrance. Translated by T. H. L. Parker. Vol. 2. Edinburgh: T. & T. Clark, 1957.

———. *The Epistle to the Romans*. Translated by Edwyn C. Hoskins. 6th ed. Oxford: Oxford University Press, 1968.

———. *The Göttingen Dogmatics: Instruction in the Christian Religion*. Edited by Hannelotte Reiffen. Translated by G. W. Bromiley. Vol. 1. Grand Rapids: Eerdmans, 1991.

———. *The Word of God and Theology*. Edited and translated by Amy Marga. London: T. & T. Clark, 2011.

———. "The Word of God as the Task of Theology." In *The Word of God and Theology*, edited and translated by Amy Marga. London: T. & T. Clark, 2011.

Bennhold, Katrin. "QAnon Is Thriving in Germany. The Extreme Right Is Delighted." *New York Times*, October 11, 2020. https://www.nytimes.com

/2020/10/11/world/europe/qanon-is-thriving-in-germany-the-extreme-right-is-delighted.html.

Berger, Peter L. "The Desecularization of the World: A Global Overview." In *The Desecularization of the World: Resurgent Religion and World Politics*, edited by Peter L. Berger, 1–18. Grand Rapids: Eerdmans, 1999.

Blair, Leonardo. "Only 13% of Evangelicals Tithe, Half Give Away Less than 1% of Income Annually: Study." *Christian Post*, October 29, 2021. https://www.christianpost.com/news/only-13-of-evangelicals-tithe-study.html.

Blowers, Paul M. *Drama of the Divine Economy: Creator and Creation in Early Christian Theology and Piety*. Oxford: Oxford University Press, 2012.

Boff, Leonardo. *Francis of Assisi: A Model for Human Liberation*. Translated by John W. Diercksmeier. Maryknoll, NY: Orbis Books, 2006.

Bonhoeffer, Dietrich. *Letters and Papers from Prison*. Edited by Eberhard Bethge. Enlarged ed. New York: Touchstone, 1997.

———. *Letters and Papers from Prison*. Vol. 8 of *Dietrich Bonhoeffer Works*, edited by John W. de Gruchy, translated by Isabel Best, Lisa E. Dahill, Reinhard Krauss, and Nancy Lukens. Minneapolis: Fortress, 2010.

Bowler, Kate. *Blessed: A History of the American Prosperity Gospel*. Oxford: Oxford University Press, 2018.

Bowler, Peter J. "Christian Responses to Darwinism in the Late Nineteenth Century." In *The Blackwell Companion to Science and Christianity*, edited by J. B. Stump and Alan G. Padgett, 37–47. Malden, MA: Wiley-Blackwell, 2012.

Boyarin, Daniel. *Dying for God: Martyrdom and the Making of Christianity and Judaism*. Stanford, CA: Stanford University Press, 1999.

Brock, Brian. *Wondrously Wounded: Theology, Disability, and the Body of Christ*. Waco, TX: Baylor University Press, 2019.

Brooks, David. "The Benedict Option." *New York Times*, March 14, 2017, sec. A23.

Brown, Callum G. *Becoming Atheist: Humanism and the Secular West*. London: Bloomsbury Academic, 2017.

Brown, Heath. *Homeschooling the Right: How Conservative Education Activism Erodes the State*. New York: Columbia University Press, 2021.

Brown, Raymond E. *The Gospel according to John (I–XII)*. Anchor Yale Bible Commentaries. New Haven, CT: Yale University Press, 2007.

"Buddhist Climate Change Statement to World Leaders." Global Buddhist Climate Change Collective, October 29, 2015. https://plumvillage.org/articles/buddhist-climate-change-statement-to-world-leaders-2015/.

Bultmann, Rudolf. *Primitive Christianity in Its Contemporary Setting*. Translated by R. H. Fuller. New York: New American Library, 1974.

Burge, Ryan P. *The Nones: Where They Came From, Who They Are, and Where They Are Going*. Minneapolis: Fortress, 2021.

Burnet, John. *Early Greek Philosophy*. Whitefish, MT: Kessinger, 2003.

Byrd, James P. *Sacred Scripture, Sacred War: The Bible and the American Revolution*. New York: Oxford University Press, 2013.

Calvin, John. *Calvin's Commentaries*. Reprint edition. Vol. 5. Grand Rapids: Baker Book House, 2003.

———. *Institutes of the Christian Religion*. Edited by John T. McNeill. Translated by Ford Lewis Battles. 2 vols. Louisville, KY: Westminster John Knox, 2006.

Campbell, Margaret M. *Critical Theory and Liberation Theology: A Comparison of the Initial Work of Jürgen Habermas and Gustavo Gutiérrez*. New York: Peter Lang, 1999.

Caputo, John D. *The Weakness of God: A Theology of the Event*. Bloomington: Indiana University Press, 2006.

Carnahan, Kevin. "Jesus Did Not Teach Nonviolent Resistance in the Sermon on the Mount." Political Theology Network, October 14, 2021. https://politicaltheology.com/jesus-did-not-teach-nonviolent-resistance-in-the-sermon-on-the-mount/.

Carr, Matthew. *Blood and Faith: The Purging of Muslim Spain*. New York: New Press, 2009.

Carter, J. Kameron. *Race: A Theological Account*. Oxford: Oxford University Press, 2008.

Catling, David C. *Astrobiology: A Very Short Introduction*. Oxford: Oxford University Press, 2013.

Cavanaugh, William. "Faith Fires Back: A Conversation with Stanley Hauerwas." *Duke University Magazine*, January–February 2002.

Chappell, Bill. "Pope Benedict XVI Failed to Stop Sex Abuse When He Was an Archbishop, Law Firm Says." *National Public Radio*, January 20, 2022. https://www.npr.org/2022/01/20/1074355457/pope-benedict-xvi-sex-abuse-report.

Christie, Nancy, Stephen J. Heathorn, and Michael Gauvreau, eds. *The Sixties and Beyond: Dechristianization in North America and Western Europe, 1945–2000*. Toronto: University of Toronto Press, 2013.

"Church and Religious Charitable Giving Statistics." Nonprofits Source. https://nonprofitssource.com/online-giving-statistics/church-giving/.

Clark, Elaine. "Institutional and Legal Responses to Begging in Medieval England." *Social Science History* 26, no. 3 (Fall 2002): 447–73.

Clayton, Philip. *God and Contemporary Science*. Edinburgh Studies in Constructive Theology. Grand Rapids: Eerdmans, 1997.

Coakley, Sarah. *God, Sexuality, and the Self: An Essay "On the Trinity."* Cambridge: Cambridge University Press, 2013.

Cobb, Jelani. "William Barber Takes on Poverty and Race in the Age of Trump." *New Yorker*, May 14, 2018. https://www.newyorker.com/magazine/2018/05/14/william-barber-takes-on-poverty-and-race-in-the-age-of-trump.

Cobb, John B. *Is It Too Late? A Theology of Ecology*. Beverly Hills, CA: Bruce, 1972.

———. *Sustainability: Economics, Ecology, and Justice*. Eugene, OR: Wipf & Stock, 2007.

Cone, James H. "The Vocation of a Theologian." *Union News*, Winter 1991.

Cox, Harvey. *The Secular City: Secularization and Urbanization in Theological Perspective*. Revised edition. Princeton, NJ: Princeton University Press, 2014.

Craig, William Lane. "Politically Incorrect Salvation." In *Christian Apologetics in the Postmodern World*, edited by Timothy R. Phillips and Dennis L. Okholm. Downers Grove, IL: InterVarsity Press, 1995.

Crick, Francis H. C., and James D. Watson. "Molecular Structure of Nucleic Acids: A Structure for Deoxyribose Nucleic Acid." *Nature* 171 (1953): 834–38.

Crossan, John Dominic, and Richard G. Watts. *Who Is Jesus? Answers to Your Questions about the Historical Jesus*. Louisville, KY: Westminster John Knox, 1996.

Daly, Mary. *Beyond God the Father: Toward a Philosophy of Women's Liberation*. Boston: Beacon, 1993.

D'Antonio, Michael. *Mortal Sins: Sex, Crime, and the Era of Catholic Scandal*. New York: Macmillan, 2013.
Darsey, James. *The Prophetic Tradition and Radical Rhetoric in America*. New York: New York University Press, 1999.
Darwin, Charles. "Autobiography of Charles Darwin." Vol. 29 of *The Works of Charles Darwin*, edited by Paul H. Barrett and R. B. Freeman. London: Routledge, 2016.
———. "Charles Darwin's Memorial of Anne Elizabeth Darwin." Darwin Correspondence Project, April 30, 1851. https://www.darwinproject.ac.uk/people/about-darwin/family-life/death-anne-elizabeth-darwin.
———. *The Descent of Man, and Selection in Relation to Sex* (1871). In *From So Simple a Beginning: The Four Great Books of Charles Darwin*, edited by Edward O. Wilson. New York: W. W. Norton, 2006.
———. "Letter No. 441." University of Cambridge, November 21, 1838. https://www.darwinproject.ac.uk/letter/DCP-LETT-441.xml.
———. "Letter No. 2814." University of Cambridge, May 22, 1860. https://www.darwinproject.ac.uk/letter/DCP-LETT-2814.xml.
———. "Letter No. 12041." University of Cambridge, May 7, 1879. https://www.darwinproject.ac.uk/letter/DCP-LETT-12041.xml.
———. *On the Origin of Species* (1859). In *From So Simple a Beginning: The Four Great Books of Charles Darwin*, edited by Edward O. Wilson. New York: W. W. Norton, 2006.
———. *The Origin of Species: 150th Anniversary Edition*. New York: Signet Classics, 2003.
Daughrity, Dyron B. *The Amazing Story of Christianity's Resurrection in the Global South*. Minneapolis: Fortress, 2018.
Dawkins, Richard. *The Blind Watchmaker: Why the Evidence of Evolution Reveals a Universe without Design*. Reprint edition. New York: W. W. Norton, 1996.
———. *The God Delusion*. Boston: Houghton Mifflin, 2006.
D'Costa, Gavin. "The Trinity in Interreligious Dialogues." In *The Oxford Handbook of the Trinity*, edited by Gilles Emery and Matthew Levering, 573–85. Oxford: Oxford University Press, 2011.
De La Torre, Miguel A. *Burying White Privilege: Resurrecting a Badass Christianity*. Grand Rapids: Eerdmans, 2019.
———, ed. *The Hope of Liberation in World Religions*. Waco, TX: Baylor University Press, 2008.
———, ed. *The Politics of Jesús: A Hispanic Political Theology*. Lanham, MD: Rowman & Littlefield, 2015.
Deckman, Melissa M. *School Board Battles: The Christian Right in Local Politics*. Washington, DC: Georgetown University Press, 2004.
Dennett, Daniel C. *Breaking the Spell: Religion as a Natural Phenomenon*. New York: Penguin, 2006.
———. *Consciousness Explained*. Boston: Little, Brown, 1991.
Derrida, Jacques. *Of Grammatology*. Translated by Gayatri Chakravorty Spivak. Baltimore: John Hopkins University Press, 1997.
———. *Specters of Marx: The State of the Debt, the Work of Mourning, and the New International*. Translated by Peggy Kamuf. New York and London: Routledge, 1994.

Devlin, Kat, Moira Fagan, and Aidan Connaughton. "Global Views of How U.S. Has Handled Pandemic Have Improved, but Few Say It's Done a Good Job." Pew Research Center, June 10, 2021. https://www.pewresearch.org/fact-tank/2021/06/10/global-views-of-how-u-s-has-handled-pandemic-have-improved-but-few-say-its-done-a-good-job/.

Diamond, Irene, and Gloria Feman Orenstein, eds. *Reweaving the World: The Emergence of Ecofeminism*. San Francisco: Sierra Club Books, 1990.

Dias, Elizabeth, Annie Karni, and Sabrina Tavernise. "Trump Tells Anti-Abortion Marchers, 'Unborn Children Have Never Had a Stronger Defender in the White House.'" *New York Times*, January 24, 2020. https://www.nytimes.com/2020/01/24/us/politics/trump-abortion-march-life.html.

Donovan, Ann. *One Right Reading? A Guide to Irenaeus*. Collegeville, MN: Liturgical Press, 2000.

Dorrien, Gary. *American Democratic Socialism: History, Politics, Religion, and Theory*. New Haven, CT: Yale University Press, 2021.

———. *Imagining Democratic Socialism: Political Theology, Marxism, and Social Democracy*. New Haven, CT: Yale University Press, 2019.

Dostoyevsky, Fyodor. *The Brothers Karamazov*. Translated by David McDuff. Revised edition. London: Penguin Books, 2003.

Dreher, Rod. *The Benedict Option: A Strategy for Christians in a Post-Christian Nation*. New York: Penguin, 2017.

Drescher, Elizabeth. *Choosing Our Religion: The Spiritual Lives of America's Nones*. Oxford: Oxford University Press, 2016.

Duca, John V., and Federal Reserve Bank of Dallas. "Subprime Mortgage Crisis: 2007–2010." Federal Reserve History, November 22, 2013. https://www.federalreservehistory.org/essays/subprime-mortgage-crisis.

Duckworth, Douglas. *Mipam on Buddha-Nature: The Ground of the Nying-Ma Tradition*. Albany: SUNY Press, 2008.

Dugatkin, Lee Alan, and Lyudmila Trut. *How to Tame a Fox (and Build a Dog): Visionary Scientists and a Siberian Tale of Jump-Started Evolution*. Reprint edition. Chicago: University of Chicago Press, 2019.

Dussel, Enrique. *A History of the Church in Latin America*. Translated by Alan Neely. Grand Rapids: Eerdmans, 1981.

Duvvuru, Kamalakar. "Is India Displaying Signs of Neo-fascism?" *Monthly Review*, July 31, 2019. https://mronline.org/2019/07/31/is-india-displaying-signs-of-neo-fascism/.

Easley, Cameron. "U.S. Conservatives Are Uniquely Inclined toward Right-Wing Authoritarianism Compared to Western Peers." *Morning Consult*, June 28, 2021. https://morningconsult.com/2021/06/28/global-right-wing-authoritarian-test/.

Ecumenical Patriarch Dimitrios, Archbishop of Constantinople and New Rome. "Encyclical Letter on the Day of Protection of the Environment," September 1, 1989. https://www.orth-transfiguration.org/wp-content/uploads/2016/05/Lecture_HAH-1989-Patr.-Dimitrios-on-Day-of-Prayer-for-Envir.pdf.

"Elijah's Covenant—New Rabbinic Statement on the Climate Crisis." The Shalom Center, January 1, 2020. https://theshalomcenter.org/content/elijahs-covenant-new-rabbinic-statement-climate-crisis.

Espín, Orlando O. *Idol and Grace: On Traditioning and Subversive Hope*. Maryknoll, NY: Orbis Books, 2014.

Evans, C. Stephen. *The Pocket Dictionary of Apologetics & Philosophy of Religion*. Downers Grove, IL: IVP Academic, 2002.

Evans, Rachel Held. *Evolving in Monkey Town: How a Girl Who Knew All the Answers Learned to Ask the Questions*. Grand Rapids: Zondervan, 2010.

———. *Searching for Sunday: Loving, Leaving, and Finding the Church*. Nashville: Nelson Books, 2015.

Evans, Rachel Held, and Jeff Chu. *Wholehearted Faith*. San Francisco: HarperOne, 2021.

Fergusson, David. *The Providence of God: A Polyphonic Approach*. Cambridge: Cambridge University Press, 2018.

Ferm, Deane W. *Third World Liberation Theologies: A Reader*. 2nd ed. Maryknoll, NY: Orbis Books, 1986.

———. *Third World Liberation Theologies: An Introductory Survey*. Maryknoll, NY: Orbis Books, 1986.

Financial Crisis Inquiry Commission. "The Financial Crisis Inquiry Report." Washington, DC: Government Printing Office, January 25, 2011. https://www.govinfo.gov/content/pkg/GPO-FCIC/pdf/GPO-FCIC.pdf.

Fitzgerald, Frances. *The Evangelicals: The Struggle to Shape America*. New York: Simon & Schuster, 2017.

Fletcher, Jeannine Hill. *The Sin of White Supremacy: Christianity, Racism, & Religious Diversity in America*. Maryknoll, NY: Orbis Books, 2017.

Flores, Nichole M. *The Aesthetics of Solidarity: Our Lady of Guadalupe and American Democracy*. Washington, DC: Georgetown University Press, 2021.

Flynn, Maureen. *Sacred Charity: Confraternities and Social Welfare in Spain, 1400–1700*. London: Macmillan, 1989.

Ford, David F. "An Interfaith Wisdom: Scriptural Reasoning between Jews, Christians and Muslims." *Modern Theology* 22, no. 3 (2006): 345–66.

Ford, David F., and C. C. Pecknold, eds. *The Promise of Scriptural Reasoning*. Malden, MA: Blackwell, 2006.

Fowler, Jeaneane D. *Perspectives of Reality: An Introduction to the Philosophy of Hinduism*. Brighton, UK: Sussex Academic Press, 2002.

Frame, John M. *Apologetics: A Justification of Christian Belief*. Edited by Joseph E. Torres. Phillipsburg, NJ: P & R Publishing, 2015.

———. *Cornelius Van Til: An Analysis of His Thought*. Phillipsburg, NJ: P & R Publishing, 1995.

Francis. "A Letter to the Rulers of the Peoples (1220)." In *Francis of Assisi—The Saint: Early Documents*, vol. 1, edited by Regis J. Armstrong, J. A. Wayne Hellmann, and William J. Short, translated by Regis J. Armstrong. New York: New City Press, 1999.

Frank, Adam. *The Constant Fire: Beyond the Science vs. Religion Debate*. Berkeley: University of California Press, 2009.

———. *Light of the Stars: Alien Worlds and the Fate of the Earth*. New York: W. W. Norton, 2018.

Freeden, Michael. *Liberalism: A Very Short Introduction*. Oxford: Oxford University Press, 2015.

Freitas, Donna. "Ex-Evangelical Rachel Held Evans Still Cherishes Her Bible." *Publishers Weekly*, May 9, 2018. https://www.publishersweekly.com/pw/by-topic/industry-news/religion/article/76494-ex-evangelical-rachel-held-evans-on-feminism-and-the-bible.html.

Fretheim, Terence E. *God and World in the Old Testament: A Relational Theology of Creation*. Translated by M. Kathryn Armistead. Nashville: Abingdon, 2010.

Fukuyama, Francis. *The End of History and the Last Man*. New York: Free Press, 1992.

García-Rivera, Alejandro. *The Community of the Beautiful: A Theological Aesthetics*. Collegeville, MN: Liturgical Press, 1999.

Gebara, Ivone. *Intuiciones ecofeministas: ensayo para repensar el conocimiento y la religión*. Translated by Graciela Pujol. Madrid: Editorial Tratto, 2000.

Gecewicz, Claire. "Key Takeaways about How Americans View the Sexual Abuse Scandal in the Catholic Church." Pew Research Center, June 11, 2019. https://www.pewresearch.org/fact-tank/2019/06/11/key-takeaways-about-how-americans-view-the-sexual-abuse-scandal-in-the-catholic-church.

Gershom, Levi ben. *Commentary on Song of Songs*. Edited and translated by Menachem Kellner. New Haven, CT: Yale University Press, 1998.

Giddens, Anthony. "Introduction." In *The Protestant Ethic and the Spirit of Capitalism*, translated by Talcott Parsons. New York: Charles Scribner's Sons, 1958.

Goizueta, Roberto S. *Caminemos Con Jesús: Toward a Hispanic/Latino Theology of Accompaniment*. Maryknoll, NY: Orbis Books, 1999.

———. *Christ Our Companion: Toward a Theological Aesthetics of Liberation*. Maryknoll, NY: Orbis Books, 2009.

———, ed. *We Are a People!* Minneapolis: Fortress, 1992.

González, Justo. *Faith and Wealth: A History of Early Christian Ideas on the Origin, Significance, and Use of Money*. Reprint edition. New York: Harper & Row, 1990.

———. "Metamodern Aliens in Postmodern Jerusalem." In *Hispanic/Latino Theology: Challenge and Promise*, edited by Ada María Isasi-Díaz and Fernando F. Segovia. Minneapolis: Fortress, 1996.

Gould, Stephen Jay. "Nonoverlapping Magisteria." *Natural History* 106 (1997): 16–22.

———. *Rocks of Ages: Science and Religion in the Fullness of Life*. New York: Ballantine Books, 1999.

Green, Emma. "Rachel Held Evans, Hero to Christian Misfits." *Atlantic*, May 6, 2019. https://www.theatlantic.com/politics/archive/2019/05/rachel-held-evans-death-progressive-christianity/588784/.

Gregory of Nyssa. *In Ecclesiasten homiliae*. In *Gregorii Nysseni Opera*, edited by Werner Jaeger, Friedrich Müller, Heinrich Dörrie, and Hadwig Hoerner, 5:334–52. Leiden: E. J. Brill, 1958.

Grenz, Stanley J. *Renewing the Center: Evangelical Theology in a Post-Theological Era*. 2nd ed. Grand Rapids: Baker Academic, 2006.

Grillmeier, Aloys. *Christ in the Christian Tradition*, vol. 1, *From the Apostolic Age to Chalcedon (451)*. Translated by John Bowden. 2nd revised edition. Atlanta: John Knox, 1975.

Grooms, Jevay, Alberto Ortega, and Alfredo-Angel Rubalcaba. "The COVID-19 Public Health and Economic Crises Leave Vulnerable Populations Exposed." Brookings Institution, August 13, 2020. https://www.brookings.edu/blog/up-front/2020/08/13/the-covid-19-public-health-and-economic-crises-leave-vulnerable-populations-exposed/.

Gschwandtner, Christina M. *Postmodern Apologetics? Arguments for God in Contemporary Philosophy*. New York: Fordham University Press, 2013.
Guidepost Solutions LLC. "Report of the Independent Investigation: The Southern Baptist Convention Executive Committee's Response to Sexual Abuse Allegations and an Audit of the Procedures and Actions of the Credentials Committee," May 15, 2022. https://www.sataskforce.net/updates/guidepost-solutions-report-of-the-independent-investigation.
Gunn, Angus M. *Intelligent Design and Fundamentalist Opposition to Evolution*. Jefferson, NC: McFarland, 2015.
Gushee, David P. *After Evangelicalism: The Path to a New Christianity*. Louisville, KY: Westminster John Knox, 2020.
———. *Changing Our Mind*. 2nd ed. Canton, MI: Read the Spirit Books, 2015.
———. *Still Christian: Following Jesus Out of American Evangelicalism*. Louisville, KY: Westminster John Knox, 2017.
Gushee, David P., and Glenn H. Stassen. *Kingdom Ethics: Following Jesus in Contemporary Context*. 2nd ed. Grand Rapids: Eerdmans, 2016.
Gutiérrez, Gustavo. "Liberation Theology and the Twenty-First Century: Celebrating Past, Present, and Future." Presented at the American Academy of Religion Annual Meeting, Denver, CO, November 19, 2001.
———. *A Theology of Liberation*. Edited and translated by Sister Caridad Inda. Maryknoll, NY: Orbis Books, 1988.
———. *We Drink from Our Own Wells: The Spiritual Journey of a People*. Maryknoll, NY: Orbis Books, 2003.
Guyatt, Nicholas. *Providence and the Invention of the United States, 1607–1876*. Cambridge: Cambridge University Press, 2007.
Habermas, Jürgen, et al. *An Awareness of What Is Missing: Faith and Reason in a Post-secular Age*. Translated by Ciaran Cronin. Malden, MA: Polity Press, 2010.
———. *Postmetaphysical Thinking: Philosophical Essays*. Cambridge, MA: MIT Press, 1992.
Hallanger, Nathan K. "Ian G. Barbour." In *The Blackwell Companion to Science and Christianity*, edited by J. B. Stump and Alan G. Padgett, 600–610. Malden, MA: Wiley-Blackwell, 2012.
Hamilton, Brian. "The Politics of Poverty: A Contribution to a Franciscan Political Theology." *Journal of the Society of Christian Ethics* 35, no. 1 (Spring/Summer 2015).
Hamilton, William. *A Quest for the Post-historical Jesus*. New York: Continuum, 1994.
Hammond, Daniel J., and Claire H. Hammond, eds. *Making Chicago Price Theory: Friedman-Stigler Correspondence 1945–1957*. London and New York: Routledge, 2006.
Hanauer, Nick. "Beware, Fellow Plutocrats, the Pitchforks Are Coming." TED Talks, August 12, 2014. https://www.ted.com/talks/nick_hanauer_beware_fellow_plutocrats_the_pitchforks_are_coming/transcript.
Hanauer, Nick, and Eric Beinhocker. "Capitalism Redefined." *Democracy: A Journal of Ideas* 31 (Winter 2014). https://democracyjournal.org/magazine/31/capitalism-redefined/.
Harris, Sam. *The End of Faith: Religion, Terror, and the Future of Reason*. New York: W. W. Norton, 2005.

Hart, David Bentley. *The Beauty of the Infinite: The Aesthetics of Christian Truth*. Grand Rapids: Eerdmans, 2004.

———. *That All Shall Be Saved: Heaven, Hell, and Universal Salvation*. New Haven, CT: Yale University Press, 2019.

———. "The 'Whole Humanity': Gregory of Nyssa's Critique of Slavery in Light of His Eschatology." *Scottish Journal of Theology* 54, no. 1 (2001): 51–69.

Harwell, Drew, Isaac Stanley-Becker, Razzan Nakhlawi, and Craig Timberg. "QAnon Reshaped Trump's Party and Radicalized Believers. The Capitol Siege May Just Be the Start." *Washington Post*, January 13, 2021. https://www.washingtonpost.com/technology/2021/01/13/qanon-capitol-siege-trump/.

Haught, John F. *Making Sense of Evolution: Darwin, God, and the Drama of Life*. Louisville, KY: Westminster John Knox, 2010.

Heim, S. Mark. *The Depth of the Riches: A Trinitarian Theology of Religious Ends*. Grand Rapids: Eerdmans, 2001.

———. *Is Christ the Only Way? Christian Faith in a Pluralistic World*. Valley Forge, PA: Judson, 1985.

———. *Salvations: Truth and Difference in Religion*. Maryknoll, NY: Orbis Books, 1995.

Hennelly, Alfred T., ed. *Liberation Theology: A Documentary History*. Maryknoll, NY: Orbis Books, 1990.

Hibbard, Scott W. *Religious Politics and Secular States: Egypt, India, and the United States*. Baltimore: John Hopkins University Press, 2010.

"Hindu Declaration on Climate Change." Parliament of the World's Religions, Melbourne, Australia, December 8, 2009. https://hinduclimatedeclaration2015.org/english.

Hinn, Costi W. *God, Greed, and the (Prosperity) Gospel: How Truth Overwhelms a Life Built on Lies*. Grand Rapids: Zondervan, 2019.

"Homeschooled Children and Reasons for Homeschooling." National Center for Education Statistics, May 2022. https://nces.ed.gov/programs/coe/indicator/tgk/homeschooled-children?tid=4.

Horsman, Reginald. *Race and Manifest Destiny: The Origins of American Racial Anglo-Saxonism*. Cambridge, MA: Harvard University Press, 2009.

Huntington, Samuel P. *The Clash of Civilizations and the Remaking of World Order*. New York: Simon & Schuster, 1996.

Ibn Rushd. *Ibn Rushd's Metaphysics: A Translation with Introduction of Ibn Rushd's Commentary on Aristotle's Metaphysics, Book Lām*. Edited and translated by Charles F. Genequand. Leiden: E. J. Brill, 1986.

Ibn Sina. *Ibn Sina's Remarks and Admonitions: Physics and Metaphysics; An Analysis and Annotated Translation*. Translated by Shams C. Inati. New York: Columbia University Press, 2014.

Investigative Staff of the Boston Globe. *Betrayal: The Crisis in the Catholic Church*. Boston: Little, Brown, 2008.

Ireland, John D., ed. *Udana and the Itivuttaka: Two Classics from the Pali Canon*. Reprint edition. Kandy, Sri Lanka: Buddhist Publication Society, 2007.

Isasi-Díaz, Ada María. *La Lucha Continues: Mujerista Theology*. Maryknoll, NY: Orbis Books, 2004.

———. *Mujerista Theology: A Theology for the Twenty-First Century*. Maryknoll, NY: Orbis Books, 1996.

———. "Preoccupations, Themes, and Proposals of Mujerista Theology." In *The Ties That Bind: African American and Hispanic American/Latino/a Theologies in Dialogue*, edited by Anthony B. Pinn and Benjamin Valentin. New York: Continuum, 2001.

"Islamic Declaration on Global Climate Change." International Islamic Climate Change Symposium, Istanbul, Turkey, August 17–18, 2015. https://www.ifees.org.uk/about/islamicdeclaration/.

Jenkins, Philip. *The New Faces of Christianity: Believing the Bible in the Global South*. New York: Oxford University Press, 2016.

Jensen, J. Vernon. "Return to the Wilberforce-Huxley Debate." *British Journal for the History of Science* 21, no. 2 (June 1988): 161–79.

Jenson, Robert W. "Jesus in the Trinity." *Pro Ecclesia* 8, no. 3 (Summer 1999): 308–18.

———. *Systematic Theology*, vol. 1, *The Triune God*. Oxford: Oxford University Press, 1997.

Jervis, Rick, Marc Ramirez, and Romina Ruiz-Goiriena. "'No Regrets': Evangelicals and Other Faith Leaders Still Support Trump after Deadly US Capitol Attack." *USA Today*, January 12, 2021. https://www.usatoday.com/story/news/nation/2021/01/12/evangelicals-donald-trump-capitol-riot-voter-fraud/6644005002/.

Johnson, Elizabeth A. *Ask the Beasts: Darwin and the God of Love*. London: Bloomsbury, 2014.

Johnson, Keith L., and Timothy Larsen, eds. *Bonhoeffer Christ and Culture*. Downers Grove, IL: IVP Academic, 2013.

Jones, Robert P. *The End of White Christian America*. New York: Simon & Schuster, 2017.

———. *White Too Long: The Legacy of White Supremacy in American Christianity*. New York: Simon & Schuster, 2020.

Jones, Robert P., Natalie Jackson, Diana Orcés, and Ian Huff. "The 2020 Census of American Religion." Public Religion Research Institute, July 8, 2021. https://www.prri.org/research/2020-census-of-american-religion/.

Joppke, Christian. *The Secular State under Siege: Religion and Politics in Europe and America*. Hoboken, NJ: John Wiley & Sons, 2015.

Joshi, Khyati Y. *White Christian Privilege: The Illusion of Religious Equality in America*. New York: New York University Press, 2020.

Juergensmeyer, Mark. *Global Rebellion: Religious Challenges to the Secular State, from Christian Militias to Al Qaeda*. Berkeley: University of California Press, 2008.

Kagay, Donald J., and Theresa M. Vann, eds. *On the Social Origins of Medieval Institutions: Essays in Honor of Joseph F. O'Callaghan*. Leiden: E. J. Brill, 1998.

Kant, Immanuel. "What Is Enlightenment?" In *Foundations of the Metaphysics of Morals and What Is Enlightenment?*, translated by Lewis White Beck. New York: Macmillan, 1959.

Keller, Catherine. *Facing Apocalypse: Climate, Democracy and Other Last Chances*. Maryknoll, NY: Orbis Books, 2021.

———. *Political Theology of the Earth: Our Planetary Emergency and the Struggle for a New Public*. New York: Columbia University Press, 2018.

Kelly, J. N. D. *Early Christian Doctrines*. Revised edition. San Francisco: HarperSanFrancisco, 1978.

Kepnes, Steven. "A Handbook for Scriptural Reasoning." *Modern Theology* 22, no. 3 (2006): 367–83.

Kerby, Lauren R. "White Christian Nationalists Want More Than Just Political Power." *Atlantic*, January 15, 2021. https://www.theatlantic.com/ideas/archive/2021/01/white-evangelicals-fixation-on-washington-dc/617690/.

Kierkegaard, Søren. *Fear and Trembling*. Translated by Walter Lowrie. Princeton, NJ: Princeton University Press, 1941.

———. *Philosophical Fragments*. Edited and translated by Howard V. Hong and Edna H. Hong. 2nd printing. Princeton, NJ: Princeton University Press, 1987.

———. *Practice in Christianity*. Edited and translated by Howard V. Hong and Edna H. Hong. Princeton, NJ: Princeton University Press, 1991.

———. *The Sickness unto Death*. Translated by Walter Lowrie. Princeton, NJ: Princeton University Press, 1941.

Kim, Elijah Jong Fil. *The Rise of the Global South: The Decline of Western Christendom and the Rise of Majority World Christianity*. Eugene, OR: Wipf & Stock, 2012.

King, Martin Luther, Jr. *A Testament of Hope: The Essential Writings and Speeches of Martin Luther King Jr.* Edited by James M. Washington. San Francisco: HarperSanFrancisco, 1991.

Kingdon, Robert M. "Calvinism and Social Welfare." *Calvin Theological Journal* 17 (1982).

———. "Social Welfare in Calvin's Geneva." *American Historical Review* 76, no. 1 (February 1971).

Klein, Linda Kay. *Pure: Inside the Evangelical Movement That Shamed a Generation of Young Women and How I Broke Free*. New York: Simon & Schuster, 2019.

Knox, Olivier, and Caroline Anders. "Fuel, Food, Finance: Brace for Impact from Russia's Ukraine War." *Washington Post*, April 21, 2022. https://www.washingtonpost.com/politics/2022/04/21/fuel-food-finance-brace-impact-russias-ukraine-war/.

Kobes Du Mez, Kristin. *Jesus and John Wayne: How White Evangelicals Corrupted a Faith and Fractured a Nation*. New York: Liveright Publishing, 2020.

Kramer, Stephanie, and Conrad Hackett. "Modeling the Future of Religion in America." Pew Research Center, September 13, 2022. https://www.pewresearch.org/religion/2022/09/13/modeling-the-future-of-religion-in-america/.

Kuhn, Thomas S. *The Structure of Scientific Revolutions: 50th Anniversary Edition*. 4th ed. Chicago: University of Chicago Press, 2012.

Larsen, Timothy. "The Evangelical Reception of Dietrich Bonhoeffer." In *Bonhoeffer, Christ and Culture*, edited by Keith L. Johnson and Timothy Larsen, 39–57. Downers Grove, IL: IVP Academic, 2013.

Larson, Edward J. *Summer for the Gods: The Scopes Trial and America's Continuing Debate over Science and Religion*. New York: Basic Books, 2020.

Laub, Malte. "The Rise of 'Authoritarian Neoliberalism' and Its Impact on Communities." King's College London, July 29, 2021. https://www.kcl.ac.uk/news/study-sheds-light-on-austerity-and-growing-sense-of-fear-in-communities.

Le Guin, Ursula K. *The Lathe of Heaven*. New York: Simon & Schuster, 2008.

L'Engle, Madeleine. *Walking On Water: Reflections on Faith and Art*. New York: North Point Press, 1995.

Lenin, Vladimir Ilyich. *The State and Revolution*. Edited by Janet B. Kopito. Reprint edition. New York: Dover Publications, 2021.
———. *The Three Sources and Three Component Parts of Marxism*. 3rd ed. Moscow: Progress Publishers, 1969.
Leonhardt, David. "What's Next for the Supreme Court? Five Republican-Appointed Justices Are Ambitious and Impatient to Change American Law." *New York Times*, June 27, 2022. https://www.nytimes.com/2022/06/27/briefing/supreme-court-abortion.html.
Levenson, Jon D. "How Not to Conduct Jewish-Christian Dialogue." *Commentary* 112, no. 5 (December 2001): 31–37.
Levinas, Emmanuel. *Totality and Infinity: An Essay on Exteriority*. Translated by Alphonso Lingis. Pittsburgh: Duquesne University Press, 1969.
Lewontin, Richard C. "Theoretical Population Genetics in the Evolutionary Synthesis." In *The Evolutionary Synthesis: Perspectives on the Unification of Biology*, 58–68. Revised edition. Cambridge, MA: Harvard University Press, 1998.
Lindbeck, George A. *The Nature of Doctrine: Religion and Theology in a Postliberal Age*. 25th Anniversary Edition. Louisville, KY: Westminster John Knox, 2009.
Liptak, Adam. "In 6-to-3 Ruling, Supreme Court Ends Nearly 50 Years of Abortion Rights." *New York Times*, June 24, 2022. https://www.nytimes.com/2022/06/24/us/roe-wade-overturned-supreme-court.html.
Lloyd, Vincent W. "Christian Responses to the Holocaust: Political Theology in Europe." In *T. & T. Clark Handbook of Political Theology*, edited by Rubén Rosario Rodríguez, 17–28. London: T. & T. Clark, 2019.
———. *Religion of the Field Negro: On Black Secularism and Black Theology*. New York: Fordham University Press, 2018.
Locke, John. *Locke's Two Treatises of Government*. Edited by Peter Laslett. Critical edition. Cambridge: Cambridge University Press, 1967.
Loncar, Samuel. "Christianity's Shadow Founder: Marcion, Anti-Judaism, and the Birth of Liberal Protestantism." *Marginalia Review*, November 19, 2021. https://themarginaliareview.com/christianitys-shadow-founder-marcion-anti-judaism-and-the-birth-of-liberal-protestantism/.
Löning, Karl, and Erich Zenger. *To Begin With, God Created . . . : Biblical Theologies of Creation*. Collegeville, MN: Liturgical Press, 2000.
Lynerd, Benjamin T. *Republican Theology: The Civil Religion of American Evangelicals*. Oxford: Oxford University Press, 2014.
Lyotard, Jean-François. *The Postmodern Condition: A Report on Knowledge*. Translated by Geoff Bennington and Brian Massumi. Minneapolis: University of Minnesota Press, 1984.
MacIntyre, Alasdair. *After Virtue: A Study in Moral Theory*. 2nd ed. Notre Dame, IN: University of Notre Dame Press, 1984.
Magris, Aldo. "Gnosticism: Gnosticism from Its Origins to the Middle Ages (Further Considerations)." In *Macmillan Encyclopedia of Religion*, edited by Lindsay Jones, 3515–16. New York: Macmillan Reference USA, 2004.
Maimonides, Moses. *The Guide for the Perplexed*. Edited and translated by Michael Friedländer. New York: Dover Publications, 1956.
Mansoor, Menaham. "The Nature of Gnosticism in Qumran." In *The Origins of Gnosticism*, edited by Bianchi. Leiden: E. J. Brill, 1970.

Marchese, David. "Rev. William Barber on Greed, Poverty and Evangelical Politics." *New York Times Magazine*, December 29, 2020. https://www.nytimes.com/interactive/2020/12/28/magazine/william-barber-interview.html.

Marsden, George M. *Fundamentalism and American Culture*. New York: Oxford University Press, 2006.

Martínez, Jessica, and Gregory A. Smith. "How the Faithful Voted: A Preliminary 2016 Analysis." Pew Research Center, November 9, 2016. https://www.pewresearch.org/fact-tank/2016/11/09/how-the-faithful-voted-a-preliminary-2016-analysis/.

Marx, Karl. *Critique of Hegel's 'Philosophy of Right.'* Translated by Annette Jolin and Joseph O'Malley. Cambridge: Cambridge University Press, 1970.

Marx, Karl, and Friedrich Engels. "Manifesto of the Communist Party." In *The Marx-Engels Reader*. 2nd ed. New York: W. W. Norton, 1978.

Masci, David, and Gregory A. Smith. "5 Facts about U.S. Evangelical Protestants." Pew Research Center, March 1, 2018. https://www.pewresearch.org/short-reads/2018/03/01/5-facts-about-u-s-evangelical-protestants/.

Massingale, Bryan. *Racial Justice and the Catholic Church*. Maryknoll, NY: Orbis Books, 2010.

Mathewes, Charles. *A Theology of Public Life*. Cambridge: Cambridge University Press, 2007.

May, Gerhard. *Creatio Ex Nihilo: The Doctrine of 'Creation out of Nothing' in Early Christian Thought*. Edinburgh: T. & T. Clark, 1995.

McClymond, Michael J. *The Devil's Redemption: A New History and Interpretation of Christian Universalism*. 2 vol. Grand Rapids: Baker Academic, 2018.

McCormack, Bruce Lindley. *The Humility of the Eternal Son: Reformed Kenoticism and the Repair of Chalcedon*. Cambridge: Cambridge University Press, 2021.

———. "'The Limits of the Knowledge of God': Theses on the Theological Epistemology of Karl Barth." In *Orthodox and Modern: Studies in the Theology of Karl Barth*. Grand Rapids: Baker Academic, 2008.

McDonough, Sean M. *Christ as Creator: Origins of a New Testament Doctrine*. Oxford: Oxford University Press, 2009.

McFague, Sallie. *The Body of God: An Ecological Theology*. Minneapolis: Fortress, 1993.

McGrath, Alister E. *A Fine-Tuned Universe: The Quest for God in Science and Theology*. The 2009 Gifford Lectures. Louisville, KY: Westminster John Knox, 2009.

McLeod, Hugh, and Warner Ustorf. *The Decline of Christendom in Western Europe, 1750–2000*. Cambridge: Cambridge University Press, 2003.

Meador, Jake. "Purity as Branding in the Evangelical Sub-Culture." *Mere Orthodoxy: A Christian Review of Ideas*, September 2, 2016. https://mereorthodoxy.com/purity-culture-branding/.

Mejido, Manuel. "A Critique of the 'Aesthetic Turn' in U.S. Hispanic Theology: A Dialogue with Roberto Goizueta and the Positing of a New Paradigm." *Journal of Hispanic/Latino Theology* 8, no. 3 (February 2001): 18–48.

Menocal, María Rosa. *The Ornament of the World: How Muslims, Jews, and Christians Created a Culture of Tolerance in Medieval Spain*. New York: Little, Brown, 2002.

Mercadante, Linda A. *Belief without Borders: Inside the Minds of the Spiritual but Not Religious*. Oxford: Oxford University Press, 2014.

Metaxas, Eric. *Bonhoeffer: Pastor, Martyr, Prophet, Spy*. Nashville: Thomas Nelson, 2011.
Micklethwait, John, and Adrian Woolridge. *God Is Back: How the Global Rise of Faith Is Changing the World*. New York: Penguin, 2009.
Midgley, Mary. *Science as Salvation: A Modern Myth and Its Meaning*. London: Routledge, 1992.
Milbank, John. "On Theological Transgression." In *The Future of Love: Essays in Political Theology*. Eugene, OR: Cascade, 2009.
———. *Theology and Social Theory: Beyond Secular Reason*. Oxford: Blackwell, 1993.
Moltmann, Jürgen. *Theology of Hope: On the Ground and the Implications of a Christian Eschatology*. New York: Harper & Row, 1967.
Monypenny, William Flavelle, and George Earle Buckle. *The Life of Benjamin Disraeli; Earl of Beaconsfield*. Vol. 4. London: John Murray, 1916.
Moore, Russell. "This Is the Southern Baptist Apocalypse." *Christianity Today*, May 22, 2022. https://www.christianitytoday.com/ct/2022/may-web-only/southern-baptist-abuse-apocalypse-russell-moore.html.
Morales Torres, José Francisco. "Review of *Dogmatics after Babel: Beyond Theologies of Word and Culture*." *Journal of Religion* 101, no. 3 (July 2021).
Moreland, J. P. *Scientism and Secularism: Learning to Respond to a Dangerous Ideology*. Wheaton, IL: Crossway, 2018.
Mountford, Brian. *Christian Atheist: Belonging without Believing*. Winchester, UK: John Hunt Books, 2011.
Moyaert, Marianne. "Scriptural Reasoning as Inter-Religious Dialogue." In *The Wiley-Blackwell Companion to Inter-Religious Dialogue*, edited by Catherine Cornille, 64–86. Malden, MA: Wiley-Blackwell, 2013.
Munch, Regina. "'Worship of a False God': An Interview with Bryan Massingale." *Commonweal*, December 27, 2020. https://www.commonwealmagazine.org/worship-false-god.
Murphy, Joseph. *Homeschooling in America: Capturing and Assessing the Movement*. New York: Simon & Schuster, 2014.
Nasr, Seyyed Hossein, Caner K. Dagli, Maria Massi Dakake, Joseph E. B. Lumbard, and Mohammed Rustom, eds. *The Study Quran: A New Translation and Commentary*. New York: HarperOne, 2015.
National Jewish Scholars Project. "Dabru Emet: A Jewish Statement on Christians and Christianity." Jewish Christian Religions: Insights and Issues in Ongoing Jewish-Christian Dialogue, July 2002. https://www.jcrelations.net/article/dabru-emet-a-jewish-statement-on-christians-and-christianity.pdf.
Nelson, Eric. *The Theology of Liberalism: Political Philosophy and the Justice of God*. Cambridge, MA: Belknap Press, 2019.
Netanyahu, Benzion. *The Origins of the Inquisition in Fifteenth-Century Spain*. New York: Random House, 1995.
Niebuhr, H. Richard. *Christ and Culture*. New York: Harper Torchbooks, 1951.
Nietzsche, Friedrich. *Beyond Good and Evil: Prelude to a Philosophy of the Future*. Edited and translated by Walter Kaufmann. New York: Vintage Books, 1989.
———. *The Gay Science: With a Prelude in German Rhymes and an Appendix of Songs*. Translated by Walter Kaufmann. New York: Vintage Books, 1974.

———. *On the Genealogy of Morality*. Edited by Keith Ansell-Pearson, translated by Carol Diethe. New York, 2007.

Nirenberg, David. *Neighboring Faiths: Christianity, Islam, and Judaism in the Middle Ages and Today*. Chicago: University of Chicago Press, 2014.

Numbers, Ronald L. *Galileo Goes to Jail and Other Myths about Science and Religion*. Reprint edition. Cambridge, MA: Harvard University Press, 2010.

Nussbaum, Martha C. *Political Emotions: Why Love Matters for Justice*. Cambridge, MA: Belknap Press, 2013.

Oakes, Kaya. "How to Make Nones and Lose Money: Study Shows Cost of Catholic Sex Abuse Scandals." Religion Dispatches, September 21, 2015. https://religiondispatches.org/how-to-make-nones-and-lose-money-study-shows-cost-of-catholic-sex-abuse-scandals/.

O'Reilly, Bill. *Culture Warrior*. New York: Broadway Books, 2006.

Osborn, Eric. *Tertullian, First Theologian of the West*. Cambridge: Cambridge University Press, 2003.

Ottati, Douglas F. *A Theology for the Twenty-First Century*. Grand Rapids: Eerdmans, 2020.

Paeth, Scott. "Walter Wink, the Powers, and the Sermon on the Mount." Political Theology Network, October 28, 2021. https://politicaltheology.com/walter-wink-the-powers-and-the-sermon-on-the-mount/.

Pahnke, Anthony Robert, and Marcelo Milan. "The Brazilian Crisis and the New Authoritarianism." *Monthly Review*, June 1, 2020. https://monthlyreview.org/2020/06/01/the-brazilian-crisis-and-the-new-authoritarianism/.

Papanikolaou, Aristotle. "Dignity: An Orthodox Perspective." In *Value and Vulnerability: An Interfaith Dialogue on Human Dignity*, edited by Matthew R. Petrusek and Jonathan Rothchild. South Bend, IN: University of Notre Dame Press, 2020.

Parker, Theodore. "Justice and the Conscience." In *Ten Sermons of Religion*. New York: Charles Francis, 1853.

Parkinson, Patrick. *Child Sexual Abuse and the Churches: Understanding the Issues*. Oxfordshire, UK: Routledge, 2003.

Pascal, Blaise. *Pensées and Other Writings*. Translated by Honor Levi. Oxford: Oxford University Press, 1999.

Pavlovitz, John. *A Bigger Table: Building Messy, Authentic, and Hopeful Spiritual Community*. Louisville, KY: Westminster John Knox, 2017.

———. *If God Is Love, Don't Be a Jerk: Finding a Faith That Makes Us Better Humans*. Louisville, KY: Westminster John Knox, 2021.

Pelikan, Jaroslav. *The Christian Tradition*, vol. 1, *The Emergence of the Catholic Tradition (100–600)*. Chicago: University of Chicago Press, 1971.

Petrella, Ivan. *The Future of Liberation Theology: An Argument and Manifesto*. Reprint edition. London: Routledge, 2014.

Pew Research Center. "America's Changing Religious Landscape." May 12, 2015. https://www.pewresearch.org/religion/2015/05/12/americas-changing-religious-landscape.

———. "The Future of World Religions: Population Growth Projections, 2010–2050." April 2, 2015. http://www.pewresearch.org/2015/04/02/religious-projections-2010-2050.

———. "The Global Religious Landscape." December 18, 2012. https://www.pewresearch.org/2012/12/18/global-religious-landscape-exec/.

———. "Global Survey of Evangelical Protestant Leaders: Evangelical Beliefs and Practices." June 22, 2011. https://www.pewresearch.org/religion/2011/06/22/global-survey-beliefs/.

———. "'Nones' on the Rise." October 9, 2012. https://www.pewresearch.org/2012/10/09/nones-on-the-rise/.

———. "When Americans Say They Believe in God, What Do They Mean?" April 25, 2018. https://www.pewresearch.org/2018/04/25/when-americans-say-they-believe-in-god-what-do-they-mean.

Phillips, Timothy R., and Dennis Okholm. "Introduction." In *Christian Apologetics in the Postmodern World*, edited by Timothy R. Phillips and Dennis Okholm, 9–23. Downers Grove, IL: InterVarsity Press, 1995.

Phillips, Timothy R., and Dennis L. Okholm, eds. *Christian Apologetics in the Postmodern World*. Downers Grove, IL: InterVarsity Press, 1995.

Pickstock, Catherine. *Aspects of Truth: A New Religious Metaphysics*. Cambridge: Cambridge University Press, 2020.

Plato. *Meno*. Translated by G. M. A. Grube. Indianapolis: Hackett, 1976.

———. *Plato's Republic*. Translated by G. M. A. Grube. Indianapolis: Hackett, 1974.

Polkinghorne, John. *Belief in God in an Age of Science*. New Haven, CT: Yale University Press, 1998.

———. *Theology in the Context of Science*. New Haven, CT: Yale University Press, 2009.

Polkinghorne, John, and Nicholas Beale. *Questions of Truth: Fifty-One Responses to Questions about God, Science, and Belief*. Louisville, KY: Westminster John Knox, 2009.

Pope Francis. "Encyclical Letter *Fratelli Tutti* of the Holy Father Francis on Fraternity and Social Friendship." Vatican website, October 3, 2020. https://www.vatican.va/content/francesco/en/encyclicals/documents/papa-francesco_20201003_enciclica-fratelli-tutti.html.

———. "Encyclical Letter *Laudato Si'* of the Holy Father Francis on Care for Our Common Home." Vatican website, May 24, 2015. https://www.vatican.va/content/francesco/en/encyclicals/documents/papa-francesco_20150524_enciclica-laudato-si.html.

———. "Encyclical Letter *Lumen Fidei* ('The Light of Faith')." Vatican website, June 29, 2013. https://www.vatican.va/content/francesco/en/encyclicals/documents/papa-francesco_20130629_enciclica-lumen-fidei.html.

Pope Paul VI. "*Nostra Aetate*: Declaration on the Relation of the Church to Non-Christian Religions." Second Vatican Council, October 28, 1965. https://www.vatican.va/archive/hist_councils/ii_vatican_council/documents/vat-ii_decl_19651028_nostra-aetate_en.html.

Pseudo-Dionysius. "The Divine Names." In *Pseudo-Dionysius: The Complete Works*, edited and translated by Paul Rorem, translated by Colm Luibheid, 47–132. New York: Paulist Press, 1987.

———. "The Mystical Theology." In *Pseudo-Dionysius: The Complete Works*, edited and translated by Paul Rorem, translated by Colm Luibheid, 133–42. New York: Paulist Press, 1987.

Rasmussen, Larry L. *Earth-Honoring Faith: Religious Ethics in a New Key*. Oxford: Oxford University Press, 2015.

———. "The Future Isn't What It Used to Be: 'Limits to Growth' and Christian Ethics." *Lutheran Quarterly* 27, no. 2 (1975): 101–11.

Rawls, John. *A Theory of Justice*. Oxford: Oxford University Press, 1971.

Rawnsley, Hardwicke Drummond. *Harvey Goodwin, Bishop of Carlisle: A Biographical Memoir*. London: John Murray, 1896.

Reagan, Ronald. "Election Eve Address 'Vision for America.'" The American Presidency Project: UC Santa Barbara, November 3, 1980. https://www.presidency.ucsb.edu/documents/election-eve-address-vision-for-america.

Renard, John. "Comparative Theology: Definition and Method." *Religious Studies and Theology* 17, no. 1 (1998): 3–18.

Ridder, Jeroen de, Rik Peels, and Rene van Woudenberg, eds. *Scientism: Prospects and Problems*. Oxford: Oxford University Press, 2018.

Rivera, Mayra. *Poetics of the Flesh*. Durham, NC: Duke University Press, 2015.

Robinson, James T., ed. and trans. *Samuel Ibn Tibbon's Commentary on Ecclesiastes: The Book of the Soul of Man*. Heidelberg, Germany: Mohr Siebeck, 2007.

Rodríguez, José David, and Loida I. Martell-Otero, eds. *Teología En Conjunto: A Collaborative Hispanic Protestant Theology*. Louisville, KY: Westminster John Knox, 1997.

Roggen, H. "¿Hizo Francisco una opción de clase?" *Selecciones de Teología* 3, no. 9 (1974): 287–95.

Rohr, Richard. *The Divine Dance: The Trinity and Your Transformation*. London: SPCK, 2016.

———. *The Universal Christ: How a Forgotten Reality Can Change Everything We See, Hope for, and Believe*. New York: Crown, 2019.

———. *Yes, and . . . : Daily Meditations*. Cincinnati: Franciscan Media, 2013.

Rorty, Richard. "Religion as Conversation-Stopper." In *Philosophy and Social Hope*, 157–70. New York: Penguin, 1999.

Rosario Rodríguez, Rubén. *Christian Martyrdom and Political Violence: A Comparative Theology with Judaism and Islam*. Cambridge: Cambridge University Press, 2017.

———. *Dogmatics after Babel: Beyond the Theologies of Word and Culture*. Louisville, KY: Westminster John Knox, 2018.

———. *Racism and God-Talk: A Latino/a Perspective*. New York: New York University Press, 2008.

Rothery, Francis. *Missional: Impossible! The Death of Institutional Christianity and the Rebirth of G-d*. Eugene, OR: Wipf & Stock, 2014.

The Royal Aal al-Bayt Institute for Islamic Thought. "The ACW Letter: A Common Word between Us and You." 2007. http://www.acommonword.com/the-acw-document/.

Rubenstein, Richard L. *After Auschwitz: Radical Theology and Contemporary Judaism*. Indianapolis: Bobbs-Merrill, 1966.

Rubin, Jennifer. "Opinion: Why Are White Evangelicals Embracing an Anti-democratic Movement? Because They're Panicking." *Washington Post*, July 12, 2021. https://www.washingtonpost.com/opinions/2021/07/12/white-evangelicals-decline-spurs-an-anti-democratic-movement/.

Ruether, Rosemary Radford. "The Biblical Vision of the Ecological Crisis." *Christian Century* 95, no. 38 (1975): 1129–32.

———. "Ecofeminism—The Challenge to Theology." *Deportate, esuli, profughe: Rivista telematica di studi sulla memoria femminile* 20 (2012): 22–33.
———. *Gaia and God: An Ecofeminist Theology of Earth Healing*. New York: HarperCollins, 1994.
———, ed. *Women Healing Earth: Third-World Women on Ecology, Feminism, and Religion*. Maryknoll, NY: Orbis Books, 1996.
Sacks, Jonathan. *The Dignity of Difference: How to Avoid the Clash of Civilizations*. Reprint edition. New York: Bloomsbury USA, 2003.
Sagan, Carl. "An Open Letter to the Religious Community." Moscow, Russia, 1990. http://earthrenewal.org/open_letter_to_the_religious_.htm.
———. *The Varieties of Scientific Experience: A Personal View of the Search for God*. Edited by Ann Druyan. 1985 Gifford Lectures. New York: Penguin, 2006.
Saint Louis University. "Saint Louis University: 2021 Profile." https://www.slu.edu/about/key-facts/slu-profile.pdf.
Salter, Emma Gurney, trans. *The Legend of St. Francis*. London: J. M. Dent & Sons, 1926.
Sarisky, Darren. "Religious Commitment in Scriptural Reasoning: A Critical Engagement with Gavin D'Costa's 'Catholics Reading the Scripture of Other Religions.'" *Modern Theology* 36, no. 2 (April 2020): 318–19.
Schmitt, Carl. *Political Theology: Four Chapters on the Concept of Sovereignty*. Translated by George Schwab. Chicago: University of Chicago Press, 2005.
Schüssler Fiorenza, Elisabeth. *In Memory of Her: A Feminist Theological Reconstruction of Christian Origins*. New York: Crossroad, 1994.
Schwöbel, Christoph. "Theology." In *The Cambridge Companion to Karl Barth*, edited by John Webster. Cambridge: Cambridge University Press, 2000.
Selby, Peter. "Christianity in a World Come of Age." In *Cambridge Companion to Dietrich Bonhoeffer*, edited by John W. de Gruchy. Cambridge: Cambridge University Press, 1999.
Shiffman, John, and Brian Grow. "U.S. Company Makes a Fortune Selling Bodies Donated to Science." *Reuters*, October 26, 2017. https://www.reuters.com/article/us-usa-bodies-science-specialreport/special-report-u-s-company-makes-a-fortune-selling-bodies-donated-to-science-idUSKBN1CV1J7.
Slater. "Scriptural Reasoning and the Ethics of Public Discourse." *American Journal of Theology and Philosophy* 38, no. 2–3 (September 2017): 123–37.
Smith, Adam. *Lectures on Justice, Police, Revenue and Arms: Delivered in the University of Glasgow*. Edited by Edwin Cannan. Oxford: Clarendon Press, 1896.
———. *The Theory of Moral Sentiments*. Reprint edition. Mineola, NY: Dover, 2006.
———. *The Wealth of Nations*. Edited by Edwin Cannan. New York: Random House, 1994.
Smith, Gregory A. "About Three-in-Ten U.S. Adults Are Now Religiously Unaffiliated." Pew Research Center, December 14, 2021. https://www.pewforum.org/2021/12/14/about-three-in-ten-u-s-adults-are-now-religiously-unaffiliated/.
Sonderegger, Katherine. *Systematic Theology*, vol. 1, *The Doctrine of God*. Minneapolis: Fortress, 2015.
———. *Systematic Theology*, vol. 2, *The Doctrine of the Holy Trinity: Processions and Persons*. Minneapolis: Fortress, 2020.

Spadaro, S.J., Antonio. "A Big Heart Open to God: An Interview with Pope Francis." *America: The Jesuit Review*, September 30, 2013. https://www.americamagazine.org/faith/2013/09/30/big-heart-open-god-interview-pope-francis.

Stackhouse, John G., Jr. "From Architecture to Argument: Historic Resources for Christian Apologetics." In *Christian Apologetics in the Postmodern World*, edited by Timothy R. Phillips and Dennis L. Okholm. Downers Grove, IL: InterVarsity Press, 1995.

———. *Humble Apologetics: Defending the Faith Today*. Oxford: Oxford University Press, 2002.

Stackhouse, Max L. *Globalization and Grace*, vol. 4 of *God and Globalization*. New York: Continuum, 2007.

"Statement by Israel Orthodox Rabbis on the Climate Crisis." Jewish Climate Initiative and The Interfaith Center for Sustainable Development. https://www.jewishecoseminars.com/statement-by-israel-orthodox-rabbis-on-the-climate-crisis/.

Stephanson, Anders. *Manifest Destiny: American Expansion and Empire of Right*. New York: Hill & Wang, 1995.

St. Ireneaus. *Proof of the Apostolic Preaching*. Translated by Joseph P. Smith. Vol. 16 of *Ancient Christian Writers: The Works of the Fathers in Translation*. Westminster, MD: Newman Press, 1952.

Stone, Glenn C., ed. *A New Ethic for a New Earth*. New York: Friendship Press, 1971.

Stott, John R. W. *Understanding Christ: An Enquiry into the Theology of Prepositions*. Grand Rapids: Zondervan, 1981.

Stout, Jeffrey. *Democracy and Tradition*. Princeton, NJ: Princeton University Press, 2004.

Tanner, Kathryn. *Christ the Key*. Cambridge: Cambridge University Press, 2010.

———. *Christianity and the New Spirit of Capitalism*. New Haven, CT: Yale University Press, 2020.

Tarico, Valerie. *Trusting Doubt: A Former Evangelical Looks at Old Beliefs in a New Light*. 2nd ed. Independence, VA: Oracle Institute Press, 2017.

Taylor, Charles. *A Secular Age*. Cambridge, MA: Harvard University Press, 2007.

———. *Sources of the Self: The Making of the Modern Identity*. Cambridge, MA: Harvard University Press, 1989.

Taylor, Mark C. *Erring: A Postmodern A/Theology*. Chicago: University of Chicago Press, 2013.

Taylor, Mark Lewis. *Remembering Esperanza: A Cultural-Political Theology for North American Praxis*. Minneapolis: Fortress, 2006.

Thatamanil, John J. *Circling the Elephant: A Comparative Theology of Religious Diversity*. New York: Fordham University Press, 2020.

"The Time to Act Is Now: A Buddhist Declaration on Climate Change." Buddhist Climate Project, May 14, 2015. https://fore.yale.edu/files/buddhist_climate_change_statement_5-14-15.pdf.

Thiselton, Anthony C. *New Horizons in Hermeneutics: The Theory and Practice of Transforming Biblical Reading*. Grand Rapids: Zondervan, 1992.

Thomas Aquinas. *Summa Contra Gentiles. Book One: God*. Edited and translated by Anton Charles Pegis. Notre Dame, IN: University of Notre Dame Press, 1975.

———. *Summa Theologiae: A Concise Translation*. Edited by Timothy McDermott. Reprint edition. Notre Dame, IN: Christian Classics, 1991.

---. *The "Summa Theologica" of St. Thomas Aquinas, Part 3*. Translated by Fathers of the English Dominican Province. New York: Benziger Brothers, 1914.
Thrush, Glenn, and Maggie Haberman. "Giving White Nationalists an Unequivocal Boost." *New York Times*, August 16, 2017, sec. A1.
Tillich, Paul. *Dynamics of Faith*. Reprint edition. Grand Rapids: Zondervan, 2001.
---. *Systematic Theology*. 2 vols. Chicago: University of Chicago Press, 1957.
---. *What Is Religion?* Edited by James Luther Adams. New York: Harper & Row, 1969.
Tirres, Christopher D. *The Aesthetics and Ethics of Faith: A Dialogue between Liberationist and Pragmatic Thought*. Oxford: Oxford University Press, 2014.
Tracy, David. *The Analogical Imagination: Christian Theology and the Culture of Pluralism*. New York: Crossroad, 1981.
---. "Comparative Theology." In *Encyclopedia of Religion*, edited by Mircea Eliade, 14:446–55. New York: Macmillan, 1987.
---. *Fragments: The Existential Situation of Our Time: Selected Essays*. Vol. 1. Chicago: University of Chicago Press, 2020.
Tsumura, David T. *The Earth and the Waters in Genesis 1 and 2: A Linguistic Investigation*. Sheffield, UK: Sheffield Academic, 1989.
United Nations. "1995 UN Copenhagen World Summit for Social Development Agreements and Final Documents," 1995. https://www.un.org/development/desa/dspd/world-summit-for-social-development-1995.html.
---. "Global Issues: Ending Poverty." https://www.un.org/en/global-issues/ending-poverty.
Uzgallis, William. "John Locke, Racism, Slavery, and Indian Lands." In *Oxford Handbook of Philosophy and Race*, edited by Naomi Zack, 21–30. Oxford: Oxford University Press, 2017.
Vahanian, Gabriel. *The Death of God: The Culture of Our Post-Christian Era*. Reprint edition. Eugene, OR: Wipf & Stock, 2009.
Van Til, Cornelius. *Christian Apologetics*. 2nd ed. Phillipsburg, NJ: P & R Publishing, 2003.
---. *The Defense of the Faith*. 3rd ed. Phillipsburg, NJ: P & R Publishing, 1972.
Volf, Miroslav. *Allah: A Christian Response*. New York: HarperOne, 2011.
---, ed. *Do We Worship the Same God? Jews, Christians, and Muslims in Dialogue*. Grand Rapids: Eerdmans, 2012.
Weber, Max. *General Economic History*. Translated by Frank H. Knight. Mineola, NY: Dover, 2003.
---. *The Protestant Ethic and the Spirit of Capitalism*. Translated by Talcott Parsons. New York: Charles Scribner's Sons, 1958.
---. "Science as a Vocation." In *From Max Weber: Essays in Sociology*, edited by H. H. Gerth and C. Wright Mills. London and New York: Routledge, 2009.
Wedgewood, Emma. "Letter No. 441." Darwin Correspondence Project, November 21, 1838. https://www.darwinproject.ac.uk/letter/DCP-LETT-441.xml.
Weed, Eric. *The Religion of White Supremacy in the United States*. Lanham, MD: Lexington Books, 2017.
Wehner, Peter. "David Brooks's Journey toward Faith." *Atlantic*, May 7, 2019. https://www.theatlantic.com/ideas/archive/2019/05/second-mountain-brooks-discusses-his-faith/588766/.

Westerlund, David, ed. *Questioning the Secular State: The Worldwide Resurgence of Religion in Politics*. London: C. Hurst, 1996.
Whitehead, Andrew L., and Samuel L Perry. *Taking America Back for God: Christian Nationalism in the United States*. Oxford: Oxford University Press, 2020.
Wildman, Wesley. *Religious Philosophy as Multidisciplinary Comparative Inquiry: Envisioning a Future for the Philosophy of Religion*. Albany: SUNY Press, 2010.
Wilken, Robert Louis. *Liberty in the Things of God: The Christian Origins of Religious Freedom*. New Haven, CT: Yale University Press, 2019.
Wilson, Edward O. "Introduction to *On the Origin of Species*." In *From So Simply a Beginning*. New York: W. W. Norton, 2006.
Wink, Walter. *Engaging the Powers: Discernment and Resistance in a World of Domination*. 25th Anniversary Edition. Minneapolis: Fortress, 2017.
———. "Neither Passivity nor Violence: Jesus' Third Way (Matt. 5:38–44 Par.)." In *The Love of Enemy and Nonretaliation in the New Testament*, edited by Willard M. Swartley. Louisville, KY: Westminster John Knox, 1992.
Winship, Michael P., and Mark C. Carnes. *The Trial of Anne Hutchinson: Liberty, Law, and Intolerance in Puritan New England*. New York: W. W. Norton, 2013.
Wittgenstein, Ludwig. *Culture and Value*. Edited by G. H. von Wright. Translated by Peter Winch. Reprint of revised edition. Chicago: University of Chicago Press, 1984.
———. *Tractatus Logico-Philosophicus*. Translated by D. F. Spears and B. F. McGuinness. Reprint edition. London: Routledge Classics, 2001.
Wollaston, A. F. R. *Life of Alfred Newton: Late Professor of Comparative Anatomy, Cambridge University 1866–1907*. New York: Dutton, 1921.
Zinsmeister, Karl. "Less God, Less Giving? Religion and Generosity Feed Each Other in Fascinating Ways." *Philanthropy Magazine*, Winter 2019. https://www.philanthropyroundtable.org/magazine/less-god-less-giving/.
Žižek, Slavoj. *The Monstrosity of Christ: Paradox or Dialectic?* Cambridge, MA: MIT Press, 2009.
Zizioulas, John D. *Communion and Otherness: Further Studies in Personhood and the Church*. Edited by Paul McPartlan. London: T. & T. Clark, 2006.
Zuckerman, Phil, Luke W. Galen, and Frank L. Pasquale. *The Nonreligious: Understanding Secular People and Societies*. Oxford: Oxford University Press, 2016.

Index of Scripture

OLD TESTAMENT

Genesis
1:1–2	200
1:3	200, 204
1:26	125
1:26–28	34, 69, 103, 152, 208, 213
1:28	129
2:7	108, 208
2:15	125
2:24	203
3:9	190

Exodus
3:13	205
20:10	161
34:14	34, 88

Leviticus
11:29–38	203
25:46	161

Deuteronomy
5:15	161
6:4–5	182

Job
4:7–9	205

Psalms
8:5–8	34, 103
90:2	106

Isaiah
61:11	62
55:8–9	106

Jeremiah
10:10	106
29:11–13	31–32

Jonah
4:2	177
4:11	177

Micah
6:8	176

NEW TESTAMENT

Matthew
3:16–17	181
5:17	196
5:38–42	81, 177
5:44	177
5:45	31
6:24	69
8:20	97
13:9	90
14:13–21	204
14:22–34	205
19:5	203
22:37–40	29
25:31–46	69
28:19	140, 181

Mark
1:9–11	181
1:10	181
4:39	106
5:7	106
6:31–44	204
6:45–53	205
8:36	70
10:8	203

Luke
4:14	162
4:18	161–62
4:21	162
4:24–27	162
4:28	162
8:3	97
9:12–17	204
12:42–46	161
14:16–24	161
15:22	161
16:13	69, 161
18:18–30	95
19:10	190

John
1:1–3	106, 200
1:3–4	200
1:5	200
1:14	197, 199, 200, 202, 204, 208, 209
2:1–11	199, 203
2:4	202
2:10	203
3:1–21	97
3:16	70, 204
4:46–54	203, 204
4:49–50	203
5:2–9	203, 204
6:1–14	199, 204
6:15	204

John, *continued*

6:19	204
6:33	210
6:35	204, 210
7:50–51	97
9:2–3	205, 213
9:5	205
9:7	205
11:1–44	199, 205
11:45–53	205
14:26	181
15:26	181
16:13	181
17:21	189
19:39–42	97
20:19–31	214

Acts

5:29	143
17:16–34	194

Romans

3:21–26	202
6:2–4	92
8:20–21	70
10:9	201

1 Corinthians

6:19–20	73
12:22–26	214
13:12	192
15:3–9	201
15:42–44	208
15:47–50	208
15:50	208

2 Corinthians

5:21	202
13:13	181

Galatians

3:27–28	163

Ephesians

2:18	181
5:31	203
6:5	163
6:9	163
6:12–13	159

Philippians

2:5–11	201, 218
2:6–8	201
2:12b–13	190

Colossians

3:11	163

1 Timothy

6:10	76

Philemon

16	163
21	163

1 Peter

3:15–16	43, 45

2 Peter

3:9	190

1 John

5:7	181

APOCRYPHA

Sirach

33:25–30a	161

QUR'AN

Sura

2:62	173
2:135–6	173
5:8	177
5:73	172
22:39–40	173
29:46	172
112:1–4	182

Index of Names and Subjects

Abrahamic religions, 168–70, 174, 176–77
  absolute poverty, 67, 69
  cooperation among, 170–71
African Methodist Episcopal Church, 129
Age of Belief, 12
Albertus Magnus, 168
Allen, Diogenes, 55, 56
Altizer, Thomas J. J., 62
Alves, Rubem 27–28, 145, 218
American Evangelicalism, 52
American exceptionalism, 36
apologetics, 33, 37, 40—45, 54–56, 58–59, 62–63, 171–97
  Bonhoeffer's reivision of, 62
  postmodern, 59
  as rationalistic, 59–60
  traditional, 61
apophatic theology, 30,191, 194, 207
Aquinas, Thomas. *See* Thomas Aquinas
Aristotle, 75–76, 168–69
Asad, Talal, 35, 48–51, 53–54
Athanasius, 209–10
Augustine of Hippo, 29–30, 105, 190, 212–14
Ayoub, Mahmoud, 173

Bakunin, Mikhail Aleksandrovich, 82
Barbour, Ian G., 118–21, 123–26
Barth, Karl, 25–27, 42, 61
  on the hiddenness of God, 26
  on the historical Jesus, 25
Benedict Option, 139
Black Lives Matter, 158

Boff, Leonardo 93–99
Bonhoeffer, Dietrich, 26, 61–63, 91
Boyarin, Daniel, 174
Brahman, 185–87, 192
Brock, Brian, 212–13
Brooks, David, 139
Brown, Raymond E., 199, 203
Buddhism, 6–7, 129, 183, 178, 187–88, 192–93, 194
Bultmann, Rudolf, 199

Calvin, John, 30–31, 71–73, 85, 105, 143
Calvinism, 71
  and doctrine of vocation, 85
  Scottish, 71
capitalism, 34, 36, 71–73, 78, 82–92, 95, 98–99, 132, 144, 151, 154–56, 198
  Christian opposition to, 90
  finance-driven, 87, 90
  Marxist critique of, 79
  neoliberalism's suppport of, 154
Caputo, John D., 11–12, 48n38
Carnahan, Kevin, 160, 163–64
Catholicism, 3, 12, 53, 57, 148
  and Conquistadors, 211
  Latino/a theology in, 146
  Orlando Espín's analysis of, 148
  patriarchy of, 3
  sex abuse scandal, 3–4
  stabilization of membership, 57
Chappell, Bill, 4n12
Chicago School, 71
Christian hegemony, 7, 10

Christianity, 6–8, 10–11, 13–15, 23, 26, 33–36, 40–41, 43, 45–46, 51–55, 57–59, 61–63, 76–77, 83, 87–93, 95, 98, 102, 105, 110–12, 117, 127, 130–31, 138–39, 142, 144, 146–47, 149, 159, 163, 167, 169–71, 173–76, 181–87, 185–86, 189–92, 195–99, 212, 217
   anti-Semitism of, 174
   and Christian atheism, 62
   and Christian nationalism, 10
   colonialism of, 130
   communal project of, 92
   decline in membership, 12
   as Eurocentric, 7, 53
   exposure to, 8
   fundamentalist, 120
   growth of, 6
   Latino/a, 147
   and socialism, 77
church and state, 10, 51–52, 121, 143–44
   separation of, 52
civil rights movement, 54
classical capitalism, 71
Clayton, Philip, 41n8
communism, 57, 68, 78, 80–82, 153, 155
comparative theology, 36, 168, 170–72, 175–77, 180, 182, 184, 186, 188
Cone, James H., 1–2, 68
COVID-19 global pandemic, 69, 141
Cox, Harvey, 46n31
Crick, Francis, 118
Crossan, John Dominic, 120

Daly, Mary, 131
Darwin, Charles, 22, 34, 102–5, 107–18
Darwinism, 105, 115, 117
   and account of human descent, 35, 105
   common descent, 22
   and human uniqueness, 34
   resistance to, 102
Dawkins, Richard, 108–9, 119
deconstruction, 10, 11–12, 14, 15, 218
De La Torre, Miguel A., 53, 144

democratic liberalism. *See* neoliberalism
Dennett, Daniel C., 119
Derrida, Jacques, 10–11, 87
divine hiddenness, 23, 25–27, 29, 37, 218
   as guiding hermeneutical principle, 25
   Karl Barth on, 26
   Ludwig Wittgenstein on, 190–91
   Pseudo-Dionysius on, 190–94
Dorrien, Gary, 35, 138
Dreher, Rod, 138–39
Drescher, Elizabeth, 2–4, 6, 8–9
Dussel, Enrique, 24

Eastern Orthodoxy, 64–66
ecofeminism, 126–27, 130–33
Engels, Friedrich, 81
Enlightenment, 12, 17–18, 22, 24–25, 33, 35, 37, 41, 43–45, 47, 49–51, 55–56, 58, 62, 71–72, 77–78, 84, 86
   and collapse of biblical authority, 35, 45
   and exclusion of religion, 17–18, 47, 62
   French Enlightenment, 122
   as Grand Narrative, 24, 84
   Marxist critique of, 78
   optimism of, 86
   postmodern criticism of, 55
   rationalism of, 12
   and secularization, 7
   socioeconomic practices of, 84
Enlightenment rationalism, 33, 37, 45
   and apologetics, 56, 58–60
Espín, Orlando, 68, 147–48
Evangelical Environmental Network, 129
Evangelicalism
   decline of, 29, 57
   and opposition to modernity and postmodernity, 61
Evans, Rachel Held, 12–14, 17

feeding of the five thousand, 199, 204, 210
fideism, 102, 122–23
Flores, Nichole, 35, 145, 148–52, 156–58, 164–65

Index of Names and Subjects

Frame, John M., 43–45
Francis of Assisi, 93, 94–99
Frank, Adam, 126n102, 133–34, 155
Freeden, Michael, 154
Fukuyama, Francis, 68, 153–54

García-Rivera, Alejandro, 150
Gebara, Ivone, 129–32, 134–35, 145, 155
Gen Z, 2–3, 8–9, 15, 63, 110, 217
Gershom, Levi ben, 168
Giddens, Anthony, 83
Goizueta, Roberto S., 150
González, Justo L., 146
Gould, Stephen Jay, 102n5, 122–23
Gregory of Nyssa, 160, 162, 184
Grenz, Stanley J., 58–59
Gschwandtner, Christina M., 54–55
Gushee, David P., 14
Gutiérrez, Gustavo, 48n37, 61, 68, 96, 144–45, 211

Habermas, Jürgen, 46–48, 50
Hamilton, William, 62
Hanauer, Nick, 154–56
Harris, Sam, 119
Hart, David Bentley, 37, 41, 111n31, 160–61, 163
Heim, S. Mark, 167, 183
Heraclitus, 18–19, 31
  metaphysics of, 185
  worldview of, 217
Hindu, 77, 88, 129, 178, 180, 184–86, 187–88, 189, 194
human uniqueness, 33–35, 103, 105, 114, 125, 127, 133, 207
Huntington, Samuel, 169n10

Ibn Rushd, 168–69
Ibn Sina, 168, 186
image of God, 34, 44, 51, 64–66, 69, 72, 89, 91, 103, 130–31, 134, 150, 152, 162, 209, 213, 218
  Calvin on, 72
  creatures as made in, 103
  Darwin's rejection of, 103
  as image of Christ, 91
imago Dei. *See* image of God

Irenaeus, of Lyon 181–82, 199, 201–2, 205, 212
Isasi-Díaz, Ada Maria, 147–49
Islam, 6, 25, 33, 35, 83, 129, 168–76, 182–87
  comparative theology in, 171–72
  growth of, 6
  Islamophobia, 54
  rejection of the Trinity in, 184
Islamism, 50–51, 54

January 6 Capitol uprising, 24, 82, 138, 141–42
Jenson, Robert W., 183
Jervis, Rick, 142
Jesus, 1, 13–15, 25–26, 29, 31, 43, 52–53, 58, 60, 62, 64, 66, 68–69, 71, 80–82, 90–93, 95–97, 106, 131, 159–65, 173–74, 181–84, 189–90, 193, 195–206, 208–10, 212, 214, 218
  historical, 27
  as image of God, 91
  in the Qur'an, 173
Johnson, Elizabeth, 120
Jones, Robert P., 57–58
Jorge Mario Bergoglio. *See* Pope Francis
Judaism, 25, 81, 83, 105, 129, 137, 162, 168, 170, 173–74, 176, 182–87, 196, 199, 202

Kant, Immanuel, 77
Keller, Catherine, 132–33
kenosis, 64
Kierkegaard, Søren, 22, 26, 39, 122, 186
King, Martin Luther, Jr., 10n34, 32, 52, 54, 158, 160, 163, 189
Kobes Du Mez, Kristin, 57n74
Kuhn, Thomas S., 119

Latino/a theology, 145–46, 150–52
Le Guin, Ursula K., 215–17
L'Engle, Madeleine, 64
Lenin, Vladimir Ilyich, 76, 80–81
liberation theology, 27–28, 30–31, 67–68, 70–71, 77, 93, 96, 129, 144–45, 219
Lindbeck, George A., 170, 175–76

248 Index of Names and Subjects

Locke, John, 72–73
Lynerd, Benjamin T., 10n34

MacIntyre, Alasdair, 138
Maimonides, Moses, 168, 182, 186
Marxism, 76–77, 80–82, 138
  anarchist critique of, 82
  atheism of, 80
  economic interpretation of, 78
  Leonardo Boff's, 94
  and opposition by conservatism, 77
  and social analysis, 77
Marx, Karl 10, 71, 72, 76–82, 84–85
Massingale, Bryan, 53
Mathewes, Charles, 137, 139–40, 142–44
McClymond, 111n31
McCormack, Bruce Lindley, 218
McGrath, Alister E., 42
#MeToo movement, 4
Middle Ages
  Abrahamic religions in the, 169
  care for the poor during, 93–94
Milbank, John, 40–41, 49–51, 88, 158
Millennials, 2–3, 6, 15, 57, 63, 110, 217
Moltmann, Jürgen, 137
Mountford, Brian, 62n99
mystery of God, 23, 25–28, 106, 139, 148, 178–79, 180–81, 182–84, 186–88, 187–90, 207, 218–19

narrative knowledge, 12, 17–18, 24–26, 32–37, 47–48, 50–51, 54, 58–59, 65, 70–71, 77–78, 86–87, 119–20, 127, 130, 132–33, 138, 142, 146, 152–55, 161–62, 167, 177, 182, 198–204, 202–3, 210, 214
natural selection, 22, 101, 103–5, 107–8, 110–15, 117–18, 123
natural theology, 21, 41–42, 44, 73, 108, 112, 122–24, 169
Nelson, Eric, 156n82
neoliberalism, 7, 82, 89, 132, 153–55
Niebuhr, H. Richard, 147n42
Nietzsche, Friedrich, 10, 84, 119, 159
Nirenberg, David, 169–70
Nones, 2–9, 23, 32, 37, 39, 40–41, 62–63, 217–19
  conception of God, 7, 9
  as demographic, 2, 5, 7, 9
  political views, 3
Nussbaum, Martha C., 42, 156–58

O'Reilly, Bill, 57n74

Paeth, Scott, 160
Papanikolaou, Aristotle, 65–66
Pascal, Blaise, 112, 114, 122–23
Pavlovitz, John A., 12–14
Perry, Samuel L., 10n34
Petrella, Ivan, 149–50
Pew Research Center, 3n11, 5–7, 33, 39, 57n73, 198
Plato, 18–21
Platonism, 10, 195–96, 199, 208–19
  of Arius, 209
  Greek neo-platonist version of, 196
  Hellenic, 195
  metaphysics of, 186
  of Philo of Alexandria, 208
  and Platonic Ideal, 21
  wordview of, 18, 217
pluralism, 9, 25, 33, 36, 40, 45, 51, 56, 127, 139, 144, 158, 167–68, 170–73, 178, 180, 182–84, 189, 194
  political, 25, 144, 158
  as relativism, 56
  religious, 36, 51, 127, 167, 173, 178, 183–84, 194
  theological, 45, 167, 171, 183
political theology, 9–10, 24, 30–31, 35, 49–50, 63, 65, 68, 77, 97, 121, 128, 137–40, 142–52, 156–58, 160–61, 171, 174, 210–12
  and legacy of Carl Schmitt, 138
  pluralism as basis for, 144
Polkinghorne, John, 112–14, 123–24, 186
Pope Francis, 70–71, 92–93, 98–99, 129, 152
  on the church as field hospital, 71, 99
  encyclical letter *Fratelli Tutti*, 98
  encyclical letter *Laudato Si'*, 98–99, 129
postliberal theology, 175
postmodernity, 54–55
  and plurality, 33

Index of Names and Subjects

post-secular age, 47
post-secular thought, 48
poverty
  decrease in, 69
  United Nation's definition of, 67
preferential option for the poor, 30–31, 132, 135, 144–45, 149–51, 165
Presbyterian Church (U.S.A.), 2
pre-Socratic worldview, 18
Protestantism
  ascetic, 86
  hospitals founded by, 94
  stabilization of membership, 57
  and war, 46
  work ethic of, 83, 86
Pseudo-Dionysius, 8, 190–94, 196, 207, 218

QAnon, 140–42

Radical Orthodoxy, 23
Rawls, John
  democratic theory of, 35
  theory of justice, 156–57
reconstruction, 14, 15
Reformation. *See* Protestantism
religious pluralism, 36, 51, 127, 167, 173, 178, 183–84, 194
religiously unaffiliated. *See* Nones
Renard, John, 171
revolution
  Chinese cultural, 82
  communist, 80–81
  nonviolent, 81
Rivera, Mayra, 36–37, 204, 206–11
Roggen, H., 93–94
Rohr, Richard, 12–13
Rorty, Richard, 137, 175
Rosario Rodríguez, Rubén, 12, 25, 28, 30, 45, 170n12
Rubenstein, Richard L., 137
Ruether, Rosemary Radford, 130

Sagan, Carl, 42, 126–28
Saint Louis University, 7
Schmitt, Carl, 35, 137–38, 145
Schwöbel, Christoph, 25

science, 8, 18, 22, 32, 35, 47–48, 101–2, 105, 118–19, 124, 128, 132, 134
  reductionist tendency, 20
  as superior knowlege, 17
scientific materialism, 119–21, 132
Scopes "Monkey Trial," 115
Scriptural Reasoning, 170, 174, 175
secularism, 6, 10, 47, 48–50
secularization, 2, 5, 6, 33, 35, 40–42, 46–47, 49, 50–51, 53, 61, 63
sense perception as knowledge, 19
Sermon on the Mount, 31, 80, 85, 159–60, 163–64, 189
slavery, 73, 130, 157, 160–63
  American, 157
  Jesus's teaching on, 161–62
  John Locke and, 73
  Paul's teaching on, 162–63
Smith, Adam, 71–75, 77, 81–84, 155
Stackhouse, John G., 56, 59–61
Stackhouse, Max L., 83
stories
  as coping mechanism, 17
  as creating community, 17
  See narrative knowledge
Stout, Jeffrey, 49, 158, 175
systematic theology, 21–23, 27–28, 29, 33, 41

Tanner, Kathryn, 9, 34, 42, 87–92
Taylor, Charles, 41, 46–50, 53
teología en conjunto, 146
Thatamanil, John J., 36, 167–68, 171, 177–92, 194
theological totalitarianism, 33, 39
theory of evolution, 107
Thomas Aquinas, 21, 30, 95, 105, 168, 186, 194
Tillich, Paul, 11, 186–88, 191, 193–94
Tracy, David, 9, 24, 186
Trinitarian, 65, 131–32, 150, 170, 180–85, 188–89, 194
Trump, Donald, 10n34, 13, 58, 140, 141–42

United Nations, 67, 69
Unite the Right Rally, 141, 151

Van Til, Cornelius, 43
violence, 24, 32, 37, 41, 70, 80–82, 86, 99, 138, 151, 159, 164, 177, 207
  Jesus' opposition to, 81
  political, 80

weak theology, 11, 63,
Weber, Max, 34, 71, 86–87
wedding at Cana, 199, 202–3

Whitehead, Andrew L., 10n34
Whitehead, Alfred North, 42
white supremacy, 30, 35, 52, 58, 145
Wink, Walter, 7, 158–60, 163–65
Wittgenstein, Ludwig, 190–91
Wollaston, A. F. R., 117

Žižek, Slavoj, 62
Zizioulas, John D., 64–66, 89

www.ingramcontent.com/pod-product-compliance
Lightning Source LLC
Chambersburg PA
CBHW020318010526
44107CB00054B/1891